The
EVERYDAY
Writer

Writing has become what I do
on a daily basis. Acting is what
I do once a year.
                    −Steve Martin

Third Edition

The EVERYDAY Writer

Andrea A. Lunsford
STANFORD UNIVERSITY

with a section for multilingual writers by

Franklin E. Horowitz
TEACHERS COLLEGE
COLUMBIA UNIVERSITY

BEDFORD/ST. MARTIN'S
Boston ◆ New York

For Bedford/St. Martin's

Developmental Editor: Sara Eaton Gaunt
Senior Production Editor: Michael Weber
Senior Production Supervisor: Nancy Myers
Marketing Manager: Kevin Feyen
Art Director: Lucy Krikorian
Text Design: Anna Palchik
Copy Editor: Judith Green Voss
Photo Research: Anita Dickhuth
Cover Design: Donna Dennison
Composition: Monotype Composition
Printing and Binding: Quebecor World Kingsport

President: Joan E. Feinberg
Editorial Director: Denise B. Wydra
Editors in Chief: Karen S. Henry and Nancy Perry
Director of Marketing: Karen Melton Soeltz
Director of Editing, Design, and Production: Marcia Cohen
Managing Editor: Erica T. Appel

Library of Congress Control Number: 2004101199

Manufactured in the United States of America.
9 8 7 6 5
f e d c

For information, write: Bedford/St. Martin's, 75 Arlington Street, Boston, MA 02116 (617-399-4000)

ISBN: 0-312-41323-8 (plastic comb)
          0-312-41328-9 (spiral)

EAN: 978-0-312-41323-1 (plastic comb)
          978-0-312-41328-6 (spiral)

Acknowledgments

Acknowledgments and copyrights appear at the back of the book on pages 519–520, which constitute an extension of the copyright page.

How to Use This Book

The Everyday Writer provides a "short and sweet" writing reference you can use easily on your own—at work, in class, even on the run. Small enough to tuck into a backpack or briefcase, this text has been designed to help you find information quickly, efficiently, and with minimal effort. I hope that this book will prove to be an everyday reference—and that the following will lead you quickly and easily to whatever information you need.

Ways into the book

QUICK ACCESS MENU. Inside the front cover you will find a list of the book's contents. Once you locate a general topic on the quick access menu, it will point you to the section of the book that contains specific information on the topic. Turn then to that tabbed section, and check the menu on the tabbed divider for the exact page.

USER-FRIENDLY INDEX. The index lists everything covered in the book. You can find information by looking up a topic ("articles," for example) or, if you're not sure what your topic is called, by looking up the word you need help with (such as *a* or *the*).

BRIEF CONTENTS. Inside the back cover, a brief, but detailed table of contents lists chapter titles and major headings.

GUIDE TO EDITING THE MOST COMMON ERRORS. The first tabbed section provides guidelines for recognizing, understanding, and editing the most common errors. This section has brief explanations, hand-edited examples, and cross references to other places in the book where you'll find more detail.

PRACTICAL ADVICE ON RESEARCH AND DOCUMENTATION. Source maps walk you step-by-step through the processes of selecting, evaluating, and citing sources. Documentation models are easy to find in two tabbed sections—one for MLA style and the other for APA, CSE, and *Chicago* styles.

REVISION SYMBOLS. If your instructor uses revision symbols to mark your drafts, consult the list of symbols at the back of the book and its cross references to places in the book where you'll find more help.

GLOSSARY OF USAGE. Chapter 41 gives quick advice on commonly confused and misused words.

Ways to navigate the pages

1 **GUIDES AT THE TOP OF EVERY PAGE.** Headers tell you what chapter or subsection you're in, the chapter number and section letter, the name of the tab, and the page number.

2 **"AT A GLANCE" BOXES.** These boxes at the beginning of most chapters—and elsewhere in the book as well—help you check your drafts with a critical eye and revise or edit as need be.

3 **BOXED TIPS THROUGHOUT THE BOOK.**

- **Tips on matters of style.** Style boxes help you make stylistic choices for various kinds of writing—in communities, jobs, and disciplines. E-style boxes offer special tips for writing online—from netiquette advice to format guidelines for readable email.
- **Tips for multilingual writers.** Advice for multilingual writers appears in a separate tabbed section and in boxes throughout the book. You can also find a list of the topics covered, including language-specific tips, at the back of the book.
- **Tips for considering disabilities.** These boxes, which also appear throughout the book, help you make your work accessible to readers with disabilities, especially when writing online. If you're a writer with a disability, these boxes also point out resources and strategies you may want to use.

4 **HAND-EDITED EXAMPLES.** Most examples are hand-edited in blue, allowing you to see the error and its revision at a glance. Blue pointers and boldface type make examples easy to spot on the page.

5 **CROSS-REFERENCES TO THE WEB SITE.** *The Everyday Writer* Web site expands the book's coverage. The cross-references to the Web site point you to practical online resources—from a tutorial on avoiding plagiarism to additional grammar exercises, model papers, a writer's almanac, and links to other Web resources.

In voice **24c** Sentences 195 — 1

AT A GLANCE

Confusing Shifts

- If you shift from one verb tense to another, check to be sure there is a reason for doing so. (24a)
- Do you see any shifts in mood—perhaps from an indicative statement to an imperative—and, if so, are they necessary? (24b)
- Check for shifts from active (*She asks questions*) to passive voice (*Questions are asked*). Are they intentional—and, if so, for what reason? (24c)
- Do you see any shifts in person or number—from *we* to *you*, for example—and, if so, what are the reasons for the shifts? (24d)
- Check your writing for consistency in tone. If your tone is serious, is it consistently so? (24f)

FOR MULTILINGUAL WRITERS

Shifting Tenses in Reported Speech

If Al said to Maria, "I will marry you," why did she then correctly tell her mom, "He said that he *would* marry me"? For guidelines on reporting speech, see 65b.

24b Check for shifts in mood.

Be careful not to shift from one mood to another without good reason. The mood of a verb can be indicative (he *closes* the door), imperative (*close* the door), or subjunctive (if the door *were closed*) (29h).

▶ Keep your eye on the ball, and ~~you should~~ bend your knees.

The sentence shifts from the imperative to the indicative; the editing makes both verbs imperative since the writer's purpose is to give orders.

bedfordstmartins.com/everyday_writer   For exercises, go to **Exercise Central** and click on **Shifts.**

24c Check for shifts in voice.

Do not shift without reason between the active voice (she *sold* it) and the passive voice (it *was sold*). Sometimes a shift in voice is justified, but often it may only confuse readers (29g).

Preface

What are hardworking students—and teachers—of writing to do these days? We blink our eyes and a new genre emerges, online and off. We listen for a few minutes and can hear vocabulary changing and growing, with spelling and capitalization changing along with it. Today, stylistic choices long unavailable to everyday writers—varied fonts, color, boxes, charts, tables, icons, photos, even sound and video—seem practically second nature. And the audiences for our writing continue to expand, calling for new thinking about how to craft messages for worldwide audiences and how to work with others across long distances.

The challenges and opportunities of writing in the twenty-first century have inspired this edition of *The Everyday Writer*—from the focus on electronic forms of writing, to increased attention to the visual "look" of writing, to the emphasis on how writing works across disciplines, to the questions the Internet raises for issues of intellectual property and for understanding and avoiding plagiarism. What remains constant is the focus on the "everydayness" of writing and on down-to-earth, practical advice for how to write well in a multitude of situations.

What also remains constant is the focus on rhetorical concerns. In a time of such challenging possibilities, taking a rhetorical perspective is particularly important. Why? Because a rhetorical perspective rejects either/or, right/wrong, black/white approaches to writing in favor of asking what choices will be most appropriate, effective, and ethical in a given writing situation. A rhetorical perspective also means paying careful attention to the purposes we want to achieve and the audiences we want to address. Writers today need to maintain such a rhetorical perspective every single day, and *The Everyday Writer,* Third Edition, provides writers with the tools for doing so.

Highlights

ATTENTION TO EVERYDAY LANGUAGE *IN* EVERYDAY LANGUAGE. This book rests on the belief that most writers have a great fund of everyday knowledge about writing and communication. Thus, each chapter opens with a brief example showing everyday use of that chapter's subject. In fact, everyday language pervades the book, giving students clear, straightforward answers, with examples from school, from the workplace, and from home.

COMPREHENSIVE ARGUMENT COVERAGE. My work on *Everything's an Argument* has strengthened my belief that argument is integral to many kinds of writing, and therefore I have expanded coverage of the topic in this handbook. Chapters 10 and 11 offer extensive instruction on argument, including attention to cultural contexts for arguments, a full student argumentative essay, and unique advice on visual argument.

HELP FOR THE MOST COMMON ERRORS. This book includes a "crisis-control" center based on nationwide research into student writing patterns and teacher responses to the writing of first-year college students. This study identified mistakes in the grammar, syntax, and use of standard written English that writers are most likely to make, as well as the larger rhetorical concerns readers are most likely to comment on. Thus, the first tabbed section of the book lists the twenty most common errors and offers advice for fixing them—all in succinct, everyday language.

SUPPORT FOR WRITING IN THE DIGITAL AGE. Building on my research into how new technologies change what writing is and the way that writing gets done, advice throughout this handbook pays special attention to the electronic texts students are composing today, the tools they are using, and the ways they are using those tools.

EMPOWERING ADVICE ABOUT LANGUAGE IN ACTION. Six chapters on language help students think about language in full context and about the consequences that their language choices have for themselves and for others with whom they communicate. This section aims to demonstrate the power of language in constructing realities, including realities that can be shared with others across languages and cultures.

SPECIAL ATTENTION TO STYLE. As always, this handbook focuses on writing that is not only correct but *good.* Style boxes throughout the book help writers make rhetorically effective stylistic choices; E-Style boxes offer style tips for working electronically and online.

THOROUGH GUIDANCE FOR MULTILINGUAL WRITERS. Written by Franklin E. Horowitz of Teachers College, Columbia University, a complete section covers grammatical and rhetorical issues of concern to multilingual writers. For this edition, I've added more boxed tips throughout the book offering advice on topics where ESL writers need extra help. Whenever possible, the advice is language-specific. I also added a new chapter on U.S. academic conventions, which gives writers insight into American academic expectations.

UNIQUE TIPS ON CONSIDERING DISABILITIES. New "Considering Disabilities" boxes help students make their work accessible to readers with disabilities, especially when writing online.

New to this edition

A more visual book

110   Media   **13a**   *Designing documents*

The National Geographic Web site uses high-contrast colors (such as yellow and blue) effectively.

• **PROXIMITY.** Parts of a page that are closely related should be together (*proximate* to one another). Your goal is to position related points, texts, and visuals as close to one another as possible and to use clear headings to identify them.

The M&M'S site Colorworks.com demonstrates proximity by placing each image next to its label and supporting text.

• **REPETITION.** Readers are guided in large part by the repetition of key words or elements. You can take advantage of this design principle by using a consistent design throughout your document for elements such as color, typestyle, and visuals.

Bartelby.com uses repetition effectively.

The navigation tabs are repeated at the top of every page on the site.

The main ways to navigate the site are repeated in the sidebar.

• **A new design.**
This edition has brighter and bolder colors that make the text easier to navigate and to use.

• **More visual explanations and examples.**
Photos, charts, and other graphics throughout the book present information both verbally and visually.

63

U.S. Academic Conventions

Xiao Ming Li, now a college teacher, reports that before she first came to the United States, she had been a "good" writer in China—both in English and Chinese. When she became a college student in the United States, however, she struggled to figure out what her teachers expected of her writing in English. Although she used appropriate words and sentence grammar, her instructors seemed to expect her to write in a whole new way, which she could not, at first, grasp.

Xiao and other multilingual students facing new writing expectations often need to call on writing-center tutors or instructors to help them write more effectively in their classes. In short, resourceful students actively tackle the question of how to write "U.S.A. style."

Of course, there is no one style of writing in any culture and surely not in the United States. Even the variety of English often referred to as "standard" covers a wide range of styles (see Chapter 38). In addition, writing styles vary considerably from field to field. In spite of this wide variation, you can learn the basic style called for most often in U.S. college writing. To begin to become an effective writer in American English, consider some of the expectations prevalent in the United States about readers, writers, and texts.

63a Understand expectations about readers.

U.S. college instructors expect you to be an actively engaged reader—to respond to class readings and to offer informed opinions on what the readings say. Such highly active reading may seem unusual or even impolite to you, but it will not seem so to your instructors and many of your classmates. Keep in mind that instructors are not asking you to be negative or combative. Rather, they want to know that you are engaged with the text and the class.

• **New images of everyday writing.**
These part-opening photos reinforce the connection between this handbook and the writing students see and do every day.

491

More on visual rhetoric to help students analyze visual texts and create their own

- **A new chapter on thinking visually.** Chapter 5 encourages students to think critically about the various ways in which images work as they prepare to use visuals in their own documents.

- **Guidelines for using visuals.** New advice throughout this handbook's coverage of the writing process helps students successfully use graphics and images in their own work.

- **Unique new sections on analyzing visual arguments.** Chapters 10 and 11 help students think about the pervasiveness and influence of images that make emotional, ethical, and logical appeals.

- **A thoroughly revised document design chapter.** Chapter 13 includes a discussion of basic design principles, guidelines for formatting documents effectively, and advice for analyzing images carefully and manipulating them ethically.

Practical treatment of research and documentation

- **Innovative new source maps.** This new feature presents annotated facsimiles of original sources along with step-by-step guidelines to help students evaluate and cite print and electronic materials.

SOURCE MAP: Evaluating Web Sources

Determine the credibility of the sponsoring organization.

1 Consider the URL, specifically the top-level domain name. (For example, .edu may indicate that the sponsor is an accredited college or university; .org may indicate it's a nonprofit organization.) Ask yourself whether such a sponsor might be biased about the topic you're researching.

2 Look for an About page or a link to the homepage for background information on the sponsor, including a mission statement. What is the sponsoring organization's stance or point of view? Does the mission statement seem biased or balanced? Does the sponsor seem to take other points of view into account? What is the intended purpose of the site? Is this site meant to inform? Or is it trying to persuade, advertise, or accomplish something else?

Determine the credibility of the author.

3 Evaluate the author's credentials. On this Web page, the authors' professional affiliations are listed, but other information about them isn't provided. You will often have to look elsewhere—such as at other sites on the Web—to find out more about an author. When you do, ask yourself if the author seems qualified to write about the topic.

Determine the currency of the Web source.

4 Look for the date that indicates when the information was posted or last updated. Here, the date is given at the beginning of the press release.

5 Check to see if the sources referred to are also up-to-date. These authors cite sources from September and October 2003. Ask yourself if, given your topic, an older source is acceptable or if only the most recent information will do.

Determine the accuracy of the information.

6 How complete is the information in the source? Examine the works cited by the author. Are sources for statistics included? Do the sources cited seem credible? Is a list of additional resources provided? Here, the authors cite the U.S. Navy and the U.S. Air Force, but they do not give enough information to track down these sources. Ask yourself whether you can find a way to corroborate what a source is saying.

- **A new chapter on integrating sources and avoiding plagiarism.** Chapter 19 helps students understand the larger issues surrounding intellectual property and provides strategies for using sources appropriately and avoiding plagiarism in the process.

- **Updated MLA, APA, CSE, and *Chicago* documentation models.** New models for citing online and other electronic and multimedia sources are based on instructors' survey responses about the most common difficulties students have working with sources.

Complete coverage of writing in the disciplines

- **A new chapter on learning to write in any discipline.**
  Chapter 59 gives student writers strategies for understanding discipline-specific assignments, expectations, vocabulary, style, use of evidence, patterns, and formats.

- **Practical advice for writing across the curriculum.**
  This edition offers two useful new chapters—Chapter 60, "Writing for Literature and the Other Humanities," and Chapter 61, "Writing for the Social Sciences and the Natural Sciences."

---

476 **Sciences** **61a** *Writing for the social sciences and natural sciences*

60d **Learn the scope of the other humanities**

In humanities disciplines other than literature, the interpretation and creation of texts are also central. The nature of these texts may vary: an art historian may "read" a painting by Leonardo Da Vinci; a philosopher may analyze a treatise by John Locke or Emmanuel Kant. But whether the text being studied is ancient or modern, literary or historical, verbal or visual, textual analysis plays a critical role in all of the reading and writing that people in the humanities undertake.

For sample pages from a student essay that uses *Chicago* style, see 58c.

bedfordstmartins.com/everyday_writer For more examples of writing in the humanities, click on **Student Writing**. For additional information, go to **Links** and click on **Writing in the Disciplines**. For other multidisciplinary resources, click on **Writer's Almanac**.

61

Writing for the Social Sciences and the Natural Sciences

The social sciences and the natural sciences call for systematic, observable studies—in offices, labs, and the field. Such studies might involve why people vote, how children learn, where birds migrate, or thousands of other phenomena. Regardless of what they are analyzing, however, both social scientists and natural scientists know that what they write, from a first grant proposal to a final scientific paper, is central to their efforts.

bedfordstmartins.com/everyday_writer For more on writing in the social sciences and natural sciences, go to **Links** and click on **Writing in the Disciplines**. For other multidisciplinary resources, click on **Writer's Almanac**.

61a **Learn the scope of the social sciences.**

The social sciences—which may include psychology, anthropology, political science, speech communication, sociology, economics, and education—attempt to identify and explain patterns of human behav-

---

- **Sample writing from across the curriculum.**
  Student examples throughout the book and on the book's companion Web site include essays that follow MLA, APA, CSE, and *Chicago* styles, as well as both print and online résumés.

Expanded coverage of media and technology

- **A new chapter on writing with computers.**
Chapter 12 offers students practical advice and strategies for using computers to collaborate, brainstorm, research, write, and revise.

12

Writing with Computers: The Basics

How often do you find yourself at a computer? Many writers today use a word-processing program to draft and revise documents from start to finish; read and write email, instant messages, and Web logs; and visit chat rooms to keep in touch with colleagues, family, and friends. In fact, many writers feel that their computers are an extension of themselves, so closely connected are they to these machines and the acts of communication they make possible. This chapter provides you with some advice, based on what writers across the country have reported, about the two most common ways of writing with computers: word processing and email.

12a Use word-processing tools.

The metaphor of word *processing* deserves attention: we use computers to literally process our words—to discover ideas, to format them in various ways, and to experiment with organization and style. An understanding of the various tools that word-processing programs provide—especially those that involve saving and sharing files, formatting, cutting and pasting, and improving your writing—can help you use these programs efficiently and effectively.

Saving and sharing files

Save each file with a clear name (*Rhetorical Analysis draft 1*, for example, instead of *Paper 1*). Doing so will save you time later on, when you're looking for a particular document. Save related files in the same folder. Here are some additional tips for saving and sharing files:

- If you are sending your draft electronically to an instructor or to someone else, include your name in the file name, along with other pertinent information, so that the recipient can easily identify it.

101

- **Advice on working with media.**
This edition offers guidelines and models for writing and designing effective print and online texts, including blogs, emails, Web pages, and presentation slides.

- **Cross-references to the book's companion Web site.**
These cross-references direct students to online materials, such as tutorials, exercises, sample student writing, and other valuable resources.

A wide array of ancillaries

PRINT RESOURCES

Instructor's Notes, Andrea Lunsford, Cheryl Glenn, and Alyssa O'Brien, ISBN 0-312-41977-5

Exercises for THE EVERYDAY WRITER, THIRD EDITION, Lex Runciman and Carolyn Lengel, ISBN 0-312-41972-4

Answer Key to Exercises for THE EVERYDAY WRITER, THIRD EDITION, ISBN 0-312-41976-7

Exercises for Multilingual Writers, Maria McCormack, ISBN 0-312-43029-9

Answer Key to Exercises for Multilingual Writers, ISBN 0-312-43028-0

The St. Martin's Pocket Guide to Research and Documentation, Second Edition, Andrea A. Lunsford and Marcia Muth, ISBN 0-312-39832-8

NEW MEDIA RESOURCES

Book Companion Site at bedfordstmartins.com/everyday_writer

The Electronic Everyday Writer 3.0 on CD-ROM, ISBN 0-312-41974-0

Comment with *The Everyday Writer*

Exercise Central at bedfordstmartins.com/exercisecentral

The Everyday Writer Exercises on **CD-ROM,** ISBNs: 0-312-43364-6 (with comb-bound book) or 0-312-43359-X (with spiral-bound book)

Electronic Diagnostic Tests at bedfordstmartins.com/lunsforddiagnostics

The St. Martin's Tutorial on Avoiding Plagiarism at bedfordstmartins.com/plagiarismtutorial

Blackboard and WebCT e-content

Acknowledgments

I am forever grateful to Sara Eaton Gaunt, who took on this editorial project at the last minute and began working miracles right away; to Fran Weinberg for invaluable, and ongoing, contributions to this text; to Anne Noyes for countless contributions to the text and its companion Web site; to Paul Stenis for outstanding work on the *Instructor's Notes* and on exercises for students; to Judy Voss for a truly superb job of copyediting; to Joelle Hann for amazing work on *The Electronic Everyday Writer 3.0* and *Comment* with *Everyday Writer;* to Michael Weber for keeping all of us organized and on track; and to Anna Palchik for her continued work on a superb interior design.

Many thanks, also, to the wonderful and supportive members of the Bedford/St. Martin's team: Kristin Bowen, Nick Carbone, Karen Melton Soeltz, Nancy Perry, Karen Henry, Denise Wydra, and Joan Feinberg.

I am especially indebted to Dànielle Nicole DeVoss at Michigan State University for her help in making this a more visual book, and to Elizabeth Trelenberg at Florida State University for her help with the *Exercises for Multilingual Writers.* I have also benefited greatly from the excellent advice of some very special colleagues: Colin Gifford Brooke, Syracuse University; Barbara Fister, Gustavus Adolphus College; Patrick Clauss, Butler University; Arnold Zwicky, Stanford University; Lisa Ede, Oregon State University; Beverly Moss, Ohio State University; and Marilyn Moller.

I owe special thanks to the group of student writers whose work appears in and enriches this book and its companion Web site: Michelle Abbot, Carina Abernathy, Eric Adamson, Milena Ateyea, Julie Baird, Valerie Bredin, Leah Clendening, David Craig, Kelly Darr, Diana Dopfel, Tara Gupta, Dana Hornbeak, Ashley Hughes, Bory Kea, Emily Lesk, Nastassia Lopez, Heather MacKintosh-Sims, Merlla McLaughlin, Laura Montgomery, Shannon Palma, Teal Pfeifer, Amrit Rao, Heather Ricker, Dawn Rodney, Melissa Schraeder, and Dennis Tyler Jr.

Once again, I have been guided by a group of hard-working and meticulous reviewers, including Thomas Amorose, Seattle Pacific University; Joseph Bartolomeo, University of Massachusetts Amherst; Jennifer Beech, The University of Tennessee at Chattanooga; Diane Belcher, The Ohio State University; Carol Bledsoe, Florida Gulf Coast University; Arnold J. Bradford, Northern Virginia Community College; Amy Braziller, Red Rocks Community College; JoAnne Bryant, Troy State University Montgomery; Zisca Burton, University of Miami; Diane Chase, University of Massachusetts Amherst; Sherry Cisler, Arizona State University West; Cynthia Cox, Belmont University; Jonathan Cullick, Northern Kentucky University; Kirk Curnutt, Troy State University Montgomery; Cherie Post Dargan, Hawkeye Community

College; Dominic Delli Carpini, York College of Pennsylvania; Suzanne Drapeau, Oakland University; Ernest J. Enchelmayer, Troy State University; Elizabeth Foreman, Edison Community College; Patricia Goldstein, University of Wisconsin Milwaukee; Charles Hill, University of Wisconsin Oshkosh; Ann Keefer, SUNY University at Buffalo; John Kerrigan, Fort Hays State University; Sarah Klock, Boston College; Jon A. Leydens, Colorado School of Mines; Gina Maranto, University of Miami; Maurice Maryanow, Troy State University Montgomery; Paul Kei Matsuda, University of New Hampshire; Donna Matsumoto, Leeward Community College; Ben McCorkle, The Ohio State University; Dana W. McMichael, Abilene Christian University; Kathy Mendt, Front Range Community College; Michael Minassian, Broward Community College; Kathleen Molloy, Santa Barbara City College; Marti L. Mundell, Washington State University; Alyssa J. O'Brien, Stanford University; Ruth Ochoa, Sacramento City College; Iswari Pandey, University of Louisville; Iris Rozencwajg, Houston Community College–Central; Richard Ruppel, Viterbo University; Gail K. Smith, Birmingham-Southern College; Laima Sruoginis, University of Southern Maine; Eleanor Sumpter-Latham, Central Oregon Community College; Rochelle Vigurs, University of Massachusetts Amherst; Robin Visel, Furman University; Jonathan Wade, Abilene Christian University; Cindy Wambeam, Arizona State University East; Eliza E. Warren, University of Nevada Reno; and Susan Youngs, Southern New Hampshire University.

Finally, and always, I continue to learn from my students, who serve as the major inspiration for just about everything I do, and from the best sisters, nieces, and nephews anyone has ever had.

–Andrea A. Lunsford

The
EVERYDAY
Writer

Learning from
COMMON
ERRORS

Error . . . is
exercise in
competence.

−GILBERT RYLE

Learning from Common Errors

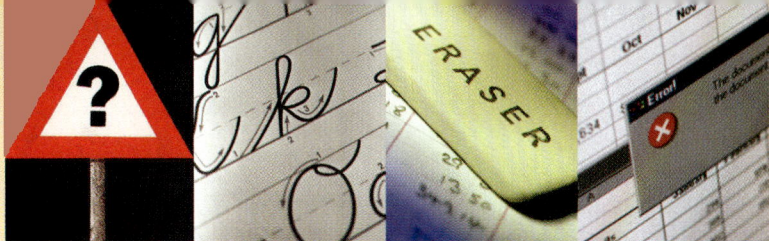

Think for a moment about how important errors have been in your life. Remember when you first learned cursive writing—and how hard it was to make those loops and how many times you had to erase and start over? Or remember learning to use new software—and all the missteps you made along the way? Such mistakes provide the kind of trial and error necessary to all learning.

So it is for all writers. Even the best writers make errors, losing track of their purpose for writing, leaving out a word or an essential comma, writing *its* instead of *it's*. The good news is that we can learn to edit our writing and to correct our errors. The first three chapters of *The Everyday Writer* will help you recognize, understand, revise—and learn from—the most common errors.

1

Broad Content Issues

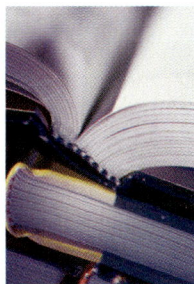

As a writer, you are in some ways like a band leader. You must orchestrate all the elements of your writing into a persuasive performance, assembling your ideas, words, and evidence into one coherent structure. Most readers in North America expect you to be their guide—to help them understand your meaning. To underscore these expectations, instructors reading college essays most often remind you about these five content issues: (1) use of supporting evidence, (2) use of sources, (3) achievement of purpose, (4) attention to audience, and (5) overall impression. Looking at the examples of such comments in this chapter will help you understand readers' responses to your own writing.

bedfordstmartins.com/everyday_writer   For additional help with broad content issues, go to **Links** and click on **The Art and Craft of Writing.**

1a   Check your use of supporting evidence.

Effective writing needs to accomplish two basic goals: to make a claim and to prove it. Readers expect that a piece of writing will make one or more points clearly and will support those points with ample evidence—good reasons, examples, or other details. When you use evidence effectively, you help readers understand your point, making abstract concepts concrete and offering proof that what you are saying is sensible and worthy of attention. In fact, according to the research conducted for this book, this issue of supporting evidence is the one that readers asked students about *most often,* accounting for 56 percent of all the comments. When readers make statements such as the following ones, they are referring to or questioning your use of supporting evidence:

> This point is underdeveloped.
>
> The details here don't really help me see your point.
>
> I'm not convinced—what's your authority?
>
> The three reasons you offer are very persuasive.
>
> Good examples. Can you offer more?

For more discussion of the use of good reasons, examples and precedents, and citing authority, see 11d and 11f. Providing supporting details in paragraphs is covered in 8b.

1b   Check your use of sources.

One important kind of supporting evidence comes from source materials. To back up the points you are making, you need to choose possible sources, evaluate them, and decide when to quote, when to summarize, and when to paraphrase them. Using sources competently not only helps support your claim but also builds your credibility as a writer: you demonstrate that you understand what others have to say about a topic and that you are fully informed about these varying perspectives. When readers make comments such as the following ones, they are referring to or questioning your use of sources:

> Only two sources? You need at least several more.
>
> Who said this? Identify your source.
>
> One of the clearest paraphrases I've seen of this crucial passage.
>
> Your summary leaves out the writer's most important points
>
> Your summary is just repetition—you fail to comment on its significance.
>
> This quotation beautifully sums up your argument.
>
> Why do you quote at such length here? Why not paraphrase?

You cite only sources that support your claim—citing one or two with dif-fering views would help show me you've considered other opinions.

For further discussion of choosing, reading, and evaluating sources, see 18a–c; for more on quoting, paraphrasing, and summarizing, see 18d. Incorporating source materials in your text is covered in Chapter 19.

1c Check to see that you achieve your purpose.

The purposes for writing vary widely. You might, for example, write to ask for a job interview, to send condolences, to summarize information for a test, or to trace the causes of World War II for an essay. In academic or professional writing, you need to pay careful attention to what an assignment asks you to do, noting particularly any key terms in the assignment, such as *analyze, argue, define,* and *summarize.* Such words are important if you are to meet the requirements of the assignment, stay on the subject, and thus achieve your purpose. Readers' questions such as the following often reveal how well you have achieved your purpose:

> Why are you telling us all this?
>
> What is the issue here, and what is your stand on it?
>
> Very efficient and thorough discussion! You explain the content very clearly and thus reveal your understanding of the article.
>
> Why simply give a lot of plot summary here—it does little to analyze character development.

For guidelines on considering purposes, see 4b.

1d Check your attention to audience.

All writing is intended to be read, even if only by the writer. The most effective writers are sensitive to readers' backgrounds, values, and needs. They pay attention to their audience by taking the time to define terms readers may not know, providing necessary background infor-mation, and considering readers' perspectives on and feelings about a topic. Following are some typical reader comments on audience:

> Careful you don't talk down to your readers.
>
> You've left me behind here. I can't follow.
>
> Your level of diction is perfect for relating to the board of trustees.
>
> I'm really enjoying reading this!
>
> Don't assume everyone shares your opinion about this issue.

For guidelines on considering your audience, see 4b and Chapter 37.

1e   Check for overall impression.

When friends, colleagues, or instructors read your writing, they often give you information about the overall impression it makes, perhaps noting how it is improving or how it needs to be improved. You will do well to note such responses carefully and to analyze them to determine your strengths and weaknesses as a writer. Setting up a conference with a writing tutor or your instructor is one way to explore these general responses. Readers tend to comment on their overall impressions at the very beginning or the very end of an essay by saying things like this:

> I was looking for more critical analysis from you, and I've found it!
>
> Much improved over your last essay.
>
> Your grasp of the material here is truly impressive.
>
> What happened here? I can't understand your point in this essay.
>
> Good job—you've convinced me!

For more specific ways of assessing the overall impression your writing creates, see 9a and b.

2

Organization and Presentation

The most important or brilliant ideas in the world will have little effect on an audience if they are difficult to recognize, read, or follow. Indeed, research confirms that North American readers depend on writers to organize and present their material in ways that aid understanding. In regard to organization and presentation, the instructors in our study most often commented on these features, in order of frequency: (1) overall organization, (2) sentence structure and style, (3) paragraph structure, (4) format, and (5) documentation.

bedfordstmartins.com/everyday_writer For additional help with organization and presentation, go to **Links** and click on **The Art and Craft of Writing.** For more on effective sentences, go to **Links** and click on **Sentences: Grammatical Choices** and **Sentences: Stylistic Choices.**

2a   Check the overall organization.

North American readers also expect a writer to provide organizational patterns and signals that will help them follow what the writer is trying to say. Sometimes such organizational cues are simple. If you are giving directions, for example, you might give chronological cues (first you do A, then B, and so on), and if you are describing a place, you might give spatial cues (at the north end is A, in the center is B, and so on). But complex issues often call for complex organizational patterns. For example, you may need to signal readers that you are moving from one problem to several possible solutions or that you are moving through a series of comparisons and contrasts. Here are some common instructor comments concerning organizational features:

> I'm confused here—what does this point have to do with the one before it?
>
> Your most important point is buried here in the middle. Why not move it up front?
>
> Organization here is chronological rather than topical; as a result, you summarize but do not analyze.
>
> How did we get here? You need a transition.
>
> Very clear, logical essay. A joy to read.

For more discussion on writing out a plan, see 7c. For more on effective patterns of development, see 8c; and on using transitions to aid organization, see p. 58.

2b   Check sentence structure and style.

Effective sentences form the links in a chain of writing, guiding readers' understanding each step along the way. If you have never looked closely at your sentences, spend a little time examining them now. How long do your sentences tend to be? Do you use strings of short sentences? Do your sentences flow logically from one thought to another, or do you make the reader work to figure out the connections between them? Do your long sentences confuse the reader or wander off the topic? How do your sentences usually begin? How do you link them to one another? Following are some typical comments about sentences:

> The pacing of your sentences here really keeps me reading—excellent variation of length and type.
>
> Can you combine sentences to make the logical connection explicit here?
>
> Your use of questions helps clarify this complex issue.
>
> This is not effective word order for a closing sentence—I've forgotten your main point. Can you find a better sentence?

These sentences all begin with nouns—the result is a kind of dull clip-clop, clip-clop.

Too many short, simple sentences here. This reads like a grocery list rather than an explanation of a complex issue.

This sentence goes on forever—how about dividing it up?

For a more detailed discussion of sentence types, see Chapter 27. Sentence conciseness is covered in Chapter 26, and sentence variety in Chapter 27.

2c Check paragraph structure.

Paragraph structure can help readers follow the thread of thought in a piece of writing. You may tend to paragraph by feel, so to speak, without thinking very much about paragraph structure as you write. In fact, the best time to examine your paragraphs is generally *after* you have completed a draft. Here are some typical readers' comments about paragraphs:

Why the one- and two-sentence paragraphs? Elaborate!

Your introductory paragraph immediately gets my attention and gives an overview of the essay—good!

I can't follow the information in this paragraph. Can you reorganize it?

What is the main idea of this paragraph?

Very effective ordering of details in this paragraph.

This paragraph skips around two or three points. It has enough ideas for three paragraphs.

For guidelines on editing paragraphs, see p. 49. For more detailed information on paragraph development in general, see Chapter 8.

2d Check format.

An attractive, easy-to-read format makes a reader's job pleasant and straightforward. Therefore, you should pay close attention to the physical presentation of your materials and to the visual effect they create. Part of your job as a writer is to know what format is most appropriate for a particular task. In the research conducted for this book, readers made the following kinds of comments about format:

You need a title, one that gets across your meaning.

Why use this tiny single-spaced type? It is almost impossible to read.

Number pages—these were not in the right order.

Your headings helped me follow this report. Why not use subheadings?

For more discussion of format, see Chapter 13 on document design.

2e   Check documentation.

Any writing that uses source materials requires careful documentation—in-text citations and endnotes or footnotes; bibliographies—to guide readers to your sources and let them know you have carried out accurate research. While very few writers carry documentation guidelines around in their heads, smart writers know which guidelines to use and where to find them. Here are some readers' comments that focus on documentation:

> I checked my copy of *Emma,* and this quotation's not on the page you list.
>
> What are you paraphrasing here? Your introduction merely drops readers into the middle of things. *Introduce the material paraphrased.*
>
> What are you summarizing here? Where do these ideas come from?
>
> I can't tell where this quotation ends.
>
> Keep in-text citations as simple as possible—see information in handbook.
>
> Why aren't works listed in alphabetical order?
>
> This is *not correct* MLA citation style. Check your book!
>
> What is the date of this publication?

For information on MLA documentation, see Chapters 52–55. APA, CSE, and *Chicago* styles are covered in Chapters 56–58.

3

The Twenty Most Common Errors

What kinds of grammar, punctuation, and other surface errors are you likely to find in your writing, and how will readers respond to them? Our study of college writing patterns revealed that spelling errors are by far the most common type of error, even with spell checkers, by a factor of more than three to one. (A list of the words most often misspelled can be found in Chapter 40.) Our study also showed that not all surface errors disturb readers, nor do instructors always mark all of them. Finally, not all surface errors are consistently viewed as errors. In fact, some of the patterns identified in our research are considered errors by some readers but stylistic options by others.

While many people think of correctness as absolute, based on hard-and-fast unchanging rules, instructors and students know better. We know that there are rules but that the rules change all the time. "Is it okay to use *I* in essays for this class?" asks one student. "My high school teacher wouldn't let us." "Will more than one comma error lower my grade?" asks another. Such questions show that rules clearly exist but that they are always shifting and thus need our ongoing attention.

A number of shifts occurred in the last century alone. Some mechanical and grammatical questions that are of little or no concern today used to be perceived as extremely important. Split infinitives represented a serious problem for many instructors of the 1950s. Nowadays, at least since the starship *Enterprise* set out "to boldly go" where no one has gone before, split infinitives seem to wrinkle fewer brows.

Shifting standards do not mean that there is no such thing as correctness in writing—only that *correctness always depends on some context.* Correctness is not so much a question of absolute right or wrong as it is a question of the way a writer's choices are perceived by readers. As writers, we are all judged by the words we put on the page. We all want to be considered competent and careful, and writing errors work against that impression. The world judges us by our control of the conventions we have agreed to use, and we all know it. As Robert Frost once said of poetry, trying to write without honoring the conventions and agreed-upon rules is like playing tennis without a net.

A major goal of this book is to help you understand and control the surface conventions of academic and professional writing. Since you already know most of these rules, the most efficient way to proceed is to focus on those that are still unfamiliar or puzzling.

To aid you in this process, we have identified the twenty error patterns (other than misspelling) most common among U.S. college students and list them here in order of frequency. These twenty errors are likely to cause you the most trouble, so it is well worth your effort to check for them in your writing. Here are brief explanations and examples of each error pattern along with cross-references to other places in this book where you can find more detail and additional examples.

FOR MULTILINGUAL WRITERS

Language-Specific Tips

Is your first language Arabic? Chinese? Spanish? something else? See the directory for multilingual writers at the back of the book to find tips about predictable error patterns in twenty different languages.

bedfordstmartins.com/everyday_writer To access the advice in this chapter online and for exercises on each of the errors, click on **20 Most Common Errors.**

1   Missing comma after an introductory element

When a sentence opens with an introductory word, phrase, or clause, readers usually need a small pause between the introductory element and the main part of the sentence. Such a pause is most often signaled by a comma. Try to get into the habit of using a comma after every introductory element, be it a word, a phrase, or a clause. When the introductory element is very short, you don't always need a comma after it. But you're never wrong if you do use a comma after an introductory element, and sometimes the comma is necessary to prevent a misreading.

▶ Frankly, we were baffled by the committee's decision.

▶ In fact, the Philippines consists of more than eight thousand islands.

▶ To tell the truth, I have never liked the Yankees.

▶ Determined to get the job done, we worked all weekend.

▶ Because of its isolation in a rural area surrounded by mountains, Crawford Notch doesn't get many visitors.

▶ Though I gave advice for revising, his draft only became worse.

   The comma is needed here to prevent a misreading; without the comma, we might read the clause as *Though I gave advice for revising his draft.*

▶ In German, nouns are always capitalized.

   This sentence would at first be misunderstood if it did not have a comma. Readers would think the introductory phrase was *In German nouns* rather than *In German.*

For more on commas and introductory elements in general, see 27b and 42a.

2   Vague pronoun reference

A pronoun is a word such as *he, she, it, they, this, that, which,* and *who* that replaces another word so that the word does not have to be repeated. Pronouns should refer clearly to a specific word or words (called the *antecedent*) elsewhere in the sentence or in a previous sentence so that readers can be sure whom or what the pronoun refers to. There are two common kinds of vague pronoun reference. The first occurs when there is more than one word that the pronoun might refer to; the second occurs when the reference is to a word that is implied but not explicitly stated.

POSSIBLE REFERENCE TO MORE THAN ONE WORD

▶ Transmitting radio signals by satellite is a way of overcoming the

the airwaves

problem of scarce airwaves and limiting how ~~they~~ are used.

What is being limited—the signals or the airwaves?

▶ Before Mary Grace physically and verbally assaulted Mrs. Turpin,

the latter

~~she~~ was a judgmental woman who created her own ranking system of

people and used it to justify her self-proclaimed superiority.

Does *she* refer to Mary Grace or Mrs. Turpin? The editing removes any doubt.

REFERENCE IMPLIED BUT NOT STATED

▶ The troopers burned a refugee camp as a result of the earlier attack.

destruction of the camp

This was the cause of the war.

What does *this* refer to? The editing makes clear what caused the war.

a policy

▶ Company policy prohibited smoking, ~~which~~ many employees resented.

What does *which* refer to—the policy or smoking? The editing clarifies the sentence.

For more on pronoun reference, see 33g.

3 Missing comma in a compound sentence

A compound sentence is made up of two or more parts that could each stand alone as a sentence. When the parts are joined by *and, but, so, yet, or, nor,* or *for,* use a comma to indicate a pause between the two thoughts.

▶ We wish dreamily upon a star **,** and then we look down to find

ourselves standing in mud.

▶ The words "I do" may sound simple **,** but they mean a life commitment.

In very short sentences, the comma is optional if the sentence can be easily understood without it. But you'll never be wrong to use a comma, and sometimes a comma is necessary to prevent a misreading.

▶ **Min wore jeans, and her feet were bare.**

   Without the comma, readers might at first think that Min was wearing her feet.

For more on using commas in compound sentences, see 28o and 42b.

4   Wrong word

Wrong-word errors can involve mixing up words that sound somewhat alike, using a word with the wrong shade of meaning, or using a word with a completely wrong meaning. Many wrong-word errors are due to the improper use of homonyms—words that are pronounced alike but spelled differently, such as *their* and *there*.

▶ **The Kings played ~~there~~ *their* best, but that was not good enough.**

▶ ***Paradise Lost* contains many ~~illusions~~ *allusions* to classical mythology.**

▶ **He noticed the ~~stench~~ *fragrance* of roses as he entered the room.**

   Wrong shade of meaning: a *stench* is a disagreeable smell; a *fragrance* is a pleasing odor.

▶ **Working at a computer all day often means being ~~sedate~~ *sedentary* for long periods of time.**

   Wrong meaning: *sedate* means "composed, dignified," and *sedentary* means "requiring much sitting."

For information about choosing the right word for your meaning, see Chapter 39. For discussion of choosing respectful words, see Chapter 37.

5   Missing comma(s) with a nonrestrictive element

Use commas to set off any part of a sentence that tells more about a word in the sentence but that your reader does *not* need in order to understand the word or sentence. A nonrestrictive element is one that is not essential to the basic meaning of the sentence.

▶ **Marina, who was the president of the club, was first to speak.**

The reader does *not* need the clause *who was the president of the club* to know the basic meaning of the sentence: who was first to speak. As a nonrestrictive (or nonessential) element, the clause is set off by commas.

▶ **Louis was forced to call a session of the Estates General, which had not met for 175 years.**

The reader does *not* need the clause *which had not met for 175 years* to understand which assembly the sentence is talking about because the *Estates General* has already been named. This clause is *not* essential to the basic meaning of the sentence and should be set off by a comma.

▶ **Kristin's first doll, Malibu Barbie, is still her favorite.**

The reader knows which doll is Kristin's favorite—her *first* one; *Malibu Barbie* is thus *not* essential to the meaning of the sentence and needs to be set off by commas.

For more on using commas with nonrestrictive elements, see 42c.

6　Wrong or missing verb ending

It is easy to forget the verb endings *-s* (or *-es*) and *-ed* (or *-d*) because they are not always pronounced clearly when spoken. In addition, some varieties of English do not use these endings in the same way as standard academic or professional English. Be on the lookout for these incorrect or omitted endings, and check carefully for them when you edit.

▶ Eliot ~~use~~ *uses* feline imagery throughout the poem.

▶ The United States ~~drop~~ *dropped* two atomic bombs on Japan in 1945.

For more on verb endings, see 29a and 29c. For subject-verb agreement, see Chapter 30.

7　Wrong or missing preposition

Many words in English are regularly used with a particular preposition to express a particular meaning. For example, throwing a ball *to* someone is different from throwing a ball *at* someone: the first ball is thrown to be caught; the second, to hurt someone. Using the wrong preposition in such expressions is a common error. Because many prepositions are short and are not stressed or pronounced clearly in speech, they are often left out accidentally in writing. Proofread carefully, and check the verb in a dictionary to see how different prepositions affect its meaning.

▶ We met ~~in~~ Union Street ~~at~~ San Francisco.
    on   *in*

In and *at* both show place, but use *on* with a street and *in* with a city.

▶ President Richard Nixon compared the United States ~~with~~ a "pitiful,
    to

helpless giant."

Compare to means "regard as similar"; *compare with* means "to examine to find similarities or differences."

▶ Who called the game yesterday?
    off

Adding *off* makes clear that the game was canceled. To *call* a game can mean either to postpone it or announce it.

For more about choosing the correct preposition, see 66a.

8   Comma splice

A comma splice occurs when only a comma separates clauses that could each stand alone as a sentence. To correct a comma splice, you can insert a semicolon or period, add a word like *and* or *although* after the comma, or restructure the sentence.

▶ Westward migration had passed Wyoming by; even the discovery of gold in nearby Montana failed to attract settlers.

▶ I was strongly attracted to her, she had special qualities.
    for

▶ I was strongly attracted to her, she had no patience at all with children.
    although

▶ ~~They always had~~ ham for Easter, this was a family tradition.
    Having

For more ways to avoid or revise comma splices, see Chapter 34.

9 Missing or misplaced possessive apostrophe

To make a noun possessive, you must add either an apostrophe and an
-s (*Ed's book*) or an apostrophe alone (*the boys' gym*). Possessive personal
pronouns, however, do *not* take apostrophes: *hers, his, its, ours, yours.*

▶ Overambitious parents can be very harmful to a ~~childs~~ well-being.
  child's

▶ Mark Prior is one of the ~~Cub's~~ most electrifying pitchers.
  Cubs'

▶ Garnet Hill is pleased to announce ~~it's~~ spring white sale.
  its

For more about possessive apostrophes, see 45a.

10 Unnecessary shift in tense

Verb tenses tell when actions take place: saying *Willie went to school* indicates a past action, whereas saying *he will go* indicates a future action.
When you shift from one tense to another with no clear reason, you can
confuse readers, who have to guess which tense is the right one.

▶ Joy laughs until she ~~cried~~ during *The Simpsons.*
  cries

▶ Pratick was watching the great blue heron take off. Then she ~~slips~~ and
  slipped
  ~~falls~~ into the swamp.
  fell

▶ Taurean is in charge of finance; she ~~will~~ always ~~keep~~ her office locked.
  keeps

For more on eliminating unnecessary shifts in tense, see 65b. For more
on using verb tenses in sequence, see 29f.

11 Unnecessary shift in pronoun

An unnecessary pronoun shift occurs when a writer who has been using
one kind of pronoun to refer to someone or something shifts to another
pronoun for no apparent reason. The most common shift in pronoun is
from *one* to *you* or *I.*

▶ When one first sees a painting by Georgia O'Keeffe, ~~you are~~ impressed
  one is
  by a sense of power and stillness.

▶ If we had known about the ozone layer, ~~you~~ *we* could have banned
aerosol sprays long ago.

For more on shifts in pronouns, see 24d.

12 Sentence fragment

A sentence fragment is a part of a sentence that is written as if it were a
whole sentence, with a capital letter at the beginning and a period, question mark, or exclamation point at the end. A fragment lacks a subject, a
complete verb, or both. Or a fragment may begin with a subordinating
word such as *because,* which indicates that it depends for its meaning on
another sentence.

NO SUBJECT

▶ Marie Antoinette spent huge sums of money on herself and her favorites.
Her extravagance helped
~~Helped~~ bring on the French Revolution.

NO COMPLETE VERB

▶ The old aluminum boat *was* sitting on its trailer.

Sitting cannot function alone as the verb of the sentence. The auxiliary
verb *was* makes it a complete verb, *was sitting,* indicating continuing action.

BEGINNING WITH SUBORDINATING WORD

▶ We returned to the drugstore, *where* ~~Where~~ we waited for our buddies.

For more ways to eliminate sentence fragments, see Chapter 35.

13 Wrong tense or verb form

Errors of wrong tense or wrong verb form include using a verb that
does not indicate clearly when an action or condition is, was, or will be
completed—for example, using *walked* instead of *had walked,* or *will go*
instead of *will have gone.* Some varieties of English use the verbs *be* and
have in ways that differ significantly from their use in standard academic or professional English; these uses may also be labeled as wrong
verb forms. Finally, many errors of this kind involve verbs with irregular forms (like *begin, began, begun* or *break, broke, broken*). Errors may
occur when a writer confuses these forms or treats these verbs as if they

followed the regular pattern—for example, using *beginned* instead of *began,* or *have broke* instead of *have broken.*

> *had*
> ► By the time Ian arrived, Jill died.

The verb *died* does not clearly state the death occurred *before* Ian arrived.

> *is*
> ► The poet ~~be~~ looking at a tree when she has a sudden inspiration.

> *broken*
> ► Mia Hamm has ~~broke~~ many soccer records.

> *built*   *brought*
> ► The Greeks ~~builded~~ a wooden horse that the Trojans ~~brung~~ into the city.

The verbs *build* and *bring* have irregular past-tense forms.

For guidelines on editing verb tenses, see 24a. For more detailed information about verb tenses and forms, see 28b and Chapters 29 and 30.

14   Lack of subject-verb agreement

A verb must agree with its subject in number and person. In many cases, the verb's form depends on whether the subject is singular or plural: *The old man is angry and stamps into the house,* but *The old men are angry and stamp into the house.* Lack of subject-verb agreement is often just a matter of leaving the *-s* ending off the verb out of carelessness, or of using a form of English that does not have this ending. Sometimes, however, this error results from particular sentence constructions.

When other words come between a subject and a verb, be careful: the noun nearest to the verb is not always the verb's subject.

> *has*
> ► A central part of my life goals ~~have~~ been to go to law school.

The subject is the singular noun *part,* not *goals.*

> *are*
> ► The two main goals of my life ~~is~~ to be generous and to have no regrets.

Here, the subject is the plural noun *goals,* not *life.*

If a subject has two or more parts connected by *and,* the subject is almost always plural. Sometimes the parts of the subject refer to the same person or thing; in such cases, as in the second example below, the subject should be treated as singular.

> ► The senator and her husband commutes every day from the suburbs.

commutes
▶ Our senator and friend ~~commute~~ every day from New York.

If a subject has two or more parts joined by *or* or *nor,* the verb should agree with the part nearest to the verb.

comes
▶ My brothers or my sister ~~come~~ every day to see Dad.

Here, the noun closest to the verb is a singular noun. The verb must agree with that singular noun. If this construction sounds awkward, consider the next edit.

sister   *brothers*
▶ My ~~brothers~~ or my ~~sister~~ commute every day from Phoenix.

Now the noun closest to the verb is plural, and the verb agrees with it.

Collective nouns such as *committee* and *jury* can be singular or plural, depending on whether they refer to a single unit or multiple individuals.

offers
▶ The committee ~~offer~~ several different solutions to that problem.
was
▶ The committee ~~were~~ honored for its fund-raising.

Some writers stumble over words like *measles* and *mathematics,* which look plural but are singular in meaning.

has
▶ Measles ~~have~~ become much less common in the United States.

Pronoun subjects cause problems for many writers. Most indefinite pronouns, such as *each, either, neither,* or *one,* are always singular and take a singular verb. The indefinite pronouns *both, few, many, others,* and *several* are always plural and take plural verb forms. Several indefinite pronouns (*all, any, enough, more, most, none, some*) can be singular or plural depending on the context in which they are used.

coordinates
▶ Each of these designs ~~coordinate~~ with the others.

▶ Many of these designs coordinates with the others.

The relative pronouns *who, which,* or *that* take verbs that agree with the word the pronoun refers to.

were
▶ Johnson was one of the athletes who ~~was~~ disqualified.

For additional information about subject-verb agreement, see Chapter 30.

15   Missing comma in a series

When three or more items appear in a series, they should be separated from one another with commas. Many newspapers do not use a comma between the last two items, but you'll never be wrong to use a series comma because a sentence can be ambiguous without one.

▶ Sharks eat mostly squid, shrimp, crabs, and other fish.
                                          ^

For more on using commas in a series, see 42d. For information on using parallel structures in a series, see 23a.

16   Lack of agreement between pronoun and antecedent

Pronouns replace another word (the antecedent) so that it does not have to be repeated. Pronouns must agree with their antecedents in gender (for example, using *he* or *him* to replace *Frederick Douglass,* and *she* or *her* to replace *Queen Elizabeth*) and in number (for example, using *it* to replace *a book,* and *they* or *them* to replace *fifteen books*).

Some problems occur with words like *each, either, neither,* and *one,* which are singular and take singular pronouns.

                                   its
▶ Each of the puppies thrived in ~~their~~ new home.
                                    ^

Problems can also occur with antecedents that are joined by *or* or *nor.*

                                   she
▶ Neither Ramón nor Susan felt that ~~they~~ had been treated fairly.
                                      ^

Some problems involve words like *audience* and *team,* which can be either singular or plural depending on whether they are considered a single unit or multiple individuals.

                                   their
▶ The team frequently changed ~~its~~ positions to get varied experience.
                                 ^

   Because *team* refers to the multiple members of the team rather than to the team as a single unit, *its* needs to change to *their.*

The other kind of antecedent that causes problems is an antecedent such as *each* or *employee,* which can refer to either men or women. Use *he* or *she, him or her,* and so on, or rewrite the sentence to make the antecedent and pronoun plural or to eliminate the pronoun altogether.

> *or her*
> ► Every student must provide his own uniform.
>
> *All students*   *their*   *uniforms.*
> ► ~~Every student~~ must provide ~~his~~ own ~~uniform.~~
>
>   *a*
> ► Every student must provide ~~his own~~ uniform.

For more on pronoun-antecedent agreement, see 33f and 33g.

17   Unnecessary comma(s) with a restrictive element

A restrictive element is one that is essential to the basic meaning of the sentence. It is *not* set off from the rest of the sentence with commas.

> ► People/who wanted to preserve wilderness areas/opposed the plan to privatize national parks.

The reader needs the clause *who wanted to preserve wilderness areas* because it announces which people opposed the plan. As an essential element, the clause should *not* be set off by commas.

> ► Shakespeare's tragedy/*Othello*/deals with the dangers of jealousy.

The reader needs to know which of Shakespeare's many tragedies this sentence is talking about. The title *Othello* is therefore essential and should *not* be set off by commas.

For additional information about restrictive phrases and clauses, see 42c and 42j.

18   Fused sentence

A fused sentence (also called a run-on sentence) is created when clauses that could each stand alone as a sentence are joined with no appropriate punctuation or words to link them. Fused sentences must either be divided into separate sentences or joined by adding words or punctuation.

> *He*
> ► The current was swift. ~~he~~ could not swim to shore.
>
>   *but*
> ► Klee's paintings seem simple, they are very sophisticated.

▶ She doubted the value of meditation; *nevertheless,* she decided to try it once.

▶ I liked the movie very much, *for* it made me laugh throughout.

For more ways to revise fused sentences, see Chapter 34.

19   Misplaced or dangling modifier

Check every modifier (whether a word, phrase, or clause) to make sure that it is as close as possible to the word it describes or relates to. Be on the lookout for misplaced modifiers that may confuse your readers by seeming to modify some other word, phrase, or clause.

▶ *With binoculars, they* ~~They~~ could see the eagles swooping and diving. ~~with binoculars.~~

     Who was wearing the binoculars—the eagles?

▶ *When he was ten years old, he* ~~He~~ had decided he wanted to be a doctor. ~~when he was ten years old.~~

     What kind of doctor would he be at age ten?

▶ The architect ~~only~~ wanted to use *only* pine paneling for decoration.

     Did the architect only consider but then reject pine paneling?

A dangling modifier hangs precariously from the beginning or end of a sentence and is attached to no other word in the sentence. The word that it modifies may exist in your mind but not on paper. Proofread carefully to ensure that each modifier refers to some other word in the sentence.

▶ A doctor should check your eyes for glaucoma every year if *you are* over fifty.

▶ Looking down the sandy beach, *we see that* people are tanning themselves.

For more on misplaced and dangling modifiers, see 32a and 32d.

20   *Its/It's* confusion

Use *its* to mean *belonging to it;* use *it's* only when you mean *it is* or *it has.*

▶ The car is lying on ~~it's~~ *its* side in the ditch. ~~Its~~ *It's* a white 2004 Subaru.

For more on distinguishing *its* and *it's,* see 45b.

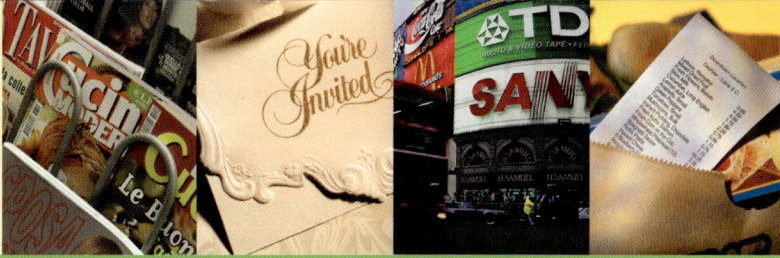

COMPOSING
in a Digital Age

... write in the kitchen, lock yourself up in
the bathroom. **Write on the bus** or the
welfare line, on the job or during meals. ...

–GLORIA ANZALDÚA

Composing in a Digital Age

4

Writing and Its Rhetorical Situations

What do a magazine article on stem-cell research, an email message to MasterCard complaining about an error on a bill, and an engineering report on a proposed new dam site all have in common? The writers of all three must analyze their rhetorical situations and then respond to them in appropriate ways. Today, Web sites, Web logs (blogs), and other forms of electronic communication allow more everyday opportunities to consider rhetorical situations than ever before.

4a Write in the twenty-first century.

Until recently, most people have defined *writing* as putting words on paper or screen, but not today. In fact, even some of the other words we associate with writing—*reading, speaking,* and *listening*—no longer get the job done. When you watch and listen to the nightly news, for example, you are "reading" the meaning of the events described, and the announcer "speaking" is likewise "reading" a text that has already been written. Since we don't have new words for these complicated and shifting acts, we need a broader definition of the old terms. Writing, for example, now includes much more than words; visual images and graphics create and carry an important part of the message. In addition, writing now can include sound and video streaming. Perhaps most important, writing today often contains many voices, as, with increasing ease, we bring ideas from the Web and other sources into what we write.

Writing in this new century is also often about collaboration and teamwork: at your job, you work with a team to produce an illustrated report, and team members then present the report to management; you and a colleague carry out an experiment together, argue over and write up the results, and explain your findings to a class or professional gathering; you work with a design artist, an illustrator, and a programmer to create a Web document for a cause close to your heart.

If it is true that "no man [or woman!] is an island," then it is equally true that no piece of writing is an island, isolated and alone. Instead, writing today is connected to a web of other writings that may be extending, responding to, or challenging it. Today, when an email message can literally circle the globe in seconds, it's important to remember this principle about writing: all writing exists within a rich and broad context in which any writer says or writes something to others for a purpose.

In short, as a writer today, you need to remember several key points:

- Writing, one of the world's oldest technologies, uses an expansive array of tools, from pencil and pen to software programs and video-streaming capacities.
- Writing is visual as well as verbal; design elements are key to the success of many documents.
- Writing is often collaborative—from planning, to designing, to producing the final product.
- Writing is increasingly multilingual, as writers bring in other languages, and as improvements in technology allow for faster and easier global communication.
- Writing has the potential to reach massive audiences in a very, very short time.
- Writing today is primarily public; once on the Web, it can take on a life of its own. As a result, writers need to consider their own—and others'—privacy.

4b Consider your rhetorical situation.

As a writer or speaker, you must think about the topic or message that you want to get across, your relationship to the audience you are writing to, and the context you are writing in. Context includes your values and beliefs and those of your audience; your background knowledge and that of the audience; your time and space limitations; your purpose; the medium and genre; your style and level of language; and a variety of other factors. Taken together, these factors constitute the rhetorical situation.

Considering your task or assignment

- If you have a specific writing assignment, what does it ask you to do? Look for words such as *analyze, classify, compare, contrast, define, describe, discuss, explain, prove,* and *survey*. Keep in mind that these words may differ in meaning from discipline to discipline or from job to job: *analyze* might mean one

The Rhetorical Situation

Writer/Speaker

Context

Audience/
Readers

Topic/
Message

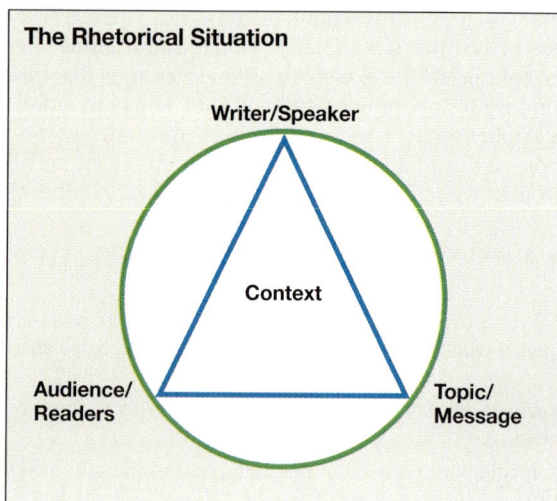

thing in literature and something rather different in biology or philosophy—
or in a corporate report.

- What information do you need to complete the assignment or task? Do you need to do research?
- Should you limit—or broaden—the topic you're writing about to make it more compelling to you and your audience? What problem(s) does the topic suggest to you? If you wish to redefine the assignment, check with the person who assigned it.
- What are the assignment's specific requirements? Consider length, format, organization, and deadline.
- What graphics or other visual information does the assignment call for?

Considering your purpose

- What is the primary purpose of the assignment—to explain? summarize? persuade? recommend? entertain? some other purpose? If you are unclear about the primary purpose, think about what you want to accomplish, or talk with the person who gave you the assignment. Are there secondary purposes to keep in mind?
- What is the purpose of the person who gave you this assignment—to make sure you have understood certain materials? to evaluate your thinking and writing abilities? to determine whether you can evaluate certain materials critically? to test your ability to think outside the box?
- What are your own purposes in this piece of writing—to respond to a question adequately and accurately? to learn as much as possible about a topic? to communicate your ideas clearly and forcefully? to make recommendations? to express certain feelings? How can you achieve these goals?

Considering your audience

- Whom do you most want to reach—people already sympathetic to your views? people who disagree with your views? members of a group you belong to? or a group you don't belong to?
- In what ways are the members of your audience different from you? from one another? Consider such factors as education, region, age, gender, occupation, social class, ethnic and cultural heritage, politics, religion, marital status, and sexual orientation.
- What assumptions can you legitimately make about your audience? What might they value? Think about brevity, originality, conformity, honesty, adventure, wit, seriousness, thrift, and so on.
- What languages and dialects do your audience use, and what special language, if any, will they expect you to use?
- What do your audience already know about your topic? Do you need to provide any special background information or define any terms?
- What sorts of information and evidence will your audience find most compelling? quotations from experts? personal experiences? photographs? diagrams or charts?
- What kinds of appeals will be most effective in reaching this audience?
- What response(s) do you want to evoke?

CONSIDERING DISABILITIES

Your Whole Audience

Remember that considering your whole audience means thinking about members with varying abilities and special needs. Current figures indicate that approximately one in five Americans were living with a disability in the year 2000. All writers need to think carefully about how their words reach out and connect with such very diverse audiences.

Considering your rhetorical stance

- How will you establish your credibility (or ethos); that is, how will you show that you are knowledgeable and trustworthy?
- What is your overall attitude toward the topic—approval? disapproval? curiosity? indifference? How strong are your opinions?
- What social, political, religious, or other factors account for your attitude?
- What do you know about the topic? What questions do you have?
- What interests you *most* and *least* about the topic? Why?
- What seems important—or unimportant—about the topic?

- What preconceptions, if any, do you have about it?
- What do you expect to conclude about the topic?
- Think about your audience. Will they have similar attitudes and interests?

Considering genre and language

- What genre, or form, of writing does your task call for—a report? a review? a poem? a letter? a blurb?
- If you need to produce academic writing, should you use any specialized varieties of English along with academic English? any occupational, professional, regional, or ethnic varieties? any words from a language other than English?

FOR MULTILINGUAL WRITERS

Bringing in Other Languages

Even when you write in English, you may want or need to include words, phrases, or whole passages in another language. If so, consider whether your readers will understand that language and whether you need to provide a translation. See 38e for more on bringing in other languages.

Considering online rhetorical situations

Before the advent of writing systems, the contexts for communication were always oral, what many now call *f2f,* for "face-to-face." Today, however, much seemingly f2f communication actually takes place online. Although the contexts for online communication are changing and multiplying daily, what can we say about them as they currently exist?

- *Online contexts offer many new ways to get information and join conversations.* As a result, you will need to learn to manage large amounts of information and to sharpen your critical-thinking skills so that you are able to distinguish the jewels from the junk.
- *Online contexts are primarily public.* Email is routinely used in court cases, and some email messages have had very serious consequences. If you don't want what you are putting online to become public, think twice before posting it.
- *Online texts travel—and travel, and travel.* Online messages may be forwarded, cut and pasted into new messages, and so on. Think about how such "traveling" may affect what you are trying to say. In the same way, be careful about forwarding anyone else's messages without permission.

AT A GLANCE

Writing Online

- What is your purpose for writing online? If it is to gather information, for example, what is the best way to phrase questions you might send out to an email discussion list or an expert on your topic?

- Have you considered your online audience carefully? How well does your audience know you? Are your tone and level of formality appropriate?

- Have you observed the rules of online etiquette? If you are writing to a listserv or a chat room, are you following expected conventions? (Chapter 12)

- Have you considered what design elements you should use? a template? color to signal response to email? graphics that can be quickly downloaded? (Chapters 13 and 14)

- If you are relying on information you found online, are you sure of its accuracy and validity? (Chapter 18)

---

bedfordstmartins.com/everyday_writer For more about online writing, go to **Links** and click on **Working Online.**

5

Thinking Visually

Today, we live in a world of words *and* visuals, in which writers routinely accompany email messages with photographs, create graphs and charts to illustrate documents, and animate their writing with many forms of media. But the ability to use color, fancy fonts, and visuals of all kinds presents writers with new challenges. This chapter will help you think about how visual information works—including the different messages it sends—and decide when to rely on plain old words, when to rely on visual data, and when to rely on both.

5a Consider document design conventions.

When you look at a document, its overall appearance—or design—often tells you the kind of document it is. For example, you can spot a standard business letter at a glance just by looking at its layout and seeing the inside address, salutation, and so on. Similarly, many academic essays have a "look" that makes them instantly identifiable.

DOCUMENTS THAT SHOW DESIGN CONVENTIONS

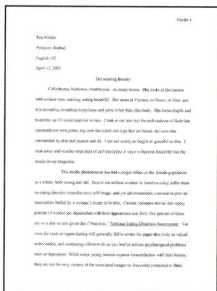

You may already recognize the design conventions in the preceding documents, but it is easy to overlook the design features of other documents you see every day. As a writer, you'll want to make sure that you are using design conventions appropriately. In other words, you want your lab report in chemistry to *look* like a lab report, just as you want your résumé to identify itself visually as one.

For help with designing your print and online documents, see Chapters 13 and 14. For more on the document conventions of different disciplines, see Chapters 59–62.

5b Consider how visuals create associations.

Visual information works by creating associations in readers' minds. When you see a popular company logo, for instance, you often make an immediate connection with the company and its product or service. Notice how quickly you can associate each logo shown in the flag on page 33 with the company it represents. This Adbusters visual of the American flag is also making a visual argument. (For advice on analyzing visual arguments, see Chapter 10.)

Regardless of the visual or the words that accompany it, writers are only partially in control of the messages they send. People will develop

AN IMAGE WITH LOGOS THAT CONVEY ASSOCIATIONS

their own associations and find their own meaning in the message. For example, the famous golden arches logo associated with McDonald's is interpreted very differently by two students.

> **JASON**   Instead of a symbol of food, I see the golden arches as a symbol of work. A child may see the "M" and think of fries or toys; I think of sweating, understaffed work crews slaving away in the back of the store.

> **DÁNIELLE**   When I was a kid, my dad would occasionally sneak me a Happy Meal. My mom must have known since the whole house would end up smelling like hot french fries. When I see the golden arches, I think of having this special secret with my dad and happily eating cheeseburgers and fries.

When you choose visuals for the documents you are creating, remember these lessons and ask what associations readers may already have with a visual you choose.

5c   Consider how visuals convey tone.

The tone of your writing can be conveyed not only by your language but also through the visuals you use in a document. Notice, for example, how each of the visuals of Albert Einstein on page 34 conveys a different tone.

A visual appropriate for one type of writing may have the wrong tone for another type of writing. In a serious academic essay about

VISUALS THAT CONVEY DIFFERENT TONES

Einstein, for example, you would not use the second and third visual shown here. When you choose a particular visual, ask yourself if it helps to convey the tone you want to achieve (humorous, serious, impassioned, and so on) and if that tone is appropriate for your audience, purpose, and topic. (For more on tone, see 9b and 24f.)

5d Consider how words and visuals work together.

Readers and writers today are usually dealing with information presented in both words and visuals. For example, Emily Lesk, a student writing about Coca-Cola as a cultural icon that shapes American identity, used the following words and visuals to help readers "see" the point she was trying to make. (You will see other examples of Emily Lesk's work in the following chapters.)

A STUDENT'S USE OF WORDS AND A VISUAL IN AN ESSAY

Even before setting foot in Israel three years ago, I knew exactly where I could find the Coke T-shirt. The tiny shop in the central block of Jerusalem s Ben Yehuda Street did offer other shirt designs, but the one with a bright white Drink Coca-Cola Classic written in Hebrew cursive across the chest was what drew in most of the dollar-carrying tourists. While waiting almost twenty minutes for my shirt (depicted in Fig. 1), I watched nearly every

Fig. 1. Hebrew Coca-Cola T-shirt. Personal photograph. Despite my dislike for the beverage, I bought this Coca-Cola T-shirt in Israel.

customer ahead of me ask for the Coke shirt, <u>todah rabah</u> [thank you very much].

At the time, I never thought it strange that I wanted one, too. Yet, I <u>had</u> absorbed sixteen years of Coca-Cola propaganda through everything from NBC s Saturday morning cartoon lineup to the concession stand at Camden Yards (the Baltimore Orioles ballpark). . . .

Getting words and visuals to work together for maximum effect isn't always easy. After the September 11, 2001, terrorist attacks, the U.S. government created a Web site (www.ready.gov) to provide information and to help people prepare for another possible attack. However, some readers found the Web site's visuals unclear—and made their point in a humorous way by rewriting the government's words, as seen below.

ORIGINAL MESSAGE	**REWRITTEN MESSAGE**	**ORIGINAL MESSAGE**	**REWRITTEN MESSAGE**
If you become aware of an unusual or suspicious release of an unknown substance nearby, it doesn't hurt to protect yourself	Don't get so preoccupied with biological weapons that you forget to put on deodorant.	**Shielding:** If you have a thick shield between yourself and the radioactive materials, more of the radiation will be absorbed, and you will be exposed to less.	If deadly radiation knocks on your door, do not answer.

To avoid misunderstandings, writers need to integrate all the elements of a document carefully, paying special attention to how well the text and visuals work together and fit the purpose of the writing and the intended audience. In addition, writers need to think carefully about when to put more emphasis on words—and when to put more emphasis on visuals.

6

Exploring Ideas

The point is so simple that we often forget it: we write best about topics we know well. This process includes everything from beginning to think about the topic to editing the final draft. One of the most important parts of the entire writing process, therefore, is choosing a topic that will engage your strengths and your interest and then exploring that topic by surveying what you know and determining what you need to find out. You can explore any topic in a number of ways; the goal is to find strategies that work well for you.

6a Try brainstorming.

One of the best ways to begin exploring a topic is also the most familiar: *talk it over* with others. Consider beginning with a brainstorming session. Brainstorming means tossing out ideas—often with other people, either in person or online. You can also brainstorm by yourself.

1. Within a time limit of five or ten minutes, with several others, list *every* word or phrase that comes to mind about the topic. Just jot down key words and phrases, not sentences. No one has to understand the list but you and your group. Don't worry about whether or not something will be useful. Just list as much as you can in this brief span of time.
2. If very little occurs to you and your group, try calling out thoughts about the opposite side of your topic. If you are trying, for instance, to think of reasons to reduce tuition and are coming up blank, try concentrating on reasons to *increase* tuition. You'll find that once you start generating ideas in one direction, you can usually move back to the other side fairly easily.
3. When the time is up, stop and read over the lists you have made. If anything else comes to mind, add it to your list. Then reread the list, looking for patterns of interesting ideas or one central idea.

6b Try freewriting.

Freewriting is a method of exploring a topic by writing about it for a period of time *without stopping.*

1. Write for ten minutes or so. Think about your topic, and let your mind wander; write down whatever occurs to you. Don't worry about grammar or spelling. If you get stuck, write anything—just don't stop.
2. When the time is up, look at what you have written. You may discover some important insights and ideas.

CONSIDERING DISABILITIES

Try Freespeaking

If you are better at talking out than writing out your ideas, try *freespeaking*, which is basically the talking version of freewriting. Begin by speaking into a tape recorder or into a computer with voice recognition software, and just keep talking about your topic for at least seven to ten minutes. Say whatever comes to your mind, and don't stop talking. You can then listen to or read the results of your freespeaking and look for an idea to pursue at greater length.

6c   Try looping.

Looping is a kind of directed freewriting that narrows a topic through a process of five-minute stages, or loops.

1. Spend five minutes freewriting about your topic *without stopping*. This is your first loop.
2. Look at what you have written. Find the central or most intriguing thought, and summarize it in a single sentence.
3. Starting with the summary sentence from your first loop, spend another five minutes freewriting. This second loop focuses on the first loop, just as the first loop focused on your topic. Look for the central idea within your second piece of freewriting—the basis of a third loop.
4. Keep this process going until you discover a clear angle or something about the topic that you can pursue in a full-length piece of writing.

FOR MULTILINGUAL WRITERS

Using Your Native Language to Explore Ideas

For generating and exploring ideas—the work of much brainstorming, freewriting, looping, and clustering—you may be most successful at coming up with good ideas quickly and spontaneously if you work in your native language. Later in the process of writing, you can choose the best of these ideas and begin working with them in English.

6d   Try clustering.

Clustering is a way of generating ideas using a visual scheme or chart. It is especially helpful for understanding the relationships among the parts of a broad topic and for developing subtopics. If you have a software program for clustering (such as Inspiration), put it to use. If not, follow these steps:

1. Write down your topic in the middle of a blank piece of paper or screen and circle it.
2. In a ring around the topic circle, write what you see as the main parts of the topic. Circle each part, and then draw a line from it to the topic.
3. Think of more ideas, examples, facts, or other details relating to each main part. Write each of these near the appropriate part, circle each one, and draw a line from it to the part.
4. Repeat this process with each new circle until you can't think of any more details. Some trails may lead to dead ends, but you will still have many useful connections among ideas.

Here is an example of the clustering Emily Lesk did for her essay about Coca-Cola and American identity:

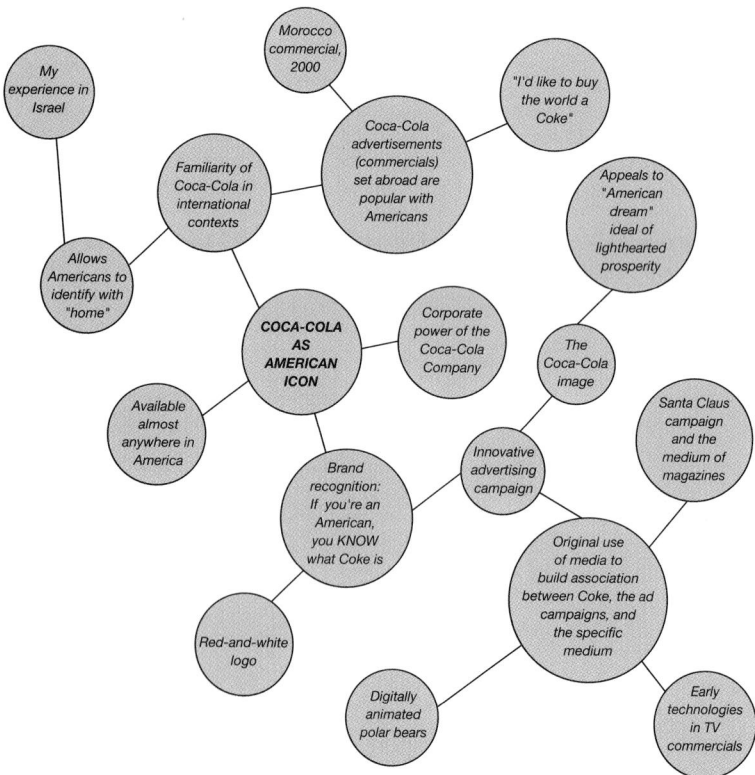

6e Ask questions.

Another basic strategy for exploring a topic and generating ideas is simply to ask and answer questions. Here are two widely used sets of questions to get you started.

Questions to describe a topic

Originally developed by Aristotle, the following questions can help you explore a topic by carefully and systematically describing it:

1. *What is it?* What are its characteristics, dimensions, features, and parts?
2. *What caused it?* What changes occurred to create your topic? How is it changing? How will it change?
3. *What is it like or unlike?* What features differentiate your topic from others? What analogies does your topic support?
4. *What larger system is your topic a part of?* How is your topic related to this system?
5. *What do people say about it?* What reactions does your topic arouse? What about the topic causes those reactions?

Questions to explain a topic

These are the well-known questions that ask *who, what, when, where, why,* and *how.* Widely used by news reporters, these questions are especially helpful for explaining a topic.

1. *Who* is doing it?
2. *What* is at issue?
3. *When* does it begin and end?
4. *Where* is it taking place?
5. *Why* does it occur?
6. *How* is it done?

6f Consult print and electronic sources.

Go to the library, and browse around for a topic you are interested in and want to learn more about. If you have a short list of possible ideas, do a quick check of encyclopedias to get overviews of the topics. You can begin with a general encyclopedia or a specialized one that focuses on a specific area such as history, music, or psychology.

Use search engines—such as Google, Yahoo!, or WebCrawler—to explore topics and ideas and to gather sources. Many search engines have directories organized by topic that you can browse and explore (see the "Issues and Causes" page on Yahoo!, for example). Some advanced searches allow you to search for only visual images, current events, and government sites and to otherwise limit your results.

6g Work collaboratively.

Most work today is done collaboratively, whether that work is on a basketball court, at a corporate meeting, or in a classroom. Writers often work together to come up with ideas, to respond to one another's drafts, or even to coauthor something. Here are some strategies for working with others:

1. Fix a regular meeting time and a system for contacting one another.
2. If you are working over a computer network, exchange email addresses, and consider exchanging ideas and drafts electronically.
3. Establish ground rules for the group. Be sure every member has an equal opportunity—and responsibility—to contribute.
4. Assign duties at each meeting: one person to take notes, another to keep the discussion on track, and so on.
5. With final deadlines in mind, set an agenda for each group meeting.
6. Listen carefully to what each person says. If disagreements arise, try paraphrasing to see if everyone is hearing the same thing.
7. Use group meetings to work together on particularly difficult problems. If an assignment is complex, have each member explain one section to all the others. If the group has trouble understanding part of the task, check with whoever made the assignment.
8. Expect disagreement, and remember that the goal is not for everyone just to "go along." The challenge is to get a really spirited debate going and to argue through all possibilities.
9. If you are preparing a group-written document, divide up the drafting duties. Set reasonable deadlines for each stage of work. Schedule at least two meetings to iron out the final draft by reading it aloud and working for consistency of tone. Have everyone proofread the final draft, with one person making the corrections.
10. If the group will be making a presentation, be sure you know exactly how much time you will have. Decide how each member will contribute to the presentation. Leave time for at least two practice sessions.
11. Make a point of assessing the group's effectiveness. What has the group accomplished? What has it done best? What has it been least successful at? What has each member contributed? How could the group function more effectively?

bedfordstmartins.com/everyday_writer If you're using **Comment** in your course, you and your classmates can easily exchange writing ideas and drafts online.

7

Drafting

One student defines drafting as that time in a writing project "when the rubber meets the road." In this sense, drafting begins the moment you start shaping your ideas for presentation to your readers. As you narrow your topic, decide on your thesis, organize materials to support that central idea, and sketch out a plan for your writing, you have already begun the drafting process.

7a   Narrow your topic.

After exploring ideas, you may have found a topic that interests you and would also be interesting to your readers. The topic, however, may be too large to be manageable. If that is the case, narrow your topic in order to focus on a more workable idea. Emily Lesk narrowed her original vast topic (American advertising) by asking herself questions.

TOPIC: American advertising

Okay, what do I most want to know about this topic? How powerful is advertising? Could advertising be related to how we define "American"?

FIRST FOCUS ATTEMPT: American advertising and national identity

Ah, I may be onto something. How about portrayals of women and how they affect U.S. identity? Better yet, how about choosing a particular company that might be linked to American identity: McDonald's? Weight Watchers? Coca-Cola? Chevrolet?

SECOND FOCUS ATTEMPT: Advertising icons that shape American identity

Yes, but how many icons are there? LOTS— and I just named a few. Better choose one.

NARROWED TOPIC: Coca-Cola as a cultural icon that shapes American identity

7b Craft a working thesis.

Most academic or professional writing contains a thesis statement, often near the beginning. The thesis functions as a promise to readers, letting them know what the writer will discuss. Though you may not have a final thesis when you begin to write, you should establish a tentative working thesis early on in your writing process.

The word *working* is important here because the working thesis may well change as you write. Even so, a working thesis focuses your thinking and research, and helps keep you on track.

A working thesis should have two parts: a topic, which states the topic, and a comment, which makes an important point about the topic.

TOPIC · COMMENT
▶ **Recent studies of depression suggest that it is much more closely**

related to physiology than scientists had previously thought.

TOPIC · COMMENT
▶ **The current health care crisis arises from three major causes.**

A successful working thesis has three characteristics:

1. It is potentially *interesting* to the intended audience.
2. It is as *specific* as possible.
3. It limits the topic enough to make it *manageable.*

You can evaluate a working thesis by checking it against each of these characteristics, as in the following example:

PRELIMINARY WORKING THESIS

▶ **Theories about global warming are being debated around the world.**

INTERESTING? The topic itself holds interest, but it seems to have no real comment attached to it. The thesis merely states a bare fact, and the only place to go from here is to more bare facts.

SPECIFIC? The thesis is not specific. Who is debating these theories? What is at issue in this debate?

MANAGEABLE? The thesis is not manageable; it would require research on global warming in many countries.

ASSESSMENT: This thesis can be narrowed by the addition of a stronger comment and a sharper focus.

REVISED WORKING THESIS

▶ **Working independently, scientists from several countries have now confirmed that global warming is demonstrably caused by humans.**

FOR MULTILINGUAL WRITERS

Stating a Thesis

In some cultures, it is considered rude to state an opinion outright. In the United States, however, academic and business practices require writers to make key positions explicitly clear.

7c   Gather information to support your thesis.

Writing will often call for research. An assignment may specify that you conduct research on your topic and cite your sources. Or you may find that you do not know enough about your topic to write about it effectively without doing some research. Sometimes you need to do research at various stages of the writing process—early on, to help you understand or define your topic, or later on, to find additional examples to support your thesis. Once you have a working thesis, consider what additional information, including any visuals, you might need. (For more on conducting research and working with sources, see Chapters 17 and 18. For more on organizing your support into paragraphs, see Chapter 8. For more on supporting your thesis, see Chapter 11.)

7d   Organize verbal and visual information.

While you're finding information on your topic, think about how you will group or organize that information to make it accessible and persuasive to readers. At the simplest level, writers most often group information in their writing projects according to four principles—space, time, logic, and association.

Organizing according to space

The organizational principle of space refers to *where* bits of information occur within a setting. If the information you have gathered is descriptive, you may choose to organize it spatially. Using spatial organization allows the reader to "see" your information, to fix it in space. You might include a map or another graphic that would help readers visualize your description. The example on the next page organizes information according to space.

I entered the forest cautiously, feeling as if many eyes were watching me. On my left loomed a fairy circle of giant redwoods, the ground below them soft with their needles. On my right, a Douglas fir stood straight and tall. And ahead of me, on the narrow path, I could see small animals scampering back and forth.

Organizing according to time

The principle of time refers to *when* bits of information occur, usually chronologically. Chronological organization is the basic method used in cookbooks, lab reports, instruction manuals, and stories. Writers of these products organize information according to when it occurs in some process or sequence of events (narrative). The example below organizes information according to time.

INFORMATION ORGANIZED CHRONOLOGICALLY

Heat oil in a skillet over medium heat. Crack four large eggs into a medium bowl. Stir with a whisk. Sprinkle with salt, pepper, parsley, and oregano. Spread egg mixture evenly in pan; top with cheese. Cook until omelet is firm.

Organizing according to logic

The principle of logic refers to how bits of information are related logically. The most commonly used logical patterns include *illustration, definition, division and classification, comparison and contrast, cause and effect, problem and solution, use of analogies,* and *narration.* The example on the next page organizes information logically, according to the principle of division. For other examples of paragraphs organized according to these logical patterns, see Chapter 8.

INFORMATION ORGANIZED LOGICALLY

Burns can be divided into three types or levels: (1) Superficial, or first-degree, burns damage the top layer of skin. They are red and painful. (2) Partial thickness, or second-degree, burns damage the outer layer of skin and the layer just below it. They are very painful and are characterized by blistering, swelling, redness, and pain. (3) Full thickness, or third-degree, burns damage deep tissues. They appear charred and black. The burn area itself is numb, but the surrounding area is very painful.

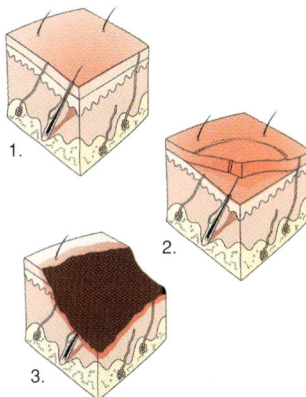

Organizing according to association

The principle of association refers to how bits of information are related in terms of visuals, motifs, personal memories, and so on. Many contemporary essays are organized through a series of associations that grow directly out of the writer's memory or experience. Thus, associational organization is often used in personal narrative, where writers can use a chain of associations to render an experience vividly for readers. The example below is built on a series of associations.

INFORMATION ORGANIZED ASSOCIATIONALLY

Flying from San Francisco to Atlanta, I looked down to see the gentle roll of the Smoky Mountains begin to appear. Almost at once, I was back on my Granny's porch, sitting next to her drinking iced tea and eating peaches. Those peaches tasted good—picked ripe, skinned, and eaten with no regard for the sweet juice trickling everywhere. And on special occasions, we'd make ice cream, and Granny would empty a bowl brimming with chopped peaches into the creamy dish. Now—that was the life!

In much of your writing, you will want to use two or more principles of organization. In addition, with the advent of electronic forms of text production you may want to include not only visuals but sound and other multimedia effects as well.

Whichever of these principles you use to begin organizing an essay or project, take special care in planning for the inclusion of visuals.

- Choose visuals that are closely related to your topic. Visuals shouldn't be just window dressing.
- Consider using visuals when you want to capture your reader's attention and interest in a vivid way; emphasize a point you have already made in your text; present information that is difficult to convey in words; or communicate with audiences with different language skills and abilities.
- Plan to place each visual as near as possible to the text it illustrates.
- Remember that, for your final draft, you need to introduce each visual clearly: *As the map to the right depicts. . . .*
- In addition, comment on the significance or effect of the visual: *Figure 1 corroborates the claim made by geneticists: while the human genome may be mapped, it is far from understood.*
- Finally, label each visual appropriately, and cite the source.

7e Make a plan.

At this point, you will find it helpful to write out an organizational plan or outline. To do so, simply begin with your thesis; review your exploratory notes, research materials, and visual sources; and then list all the examples and other good reasons you have to support the thesis.

A sample organizational plan

One informal way to organize your ideas is to figure out what belongs in your introduction, body paragraphs, and conclusion. Here is how one student, who was writing about solutions to a problem, used this kind of plan:

WORKING THESIS

▶ **Increased motorcycle use demands the reorganization of campus parking lots.**

INTRODUCTION

give background and overview (motorcycle use up dramatically) and use a photograph of overcrowding in a lot

state purpose—to fulfill promise of thesis by offering solutions

BODY

describe the current situation (tell of my research at area parking lots)

describe the problem in detail (report on statistics: cars vs. cycles) and include a graph representing findings

present two possible solutions (enlarge lots or reallocate space)

CONCLUSION

recommend against first solution because of cost and space

recommend second solution, and summarize benefits of it

A formal outline

Even if you have made an informal written plan before drafting, you may also want—or be required—to prepare a formal outline, which can help you see exactly how the parts of your writing will fit together—how your ideas relate, where you need examples, and what the overall structure of your work will be. Your word-processing program probably has an outline feature. (To prepare an outline in Microsoft Word, click on FORMAT, BULLETS AND NUMBERING, and then OUTLINE NUMBERED.)

Most formal outlines follow a conventional format of numbered and lettered headings and subheadings, using roman numerals, capital letters, arabic numerals, and lowercase letters to show the levels of importance of the various ideas and their relationships. Each new level is indented to show its subordination to the preceding level.

Thesis statement

I. First main idea
   A. First subordinate idea
      1. First supporting detail or point
      2. Second supporting detail
      3. Third supporting detail
   B. Second subordinate idea
      1. First supporting detail
      2. Second supporting detail

II. Second main idea
   A. First subordinate idea
      1. First supporting detail
      2. Second supporting detail
   B. Second subordinate idea
      1. First supporting detail
      2. Second supporting detail
         a. First supporting detail
         b. Second supporting detail

Note that each level contains at least two parts, so there is no A without a B, no 1 without a 2. Also keep in mind that headings should be stated in parallel form—either all sentences or all grammatically parallel structures.

Whatever form your plan takes, you may want or need to change it along the way. Writing has a way of stimulating thought, and the process of drafting may generate new ideas. Or you may find that you need to reexamine some data or information or gather more material.

7f Write out a draft.

No matter how good your planning, investigating, and organizing have been, chances are you will need to do more work as you draft. This fact of life leads to the first principle of successful drafting: be flexible. If you see that your plan is not working, do not hesitate to alter it. If some information now seems irrelevant, leave it out—even if you went to great lengths to obtain it. Throughout the drafting process, you may need to refer to points you have already written about. You may learn that you need to do more research, that your whole thesis must be reshaped, or that your topic is still too broad and should be narrowed further. Very often you will continue planning, investigating, and organizing throughout the writing process.

AT A GLANCE

Drafting

- *Set up a computer folder or file for your essay.* Give the file a clear and relevant name, and save to it often.

- *Have all your information close at hand and arranged according to your organizational plan.* Stopping to search for a piece of information can break your concentration or distract you.

- *Try to write in stretches of at least thirty minutes.* Writing can provide momentum, and once you get going, the task becomes easier.

- *Don't let small questions bog you down.* Just make a note of them in brackets—or in all caps—or make a tentative decision and move on.

- *Remember that first drafts aren't perfect.* Concentrate on getting all your ideas onscreen, and don't worry about anything else.

- *Stop writing at a place where you know exactly what will come next.* Doing so will help you start easily when you return to the draft.

---

bedfordstmartins.com/everyday_writer To see some student drafts, click on **Student Writing.**

8

Constructing Strong Paragraphs

Paragraphs serve as signposts—pointers that help guide readers through a piece of writing. A look through a popular magazine will show paragraphs working this way: the first paragraph of an article almost always aims to get our attention and to persuade us to read on, and subsequent ones often indicate a new point or a shift in focus or tone.

Put most simply, a paragraph is a group of sentences or a single sentence set off as a unit. Usually all the sentences in a paragraph revolve around one main idea.

AT A GLANCE

Editing Paragraphs

- Is there a sentence that makes the main idea of each paragraph clear? If not, should there be? (8a)

- Does the first sentence of each paragraph let readers know what that paragraph is about? Does the last sentence in some way conclude that paragraph's discussion? If not, does it need to?

- Within each paragraph, how does each sentence relate to the main idea? Revise or eliminate any that do not. (8a)

- How completely does each paragraph develop its main idea? What details are used? Are they effective? Do any paragraphs need more detail? (8b) What other methods of development might be used— definition? example? comparison and contrast? analogy? (8c)

- Is each paragraph organized in a way that is easy to follow? Are sentences within each paragraph clearly linked? Do any of the transitions try to create links between ideas that do not really exist? (8e)

- Are the paragraphs clearly linked? Do any links need to be added? Are any of the transitions from one paragraph to another artificial? (8e)

- How does the introductory paragraph catch readers' interest? How does the last paragraph draw the piece to a conclusion? (8f)

- If you are writing an email or creating a Web text, are your paragraphs effective and visually clear? (8g)

8a   Focus on a main idea.

An effective paragraph often focuses on one main idea. A good way to achieve such paragraph unity is to state the main idea clearly in one sentence and then relate all the other sentences in the paragraph to that idea. The sentence that presents the main idea is called the topic sentence.

FOR MULTILINGUAL WRITERS

Being Explicit

Native readers of English generally expect that paragraphs will have an explicitly stated main idea and that the connections between points in a paragraph will also be stated explicitly. Such step-by-step explicitness may strike you as unnecessary or ineffective, but it follows the traditional paragraph conventions of English.

Announcing the main idea in a topic sentence

The following paragraph opens with a clear topic sentence, and the rest of the paragraph builds on the idea stated in that sentence:

> *Our friendship was the source of much happiness and many memories.* We danced and snapped our fingers simultaneously to the tunes of Lenny Kravitz and Sheryl Crow. We sweated together in the sweltering summer sun, trying to win the championship for our softball team. I recall the taste of pepperoni and sausage pizza as we discussed the highlights of our team's victory. Once we even became attracted to the same person, but luckily we were able to share his friendship.

A topic sentence does not always come at the beginning of a paragraph; it may come at the end. Occasionally a paragraph's main idea is so obvious that it need not be stated explicitly in a topic sentence.

Relating each sentence to the main idea

Whether the main idea of a paragraph is stated in a topic sentence or is implied, make sure that all other sentences in the paragraph contribute to the main idea. In the preceding example about friendship, all of the sentences clearly relate to the point that is made in the first sentence. The result is a unified paragraph.

8b Provide details.

An effective paragraph develops its main idea by providing enough details to hold the reader's interest. Without such development, a paragraph may seem lifeless and abstract.

No such thing as human nature compels people to behave, think, or react in certain ways. Rather, from the time of our infancy to our death, we are constantly being taught, by the society that surrounds us, the customs, norms, and mores of our distinct culture. Everything in culture is learned, not genetically transmitted.

This paragraph is boring. Although its main idea is clear and its sentences hold together, it fails to gain our interest or hold our attention because it lacks any specific examples or details. Now look at the paragraph revised to include needed specifics.

Imagine a child in Ecuador dancing to salsa music at a warm family gathering while a child in the United States is decorating a Christmas tree with bright, shiny red ornaments. Both of these children are taking part in their countries' cultures. It is not by instinct that one child knows how to dance to salsa music, nor is it by instinct that the other child knows how to decorate the tree. No such thing as human nature compels people to behave, think, or react in certain ways. Rather, from the time of our infancy to our death, we are constantly being taught, by the society that surrounds us, the customs, norms, and mores of our distinct culture. A majority of people feel that the evil in human beings is human nature. However, the Tasaday, a tribe discovered not long ago in the Philippines, do not even have equivalents in their language for the words *hatred, competition, acquisitiveness, aggression,* and *greed.* Such examples suggest that everything in culture is learned, not genetically transmitted.

Though both paragraphs present the same point, only the second one comes to life. It does so by bringing in specific details *from* life. We want to read this paragraph because it appeals to our senses (a child dancing; bright, shiny red ornaments) and our curiosity (who are the Tasaday?).

8c Use effective methods of development.

As noted in Chapter 7, there are several common methods of development. You can use them to develop paragraphs.

Narrative

A narrative paragraph uses the chronological elements of a story to develop a main idea. The following is one student's narrative paragraph that tells a personal story to support a point about the dangers of racing bicycles with flimsy alloy frames.

People who have been exposed to the risk of dangerously designed bicycle frames have paid too high a price. I saw this danger myself in last year's Putney Race. An expensive graphite frame failed, and the rider was catapulted onto Vermont pavement at fifty miles per hour. The pack of riders behind him was so dense that other racers crashed into a tangled, sliding heap. The aftermath: four hospitalizations. I got off with some stitches, a bad road rash, and severely pulled tendons. My Italian racing bike was pretzled, and my racing was over for that summer. Others were not so lucky. An Olympic hopeful, Brian Stone of the Northstar team, woke up in a hospital bed to find that his cycling was over—and not just for that summer. His kneecap had been surgically removed. He couldn't even walk.

Description

A descriptive paragraph uses specific details to create a clear impression. Notice how the following paragraph includes details about an old schoolroom; they convey a strong impression of a room where "time had taken its toll." Notice as well how the writer uses spatial organization, moving from the ceiling to the floor.

The professor's voice began to fade into the background as my eyes wandered around the classroom in the old administration building. The water-stained ceiling was cracked and peeling, and the splitting wooden beams played host to a variety of lead pipes and coils. My eyes followed these pipes down the walls and around corners until I eventually saw the electric outlets. I thought it was strange that they were exposed, and not built in, until I realized that there probably had been no electricity when the building was built. Below the outlets the sunshine was falling in bright rays across the hardwood floor, and I noticed how smoothly the floor was worn. Time had taken its toll on this building.

Definition

You may often need to write an entire paragraph in order to define a word or concept, as in the following paragraph:

> Economics is the study of how people choose among the alternatives available to them. It's the study of little choices ("Should I take the chocolate or the strawberry?") and big choices ("Should we require a reduction in energy consumption in order to protect the environment?"). It's the study of individual choices, choices by firms, and choices by governments. Life presents each of us with a wide range of alternative uses of our time and other resources; economists examine how we choose among those alternatives.
>
> —TIMOTHY TREGARTHEN, *Economics*

Example

One of the most common ways of developing a paragraph is by illustrating a point with one or more examples.

> The Indians made names for us children in their teasing way. Because our very busy mother kept my hair cut short, like my brothers', they called me Short Furred One, pointing to their hair and making the sign for short, the right hand with fingers pressed close together, held upward, back out, at the height intended. With me this was about two feet tall, the Indians laughing gently at my abashed face. I am told that I was given a pair of small moccasins that first time, to clear up my unhappiness at being picked out from the dusk behind the fire and my two unhappy shortcomings made conspicuous.
>
> —MARI SANDOZ, "The Go-Along Ones"

Division and classification

Division breaks a single item into parts. Classification groups many separate items according to their similarities. A paragraph evaluating one history course might divide the course into several segments—textbooks, lectures, assignments—and examine each one in turn. A paragraph giving an overview of many history courses might classify the courses in a number of ways—by time periods, by geographic areas, by the kinds of assignments demanded, by the number of students enrolled, or by some other principle.

DIVISION

> We all listen to music according to our separate capacities. But, for the sake of analysis, the whole listening process may become clearer if we break it up into its component parts, so to speak. In a certain sense, we all listen

to music on three separate planes. For lack of a better terminology, one might name these: (1) the sensuous plane, (2) the expressive plane, (3) the sheerly musical plane. The only advantage to be gained from mechanically splitting up the listening process into these hypothetical planes is the clearer view to be had of the way in which we listen.

— AARON COPLAND, *What to Listen For in Music*

CLASSIFICATION

Many people are seduced by fad diets. Those who have always been overweight turn to them out of despair; they have tried everything, and yet nothing seems to work. A second group to succumb appear perfectly healthy but are baited by slogans such as "look good, feel good." These slogans prompt self-questioning and insecurity—do I really look good and feel good?—and as a direct result, many healthy people fall prey to fad diets. With both types of people, however, the problems surrounding such diets are numerous and dangerous. In fact, these diets provide neither intelligent nor effective answers to weight control.

Comparison and contrast

When you compare two things, you look at their similarities; when you contrast two things, you focus on their differences. You can structure paragraphs that compare or contrast in two basic ways. One way is to present all the information about one item and then all the information about the other item, as in the following paragraph:

You could tell the veterans from the rookies by the way they were dressed. The knowledgeable ones had their heads covered by kerchiefs, so that if they were hired, tobacco dust wouldn't get in their hair; they had on clean dresses that by now were faded and shapeless, so that if they were hired they wouldn't get tobacco dust and grime on their best clothes. Those who were trying for the first time had their hair freshly done and wore attractive dresses; they wanted to make a good impression. But the dresses couldn't be seen at the distance that many were standing from the employment office, and they were crumpled in the crush.

— MARY MEBANE, "Summer Job"

Or you can switch back and forth between the two items, focusing on particular characteristics of each in turn.

Malcolm X emphasized the use of violence in his movement and employed the biblical principle of "an eye for an eye and a tooth for a tooth." King, on the other hand, felt that blacks should use nonviolent civil disobedience and employed the theme "turning the other cheek," which Malcolm X rejected as "beggarly" and "feeble." The philosophy of Malcolm X was one of revenge, and often it broke the unity of black Americans. More radical blacks supported him, while more conservative ones supported King. King thought that blacks should transcend their humanity. In contrast, Malcolm X thought they should embrace it and reserve their love for one another, regarding whites as "devils" and the "enemy." King's politics were those of a rainbow, but Malcolm X's rainbow was insistently one color—black. The distance between Martin Luther King Jr.'s thinking and Malcolm X's was the distance between growing up in the seminary and growing up on the streets, between the American dream and the American reality.

Analogy

Analogies (comparisons that explain an unfamiliar thing in terms of a familiar one) can also help develop paragraphs. In the following paragraph, the writer draws an unlikely analogy—between the human genome and Thanksgiving dinner—to help readers understand what scientists know about the human genome.

> Think of the human genome as the ingredients list for a massive Thanksgiving dinner. Scientists long have had a general understanding of how the feast is cooked. They knew where the ovens were. Now, they also have a list of every ingredient. Yet much remains to be discovered. In most cases, no one knows exactly which ingredients are necessary for making, for example, the pumpkin pie as opposed to the cornbread. Indeed, many, if not most, of the recipes that use the genomic ingredients are missing, and there's little understanding why small variations in the quality of the ingredients can "cook up" diseases in one person but not in another.
> —*USA Today*, "Cracking of Life's Genetic Code Carries Weighty Potential"

Cause and effect

You can often develop paragraphs by explaining the causes of something or the effects that something brings about. The following paragraph discusses the effects of television on the American family:

Television's contribution to family life has been an equivocal one. For while it has, indeed, kept the members of the family from dispersing, it has not served to bring them together. By its domination of the time families spend together, it destroys the special quality that distinguishes one family from another, a quality that depends to a great extent on what a family does, what special rituals, games, recurrent jokes, familiar songs, and shared activities it accumulates.

—MARIE WINN, *The Plug-in Drug: Television, Children, and the Family*

Process

Paragraphs that explain a process often use the principle of time or chronology to order the stages in the process.

By the late 20s, most people notice the first signs of aging in their physical appearance. Slight losses of elasticity in facial skin produce the first wrinkles, usually in those areas most involved in their characteristic facial expressions. As the skin continues to lose elasticity and fat deposits build up, the face sags a bit with age. Indeed, some people have drooping eyelids, sagging cheeks, and the hint of a double chin by age 40 (Whitbourne, 1985). Other parts of the body sag a bit as well, so as the years pass, adults need to exercise regularly if they want to maintain their muscle tone and body shape. Another harbinger of aging, the first gray hairs, is usually noticed in the 20s and can be explained by a reduction in the number of pigment-producing cells. Hair may become a bit less plentiful, too, because of hormonal changes and reduced blood supply to the skin.

—KATHLEEN STASSEN BERGER, *The Developing Person through the Life Span*

Problem and solution

Another way to develop a paragraph is to open with a topic sentence that states a problem or asks a question about a problem and then to offer a solution or answers in the sentences that follow.

How prepared is America for the next 9/11? The Bush administration's response to the U.S. intelligence and law-enforcement agencies' failure to communicate is the Terrorist Threat Integration Center. Launched last May, TTIC is an independent body manned with analysts from more than a dozen agencies, including the CIA, FBI, Immigration and Customs Enforcement, the National Security Agency, the Coast Guard, Homeland Security and the Secret Service. Each day TTIC analysts are supposed to share whatever they hear about potential threats and produce a report that goes to the White House, Pentagon and other major "customers."

—MICHAEL HIRSCH AND MARK HOSENBALL, "Spies: Too Little Sharing"

Reiterating

Increasingly an important method of development, reiterating calls for an early statement of the main point of a paragraph. The paragraph then goes on to restate the point, hammering home the point and often building in intensity as well.

> *We are on the move now.* The burning of our churches will not deter us. *We are on the move now.* The bombing of our homes will not dissuade us. *We are on the move now.* The beating and killing of our clergymen and young people will not divert us. *We are on the move now.* The arrest and release of known murderers will not discourage us. *We are on the move now.* Like an idea whose time has come, not even the marching of mighty armies can halt us. *We are moving* to the land of freedom.
> —MARTIN LUTHER KING JR., "Our God Is Marching On"

8d Consider paragraph length.

Paragraph length is determined by content and purpose. Paragraphs should develop an idea, create any desired effects (such as suspense or humor), and advance the larger piece of writing. Fulfilling these aims will sometimes require short paragraphs, sometimes long ones. For example, if you are writing a persuasive piece, you may put all your evidence into one long paragraph to create the impression of a solid, overwhelmingly convincing argument. In a story about an exciting event, on the other hand, you may use a series of short paragraphs to create suspense, to keep the reader rushing to each new paragraph to find out what happens next.

Reasons to start a new paragraph

- to turn to a new idea
- to emphasize something (such as an idea or an example)
- to change speakers (in dialogue)
- to lead readers to pause
- to take up a subtopic
- to start the conclusion

8e Make paragraphs flow.

A paragraph has coherence—or flows—if its details fit together clearly in a way that readers can easily follow. When you arrange information in a particular order (as described in 7d and 8c), you help readers move from one point to another. Regardless of your organization, however, be aware of several other ways to achieve paragraph coherence.

Repeating key words and phrases

Weaving in repeated key words and phrases—or pronouns that point to them—not only links sentences but also alerts readers to the importance of those words or phrases in the larger piece of writing. Notice in the following example how the repetition of the italicized key words and the use of pronouns that refer to those words help hold the paragraph together:

> Over the centuries, *shopping* has changed in function as well as in style. Before the Industrial Revolution, most consumer goods were sold in open-air *markets, customers* who went into an actual *shop* were expected to *buy* something, and *shoppers* were always expected to *bargain* for the best possible *price.* In the nineteenth century, however, the development of the department *store* changed the relationship between buyers and sellers. Instead of visiting several *market* stalls or small *shops, customers* could now *buy* a variety of merchandise under the same roof; instead of feeling expected to *buy,* they were welcome just to look; and instead of *bargaining* with several merchants, they paid a fixed *price* for each *item.* In addition, *they* could return an *item* to the *store* and exchange *it* for a different one or get their money back. All of these changes helped transform *shopping* from serious requirement to psychological recreation.

Using parallelism

Parallel structures can help connect the sentences within a paragraph. As readers, we feel pulled along by the force of the parallel structures in the following example:

> William Faulkner's "Barn Burning" tells the story of a young boy trapped in a no-win situation. If he betrays his father, he loses his family. If he betrays justice, he becomes a fugitive. In trying to free himself from his trap, he does both.

Using transitions

Transitions are words such as *so, however,* and *thus* that signal relationships between sentences and paragraphs. Transitions help guide the reader from one idea to another. To understand how important transitions are in directing readers, try reading the following paragraph, from which all transitions have been removed.

A PARAGRAPH WITH NO TRANSITIONS

In "The Fly," Katherine Mansfield tries to show us the real personality of the boss beneath his exterior. The fly helps her to portray this real self. The boss goes through a range of emotions and feelings. He expresses these feelings to a small but determined fly, whom the reader realizes he unconsciously relates to his son. The author basically splits up the story into three parts, with the boss's emotions and actions changing quite measurably. With old Woodifield, with himself, and with the fly, we see the boss's manipulativeness. Our understanding of him as a hard and cruel man grows.

We can, if we work at it, figure out the relationship of these sentences to one another, for this paragraph is essentially unified by one major idea. But the lack of transitions results in an abrupt, choppy rhythm; the paragraph lurches from one detail to the next, dragging the confused reader behind. See how much easier the passage is to read and understand with transitions added.

THE SAME PARAGRAPH WITH TRANSITIONS

In "The Fly," Katherine Mansfield tries to show us the real personality of the boss beneath his exterior. The fly in the story's title helps her to portray this real self. In the course of the story, the boss goes through a range of emotions. At the end, he finally expresses these feelings to a small but determined fly, whom the reader realizes he unconsciously relates to his son. To accomplish her goal, the author basically splits up the story into three parts, with the boss's emotions and actions changing measurably throughout. First with old Woodifield, then with himself, and last with the fly, we see the boss's manipulativeness. With each part, our understanding of him as a hard and cruel man grows.

Commonly used transitions

TO SIGNAL SEQUENCE

again, also, and, and then, besides, finally, first . . . second . . . third, furthermore, last, moreover, next, still, too

TO SIGNAL TIME

after a few days, after a while, afterward, as long as, as soon as, at last, at that time, before, earlier, immediately, in the meantime, in the past, lately, later, meanwhile, now, presently, simultaneously, since, so far, soon, then, thereafter, until, when

TO SIGNAL COMPARISON

again, also, in the same way, likewise, once more, similarly

TO SIGNAL CONTRAST

although, but, despite, even though, however, in contrast, in spite of, instead, nevertheless, nonetheless, on the contrary, on the one hand . . . on the other hand, regardless, still, though, yet

TO SIGNAL EXAMPLES

after all, for example, for instance, indeed, in fact, of course, specifically, such as, the following example, to illustrate

TO SIGNAL CAUSE AND EFFECT

accordingly, as a result, because, consequently, for this purpose, hence, so, then, therefore, thereupon, thus, to this end

TO SIGNAL PLACE

above, adjacent to, below, beyond, closer to, elsewhere, far, farther on, here, near, nearby, opposite to, there, to the left, to the right

TO SIGNAL CONCESSION

although it is true that, granted that, I admit that, it may appear that, naturally, of course

TO SIGNAL SUMMARY, REPETITION, OR CONCLUSION

as a result, as has been noted, as I have said, as mentioned earlier, as we have seen, in any event, in conclusion, in other words, in short, on the whole, therefore, to summarize

8f Work on opening and closing paragraphs.

Opening paragraphs

Even a good piece of writing may remain unread if it has a weak opening paragraph. In addition to announcing your topic, an introductory paragraph must engage readers' interest and focus their attention on what is to follow. One common kind of opening paragraph follows a general-to-specific sequence, in which the writer opens with a general statement and then gets more and more specific, concluding with the thesis. The following paragraph illustrates such an opening:

Throughout Western civilization, places such as the ancient Greek agora, the New England town hall, the local church, the coffeehouse, the village square, and even the street corner have been arenas for debate on public affairs and society. Out of thousands of such encounters, "public opinion" slowly formed and became the context in which politics was framed. Although the public sphere never included everyone, and by itself did not determine the outcome of all parliamentary actions, it contributed to the spirit of dissent found in a healthy representative democracy. Many of these public spaces remain, but they are no longer centers for political discussion and action. They have largely been replaced by television and other forms of media—forms that arguably isolate citizens from one another rather than bringing them together.

–Mark Poster, "The Net as a Public Sphere"

In this paragraph, the opening sentence introduces a general subject— sites of public debate throughout history; subsequent sentences focus more specifically on political discussion; and the last sentence presents the thesis, which the rest of the essay will develop.

OTHER EFFECTIVE WAYS OF OPENING

- with a quotation: *There is a bumper sticker that reads, "Too bad ignorance isn't painful."* –Nikki Giovanni, "Racism 101"
- with an anecdote: *I first met Angela Carter at a dinner in honor of the Chilean writer José Donoso at the home of Liz Calder, who then published all of us.* –Salman Rushdie, "Angela Carter"
- with a question: *Why are Americans terrified of using nuclear power as a source of energy?*
- with a strong opinion: *Men need a men's movement about as much as women need chest hair.* –John Ruszkiewicz, *The Presence of Others*

Concluding paragraphs

A good conclusion wraps up a piece of writing in a satisfying and mem- orable way. A common and effective strategy for concluding is to restate the central idea (but not word for word), perhaps specifying it in several sentences, and then ending with a much more general statement:

Lastly, and perhaps greatest of all, there was the ability, at the end, to turn quickly from war to peace once the fighting was over. Out of the way these two men [Generals Grant and Lee] behaved at Appomattox came the possibility of a peace of reconciliation. It was a possibility not wholly real- ized, in the years to come, but which did, in the end, help the two sections to become one nation again . . . after a war whose bitterness might have seemed to make such a reunion wholly impossible. No part of either man's life became him more than the part he played in this brief meeting in the McLean house at Appomattox. Their behavior there put all succeeding gen- erations of Americans in their debt. Two great Americans, Grant and Lee— very different, yet under everything very much alike. Their encounter at Appomattox was one of the great moments of American history.

–Bruce Catton, "Grant and Lee: A Study in Contrasts"

OTHER EFFECTIVE WAYS OF CONCLUDING

- with a quotation
- with a question
- with a vivid image
- with a call for action
- with a warning

8g Create effective paragraphs online.

Email, online discussion lists, hypertext—all pose challenges for writers creating effective paragraphs. Both the limitations of electronic communication (such as a lack of indentation in some email software) and the dizzying possibilities (for example, alternative ways to arrange hypertext) call for special creativity. When designing paragraphs to send electronically or post to the Web, keep the following pointers in mind:

- Break up large blocks of text; long, dense clumps of text are hard to read.
- Create paragraphs by skipping a line to leave a space every time you shift topics or introduce a new idea.

For more information on document and Web design, see Chapters 13 and 14.

bedfordstmartins.com/everyday_writer For more help with writing, go to **Links** and click on **The Art and Craft of Writing.**

9

Revising and Editing

Whether you are writing a wedding invitation, an email to a client, or a history essay, you will want to make time to revise, edit, and proofread what you write. Revising involves taking a fresh look at your draft, making sure that it includes all the necessary information and that the presentation is clear and effective. Editing involves fine-tuning your prose, attending to details of sentence structure, grammar, usage, punctuation, and spelling. Finally, careful proofreading aims at a perfect copy.

A MATTER OF STYLE

Revising Online Writing

The revising you do online will depend on your rhetorical situation. If a lot is at stake (a promotion or a scholarship, for example), then you will want to devote time and effort to revising: the writing must be correct, accurate, and persuasive. However, many less formal situations (casual email, for example) may call for conveying information quickly and easily; in such cases, the messages you write probably need to be revised only for clarity.

9a Revise.

If at all possible, put the draft away for a day or two to clear your mind and get some distance from your writing.

Rereading for meaning

At this point, don't sweat the small stuff. Instead, concentrate on your message and on whether you have expressed it clearly. Note any places where the meaning seems unclear.

Remembering your purpose

Does your draft achieve its purpose? If you wrote for an assignment, make sure that you have produced what was asked for. If you set out to prove something, make sure you have succeeded. If you intended to propose a solution to a problem, make sure you have set forth a well-supported solution rather than just an analysis of the problem.

Reconsidering your stance

Take time to look at your draft with one central question in mind: where are you coming from in this draft? Articulate the stance you take, and ask yourself what factors have led you to that position.

Considering your audience

How appropriately do you address your audience? Think carefully about your audience's experiences and expectations. Will you catch their interest, and will they be able to follow your discussion? Is the language formal or informal enough for these readers? Have you defined any terms they may not know? What objections might they raise?

Analyzing organization

One way to check the organization of a draft is to outline it. After numbering the paragraphs in the draft, read through each one, jotting down the main idea or topic. Do the main ideas clearly relate to the thesis and to one another? Can you identify any confusing leaps from point to point? Have you left out any important points?

Considering your use of visuals

Have you used any visuals? If so, do they help make a point and get your meaning across? Are all visuals clearly labeled? Are their sources given? Are they referred to in the text? Have you commented on their significance? Consider whether there is information in your draft that would be better presented as a visual.

Getting response

In addition to your own critical appraisal and that of an instructor or supervisor, you may want to get responses to your draft from friends, classmates, or colleagues. Use the questions here to respond to someone else's draft or to analyze your own. If you ask other people to evaluate your draft, be sure that they know your assignment, intended audience, and purpose.

FOR MULTILINGUAL WRITERS

Asking a Native Speaker to Review Your Draft

One good way to make sure that your writing is well developed and easy to follow is to have someone else read it. You might find it especially helpful to ask a native speaker to read over your draft and to point out any words or patterns that are unclear or not idiomatic. (See Chapter 66 for more on words used idiomatically.)

AT A GLANCE

Some Guidelines for Peer Response

- *Initial thoughts.* What are the main strengths and weaknesses of the draft? What might be confusing to readers? What is the single most important thing the writer says in the draft? What will readers want to know more about?
- *Assignment.* Does the draft carry out the assignment?
- *Title and introduction.* Does the title tell readers what the draft is about? How does it catch readers' interest? Does the opening make readers want to continue? How else might the draft begin?
- *Thesis and purpose.* Paraphrase the thesis as a promise: *In this paper, the writer will . . . .* Does the draft fulfill that promise? Does it carry out the writer's purpose?
- *Audience.* How does the draft interest and appeal to its audience? Is it written at the right level for the intended readers?
- *Rhetorical stance.* Where does the writer stand? What words indicate the stance? What influences have likely contributed to that stance?
- *Supporting points.* List the main points, and review them one by one. How does each one support the thesis? Do any points need to be explained more or less? Do any seem confusing or boring? Should any points be eliminated or added? How well is each point supported by details?
- *Visuals.* Do any visuals add to the key points? Are they clearly referred to in the draft? Are they labeled appropriately?
- *Organization and flow.* Is the writing easy to follow? Are the ideas presented in an order that will make sense to readers?
- *Transitions.* Are there effective transitions within sentences, between paragraphs, and from one idea to the next?
- *Conclusion.* Does the draft conclude in a memorable way, or does it seem to end abruptly or trail off into vagueness? Is there another way it might end?

FOR MULTILINGUAL WRITERS

Understanding Peer Review

If your language or culture discourages direct criticism of others or considers it rude, you may be concerned if some classmates question or even challenge your work. As long as the questions and suggestions are constructive, however, they are appropriate to peer-review collaboration. Your peers will expect you to join in, too, so be sure to offer your questions, suggestions, and insights.

Reviewing a draft online

If you are doing a peer review in the body of an email message, you can copy the message into an email of your own and then insert your comments directly into the writer's text by putting them in brackets. Use a subject line that alerts your classmate that you are sending back a review of a draft. If the draft comes as an attachment, save the document in a peer-review folder under a name you will recognize, and use your word-processor's tools to insert your remarks into the text. You can also use the footnote feature in your word-processing program. Finally, you can always simply insert your remarks in brackets, boldface, all caps, color, or italics. If you can't insert comments directly into a text, be sure to let the writer know what line, passage, or paragraph you are commenting on (for example, *par. 1, line 4*).

bedfordstmartins.com/everyday_writer To explore tools for peer review, go to **Working Online** and click on **Word Processors.** If you're using **Comment** in your course, you and your classmates can take part in peer-review activities online.

9b Edit.

Once you have revised a draft for content and organization, it is time to look closely at your sentences and words. Turning a "blah" sentence into a memorable one—or finding exactly the right word to express a thought—can result in writing that is really worth reading.

As with life, variety is the spice of sentences. You can add variety to your sentences by looking closely at their length, structure, and opening patterns.

Varying sentence length

Too many short sentences, especially one following another, can sound like a series of blasts on a car horn, whereas a steady stream of long sentences may tire or confuse readers. Most writers aim for some variety in length, breaking up a series of fairly long sentences with a very brief one.

In examining the following paragraph from her essay, Emily Lesk discovered that the sentences were all fairly long. In revising, she decided to cut the second sentence from twenty-six to fourteen words, thereby offering a shorter sentence between two long ones.

Effective magazine advertising is just one example of the media

~~In other words, Coca-Cola has hammered itself into our perceptions--both~~

strategies Coca-Cola has used to encourage us to equate Coke with the

~~conscious and subconscious--of an American cultural identity by equating itself~~

"happy life" element of American identity. *As*

~~with media that define American culture. When~~ the omnipresent ~~general~~

gave way to

magazine ~~that marked the earlier part of the century fell by the wayside under~~

television~~'s power,~~ Coke was there from the beginning. In its 1996 recap of the

previous fifty years in industry history, the publication Beverage Industry cites

Coca-Cola as a frontrunner in the very first form of television advertising:

sponsorship of entire programs such as, in the case of Coke, The Bob Dixon Show

and The Adventures of Kit Carson.

Varying sentence openings

Opening sentence after sentence in the same way results in a jerky, abrupt, or choppy rhythm. You can vary sentence openings by beginning with a dependent clause, a phrase, an adverb, a conjunctive adverb, or a coordinating conjunction (27b).

Another paragraph in Emily Lesk's essay tells the story of how she got her Coke T-shirt in Israel. Before she revised, every sentence in the paragraph opened with the subject, so Emily decided to delete some examples and vary her sentence openings. The final version (part of which also appears on p. 34) is a dramatic and easy-to-read paragraph.

~~I have a favorite T-shirt that says "Drink Coca-Cola Classic" in Hebrew. It's~~

~~Israel's standard tourist fare, like little nested dolls in Russia or painted horses~~

Even *exactly*

~~in Scandinavia, and~~ before setting foot in Israel three years ago, I knew where I

's

could find the Coke T-shirt. The tiny shop in the central block of a Jerusalem

Ben Yehuda Street

~~shopping center~~ did offer other shirt designs ~~("Macabee Beer" was a favorite),~~

While waiting
but ~~that Coca-Cola shirt~~ was what drew in most of the dollar-carrying tourists. ~~I~~

my shirt
~~waited~~ almost twenty minutes for ~~mine, and~~ I watched nearly everyone ahead of

, todah rabah [thank you very much]."
me ask for "the Coke shirt" ~~(and "thanks" in Hebrew).~~

the one with a bright white "Drink Coca-Cola Classic" written in Hebrew cursive across the chest

Checking for sentences opening with it and there

As you go over the opening sentences of your draft, look especially at those beginning with *it* or *there*. Sometimes these words can create a special emphasis, as in *It was a dark and stormy night*. But they can also be easily overused or misused. Another, more subtle problem with these openings is that they may be used to avoid taking responsibility for a statement. The following sentence can be improved by editing:

The university must
▶ ~~It is necessary to~~ raise student fees.

Examining words

Even more than paragraphs and sentences, word choice—or diction— offers writers an opportunity to put their personal stamp on a piece of writing. Becoming aware of the kinds of words you use should help you get the most mileage out of each word.

Using spell checkers

While these software tools won't catch every spelling error or identify all problems of style, they can be very useful. Most professional writers use their spell checkers religiously. Remember, however, that spell checkers are limited; they don't recognize most proper names, foreign words, or specialized language, and they do not recognize homonym errors (misspelling *there* as *their*, for example). (For advice on using grammar checkers, see pp. 103–4).

Examining tone

Tone refers to the attitude that a writer's language conveys toward the topic and the audience. In examining the tone of your draft, think about the nature of the topic, your own attitude toward it, and that of your

---

AT A GLANCE

Studying Word Choice

- Are the nouns primarily abstract and general or concrete and specific? Too many abstract and general nouns can result in boring prose. To say that you bought a new car is much less memorable and interesting than to say you bought a new red Miata convertible.

- Are there too many nouns in relation to the number of verbs? The *effect* of the *overuse* of *nouns* in *writing* is the *placing* of too much *strain* on the inadequate *number* of *verbs* and the resultant *prevention of movement* of the *thought*. In the preceding sentence, one tiny verb (*is*) has to drag along the entire weight of eleven nouns. The result is a heavy, boring sentence. Why not say instead, *Overusing nouns places a big strain on the verbs and consequently slows down the prose*?

- How many verbs are forms of *be*—*be, am, is, are, was, were, being, been*? If *be* verbs account for more than about a third of your total verbs, you are probably overusing them (29a and b).

- Are verbs *active* wherever possible? Passive verbs are harder to read and remember than active ones. Although the passive voice has many uses, your writing will often be stronger, more lively, and more energetic if you use active verbs (29g).

- Are your words *appropriate*? Check to be sure they are not too fancy—or too casual.

intended audience. Check for connotations, or specific associations, of words as well as slang, jargon, emotional language, and your level of formality. Is your language creating the tone you want to achieve (humorous, serious, impassioned, and so on), and is that tone an appropriate one, given your audience and topic?

Reviewing document design

Before you produce a copy for final proofreading, reconsider issues of format and the "look" you want your document to have. This is one last opportunity to think carefully about the visual appearance of your final draft. (For more on document and Web design, see Chapters 13 and 14. For more on the document conventions of different disciplines, see Chapters 59–62.)

Proofreading the final draft

Take time for one last, careful proofreading, which means reading to correct any typographical errors or other inconsistencies in spelling and punctuation. To proofread most effectively, read through the copy aloud, making sure that you've used punctuation marks correctly and consistently, that all sentences are complete—except for intentional fragments or run-ons used to create special effects (see p. 271)—and that no words are missing. Then go through the copy again, this time reading backward so that you can focus on each individual word and its spelling.

10

Analyzing Verbal and Visual Arguments

In one important sense, all language use has an argumentative edge. When you greet friends warmly, you wish to convince them that you are genuinely glad to see them. When you end an email message with a smiley face, you use a visual representation to indicate your mood to your reader. By putting a particular story or photo on the front page, a newspaper argues that it is more important than other stories; by using emotional language and intense video footage, a newscaster tries to persuade us to view an event in a particular way. What one reporter might call a *massive demonstration* another might call a *noisy protest,* and yet another an *angry march.* In much academic writing, however, *argument* is more narrowly defined as a text that makes a claim (usually in the form of an argumentative thesis) and supports it fully.

10a Recognize cultural contexts for arguments.

If you really want to understand the arguments of others, begin by paying attention to clues to cultural context and to where the writer or creator is coming from. It may help to put yourself in the position of the person creating the argument—in order to see the topic from that person's point of view—before looking skeptically at every claim and examining every piece of evidence. Above all, watch out for your own assumptions as you analyze what you read or see. For example, just because you assume that statistical evidence is more persuasive than, say, precedent drawn from religious beliefs, you can't assume that all writers agree with you. Take a writer's cultural beliefs into account before you begin to analyze an argument.

AT A GLANCE

Analyzing Arguments

Here are some questions to help you analyze verbal and visual arguments:

- What cultural contexts inform the argument—and what do they tell you about where the writer or creator is coming from? (10a)
- What is the main issue (or stasis) of the argument? (10b)
- What emotional, ethical, and logical appeals is the argument making? (10c)
- How has the writer or creator established credibility? (10c)
- What sources does the argument rely on? How current and reliable are they? Are some perspectives left out? What effect does this exclusion have on the argument? (10c)
- What claim does the verbal or visual argument make? What reasons and warrants support and underlie the claim? What additional evidence backs up the warrant and claim? (10d)
- Does the argumentative thesis reflect the claim accurately?
- What fallacies can you identify, and what effect do they have on the argument's persuasiveness? (10e)
- How has the writer or creator used visuals to make or support the argument? (10f)
- What overall impression does the argument create? Are you convinced?

10b Get to the main issue: stasis theory.

Greek and Roman rhetoricians used four questions to identify the main issue of any argument. Referred to as *stasis theory* (in Greek, the word *stasis* means "a stand"—literally, where an arguer takes a stand), these questions can be very useful in analyzing arguments:

1. Did the act occur?
2. How is the act defined?
3. How important or serious is the act?
4. What actions should be taken as a result of this act?

If you are reading an article arguing that the attacks on Islamic centers and mosques following September 11, 2001, were acts of patriotism, for example, you can use these questions to good effect:

1. *Did the act occur?* Yes, the article identifies five major attacks on such centers in Ohio alone.
2. *How is the act defined?* In the article, the writer argues that these acts should be defined as patriotic, as part of ongoing homeland security.

3. *How important or serious is the act?* The writer argues that the act is defensive, not offensive, thus supporting the definition offered earlier.
4. *What actions should be taken?* According to the writer, no punitive action should be taken since no crime has been committed.

You, as a reader, have now opened the heart of the writer's argument and should be ready to analyze the claims and the evidence. In other words, you have identified the argument's key parts, and you can now examine each part separately to identify the weak points.

bedfordstmartins.com/everyday_writer For more on stasis theory, click on **Additional Resources.**

10c Identify an argument's basic appeals.

Aristotle categorized argumentative appeals into three types: emotional appeals (those that appeal to our hearts and values), ethical appeals (those that appeal to character), and logical appeals (those that involve factual information and evidence). Using these categories can give you a way into any argument and thus help you begin analyzing—and evaluating—it.

Identifying emotional appeals

Emotional appeals stir our emotions and remind us of deeply held values. When politicians argue that the country needs more tax relief, they almost always mention one or more families they have met, stressing the concrete ways in which a tax cut would improve the quality of the families' lives. Doing so creates a strong emotional appeal. Although emotional appeals are sometimes criticized as a way to manipulate or mislead an audience, they are an important part of almost every argument. Critical readers can combat unfair emotional appeals by analyzing them carefully.

Identifying ethical appeals

Ethical appeals are those that support the credibility, moral character, and goodwill of the writer. These appeals are especially important for critical readers to recognize and evaluate. We may respect and admire the acting skills of certain movie stars, for example, but does that mean we should automatically believe them when they argue in favor of a particular law or politician? To identify ethical appeals in arguments, ask yourself these questions: What is the writer or creator doing to show that he or she is knowledgeable and credible about the subject—has really done homework on it? What sort of character does the writer or creator build, and how does he or she do so? More important, is that character trustworthy? What does the writer or creator do to show that he or she has the best interests of the audience in mind? Do those best interests match your own, and, if not, how is the power of the argument affected?

Identifying logical appeals

Logical appeals are perhaps the most familiar to us in the Western world because they are viewed as especially trustworthy: as some say, "the facts don't lie." Of course, facts are not the only type of logical appeals, which also include firsthand evidence drawn from observations, interviews, surveys and questionnaires, experiments, and personal experience; and secondhand evidence drawn from authorities, the testimony of others, statistics, and other print and online sources. Critical readers need to examine logical appeals just as carefully as emotional and ethical ones because the data presented may be out of date or unreliable. Ask yourself the following questions: What is the source of the logical appeal—and is that source trustworthy? Are all terms defined clearly? Has the evidence presented been taken out of context? Does taking something out of its context change its meaning?

10d Identify the elements of arguments.

According to philosopher Stephen Toulmin, most arguments contain common features: a claim or claims; reasons for the claim(s); warrants (often in the form of assumptions, whether stated or not) that connect the claim(s) to the reasons; evidence (facts, authoritative opinion, examples, statistics, and so on); and qualifiers that limit the claim in some way. The diagram on the next page shows how these elements might be used to analyze an argument about sex education.

Whether you are examining a verbal or a visual argument, nailing down the major claim(s)—and the reasons, warrants, and evidence that support the claim(s)—will put you well on your way to an effective analysis.

10e Recognize fallacies.

Fallacies have traditionally been viewed as serious flaws that damage the effectiveness of arguments. But arguments are ordinarily pretty complex, so what looks like a fallacy in one argument might not be a fallacy in another. The best advice may be to learn to identify fallacies but to be cautious in jumping to quick conclusions about them. Rather than

TOULMIN'S SYSTEM APPLIED TO SEX-EDUCATION ARGUMENT

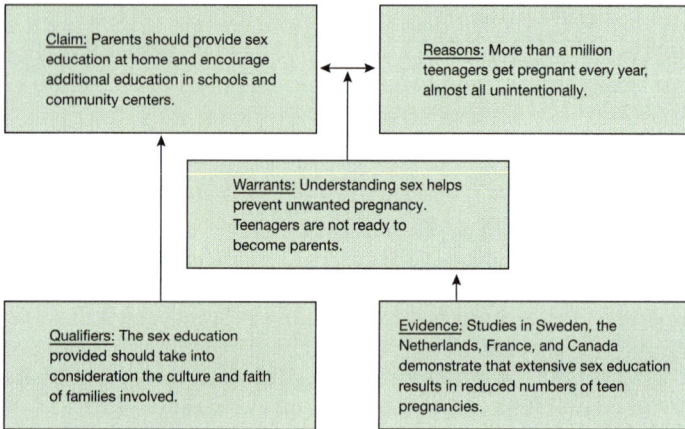

Claim: Parents should provide sex education at home and encourage additional education in schools and community centers.

Reasons: More than a million teenagers get pregnant every year, almost all unintentionally.

Warrants: Understanding sex helps prevent unwanted pregnancy. Teenagers are not ready to become parents.

Qualifiers: The sex education provided should take into consideration the culture and faith of families involved.

Evidence: Studies in Sweden, the Netherlands, France, and Canada demonstrate that extensive sex education results in reduced numbers of teen pregnancies.

thinking of them as errors you can use to discredit an argument, you might think of them as barriers to common ground (11e) and understanding, since they often shut off debate.

Recognizing emotional fallacies

Unfair or overblown emotional appeals attempt to overcome readers' good judgment.

BANDWAGON APPEAL

Bandwagon appeal suggests that a great movement is under way and the reader will be a fool or a traitor not to join it.

▶ Voters are flocking to candidate X by the millions, so you'd better cast your vote the right way.

FLATTERY

Flattery tries to persuade readers to do something by suggesting that they are thoughtful, intelligent, or perceptive enough to agree with the writer.

▶ We know you have the good taste to recognize that an investment in an Art-Form ring will pay off in the future.

IN-CROWD APPEAL

In-crowd appeal, a kind of flattery, invites readers to identify with a select group.

▶ Want to know a secret that more and more successful young professionals are finding out about? It's Mountainbrook Manor, the best new condominiums.

VEILED THREATS

Veiled threats try to frighten readers into agreement.

▶ If Public Service Electric does not get an immediate 15 percent rate increase, its services to you will be seriously affected.

FALSE ANALOGIES

False analogies make comparisons between two situations that are *not* alike in most respects.

▶ The volleyball team's sudden defeat seemed reminiscent of the sinking of the *Titanic.*

Recognizing ethical fallacies

Ethical fallacies focus not on establishing the credibility of the writer but on destroying the credibility of an opponent.

AD HOMINEM

Ad hominem charges directly attack someone's character rather than focusing on the issue at hand. They suggest that because something is wrong with this person, whatever he or she says must also be wrong.

▶ Patricia Ireland is just a hysterical feminist. We shouldn't listen to her views on abortion.

GUILT BY ASSOCIATION

Guilt by association attacks someone's credibility by linking that person with a person or an activity the audience considers bad, suspicious, or untrustworthy.

▶ Senator Fleming does not deserve reelection; one of her assistants turned out to be involved with organized crime.

FALSE AUTHORITY

False authority is often used by advertisers who show famous actors and sports figures testifying to the greatness of a product about which they probably know very little, if anything.

▶ Michael Jordan says using 1-800-COLLECT to make collect calls results in "big savings."

Recognizing logical fallacies

Logical fallacies are usually defined as errors in formal reasoning, but they can work very effectively to convince audiences.

BEGGING THE QUESTION

Begging the question is a kind of circular argument that treats a question as if it has already been answered.

▶ **That TV news provides accurate and reliable information was demonstrated conclusively on last week's *60 Minutes*.**

POST HOC FALLACY

The *post hoc* fallacy, from the Latin *post hoc, ergo propter hoc* ("after this, therefore caused by this"), assumes that just because B happened *after* A, it must have been *caused* by A.

▶ **We should not rebuild the docks. Every time we do, a hurricane comes along and damages them.**

NON SEQUITUR

A non sequitur (Latin for "it does not follow") attempts to tie together two or more logically unrelated ideas as if they *were* related.

▶ **If we can send a spacecraft to Mars, then we can cure all cancers.**

EITHER-OR FALLACY

The either-or fallacy asserts that a complex situation can have only two possible outcomes, one of which is necessary.

▶ **If we do not build the aqueduct, businesses in the area will be forced to shut down because of lack of water.**

HASTY GENERALIZATION

A hasty generalization bases a conclusion on too little (or misunderstood) evidence.

▶ **I couldn't understand the lecture, so I know this course will be impossible.**

OVERSIMPLIFICATION

Oversimplification of the relation between causes and effects is another fallacy based on careless reasoning.

▶ **If we prohibit the sale of alcohol, we will get rid of binge drinking.**

10f Examine visual arguments.

We usually think of arguments as being made with words—in writing, as part of an essay or a report, and orally, as part of a debate or conversation. But arguments can also be made only with images or with a combination of words and images.

You analyze a visual argument in much the same way that you analyze *any* argument. You try to determine whether any cultural values are evident (10a). You also look at content: the emotional, ethical, and logical appeals (10c) as well as the claims, reasons, and warrants (10d). However, for visual arguments, you must also consider the effects of design very carefully.

AT A GLANCE

Analyzing Visual Arguments

- What detail(s) is your eye first drawn to? Why is your attention drawn to that spot, and what effect does this attention-getting device have on your response to the argument?

- What is in the foreground, and what is in the background? What is placed in the center or high up as opposed to low? What effect do these choices have on the argument itself?

- Are any words or images tucked away in a corner or downplayed? What effect do they have on the argument?

- Do the colors that are used "match" the argument being made, or are they somehow in conflict with it? Does the use of color enhance the argument, and, if so, in what ways? If black and white are used instead of color, are they appropriate for the particular argument?

- If sound or video is used, how effective is it in conveying the argument's message?

- What is the relationship between words and images in the argument? How well do they work together to make the point?

- Are any words or images repeated? If so, does the repetition help to get the point across?

- If you are analyzing a Web page, what overall impression does it create at first glance, and how does closer inspection either change or reaffirm that impression? How are you guided along the Web page; how easy is it to negotiate? Do such considerations affect the argument the page is making?

A CARTOON THAT MAKES A VISUAL ARGUMENT

The cartoon here contains very few words, yet it makes a series of subtle arguments.

A group of students discussed the cartoon and came up with several possible claims:

POSSIBLE CLAIM   The threat of bioterrorism affects people in different ways.

POSSIBLE CLAIM   A symbolic security blanket no longer offers protection.

POSSIBLE CLAIM   In the face of bioterrorism, the best thing to do is to continue on as normal.

The students also talked about the cartoon's appeals and cultural values. What feelings does the cartoon elicit? nostalgia? anger? fear? sadness? In the lower left-hand corner, Luckovich says "apologies to Schulz." What kinds of appeals does this remark make?

You might also study the cartoon's design. Is your eye first drawn to the left side, which features a sickly looking tree, ominous (gas?) clouds, and Linus wearing the gas mask, or to some other point? The bubble with words partially obscures one of the clouds—what do you think that suggests about the girls' attitude? What is the significance of Linus's standing still while the girls are marching along? How might the effect of the cartoon be different if it appeared in color?

bedfordstmartins.com/everyday_writer   For additional help with argumentation, go to **Links** and click on **Argument.** For exercises, go to **Exercise Central** and click on **Analyzing Verbal and Visual Arguments.**

11

Constructing Arguments

We respond to arguments all the time—when we see a STOP sign, for example, and dutifully come to a halt, we've agreed to accept the argument that stopping at such signs is a sensible thing to do. Unfortunately, constructing an effective argument of your own is not as easy as putting up a stop sign. In fact, it's often remarkably difficult to create a thorough and convincing argument. It is especially hard to present arguments to complete strangers in cyberspace. This chapter guides you in taking up the challenges of crafting effective arguments.

11a Understand what counts as argument.

For many years, traditional Western notions of argument tended to highlight one purpose—winning. Although winning is still one important purpose of argument, it is by no means the only purpose.

AT A GLANCE

Reviewing Your Argument

- What is the purpose of your argument—to win? to convince others? to explore an issue? (11a)
- Is the point you want to make arguable? (11a)
- Have you formulated a clear claim and a strong argumentative thesis? (11b)
- Have you considered your audience in shaping your appeals? (11c)
- Have you attached good reasons to support your claim? (11d)
- How have you established your own credibility in the argument? (11e)
- How have you incorporated logical and emotional appeals into your argument? (11f and g)
- How have you used visuals to help make your argument? (11e, f, and g)
- How have you used sources and how effectively are they integrated into your argument? (11h)
- How is your argument organized? Have you used either the classical or the Toulmin system to guide your organization? (11i)
- What design elements help you make your argument? (11j)

TO WIN The most traditional purpose of academic argument, arguing to win, is used in campus debating societies, in political debates, in trials, and often in business. The writer or speaker aims to present a position that prevails over some other position.

TO CONVINCE Often, out-and-out defeat of another's position is not only unrealistic but undesirable. Instead, the goal might be to convince another person to change his or her mind. Doing so calls on a writer to provide *compelling reasons* for an audience to accept the writer's conclusion.

TO EXPLORE AN ISSUE Argument to explore an issue or reach a decision seeks a sharing of information and perspectives in order to make informed choices.

Checking whether a statement can be argued

In much of your work at school or on the job, you will be asked to take a position and argue for that position—whether to prove a mathematical equation or analyze a trend in your company's sales. Such work will usually call for you to convince or decide and will, therefore, require you to consider an arguable statement, to make a claim based on the statement, and finally to present good reasons in support of the claim. An arguable statement, to begin with, should have three characteristics:

1. It should attempt to convince readers of something, change their minds about something, or urge them either to do something or to explore a topic in order to make a wise decision.
2. It should address a problem for which no easily acceptable solution exists or ask a question to which no absolute answer exists.
3. It should present a position that readers might realistically have varying perspectives on.

ARGUABLE   Video games lead to violent behavior.

This statement seeks to convince, suggests a causal relationship that is difficult to prove, and takes a position many disagree with.

UNARGUABLE   Video games earn millions of dollars every year for the companies that produce them.

This statement can easily be verified and thus does not offer a basis for argument.

11b   Make a claim and formulate an argumentative thesis.

Once you have an arguable statement, you need to make a claim about it, one you will then ask readers to accept. The following initial claim is arguable because it aims to convince, it addresses an issue with no one identifiable answer, and it can realistically be disputed.

ARGUABLE STATEMENT (OR INITIAL CLAIM)	Pesticides should be banned.

Although the preceding statement does make a kind of claim—that pesticides should be banned—it offers no reason for doing so. To develop a claim that can become the working thesis for an argument, you need to include at least one good reason to support the arguable statement.

REASON	because they endanger the lives of farm workers.
ARGUMENTATIVE THESIS (CLAIM WITH REASON ATTACHED)	Because they endanger the lives of farm workers, pesticides should be banned.

In academic writing, you will often make a claim that urges readers not to take action but to interpret something in a certain way. In such cases, the claim of the argumentative thesis may be implied rather than stated.

▶ **Moral opposition to slavery was the major cause of the Civil War.**

Implied, but not stated, is the claim that economic or constitutional causes were far less important than this one was.

11c Shape your appeal to your audience.

Arguments and the claims they make are effective only insofar as they appeal to particular audiences. For example, if you want to argue for increased lighting in parking garages on campus, you might appeal to students by citing examples drawn from student experiences of the safety problems in such dimly lit garages. If you are writing to university administrators, however, you might focus on the negative publicity associated with past attacks in campus garages and evoke the anger that such attacks cause in parents, alumni, and other important groups.

Keep your audience in mind as you develop any argument.

- Establish common ground (11e) with your readers wherever possible.
- Show that you respect your audience's interests and views.
- Choose examples and other pieces of verbal and visual evidence that your audience will understand and relate to.
- Choose language, style, and level of formality appropriate to your audience.

11d Formulate good reasons to support your claim.

Torture, wrote Aristotle, makes for a very convincing argument but not one that reasonable people will accept. In effecting real changes in minds and hearts, we need instead to rely on *good reasons*—reasons that establish our credibility, reasons that appeal to logic, and reasons that appeal to emotion. These appeals, which were presented in Chapter 10 to help you analyze the arguments of others, will also help you construct arguments of your own.

11e   Establish your credibility through ethical appeals.

To make your argument convincing, you must first gain the respect and trust of your readers, or establish your credibility with them. In general, writers can establish credibility in four ways.

Demonstrating knowledge

A writer can establish credibility first by establishing his or her credentials. To decide whether you know enough to argue an issue credibly, consider the following questions:

- Can you provide information about your topic from sources other than your own knowledge?
- What are the sources of your information?
- How reliable are your sources?
- Do any sources contradict one another? If so, can you account for or resolve the contradictions?
- If you have personal experience relating to the issue, would telling about this experience help support your claim?

These questions may well show that you must do more research, check sources, resolve contradictions, refocus your working thesis, or even change your topic.

Establishing common ground

Many arguments between people or groups are doomed to end without resolution because the two sides occupy no common ground, no starting point of agreement. The following questions can help you find common ground in presenting an argument:

- What are the differing perspectives on this issue?
- What common ground can you find—aspects of the issue on which all sides agree?
- How can you express such common ground clearly to all sides?
- How can you discover—and consider—opinions on this issue that differ from your own?

- How can you use language—occupational, regional, or ethnic varieties of English, or languages other than English—to establish common ground with those you address?

You can read more about common ground in Chapter 37.

Demonstrating fairness

In arguing a position, writers must demonstrate fairness toward opposing arguments (often called counterarguments). Audiences are more inclined to give credibility to writers who seem to be considering and representing their opponents' views fairly than to those who seem to be ignoring or distorting such views.

Using visuals that make ethical appeals

In arguments and in other kinds of writing, visuals that make ethical appeals can help establish credibility and fairness. That's why so many universities, nonprofit organizations, and government agencies are following the lead of business and creating branding images for themselves. The Environmental Protection Agency, for example, includes its seal—and usually its motto, *Protecting human health, safeguarding the natural environment*—on its reports and documents. As shown here, the seal and motto help establish the credibility of the agency.

A VISUAL THAT MAKES AN ETHICAL APPEAL

U.S. Environmental Protection Agency

Protecting human health, safeguarding the natural environment

Recent Additions | Contact Us | Print Version   Search: GO Advanced Search

---

FOR MULTILINGUAL WRITERS

Counting Your Own Experience

You may have been told that your own personal experience doesn't count in making academic arguments. If so, reconsider this advice, for showing an audience that you have personal experience with a topic can carry strong persuasive appeal with many English-speaking readers. As with all evidence used in an argument, however, evidence based on your own experience must be pertinent to the topic, understandable to the audience, and clearly related to your purpose.

11f Use effective logical appeals.

Our credibility alone cannot and should not carry the full burden of persuading readers. Indeed, many view the logic of the argument—the reasoning behind it—as equally, if not more, important.

Providing examples, precedents, and narratives

Just as a picture can be worth a thousand words, a well-conceived **example** can also be valuable in arguing a point. Examples are used most often to support generalizations or to bring abstractions to life. In an argument about violence and video games in which you make the general claim that such games send a message that violence is fun, you might then illustrate that generalization with these examples:

> For instance, the makers of the game *Quake* present deadly and deranged acts of violence as fun entertainment, while the makers of *Postal* imply that preying on the defenseless is acceptable behavior by marketing a game in which players kill innocent, helpless victims.

Precedents are particular kinds of examples taken from the past. If, as part of a proposal for increased lighting in the library garage, you point out that the university has increased lighting in four similar garages in the past year, you are arguing on the basis of precedent.

In research writing (see Chapters 16–20), you identify your sources for any examples or precedents not based on your own knowledge.

Because storytelling is universal, **narratives** can be very persuasive in helping readers understand and accept an argument. In arguing for increased funding for the homeless, for instance, you might include a brief narrative about a day in the life of a homeless person to dramatize the issue and help readers see the need for more funding.

The following questions can help you check any use of example, precedent, and narrative:

- How representative are the examples?
- Are they sufficient in strength or number to lead to a generalization?
- In what ways do they support your claim?
- How closely does the precedent relate to the claim you're trying to make? Are the situations really similar?
- How timely is the precedent? (What would have been applicable in 1920 is not necessarily applicable today.)
- Does the narrative support your claim?
- Will the story's significance to the argument be clear to your readers?
- Is the story one of several good reasons, or does it have to carry the main burden of the argument?

Citing authority and testimony

Another way to support an argument logically is to cite an authority. The use of authority has figured prominently in the controversy over smoking. Since the U.S. surgeon general's 1964 announcement that smoking is hazardous to health, many Americans have quit smoking, largely persuaded by the authority of the scientists offering the evidence.

Ask yourself the following questions to be sure you are using authorities effectively:

- Is the authority timely? (The argument that the United States should pursue a policy just because it was supported by Thomas Jefferson will probably fail because Jefferson's time was so radically different from ours.)
- Is the authority qualified to judge the topic at hand? (To cite a fan's Web site on Tom Cruise in an essay on film history is not likely to strengthen your argument.)
- Is the authority likely to be known and respected by readers? (To cite an unfamiliar authority without some identification will lessen the impact of the evidence.)
- Are the authority's credentials clearly stated and verifiable? (Especially with Web-based sources, it is crucial to know whose authority guarantees the reliability of the information.)

Testimony—the evidence that an authority presents in support of a claim—is a feature of much contemporary argument. If testimony is timely, accurate, representative, and provided by a respected authority, then it, like authority itself, can add powerful support.

In research writing (see Chapters 16–20), you should cite your sources for authority and testimony not based on your own knowledge.

Using visuals that make logical appeals

Visuals that make logical appeals can be especially useful in arguments, since they present factual information that can be taken in at a glance. As shown on page 87, *Business Week* used a simple bar graph to carry a big message about equality of pay for men and women. Consider how long it would take to explain all the information in this graph with words alone.

Establishing causes and effects

Showing that one event is the cause—or the effect—of another can help support an argument. Suppose you are trying to explain, in a petition to change your grade in a course, why you were unable to take the final examination. You would probably try to trace the causes of your failure to appear—your severe illness and the theft of your car, perhaps—so

that the committee reading the petition would reconsider the effect—
your not taking the examination.

Tracing causes often lays the groundwork for an argument, particularly if the effect of the causes is one we would like to change. In an
environmental science class, for example, a student may argue that a
national law regulating smokestack emissions from utility plants is
needed because (1) acid rain on the East Coast originates from emissions at utility plants in the Midwest, (2) acid rain kills trees and other
vegetation, (3) utility lobbyists have prevented midwestern states from
passing strict laws controlling emissions from such plants, and (4) in the
absence of such laws, acid rain will destroy most eastern forests by 2020.
In this case, the fourth point ties all of the previous points together to
provide an overall argument from effect: unless X, then Y.

Using inductive and deductive reasoning

Traditionally, logical arguments are classified as using either inductive or
deductive reasoning; in practice, the two almost always work together.
Inductive reasoning is the process of making a generalization based on a
number of specific instances. If you find you are ill on ten occasions after
eating seafood, for example, you will likely draw the inductive generalization that seafood makes you ill. It may not be an absolute certainty
that seafood is to blame, but the *probability* lies in that direction.

Deductive reasoning, on the other hand, reaches a conclusion by
assuming a general principle (known as a major premise) and then
applying that principle to a specific case (the minor premise). In practice, this general principle is usually derived from induction. The inductive generalization *Seafood makes me ill,* for instance, could serve as the
major premise for the deductive argument *Since all seafood makes me ill,
the shrimp on this buffet is certain to make me ill.*

Deductive arguments have traditionally been analyzed as syllogisms—three-part statements containing a major premise, a minor
premise, and a conclusion.

MAJOR PREMISE	All people die.
MINOR PREMISE	I am a person.
CONCLUSION	I will die.

Syllogisms, however, are too rigid and absolute to serve in arguments
about questions that have no absolute answers, and they often lack any
appeal to an audience. From Aristotle came a simpler alternative, the
enthymeme, which calls on the audience to supply the implied major
premise. Consider the following example:

> Since violent video games can be addictive and cause psychological harm,
> players and their parents must carefully evaluate such games and monitor
> their use.

You can analyze this enthymeme by restating it in the form of two premises and a conclusion.

MAJOR PREMISE	Games that cause harm to players should be evaluated and monitored.
MINOR PREMISE	Violent video games cause addiction and psychological harm to players.
CONCLUSION	These games should be evaluated and monitored.

Note that the major premise is one the writer can count on an audience agreeing with or supplying: safety and common sense demand that potentially harmful games should be used with great care. By implicitly asking an audience to supply this premise to an argument, a writer engages the audience's participation.

As noted in Chapter 10, Toulmin's system looks for claims, reasons, and warrants instead of major and minor premises. In Toulmin's terms, the argument about video games would look like this:

CLAIM	Violent video games should be carefully evaluated and their use monitored.
REASON(S)	Violent video games cause addiction and psychological harm to players.
WARRANT	Games that cause harm to players should be evaluated and monitored.

Whether it is expressed as a syllogism, an enthymeme, or a claim, a deductive conclusion is only as strong as the premise or reasons on which it is based.

A VISUAL THAT MAKES A LOGICAL APPEAL

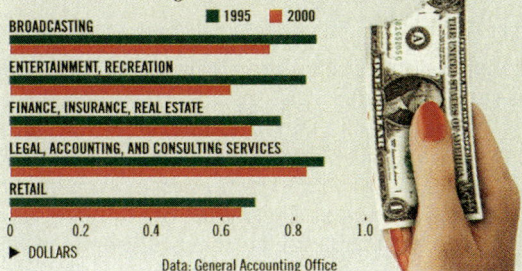

THE BIG PICTURE

THIS IS PROGRESS?

Pay equality between men and women worsened for many professions in the late '90s. For each dollar earned by men, women at the same age and education levels earned:

■ 1995 ■ 2000

BROADCASTING

ENTERTAINMENT, RECREATION

FINANCE, INSURANCE, REAL ESTATE

LEGAL, ACCOUNTING, AND CONSULTING SERVICES

RETAIL

0   0.2   0.4   0.6   0.8   1.0

▶ DOLLARS

Data: General Accounting Office

11g Use effective emotional appeals.

Most successful arguments appeal to our hearts as well as to our minds. This principle is vividly demonstrated by the AIDS epidemic in Africa. Facts and figures (logical appeals) convince us that the problem is real and serious. What elicits an outpouring of support, however, is the arresting emotional power of televised images and photographs of suffering individuals.

Using concrete descriptive details

Like photographs, vivid description can bring a moving immediacy to any argument. A student may amass facts and figures, including diagrams and maps, to illustrate the problem of wheelchair access to the library. But only when the student asks a friend who uses a wheelchair to accompany her to the library does the student writer discover the concrete details necessary to move readers. The student can then write, "Marie inched her heavy wheelchair up the narrow, steep entrance ramp, her arms straining to pull up the last twenty feet, her face pinched with the sheer effort."

Using figurative language

Figurative language, or figures of speech, paint a detailed and vivid picture by making striking comparisons between something you are writing about and something else that helps a reader visualize, identify with, or understand it (39d).

Figures of speech include metaphors, similes, and analogies. Most simply, metaphors compare two things directly: *Richard the Lion-Hearted; old age is the evening of life.* Similes make comparisons using *like* or *as: Richard is as brave as a lion; old age is like the evening of life.* Analogies are extended metaphors or similes that compare an unfamiliar concept or process to a more familiar one (see pp. 55–56).

Using visuals that make emotional appeals

Visuals that make emotional appeals can add substance to your argument as well. To make sure that such visual appeals will enhance your argument, test them out with several potential readers. In a "My Turn" essay from *Newsweek,* writer and actor Joseph C. Phillips argues that black Americans should claim the American freedom they have fought so long to gain rather than reject America. The picture of Phillips accompanied this argument, a visual that captures his identification with flag and country.

A VISUAL THAT MAKES AN EMOTIONAL APPEAL

11h   Cite sources in an argument.

In constructing a written argument, it is usually necessary—and often essential—to use sources. The key to persuading people to accept your argument is good reasons; and even if your assignment doesn't specify that you must consult outside sources, they are often the most effective way of finding and establishing these reasons. Sources can help you

- provide background information on your topic
- demonstrate your knowledge of the topic to readers
- cite authority and testimony in support of your argumentative thesis
- find opinions that differ from your own, which can help you sharpen your thinking, qualify your argumentative thesis if necessary, and demonstrate fairness to opposing arguments

For a thorough discussion of finding, gathering, and evaluating verbal and visual sources, both off- and online, see Chapters 17 and 18.

11i   Organize an argument.

Once you have assembled good reasons in support of an argumentative thesis, you must organize your material to present the argument convincingly. Although there is no ideal or universally favored organizational framework, you may find it useful to try one of the following.

The classical system

The system of argument often followed by ancient Greek and Roman orators is now referred to as *classical*. You can adapt the ancient format to written arguments as follows:

1. Introduction
   - Gain readers' attention and interest.
   - Establish your qualifications to write about your topic.
   - Establish common ground with readers.
   - Demonstrate fairness.
   - State or imply your thesis.
2. Background
   - Present any necessary background information, including pertinent personal narrative.
3. Lines of argument
   - Present good reasons (including logical and emotional appeals) in support of your thesis.
   - Generally present reasons in order of importance.
   - Demonstrate ways your argument may be in readers' best interest.
4. Alternative arguments
   - Examine alternative points of view.
   - Note advantages and disadvantages of alternative views.
   - Explain why one view is better than other(s).
5. Conclusion
   - Summarize the argument if you choose.
   - Elaborate on the implication of your thesis.
   - Make clear what you want readers to think or do.
   - Reinforce your credibility.

The Toulmin system

As noted earlier, another useful system of argument was developed by Stephen Toulmin. This simplified form of the Toulmin system can help you organize an argumentative essay:

1. Make your claim (a statement that is debatable or controversial).

   ▶ **The federal government should ban smoking.**

2. Qualify your claim if necessary.

   ▶ **The ban would be limited to public places.**

3. Present good reasons to support your claim.

- ▶ **Smoking causes serious diseases in smokers.**
- ▶ **Nonsmokers are endangered by others' smoke.**

4. Explain the warrant(s) (underlying assumptions) that connect your claim and your reasons. If the warrants are controversial, provide backing for them.

WARRANT	The Constitution was established to "promote the general welfare."
WARRANT	Citizens are entitled to protection from harmful actions by others.
BACKING	The United States is based on a political system that is supposed to serve the basic needs of its people, including their health.

5. Provide additional evidence to support your claim (facts, statistics, testimony, and other logical, ethical, or emotional appeals).

STATISTICS	Cite the incidence of deaths attributed to secondhand smoke.
FACTS	Cite lawsuits won recently against large tobacco companies, including one that awarded billions of dollars to states in reparation for smoking-related health care costs.
FACTS	Cite bans on smoking already imposed in many public institutions and places of employment— such as Ohio State University and all restaurants in California.
AUTHORITY	Cite the surgeon general.

6. Acknowledge and respond to possible counterarguments.

COUNTERARGUMENT	Smokers have rights, too.
RESPONSE	The suggested ban applies only to public places; smokers could smoke in private.

7. Finally, draw your conclusion, stated in the strongest way possible.

11j Consider design issues.

Most arguments today are carefully designed to make the best use of space, font style and type size, color, visuals, and contemporary technology. The following tips will get you thinking about how to produce and design a document that will add to the ethical, logical, and emotional appeals you are making:

- Before you begin, check out any conventions that may be expected in the kind of argument you are writing. Look for examples of similar arguments, or ask your instructor for information about such conventions.

- To emphasize an important part of your argument, consider using a special design element. For example, you might put a list of essential evidence in a carefully labeled box.

- Choose colors carefully, keeping in mind that colors call up many responses: red for war, for example, or blue for purity.

For more on document design, see Chapter 13.

11k A student argument essay

In this essay, Teal Pfeifer argues that images in the media affect how women see themselves, and she offers a solution to a problem. Her essay has been annotated to point out the various parts of her argument as well as her use of good reasons, evidence, and appeals to logic and emotion. Teal also uses a key visual for additional support.

Student Writer

Teal Pfeifer

bedfordstmartins.com/everyday_writer For additional help with argumentation, go to **Links** and click on **Argument.** To read another sample argument essay, click on **Student Writing.**

Pfeifer 1

Teal Pfeifer

Professor Rashad

English 102

April 13, 2003

Devastating Beauty ──────────── Title uses
play on
words to
pique
interest

Collarbones, hipbones, cheekbones — so many bones. She looks
at the camera with sunken eyes, smiling, acting beautiful. Her dress
is Versace, or Gucci, or Dior, and it is revealing, revealing every bone
and joint in her thin, thin body. She looks fragile and beautiful, as if
I could snap her in two. I look at her and feel the soft cushion of ──── Opening
uses emo-
flesh that surrounds my own joints, my own shoulders and hips that tional
appeals
are broad, my own ribs surrounded by skin and muscle and fat. I am and tries to
establish
not nearly as fragile or graceful or thin. I look away and wonder common
ground with
what kind of self-discipline it takes to become beautiful like the readers
model in my magazine.

By age seventeen a young woman has seen an average of
250,000 ads featuring a severely underweight woman whose body
type is, for the most part, unattainable by any means, including
extreme ones such as anorexia, bulimia, and drug use, according to
Allison LaVoie (par. 4). The media promote clothing, cigarettes, ──── Presents
background
fragrances, and even food with images like these. In a culture that information
on the
has become increasingly visual, the images put out for public problem and
cites sources
consumption feature women that are a smaller size than ever before.
In 1950, the White Rock Mineral Water girl was 5'4" tall and weighed
140 pounds; now she is 5'10" tall and weighs only 110 pounds,
signifying the growing deviation between the weight of models and
that of the normal female population (Pipher 184).

This media phenomenon has had a major effect on the female
population as a whole, both young and old. Five to ten million women ── Introduces
problem: ads
in America today suffer from an eating disorder related to poor self- encourage
women's
image, and yet advertisements continue to prey on insecurities fueled poor body
image
by a woman's desire to be thin. Current estimates reveal that 80

Pfeifer 2

percent of women are dissatisfied with their appearance and 45
percent of those are on a diet on any given day ("Statistics"). Yet

Good reason for thesis: stringent dieting can cause psychological problems — even the most stringent dieting will generally fail to create the paper-
thin body so valued in the media, and continuing efforts to do so can
lead to serious psychological problems such as depression.

While many women express dissatisfaction with their bodies, they
are not the only victims of the emaciated images so frequently

Provides statistical evidence that problem extends across age groups — presented to them. Young girls are equally affected by these images, if
not more so. Eighty percent of girls under age ten have already been
on a diet and expressed the desire to be thinner and more beautiful
(Slim Hopes). Thus from a young age, beauty is equated with a
specific size. The message girls get is an insidious one: in order to be
your best self, you should wear size 0 or 1. The pressure only grows
more intense as girls grow up. According to results from the Kaiser
Family Foundation Survey "Reflections of Girls in the Media," 16
percent of ten- to seventeen-year-old girls reported that they had

Uses logical appeals — dieted or exercised to look like a TV character. Yet two-thirds of
teenage girls acknowledged that these thin characters were not an
accurate reflection of "real life" (qtd. in Dittrich, "Children" pars. 2-3).

It is tragic to see so much of the American population obsessed
with weight and reaching an ideal that is, for the most part,

Good reason for thesis: magazines feed obsession with dieting — ultimately unattainable. Equally troubling is the role magazines play
in feeding this obsession. When a researcher asked female students
from Stanford University to flip through several magazines containing
images of glamorized, super-thin models, 68 percent of the women
felt significantly worse about themselves after viewing the magazine

Backs up reasons with research and expert opinion — models (qtd. in Dittrich, "Media" par. 16). Another study showed that
looking at models on a long-term basis leads to stress, depression,
guilt, and lowered self-worth (qtd. in Dittrich, "Media" par. 19). As
Naomi Wolfe points out in The Beauty Myth, thinking obsessively
about fat and dieting has actually been shown to change thought
patterns and brain chemistry.

Pfeifer 3

Fig. 1. <u>Young woman reading magazine</u>. Personal photograph. This magazine's cover image exemplifies the sexy, thin stereotype.

How do we reject images that are so harmful to the women and young girls who view them (such as those appearing in magazines like the one in Fig. 1)? Legislation regarding what can be printed and distributed is not an option because of First Amendment rights. Equally untenable is the idea of appealing to the industries that hire emaciated models. As long as the beauty and clothing industries are making a profit from the physically insecure girls and women who view their ads, nothing will change.

What, however, might happen if those females stopped buying the magazines that print such destructive images? A boycott is the most effective way to rid the print medium of emaciated models and eliminate the harmful effects they cause. If women stopped buying magazines that target them with such harmful advertising, magazines would be forced to change the kinds of ads they print. Such a

Considers and rejects alternative solutions

States argumentative thesis: a boycott would effectively solve problem

boycott would send a clear message: women and girls reject the victimization that takes place every time they look at a skeletally thin model and then feel worse about themselves. Consumers can ultimately control what is put on the market: If we don't buy, funding for such ads will dry up fast.

Good reason: boycotts have been effective

Presents a precedent/ example as evidence

In the past, boycotts have been effective tools for social change. Rosa Parks, often identified as the mother of the modern-day civil rights movement, played a pivotal role in the Montgomery bus boycott in December 1955. When Parks refused to give up her seat to a white bus rider, she was arrested, and this incident inspired the boycott. For more than a year, the vast majority of African Americans in Montgomery chose to walk instead of ride the buses. Many of them were terrorized or harassed, but the boycott was eventually successful: segregation on buses was declared illegal by the U.S. Supreme Court.

Presents a second precedent/ example as evidence

Between 1965 and 1973, Cesar Chavez also used boycotts successfully to change wage policies and working conditions for millions of Mexicans and Mexican Americans who were being exploited by growers of grapes and lettuce. In his boycott efforts, Chavez moved on two fronts simultaneously: he asked the workers to withhold their labor, and he asked consumers to refrain from purchasing table grapes (and later, lettuce) in order to show their support for the workers. In this situation, not only did the boycott force an industry to improve existing conditions, but it also made the public aware of pressing labor issues. Thus a bond was formed between the workers and the community their labor was benefiting.

Appeals directly to audience by using "we" in conclusion

As a society, we have much to learn from boycotts of the past, and their lessons can help us confront contemporary social ills. As I have shown, body-image dissatisfaction and eating disorders are rising at an alarming rate among young girls and women in American society. This growing desire for an unrealistically thin body affects our minds and our spirits, especially when we are pummeled dozens

Pfeifer 5

of times a day with glamorized images of emaciated and unhealthy — *Reinforces severity of problem and appeals to emotion*
women. The resulting anorexia and bulimia that women suffer from
are not only diseases that can be cured; they are also ones that can
be prevented — if women will take a solid stand against such
advertisements and the magazines that publish them. While we are
not the publishers or advertisers who choose the pictures of starving
women represented in magazines, we are the ones who decide — *Restates thesis as a call to action*
whether or not these images will be purchased. This is where power
lies — in the hands of those who hand over the dollars that support
the glorification of unhealthy and unrealistic bodies. It is our choice
to exert this power and to reject magazines that promote such
images.

Pfeifer 6

Works Cited

Dittrich, Liz. "About-Face Facts on the Children and the Media."
<u>About-Face</u>. 10 Mar. 2003 <http://www.about-face.org/r/facts/
childrenmedia.shtml>.

---. "About-Face Facts on the Media." <u>About-Face</u>. 10 Mar. 2003
<http://www.about-face.org/r/facts/media.shtml>.

LaVoie, Allison. "Media Influence on Teens." <u>The Green Ladies</u>. 11
Mar. 2003 <http://kidsnrg.simplenet.com/grit.dev/london/
g2_jan12/green_ladies/media/>.

Pipher, Mary. <u>Reviving Ophelia: Saving the Selves of Adolescent Girls</u>.
New York: Ballantine, 1994.

<u>Slim Hopes</u>. Dir. Sut Jhally. Prod. Jean Kilbourne. Videocassette.
Media Education Foundation, 1995.

"Statistics." <u>National Eating Disorders Association</u>. 2002. 14 Mar.
2003 <http://www.nationaleatingdisorders.org>.

Wolfe, Naomi. <u>The Beauty Myth</u>. New York: Harper, 2002.

Young woman reading magazine. Personal photograph by author. 14
Mar. 2003.

Focusing on MEDIA and DESIGN

Design means **being good, not just looking good.**

—CLEMENT MOK

LOG IN

My Portfolio

Quotes & News

YOU have mail!

Message:
Are we still on
for tomorrow?
OK ↔ ABC

SEND

Focusing on Media and Design

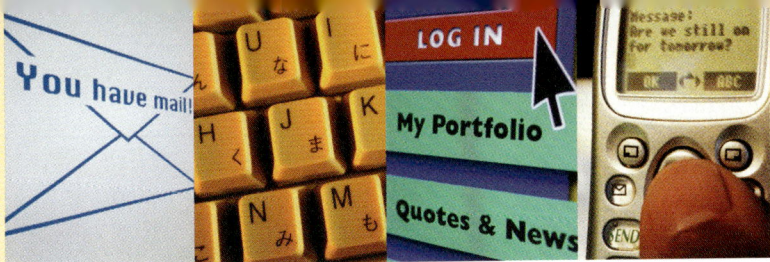

12

Writing with Computers: The Basics

How often do you find yourself at a computer? Many writers today use a word-processing program to draft and revise documents from start to finish; read and write email, instant messages, and Web logs; and visit chat rooms to keep in touch with colleagues, family, and friends. In fact, many writers feel that their computers are an extension of themselves, so closely connected are they to these machines and the acts of communication they make possible. This chapter provides you with some advice, based on what writers across the country have reported, about the two most common ways of writing with computers: word processing and email.

12a Use word-processing tools.

The metaphor of word *processing* deserves attention: we use computers to literally process our words—to discover ideas, to format them in various ways, and to experiment with organization and style. An understanding of the various tools that word-processing programs provide—especially those that involve saving and sharing files, formatting, cutting and pasting, and improving your writing—can help you use these programs efficiently and effectively.

Saving and sharing files

Save each file with a clear name (*Rhetorical Analysis draft 1,* for example, instead of *Paper 1*). Doing so will save you time later on, when you're looking for a particular document. Save related files in the same folder. Here are some additional tips for saving and sharing files:

- If you are sending your draft electronically to an instructor or to someone else, include your name in the file name, along with other pertinent information, so that the recipient can easily identify it.

- Always check on the file type another person can receive before sending a draft electronically, since not all users will have the same edition or type of software you do. Adding visuals and multimedia will increase the file size, and some email accounts limit the size of files. In addition, larger files take longer to download.

- Make sure that your word processor's AUTO SAVE function is set; if it's not, remember to save your files every five minutes or right after you've made an important change, since few things are more frustrating to writers than losing part of their work.

- Take the extra precaution of saving a second copy of every file and giving it a slightly different name (*Rhetorical Analysis draft 1 dup*) on a disc, in another location, or with a "one touch" backup system if you have it.

CONSIDERING DISABILITIES

Accessible Files

When you are sharing files with other members of your class for peer review or other group activities, remember to consider the different needs of group members. You may have a classmate who uses a voice-screen-reader program (such as JAWS); these programs typically do not read visuals very well. You can help your group get off to a good start by making a plan for accommodating everyone's needs.

Formatting

The advantage of using specific formatting tools is that your formatting choices will remain intact even if you change the content. The following list of format recommendations includes some keywords (in *italics*) that you can search for in your word processor's HELP menu to learn how to use each specific feature.

- Most word processors set the default *margins* at 1 inch for top and bottom and 1.25 inches for left and right sides. You may need to adjust margins for some documents.

- For text you want to *indent*, don't use the *enter* key for hard returns. Instead, highlight the text, and then use the FORMAT menu or ruler bar to align the text as needed.

- Use the word processor to insert *page numbers* automatically and to adjust them if you add or delete pages. Include additional information with the page number by using *headers and footers*. You can also automatically add and number *footnotes and endnotes*.

- Format your lists by using *bullets* and *numbering*. For some documents, you may want to try highlighting your text and creating *columns*.

- Many word processors include graphics tools for creating charts, graphs, tables, and other illustrations. Choosing *insert* may also help you easily add a *picture*, *symbol*, or *hyperlink* to your document.
- Use PRINT PREVIEW before printing a document. You'll save paper and toner by first checking to be sure that your format looks correct.

Cutting and pasting

Here are some tips to help you CUT, COPY, and PASTE text efficiently as you revise:

- You can select text for copying by highlighting a passage and then clicking on COPY in the EDIT menu. Copied text will stay where it was in your document while you experiment with moving it to a more appropriate place. If the passage fits better somewhere else, you can paste it there and then go back and delete it from its original location.
- If you plan to revise the organization of a document extensively, work from a copy of the file before making additions, cutting, copying, pasting, and so on.
- If you're reluctant to cut passages you particularly like, paste them into a new file so that you can save them for future writing projects.
- Remember that too much cutting and pasting can result in an incoherent text fairly quickly. After cutting and pasting, reread your entire text to make sure it still moves logically from point to point.

Improving your writing with other basic tools

Several other word-processing tools may help you improve the quality of your writing.

- Use the OUTLINE function to check the logical connections in a document you create.
- Spell checkers can go a long way toward identifying typos and other misspellings. But a spell checker will fail, for instance, to flag misspelled proper names; confused homonyms (*there, their, they're*); and wrong words that are nevertheless spelled correctly (*form* when it should be *from*). In short, there is no substitute for careful proofreading.
- Grammar and style checkers can be more problematic than spell checkers for one simple reason: they are looking at your text out of context, without knowing your purpose or audience. Furthermore, grammar and style checkers sometimes give the wrong advice, as shown on page 104. Nevertheless, grammar checkers can help you spot typos and grammatical errors.
- If you're using Microsoft Word, experiment with TRACK CHANGES and COMMENT tools. The TRACK CHANGES function records additions, deletions, and so on, and allows you to later accept or reject those changes. As the names imply, both of these tools are useful for revising and working collaboratively.

INCORRECT SUGGESTION FROM A GRAMMAR CHECKER

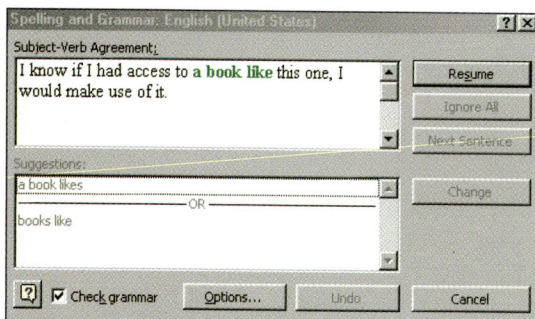

- Use the FIND and REPLACE functions to help you search for certain kinds of errors. For example, if you sometimes mistype *it's* for *its,* you can search for all uses of *it's* and correct them if necessary.

bedfordstmartins.com/everyday_writer For tips on using FIND and REPLACE, go to **Working Online** and click on **Word Processors**.

12b Follow conventions for email, discussion lists, and Web logs (blogs).

Because online communication is so common, many writers fall into habits based on the way they write most often—very informally. Sometimes, then, by failing to adjust style and voice for different occasions and audiences, they undermine their own intentions.

Email

As with any kind of writing, email calls on you to consider your purpose and audience when you write messages. The following advice will help ensure that your email is effective:

- Use a subject line that states your topic accurately and clearly—whether you are writing an email message or responding to one.

- Avoid flaming—using intentionally rude or insulting language—and remember that tone is very hard to convey in online postings: what you intend as a joke may come across as an insult. In addition, remember that many readers find messages in ALL CAPS irritating, as if someone were shouting at them. For more on tone, see 9b.

- Be pertinent. Consider your readers by giving them only the information they need. The length and style of your messages will vary, depending on the subject at hand and your recipients' expectations.

- Break your long paragraphs into shorter paragraphs, and when a message has several points, create sections with headings.

- Use a more formal tone along with a formal greeting and closing when writing to someone you don't know or to an authority, such as a supervisor or instructor (*Dear Ms. Aulie* rather than *Hello*).

- Except in very informal situations, use the conventions of academic English (38a). If you want your message to be taken seriously, be sure it is clearly written and error free. Proofread email messages just as you would other writing.

- Avoid using color fonts or other special formatting unless you know the formatting will appear as you intend on your reader's screen.

- Remember that the Internet is public and that online readers can easily print or forward your messages. When privacy is important, think twice before communicating by email.

- Before attaching files of text or visuals, check with your recipients to make sure they will be able to download them.

- Conclude your message with your name and email address. Your email program likely includes a command that lets you place this information in a signature file.

EMAIL

```
To: techsoup@indirect.com
From: Andrea Lunsford <lunsford@stanford.edu>
Subject: help finding a correct address

Dear Techsoup:

I am trying to send a message to Irene Whitney
at Pacific Synergies, which is headquartered
in Whistler, B.C.  The email address she gave
me is pacsyn@direct.net -- which is obviously
not right since you returned it as undeliver-
able.  If you have an address for Pacific
Synergies, I would be very grateful to receive
it.

Andrea Lunsford, Department of English
<lunsford@stanford.edu>
Stanford University
450 Serra Mall
Stanford, CA 94305-2087
(650) 723-0682 phone
(650) 723-0631 fax
```

Subject line provides accurate and specific information

Double spacing between salutation and message

Message kept succinct and direct

Double spacing between end of message and signature line

Signature gives name and contact information of sender

Following Email Conventions

Email conventions are still evolving, and they differ from one cultural context to another. Especially if you do not know the recipients of your email, stick to a more formal tone (*Dear Ms. Ditembe* and *Sincerely yours,* for example), and follow the conventions of print letter writing— complete sentences, regular capitalization, and so on.

Email lists and discussion forums

People who sign up with discussion lists (sometimes called listservs) receive a copy of messages sent to that list by other members and can send messages to the list themselves. As members respond to one another, the email accumulates, creating a chain or thread that forms an online discussion. When taking part in a discussion-list conversation, keep the following tips in mind:

- Avoid unnecessary criticism of spelling or other obvious language errors. If you disagree with an assertion of fact, offer what you believe to be the correct information, but don't insult the writer for making a mistake.

- If you think you've been flamed, give the writer the benefit of the doubt. Replying with patience establishes your credibility and helps you come across as mature and fair.

- In general, follow the conventions of a particular discussion forum regarding the use of a growing number of acronyms (such as *IOW* for *in other words*). If readers might not understand a particular acronym, write it out.

- Keep in mind that many email discussion lists are archived, so more people than you think may be reading your messages. Remember that your postings create an impression of you.

Web logs (blogs)

You have probably run into more than a few Web logs, or blogs, since current figures estimate that millions of blogs are now on the Web. So what are blogs? Most would agree that they are Web texts written by one or more persons focusing on a single topic and updated regularly, often daily. For those writing and reading them, blogs provide an ongoing record of thinking, one that is easily recoverable: think of an interactive electronic journal you write in as often as possible. It's easy to create a blog using sites such as <blogger.com>. (For information on using blogs in research assignments, see p. 143.) Here are some basic tips for using blogs effectively:

- If you are composing a blog, remember that it, like email, is public—what you wish to remain private should not go on a blog.

- To comment on a blog, follow the same conventions you would for a discussion-list posting (see the previous section). In addition, experienced bloggers recommend that you become familiar with the conversation before you add a comment of your own and that you avoid commenting on blog entries that are several days old.

- Remember that a blog can serve as a personal journal, as a place to comment on other blogs, as a research log, or as a way to share writing with classmates. A blog makes it easy to post writing to the Web, but how you use a blog is determined by your purpose, audience, and imagination.

POSTING TO A DISCUSSION LIST

Subject line provides specific information

```
To: alenglh167@lists.acs.ohio-state.edu
From: Kristen Convery <convery.8@osu.edu>
Subject: Re: class discussion of "self"

At 03:48 PM 04/17/04 -0500, Kate wrote:

>Has anyone had any interesting or pertinent
>discussions of the "self" in other classes
>this term?

I'm taking psychology this quarter and have
found some information that pertains to our
discussion on the self.

Carl Rogers studied the self and self-concept,
theorizing that people do things in line with
their concept of themselves in order to avoid
having to rework that self-concept.  For
instance, if I think of myself as an artist and
not as a musician and I want to go to a con-
cert, I will go to the art museum just so that
I do not have to rethink and maybe change the
way I view myself.

It strikes me as interesting that we seem to
feel as if we must fit one mold, and that that
mold nullifies all other concepts of the self.
Why can't we be both artists and musicians?
Comments from other class members?

Kristen C.
```

Part of an earlier posting included, which helps other list members follow the conversation

Posting responds to query raised by another member and then calls for further comments. Tone is engaged, friendly, and polite

Writer gives only first name and initial because this is a closed discussion list for class members

A WEB LOG (BLOG)

Responses to email and postings

When responding to a particular message, keep these guidelines in mind:

- Change the subject line if you are writing about something different from the original subject.

- Check to make sure you are responding to the appropriate person or persons. If you receive a message that is copied to several others, decide whether you want to reply to the author (REPLY) or to the whole group (REPLY TO ALL). Writers often accidentally send personal messages to an entire group, and doing so can be embarrassing.

- Include only those parts of the original message that you are writing about, and delete the rest.

13

Designing Documents

Computers have made it easier for us to use headings, lists, graphics, and other visuals when we write. Because these visual elements can help us get and keep a reader's attention, they bring a whole new dimension to writing—what some refer to as *visual rhetoric*. This chapter will help you use design elements effectively in your print and online documents.

13a Create a visual structure.

Effective writers of both print and Web-based documents use visual elements such as white space (or negative space) and color, and they choose type styles and sizes that guide readers by presenting them with documents that are easy on the eyes and easy to understand.

Choosing the mode of delivery

One of your first document design decisions will be choosing between print delivery and electronic delivery. In general, print documents are easily portable, often fast to produce, and more familiar than Web documents. In addition, the tools for producing print texts are highly developed and stable. On the other hand, Web-based documents have significant advantages: sound, color, and other illustrative materials are cost-effective options; updates are easy to make; distribution is fast and efficient; and feedback can be swift. In many writing situations, the assignment will tell you which delivery mode to use. Whether you are working to produce a print or a Web-based document, however, you should rely on some basic design principles.

Understanding Design Principles

Most design experts begin with several very simple principles that guide the design of print and Web-based texts. These principles are illustrated in the Web sites shown on pp. 110–111. (For more on the design of nonprint documents, see Chapter 14.)

- **CONTRAST.** The contrast in a design is what attracts your eye to the page and guides you around it. You may achieve contrast through the use of color, icons, boldface or large type, headings, and so on. If you are trying to capture your readers' attention, give careful consideration to contrast. Begin with a focal point—the dominant point, visual, or words on the page—and structure the flow of your visual information from this point. White space (13b) also helps guide readers through your document and provides pauses or breaks.

The National Geographic Web site uses high-contrast colors (such as yellow and blue) effectively.

- **PROXIMITY.** Parts of a page that are closely related should be together (*proximate* to one another). Your goal is to position related points, texts, and visuals as close to one another as possible and to use clear headings to identify them.

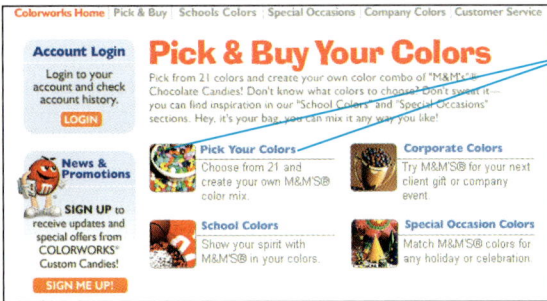

The M&M'S site Colorworks.com demonstrates proximity by placing each image next to its label and supporting text.

- **REPETITION.** Readers are guided in large part by the repetition of key words or elements. You can take advantage of this design principle by using a consistent design throughout your document for elements such as color, typestyle, and visuals.

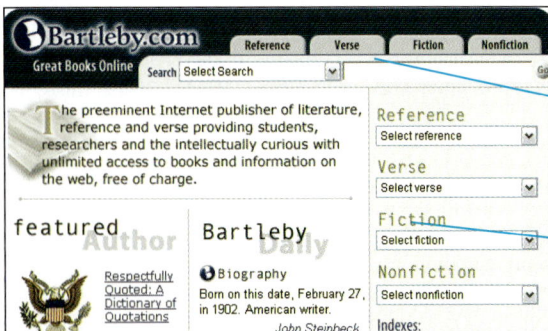

Bartelby.com uses repetition effectively.

The navigation tabs are repeated at the top of every page on the site.

The main ways to navigate the site are repeated in the sidebar.

- **ALIGNMENT.** This principle refers to how visuals and text on a page are lined up, both horizontally and vertically. The headline, title, or banner on a document, for example, should be carefully aligned horizontally so that the reader's eye is drawn easily along one line from left to right. Vertical alignment is equally important. In general, you can choose to align things with the left side, the right side, or the center. If you begin with left alignment, for example, stick with it. The result will be a cleaner and more organized look.

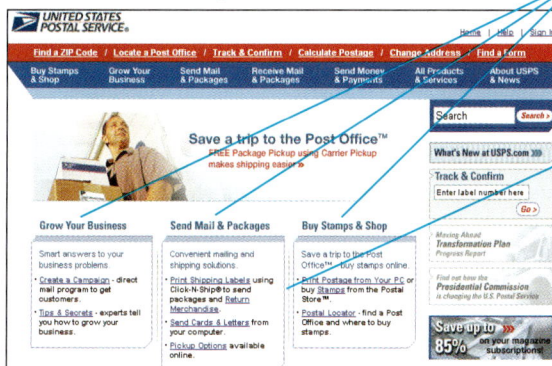

On its site, the U.S. Postal Service effectively aligns content under three major headings.

The box rules and the vertical lines in between them help make the alignment clear.

Text under each heading is aligned at left.

- **OVERALL IMPRESSION.** Aim for a design that creates the appropriate overall impression, or mood, for your document. For an academic essay, you will probably make conservative choices that strike a serious scholarly note. In a newsletter for a campus group, you might choose bright colors and arresting images.

13b Use format effectively.

Because writers have so many design possibilities to choose from, it's important to spend some time thinking about the most appropriate format for a document. Although the following basic formatting guidelines often apply, remember that print documents, Web pages, slide shows or other multimedia presentations, videos, or radio essays have their own special formatting conventions.

Margins and white space

For most print documents, frame your page with margins of between 1 inch and 1.5 inches (Web pages require wider margins). Since the eye takes in only so much data in one movement, very long lines can be hard to read. Wider margins help, particularly if the information is dif-

A BROCHURE USING WHITE SPACE EFFECTIVELY

a   Wide margins and short, easy-to-read lines

b   White space before heading signals beginning of new section

c   White space before and after visual helps it stand out from figure title and footnotes

ficult or dense. To make Web pages easier to read, set margins so that the average text line includes about 10 words (or 75 characters).

Use white space, or negative space, to emphasize and direct readers to parts of the page. For example, you can use white space around graphics, headings, or lists to make them stand out.

Color

Many software programs and printers allow you to use color in print and Web documents. Your use of color should depend on the purpose(s) of your document and its intended audience. As you design documents, keep in mind that some colors (red, for example) can evoke powerful responses, so take care that the colors you use match the message you are sending and the mood you want to create. Here are some other tips for using color:

- Use color to draw attention to elements you want to emphasize: headings and subheadings, bullets, text boxes, parts of charts or graphs, other visuals.

- Be consistent in your use of color; use the same color for all main headings, for example.

- For most documents, keep the number of colors fairly small; too many colors can create a jumbled or confused look. In addition, avoid colors that clash or that are hard on the eyes (certain shades of yellow, for example). Check to make sure that all color visuals and text are legible.

- Remember that when colors are printed or projected, they may not look the same as they do on your computer screen.

- Look for examples of effective use of color. Find color combinations that you think look especially good—and then try them out.

Certain color combinations clash and are hard to read.

Other combinations are easier on the eyes.

CONSIDERING DISABILITIES

Color for Contrast

Remember that not everyone will see color as you do. Some individuals don't perceive color at all; others perceive color in a variety of ways. When putting colors next to one another, then, try to use those that reside on opposite sides of the color spectrum, such as purple and gold, in order to achieve high contrast. Doing so will allow readers to see the contrast, if not the nuances, of color.

Paper

The quality of the paper and the readability of the type affect the overall look and feel of print documents. Although inexpensive paper is fine for your earlier drafts, use $8\frac{1}{2}$" × 11" good-quality white bond paper for your final drafts. For résumés, you may wish to use parchment or cream-colored bond. For brochures and posters, colored paper may be most appropriate. Try to use the best-quality printer available to you for your final product.

Pagination

Except for a separate title page, which is usually left unnumbered, number every page of your print document. Your instructor may ask that you follow a particular format (see Chapters 52–55 for format preferences of the Modern Language Association, for example); if not, beginning with the first page of text, place your last name and an Arabic numeral in the upper-right-hand corner of the page, about one-half inch from the top and aligned with the right margin. Most personal computers will paginate a document for you.

Type

Most personal computers allow writers to choose among a great variety of type sizes and typefaces, or fonts. For most college writing, 10- to 12-point type sizes are best. A serif font (as used in the main text of this book) is generally easier to read than a sans serif font. And although unusual fonts might seem attractive at first glance, readers may find such fonts distracting and hard to read over long stretches of material.

Remember that typefaces help you create the tone of a document, so consider your audience and purpose when selecting type.

Different fonts convey different feelings.

Different fonts convey different feelings.

DIFFERENT FONTS CONVEY DIFFERENT FEELINGS.

Different fonts convey different feelings.

Most important, be consistent in the size and style of type you choose. Unless you are striving for some special effect, shifting sizes and fonts can give an appearance of disorderliness.

Spacing

Final drafts for most of your college writing should be double-spaced, with the first line of paragraphs indented one-half inch or five spaces. Other documents, however, may call for different spacing. Letters, memorandums, lab reports, and Web texts, for example, are usually single-spaced, with no paragraph indentation. Single-spaced text usually adds a blank line between paragraphs instead of indenting paragraphs to make the text easier to read. Other kinds of documents, such as flyers and newsletters, may call for multiple columns of text. Consult a style guide (such as the *MLA Handbook*), or ask your instructor about appropriate spacing.

13c   Use headings effectively.

In longer documents, headings call attention to the organization of the text and thus aid comprehension. Some kinds of reports have standard headings (like *Abstract* or *Summary*), which readers expect (and writers therefore should provide). If you use headings, you need to decide on type size and style, wording, and placement.

Type size and style

This book uses multiple levels of headings distinguished by different type sizes and fonts as well as by color. In a college paper, you will usually distinguish levels of headings using only type—for example, all capitals for the first-level headings, capitals and lowercase boldface for the second level, capitals and lowercase italics for the third level, and so on.

FIRST-LEVEL HEADING
Second-Level Heading
Third-Level Heading

On page 114, "13c Use headings effectively" is a first-level head; "Type size and style" is a second-level head.

Consistent headings

Look for the most succinct and informative way to word your headings. Most often, state the topic in a single word, usually a noun (*Toxicity*); in a phrase, usually a noun phrase (*Levels of Toxicity*) or a gerund phrase (*Measuring Toxicity*); in a question that will be answered in the text (*How Can Toxicity Be Measured?*); or in an imperative that tells readers what steps to take (*Measure the Toxicity*). Whichever structure you choose, make sure you use it consistently for all headings of the same level.

Typically, place a first-level heading at the left margin; indent a second-level heading five spaces from the left. Just remember to position each level of heading consistently throughout your paper.

bedfordstmartins.com/everyday_writer   For more on effective design, click on **Roger Munger's Tutorial on Designing Documents with a Word Processor.**

13d Use visuals effectively.

Visuals can often make a point more vividly and succinctly than words alone could. In this way, visuals help draw your audience into your document. Try to choose visuals that will help you make your points most emphatically and will help your audience understand your document. (See the table on p. 116 for advice on using a variety of visuals.)

Number your visuals (number tables separately from other visuals) and give them informative titles. In some instances, you may need to provide captions to give readers additional data such as source information.

Figure 1. College Enrollment for Men and Women by Age, 2003 (in millions)

Table 1. Word Choice by Race: *Seesaw* and *Teeter-totter*, Chicago 1986

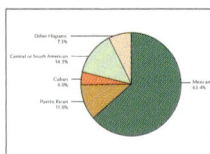

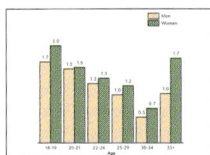

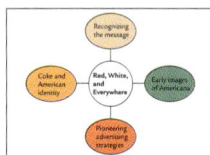

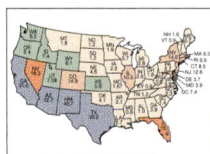

Type of Visual	When to Use It
Pie Chart	Use *pie charts* to compare a part to the whole.
Bar Graph	Use *bar graphs* and *line graphs* to compare one element with another, to compare elements over time, to demonstrate correlations, and to illustrate frequency.
Table	Use *tables* to draw attention to particular numerical information.
Diagram	Use *drawings* or *diagrams* to draw attention to dimensions and to details.
Map	Use *maps* to draw attention to location and to spatial relationships.
Cartoon	Use *cartoons* to illustrate or emphasize a point dramatically or comically.
Photo	Use *photographs* to draw attention to a graphic scene (such as devastation following an earthquake) or to depict people or objects.

Using scanners and image editors

Tools such as scanners and image editors give today's writers much more control over the visuals they insert into their documents. Remember that resolution affects the quality of the visual you are scanning. Choose a higher resolution for a sharper picture—but remember, too, that the higher the resolution the bigger the file size.

Using photo-editing software (such as Adobe Photoshop or Macromedia Fireworks) allows you to sharpen a visual or create particular effects and then turn the image file into the right form for printing or posting to a Web page. Here are some things you can do with an image editor:

• make visuals larger or smaller
• adjust or rotate a visual to a particular angle
• adjust colors to make them brighter or to heighten contrast
• crop visuals to create close-ups or emphasis

Analyzing and altering visuals

Because of the technical tools available to writers and designers today, many people can create and publish visuals on the Web. Sometimes, however, the visuals are manipulated or taken out of context. For example, the image below on the far left was circulated widely via email as a *National Geographic* Photo of the Year. The National Geographic Society had to step in to clarify that the picture was a prank and not real. Instead, the photograph was a collage a digital artist had made of two separate pictures—the photo in the middle, from *National Geographic,* and the photo on the right, from the U.S. Air Force Web site.

As you would with any source material, carefully assess any visuals you find online for effectiveness, appropriateness, and validity. Here are additional tips for evaluating visuals:

• Check the context in which the visual appears. Is it part of an official government, company, or library site?
• If the visual is a photograph, is the date, time, place, and setting shown or explained? If the visual is a chart, graph, or diagram, are the numbers and labels explained? Are the sources of the data given?

- Is biographical and contact information for the designer, artist, or photographer given?

If you *do* alter a visual, do so ethically:

- Make sure the visual does not attempt to mislead readers. Show things as accurately as possible.
- Tell your audience what changes you have made.
- Include all relevant data and information about the visual, including the source.

AT A GLANCE

Using Visuals Effectively

- Use visuals as a part of your text, never as decoration.
- In print texts, refer to the visual before it actually appears. For example: *As Table 1 demonstrates, the cost of a college education has risen dramatically in the last decade.*
- Tell the audience explicitly what the visual demonstrates, especially if it presents complex information. Do not assume readers will "read" the visual the way you do; your commentary on it is important.
- Number and title all visuals. Number tables and figures separately.
- Follow established conventions for documenting visual sources, and ask permission for use, if necessary. (19c and e)
- Use clip art sparingly, if at all. Clip art is so easy to cut and paste that you may be tempted to slip it in everywhere, but resist this urge.
- Get responses to your visuals in an early draft. If readers can't follow them or are distracted by them, revise accordingly.
- Do a test-run printout of all visuals just to make sure your printer is adequate for the job.
- Use scanners and image editors to prepare drawings, photographs, or other illustrations for insertion into your document. But *remember* to do so ethically.

13e Sample documents

A group of annotated documents collected from college students and others follow; these samples should help you create similar documents of your own. (For examples of academic essays, see Chapters 11 and 55–58.)

bedfordstmartins.com/everyday_writer For more sample documents, click on **Student Writing.**

PAGES FROM A BROCHURE

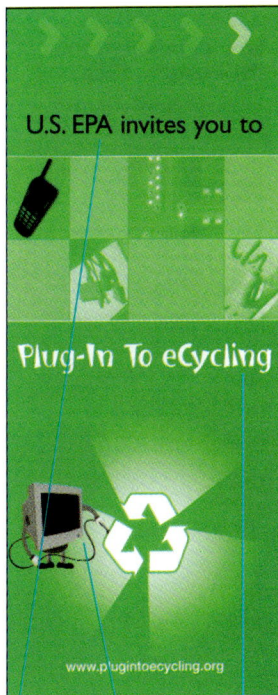

U.S. EPA invites you to

Plug-In To eCycling

www.plugintoecycling.org

Electronics Recycling Gives Old Electronics A Second Chance!

Our "plugged in" world relies on an ever-growing and constantly changing supply of electronics products. The introduction of better, smaller, and cheaper electronics has prompted us to replace older models at a rapid rate. As a result, electronics are a fast growing portion of America's trash—more than 3 million tons of electronic waste are discarded in landfills annually. This trend has given rise to a new environmental challenge: safe and resource-wise management of electronic waste.

Why Is Electronics Waste an Issue?

- Nearly 250 million computers will become obsolete in the next 5 years.
- Mobile phones will be discarded at a rate of 130 million per year by 2005, resulting in 65,000 tons of waste containing lead and brominated flame retardants.
- TVs and computers can contain an average of 4 pounds of lead as well as other toxics like chromium, cadmium, mercury, nickel, zinc, and flame retardants.

Photo shows e-cycling in action

Bulleted list succinctly gives facts for a persuasive message

Bold heading clearly explains purpose

Appropriate visuals help convey meaning

High-contrast title in large, eye-catching type

FIRST PAGE OF A REPORT (ON THE WEB)

Identifies action-group sponsor

Unusual font and all caps for the logo and graphic

Color used only in headings, graphics, and margins

Large type used for title of report

Introduction to the problem

Single spacing within paragraphs

Double spacing between paragraphs

Left alignment used consistently

BAY AREA ACTION

EDUCATION THROUGH ENVIRONMENTAL ACTION

ABOUT   PROJECTS   NEWS   JOIN   CONTACT   ECOCALENDAR

Environmental Gift Catalog
▸ Buy an eco-gift for yourself.

March is BAA Experience Month!
▸ A full month of cool events!

HOME

RECENT ARTICLES
ARCHIVED ARTICLES
OUR NEWSLETTER
MEDIA CONTACT
SEARCH

News

Water fluoridation
Tooth protectant or protected pollutant?

By Cindy L. Russell, M.D.
and David Smernoff, Ph.D.

FOR NEARLY 50 YEARS, the US government and media have been telling the public that fluoride compounds are safe and effective at reducing cavities. Recent evidence clearly shows that neither claim is true. Nevertheless, in 1995 the California legislature mandated fluoridation of the re-maining 85% of state water supplies.

In 1997, 1,500 members of the National Federation of Federal Employees local 2050, representing toxicologists, chemists, biologists and other professionals at EPA headquarters in Washington D.C., voted unanimously to oppose water fluoridation by co-sponsoring the California Safe Drinking Water Initiative. They did this after reviewing scientific evidence, including animal and human epidemiology studies, that indicate a causal link between fluoride/fluoridation and cancer, genetic damage, neurological impairment and bone pathology. Of particular concern are recent studies linking fluoride exposure to lowered IQ in children.

Recently declassified documents from the Manhattan Project remind us that fluoride emissions from uranium processing facilities caused widespread animal death and severe crop damage. A large public relations campaign was conducted to protect the government from lawsuits and to change public perceptions about fluoride. In fact, fluoride was promoted as a tooth protectant by the same people within the Atomic Energy Commission that injected plutonium into prisoners to test the effects of radiation on humans!

Fun Fluoride Facts, or Do you really want this in your water?

- Fluoride compounds are toxic byproducts of phosphate mining, aluminum refining and

More info:

NoFlouride.com

International

NEWSLETTER

NEWS

WEST COAST
environmental law

Volume 26:01 June 12, 2000

FROM WEST COAST ENVIRONMENTAL LAW

Public interest environmental law for British Columbia

Safe to Drink?

The events in Walkerton, Ontario, provide an urgent wake-up call: BC has the highest per capita incidence of water-borne disease of any province in Canada, and the province is not adequately protecting drinking water sources from human related impacts.

The tragic events that have recently unfolded in Walkerton, Ontario, should be a wake-up call to governments across the country because the agenda of downsizing environment ministries, privatizing government inspection and monitoring services, and abandoning environmental regulation is not unique to the Harris government. We have known for some time that there are very real human costs associated with failing to protect the air we breathe and the water we drink -- the horrendous impacts of the E. coli contamination of drinking water in Walkerton remind us of how immediate those consequences can be.

BC's drinking water is at risk
There is certainly no reason for BC residents to be complacent when it comes to water quality. In fact this province has an ignominious record when it comes to safe drinking water. Here are the troubling statistics:

• BC has the highest per capita incidence of water-borne disease of any province in Canada. A 1998 government study reported that there had been 27 outbreaks of toxoplasmosis, cryptosporidium, giardia, and other diseases in the past eighteen years.

• The GVRD's water supply frequently exceeds the minimum federal guidelines for water turbidity. It is the only unfiltered Canadian water

supply which often exceeds the standards on which Canada's safe drinking water guidelines are based.

• Contamination is a serious problem for some provincial groundwater sources. For example, drinking water guidelines for nitrate-nitrogen are not being met in certain aquifers because of contamination from manure and fertilizers.

• The government's first Water Quality Status Report of April 1996 found that of 124 water-bodies surveyed, only 60% had source waters which fell into the "good to excellent" category for drinking water purposes. Even for the 60% in that category, disinfection was still required.

• Over 200 BC communities are on permanent "boil water" advisories, i.e. they cannot safely drink the water from their tap without boiling it first

Audit brings bad news
A disturbing indictment of the province's efforts to ensure safe drinking water for BC residents was recently offered by the Auditor General (Protecting Drinking Water Sources 1998/99). According to the Auditor: "...the province is not adequately protecting drinking water sources from human

related impacts, and this could have significant cost implications in the future for the province, for municipal governments and for citizens in general."

The Auditor pointed the finger at the lack of a coherent and integrated approach to land use management. The role of the Ministry of Forests in watershed and agricultural land management is particularly problematic because it bears so little responsibility for the impact or costs associated with poor management decisions. Unfortunately, the Auditor's mandate didn't extend to examining the adequacy of the province's legislative framework for protecting water. Had it, he would have no doubt noted the inadequate patchwork of water quality regulation in BC.

For instance, BC is the only Canadian province with no groundwater protection legislation. While safe drinking water regulations have been established under the *Health Act*, only one of hundreds of water quality guidelines is actually given the force of regulatory protection. Even where regulatory controls exist, inadequate monitoring and indifferent enforcement policies often render them ineffective.

see **Safe to Drink?**, continued on page 2

2 Emissions Trading: the great leap forward?
3 Is Canada Sinking Kyoto?

4 Blowing Cold over Hot Air
5 Chinese brochures
5 Fish habitat workshops

6 Environmental Dispute Resolution Fund in Action
7 In Good Company

Annotations:
- Organization logo uses distinctive visual
- Sponsoring organization identified
- Question used as attention-getting title
- Italics signal overview of problem
- Text wraps around appropriate visual
- Double spacing between sections of text
- Bullets call out important statistics
- Visuals indicate what's coming up inside the newsletter

FLYER

Use of white background with clearly contrasting colors gets attention

Central image draws attention and makes a playful allusion to a popular film, *The Usual Suspects*

Typefaces and sizes used consistently to differentiate sections of the flyer

Related information grouped together makes for easy reading

Web-site address featured prominently for further information

five tutors. two dorms. no coincidence

The Usual Subjects

Katy Barglow	**Sheba Najmi**	**Tania Lombrozo**	**Manish Patel**	**Leo Alekseyev**
Good with chemicals and biological agents.	Armed with potentially destructive writing skills.	Always right on when it comes to documents and verbal combat.	Implicated in devious econ calculations.	Easily provoked to be physical and mathematical.
Can be found in:	*Can be found in:*	*Can be found in:*	*Can be found in:*	*Can be found in:*
Castano 218 *Mon, Thu* 9 – 11 PM	Lantana 205 *Tue, Thu* 9 – 10:30 PM	Castano 319 *Tue* 8 – 10 PM *Thu* 9 – 10 PM	Castano 205 *Sun* 9 – 11 PM	Lantana 303 *Mon* 7:30 – 9:30 PM

Visit us during our office hours, or make an appointment.
For complete tutoring schedule or more info, see

uac-tutoring.stanford.edu/tutor

14

Creating Web Texts

You're probably growing more and more accustomed to the advantages, demands, and different styles of Web sites. Unlike print texts, most Web texts can use links to take readers to other parts of a site—or to other sites altogether; can organize information as a cluster of associations; can be revised and updated hourly; can use sound and animation; and can reach a very wide audience very quickly. This chapter aims to help you take advantage of the opportunities Web texts offer and to think carefully about the design of effective Web pages.

14a Plan your Web text carefully.

As in preparing any important document, you need to plan your Web text with a keen eye on your rhetorical situation, including purpose, audience, topic, and stance. Once you've considered these general factors—along with your deadlines and other time-management issues—you can use the following tips to begin planning your Web text:

- Make sure you have access to space on a server so that you can preview your pages as you design them and so that you can post them "live" to the Web.
- Consider the overall impression you want to create. Do you want your site to be bold? soothing? serious? This overall impression should guide your decisions about text, navigational aids, visuals, color, video, sound clips, and so on.
- Visit several Web sites you admire. Look for effective design ideas and ways of organizing navigation and information (note the placement of visuals, how links are named, how color is used, and so on).
- Map (or storyboard) your Web document, and be ready to move elements around to improve organization. (14b) Think about creating a template for consistent layout of pages or sections.
- Plan your use of visuals very carefully, making sure that each one helps to get your message across. Make sure your visuals are saved in browser-supported formats such as GIF or JPEG. Check the file size and resolution of photos and other visuals to make sure they can be downloaded quickly. (14e)
- Give considerable thought to the colors you will use, remembering that colors carry strong emotional associations. (13b)
- Consider the technical limitations readers of your Web text may face, and test your Web text from a dial-up modem and in different browsers to see how it loads and looks.
- Remember that Web texts are dynamic—so you should plan to reassess, revise, and maintain your Web text on an ongoing basis and to note when the site was last updated.

CONSIDERING DISABILITIES

Special Coding and Features for Web Texts

For those with certain disabilities, much on the Web remains hard to access and read. Keep these priorities in mind:

• For readers whose vision is impaired, provide a text-only version of your document, including descriptions of all visuals.

• Don't rely solely on color to carry the meaning of your message. For readers who may be color-blind, make sure to choose colors that create a sharp contrast. (13b)

• For readers whose hearing is impaired, provide captions for any sound on your Web site.

PROCESS FOR CREATING A WEB TEXT

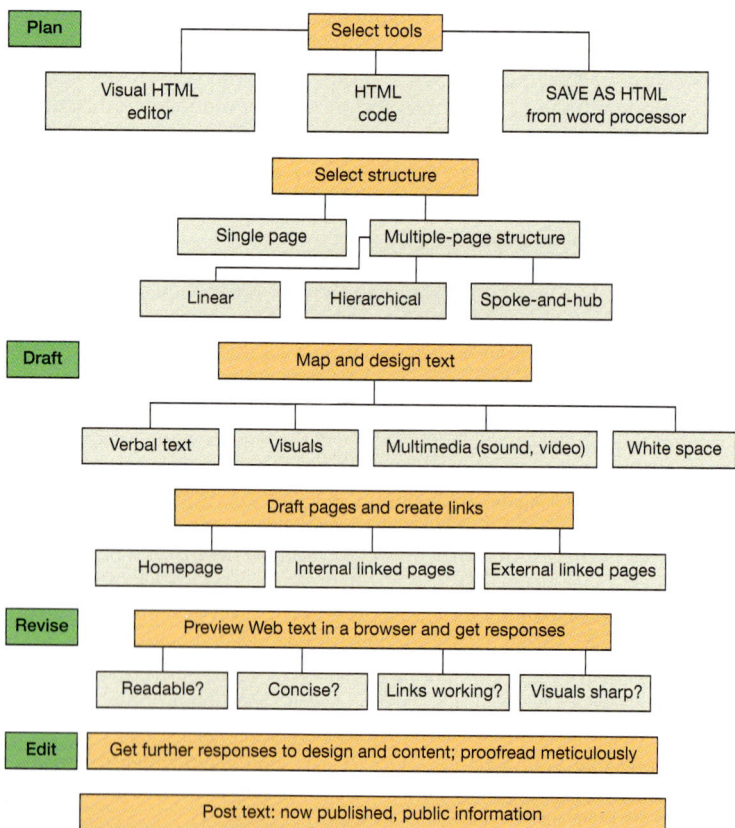

Plan

Select tools

| Visual HTML editor | HTML code | SAVE AS HTML from word processor |

Select structure

Single page | Multiple-page structure

Linear | Hierarchical | Spoke-and-hub

Draft

Map and design text

Verbal text | Visuals | Multimedia (sound, video) | White space

Draft pages and create links

Homepage | Internal linked pages | External linked pages

Revise

Preview Web text in a browser and get responses

Readable? | Concise? | Links working? | Visuals sharp?

Edit

Get further responses to design and content; proofread meticulously

Post text: now published, public information

14b   Use mapping to organize your Web texts.

Just as you might outline a print document, you should develop a clear structure for a Web text. Many Web sites are organized according to one of three basic patterns: linear, hierarchical, or spoke-and-hub.

LINEAR ORGANIZATION

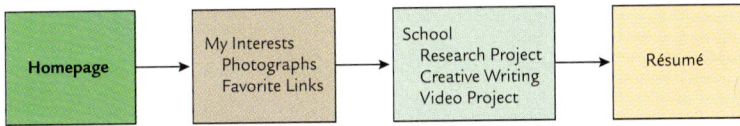

| Homepage | → | My Interests
Photographs
Favorite Links | → | School
Research Project
Creative Writing
Video Project | → | Résumé |

HIERARCHICAL ORGANIZATION

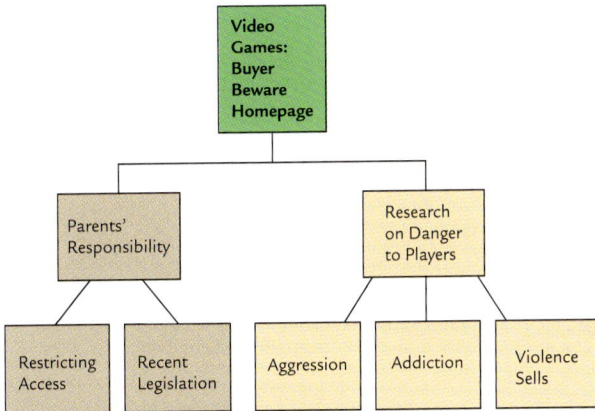

Video Games: Buyer Beware Homepage

- Parents' Responsibility
  - Restricting Access
  - Recent Legislation
- Research on Danger to Players
  - Aggression
  - Addiction
  - Violence Sells

SPOKE-AND-HUB ORGANIZATION

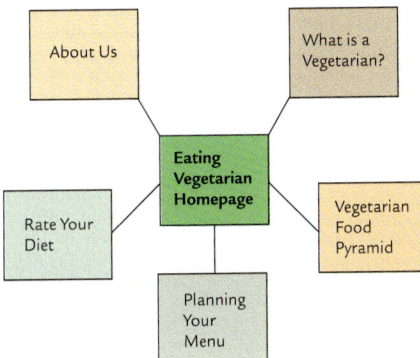

Eating Vegetarian Homepage

- About Us
- What is a Vegetarian?
- Rate Your Diet
- Vegetarian Food Pyramid
- Planning Your Menu

These tips can help you map your Web text:

1. Inventory the content material you have, and make a list of what you still need to find or create.
2. Using a word-processing program or old-fashioned pencil and paper, sketch the basic text and visuals for each page of your text, beginning with the homepage.
3. Indicate the links among the pages—and make sure all sections of your Web text link to the homepage.

14c Follow good design principles.

For any Web document, you should follow some basic principles of good design (see Chapter 13). In addition, use these design tips to get the best results:

- At the top of the homepage, put a title (and subtitle, if necessary) along with an eye-catching and easy-to-process visual or statement that makes clear what the Web site is about.
- Think of each page beyond the homepage as having two main parts: navigation areas (such as menus or links) and content areas. Your goal is to make these two areas distinct from one another and to make the navigation clear to your readers.
- Use an existing design template, or create one of your own, to make the elements on each page consistent. You can find such templates in some Web-writing tools and on Web design sites; or you may take cues from existing Web designs (but be sure to give proper credit).
- Create a navigation area for every main page, listing links to the key sections of the site. Remember that every page should include a link back to the homepage.
- Use visuals that can be downloaded quickly and easily by your readers. (14e)
- Remember that the top left of a page is always visible and thus the most important spot.
- Include your name and contact information on every page.
- Get responses to a rough draft of your pages, especially the homepage. How understandable and readable are these pages? How easy are they to navigate? How effective is your use of color, visuals, fonts, sound, and so on?

14d Code your Web text.

Essentially, codes tell a Web browser how to interpret the various elements on a page. One set of codes (usually called document tags) governs the larger aspects of the text (such as the title, body elements, background color, and so on), while another set (usually called appearance tags) governs smaller aspects (italics, boldface, underlining, and so on). The figures below show part of a simple Web page and the HTML (Hypertext Markup Language) code used to produce it.

A STUDENT WEB PAPER AND ITS HTML CODE

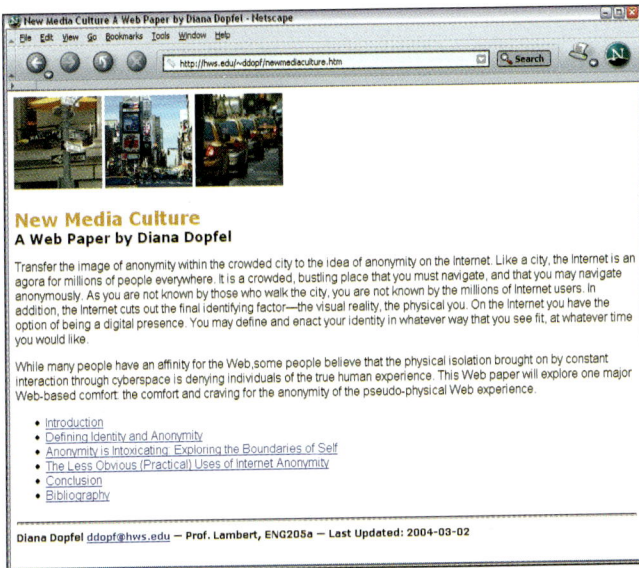

You're no doubt familiar with HTML code, like that depicted on page 127, but richer and more complex markup languages—such as XHTML, SMGL, and XML—are becoming more popular.

You can write your own code from scratch. Or you can write your document using your word processor and save the material as HTML. But you will most likely use a text editor (such as Microsoft FrontPage, Netscape Composer, PageMill, or Dreamweaver) that does the bulk of the hard work for you and lets you see each page and content as it is created.

No matter how you've decided to code your document, asking for responses from readers is crucial to your overall success. Before you make your document available on the Web, therefore, you and others should preview your text.

- Proofread every page, looking for any typos, errors, or confusing passages.
- Check the navigation of the site, verifying that all links work and that readers can find their way around with ease.
- Check the site using several different browsers and computers, if possible, to see that each page displays properly.

14e   Use visuals and multimedia appropriately.

The visual and multimedia possibilities of the Web can at times seem overwhelming. The following tips will help you think carefully about how best to use visuals and multimedia in your Web texts:

- Visuals may add to but are not a substitute for text, so integrate the two very carefully. Don't use visuals for mere decoration.
- As noted in Chapter 13, readers may not see the connection between a visual and text: you need to make that relationship clear in the text or in labels or captions.
- Most work on the Web is protected by copyright, so unless there is an explicit statement that the information is available for free use, you need to request permission to use a visual, sound clip, and so on that you have not created yourself. Free icons, clip art, and other visuals are widely available on the Web; you can check most search engines or other archives of free visuals. In addition, government documents are in the public domain and thus free for use, but always include source information.
- To download and save a visual image from the Web using Windows on a PC, place your cursor over the visual, right click with your mouse, and select SAVE IMAGE AS. To download a visual image on a Mac, hold down the mouse until a menu appears, and select SAVE THIS IMAGE AS.
- The file space a JPEG or GIF visual takes up may make downloading the image difficult, so limit individual visuals to 30 to 40 kilobytes—or use a smaller thumbnail version as a link to the original, larger file.
- Experiment with scanning objects and taking pictures with a digital camera—and using photo-editing software to clarify and improve them. (13d)

- Remember that visuals and audio often will not be accessible to those with disabilities and to those with browsers that can't display them. You need to test your Web site to see how accessible it is.

AT A GLANCE

Evaluating Your Web Text

- Does your Web text accomplish its purpose? Is every page relevant to your topic? (14a)
- Who is the intended audience? Does the homepage invite those readers in? Is your site accessible to those with disabilities? (14a and c)
- How effective is the organization of your site? How easy is it to navigate? Have you maintained consistency among your pages? (14b and c)
- Does your site adhere to basic design principles? (13a)
- Is your name and contact information on every page? (14c)
- Have you tested your site on different browsers and computers? (14d)
- How have you used visuals, color, and multimedia? Do they all help convey the meaning you intended? Check to be sure you have struck an appropriate balance between the visuals and the text of your document. If you have used visuals or multimedia created by someone else, have you obtained permission and given proper credit to your source? (14e)

---

bedfordstmartins.com/everyday_writer For resources and more information, click on **Working Online.** For additional help, click on **Mike Markel's Tutorial on Designing for the Web.**

15

Making Oral and Multimedia Presentations

When the Gallup Poll reports on what U.S. citizens say they fear most, the findings are always the same: public speaking is apparently more frightening to us than almost anything else, even scarier than an attack from outer space. This chapter aims to allay any such fears you may have by offering guidelines that can help you prepare for and deliver successful presentations.

AT A GLANCE

Preparing for Presentations

- How effectively are you contributing to class discussions? (15a)
- How does your presentation fulfill your purpose, including the goals of the assignment? (15b)
- How do you appeal to your audience's interests? (15b)
- How do the introduction and conclusion hold the audience's attention? (15b)
- Is your organizational structure crystal clear? How do you guide listeners? Are your transitions and signpost language explicit? Do you repeat key words or ideas? (15b)
- Have you practiced your presentation and gotten some response to it? (15b)
- Have you marked the text you are using for pauses and emphasis? (15b)
- Have you prepared all necessary visuals, including presentation slides and other multimedia? Are they large enough to be seen? Would other visuals be helpful? (15b and c)

15a   Contribute to class discussions.

Remember that the contributions you make to class discussions are mini presentations. Here are some tips for making sure your contributions are effective ones:

- Be prepared so that the comments you make will be relevant to the discussion.
- Listen purposefully, jotting down related points and following the flow of the conversation.
- If you think you might lose track of your ideas while speaking, jot down key words to keep you on track.
- Make your comments count by asking a key question, by taking the conversation in a new direction, or by summarizing or analyzing what has been said.
- Respond specifically to questions or comments by others (*The passage on p. 42 provides evidence in support of your point* rather than *I agree*).
- If you have trouble speaking up, set a goal of making at least one comment a day.

FOR MULTILINGUAL WRITERS

Speaking Up in Class

Speaking up in class is viewed as inappropriate or even rude in some cultures. In the United States, however, doing so is expected and encouraged. Some instructors even assign credit for class participation.

15b Make effective oral presentations.

More and more students report that formal presentations are becoming part of their work both in and out of class. As you begin to plan for such a presentation, you should consider a number of issues.

Considering your task, purpose, and audience

Think about how much time you have to prepare; where the presentation will take place; how long the presentation is to be; whether you will use written-out text or notecards; whether visual aids, handouts, or other accompanying materials are called for; and what equipment you will need. If you are making a group presentation, you will need time to divide duties and to practice with your classmates.

Consider the purpose of your presentation. Are you to lead a discussion? teach a lesson? give a report? engage a group in an activity? Also consider your audience. What do they know about your topic, what opinions do they already hold about it, and what do they need to know to follow your presentation and perhaps accept your point of view?

CONSIDERING DISABILITIES

Accessible Presentations

Do all you can to make your presentations accessible.

- Do not rely on color or visuals alone to get across information—some individuals may be unable to pick up such cues.
- If you use video, provide captions to explain any sounds that won't be audible to some audience members.

Emphasizing your introduction and conclusion

Listeners tend to remember beginnings and endings most readily, so try to make these elements memorable. Consider, for example, using a startling statement, opinion, or question; a vivid anecdote; or a powerful quotation. Getting and holding the attention of your listeners will help them remember your presentation.

Using an explicit structure and signpost language

Organize your presentation clearly and carefully, and give an overview of your main points at the outset. (You may wish to recall these points toward the end of the talk.) Throughout your presentation, pause between major points, and use signpost language as you move from one idea to the next. Such signposts should be clear and concrete: *The second crisis point in the breakup of the Soviet Union occurred hard on the heels of the first* instead of *Another thing about the Soviet Union's problems. . . .* (For a list of transitions, see 8e.) You can also offer signposts by repeating key words and ideas. Avoid long, complicated sentences, and remember that listeners prefer action verbs and concrete nouns. If you are talking about abstract ideas, try to provide concrete examples for each.

Turning writing into speaking

Even though you will rely on some written material for your presentation, that material will need to be adapted for speech. If you decide to prepare a full text of your presentation, double- or triple-space it, and use fairly large print so that it will be easy to see. Try to end each page with the end of a sentence so that you won't have to pause while you turn a page. Or you may prefer to work from a detailed topic outline, from note cards, or from points on flip charts, overhead transparencies, or slides. In any case, be sure to mark the places where you want to pause and to highlight the words you want to emphasize.

The first example that follows is from an essay that is intended to be read by its audience. The second example contains the same information, but it is intended for oral presentation. Note how this second version uses signpost language; repetition; vivid, concrete examples; and uncomplicated sentence structure to make it easy to follow by ear. Note also how the student writer has marked his text for emphasis and pauses.

TEXT FROM A WRITTEN ESSAY

The Simpson family has occasionally been described as a "nuclear" family, which obviously has a double meaning: first, the family consists of two parents and three children, and, second, Homer works at a nuclear power plant with very relaxed safety codes. The overused label *dysfunctional,* when applied to the Simpsons, suddenly takes on new meaning. Every episode seems to include a scene in which son Bart is being choked by his father, the baby is being neglected, or Homer is sitting in a drunken stupor transfixed by the television screen. The comedy in these scenes comes from the exaggeration of commonplace household events (although some talk shows and news programs would have us believe that these exaggerations are not confined to the madcap world of cartoons).

TEXT REVISED FOR ORAL PRESENTATION

What does it mean to pick an overused label and to describe the Simpsons as a *nuclear* family? Clearly, a double meaning is at work. First, the Simpsons fit the dictionary meaning — a family unit consisting of two parents and some children. The second meaning, however, packs more of a punch. You see, Homer works at a nuclear power plant [pause here] with *very* relaxed safety codes!

Another overused family label describes the Simpsons. Did everyone guess I was going to say *dysfunctional*? And like "nuclear," when it comes to the Simpsons, "dysfunctional" takes on a whole new meaning.

Remember the scenes when Bart is being choked by his father?

How about the many times the baby is being neglected?

Or the classic view — Homer sitting in a drunken stupor transfixed by the TV screen!

My point here is that the comedy in these scenes often comes from double meanings — and from a lot of exaggeration of everyday household events.

Using visuals

Think of visuals — charts, graphs, photographs, or lists — not as add-ons but as a major way to convey information. Many speakers use presentation software to help keep themselves on track and to guide members of the audience, especially those who learn better by reading *and* listening (see 15c). Transparencies, posters, flip charts, and chalkboards can make strong visual statements as well.

Because of their importance, visuals must be large enough to be easily seen and read by your audience. Be sure that the information on any visual is simple, clear, and easy to read and understand. And remember *not* to simply read from visuals (such as PowerPoint slides) or to turn your back on your audience while you refer to any visuals.

Most important, make sure that all visuals engage and help your listeners rather than distract them from your message. Check the effectiveness of your visuals by trying them out on other people before you give your presentation.

You may also want to prepare handouts for your audience: pertinent bibliographies, for example, or text too extensive to be presented otherwise. Unless the handouts include material you want your audience to consult while you speak, distribute them at the end of the presentation.

Practicing your presentation

Prepare a draft of your presentation, including all visuals, far enough in advance to allow for several run-throughs. Some speakers audiotape or videotape their rehearsals and then base their revisions on the taped performance. Others practice in front of a mirror or in front of colleagues or friends, who can give comments on content and style.

Make sure you will be heard clearly. If you are soft-spoken, concentrate on projecting your voice; if your voice tends to rise when you're in the spotlight, practice lowering the pitch. If you speak rapidly, practice slowing down. Remember, too, that tone of voice affects listeners, so it's usually best to avoid sarcasm in favor of a tone that conveys interest in your topic and listeners.

Once you are comfortable giving the presentation, make sure you will stay within the allotted time. One good rule of thumb is to allow roughly two and a half minutes per double-spaced $8\frac{1}{2}$" $\times$ 11" page of text (or one and a half minutes per 5" $\times$ 7" card)—and then time yourself precisely.

Making your presentation

The best strategy for calming your nerves and getting off to a good start seems to be to know your material really well. You may also be able to use the following strategies to good advantage:

- Consider how you will dress and how you will move around, making sure that both are appropriate to the situation.
- Visualize your presentation with the aim of feeling comfortable during it; go over the scene of your presentation in your mind.
- Consider doing some deep-breathing exercises before the presentation, and concentrate on relaxing; avoid too much caffeine.
- Remember that most speakers make a stronger impression standing rather than sitting.
- Pause before you begin, concentrating on your opening lines.
- Interact with your audience during the presentation, facing them at all times and making eye contact as much as possible.
- Allow time for the audience to respond and ask questions, and keep your answers short so that others can participate in the conversation.
- Thank your audience at the end of your presentation.

15c   Use presentation slides effectively.

Using multimedia—combining text, sound, graphics, video, and interactivity—in a presentation is now an everyday thing. Many speakers use presentation software, such as PowerPoint, to help them create a memorable multimedia presentation. (See the examples on p. 136.) Before you begin designing such a presentation, make sure that the computer equipment and projector you need will be available. Then keep some simple principles in mind:

- Make sure your audience can read all text: 44- to 50-point type for headings, 30- to 34-point type for subheads, smaller but still readable type for other text.
- For slides that contain text, use bulleted or numbered lists instead of paragraphs. Keep these items concise, and use clear language. Make sure the points are logically related and will actually guide both you and the audience.
- Don't try to put too much information on one slide—a good rule of thumb is to use no more than three to five bullet points or no more than fifty words.
- Create a clear contrast between any text or visuals and the background. As a general rule, light backgrounds work better in a darkened room, dark backgrounds in a lighted one.
- Be careful of becoming overly dependent on presentation-software templates. The choices of layout, color, font, and so on offered by such "wizards" may not always match your goals or fit your topic.
- Use the slides to illustrate or summarize points. *Never* simply read the text of slides to your audience: some pundits refer to this as "death by Power-Point."
- Make sure all visuals—photos, graphs, and so on—are sharp and large enough to be clearly visible to your audience.
- If you add sound or video clips, make sure that they are audible and that they relate directly to your topic.

bedfordstmartins.com/everyday_writer   For other examples of effective presentations, click on **Student Writing**. For additional help, click on **Jon Battalio's Tutorial on Preparing Presentation Slides**.

SAMPLE SLIDES FROM AN EFFECTIVE POWERPOINT PRESENTATION

The Problem or a Solution?

The Role of Divorce in
American Family Life

Myles Morrison
PWR-3, Section 18
Dr. Stacey Stanfield Anderson
January 16, 2003

Heading in large,
easy-to-read type

Clear contrast
between light-
colored type and
dark background

Presenter, course,
instructor, and date
identified

Divorce Rate, 1889-1999

Heading clearly
identifies the topic
of the graph

Arrows point out
specific years for
the purpose of this
presentation

Source of statistics
included at bottom
of graph

Statistics from U.S. Department of Health and Human Services

Overview

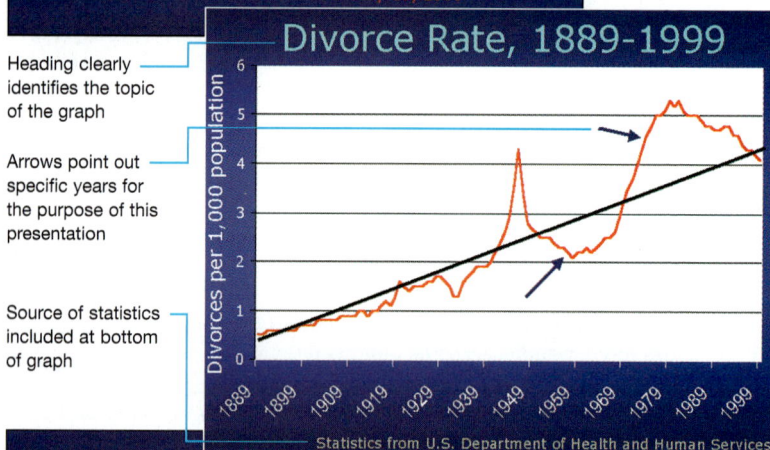

- Many factors contribute to rise in
  divorce rate over the last 50 years
  - Diminished influence of religion
  - Evolution of gender roles within marriages
  - Economically viable alternatives to marriage
  - Changed societal expectations
- Changes generally considered constructive
  have contributed to increase in the divorce rate.

Light type against
dark background is
easy to read
onscreen in a well-
lit room

Bulleted points
announce presen-
tation's topics and
subtopics

Bulleted points
kept brief

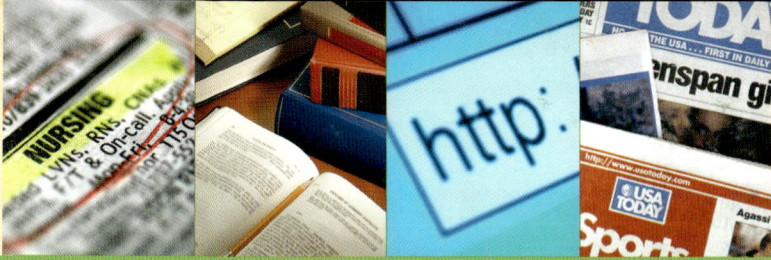

Conducting
RESEARCH

**Research is formalized curiosity.
It is poking and prying with a purpose.**

−ZORA NEALE HURSTON

Conducting Research

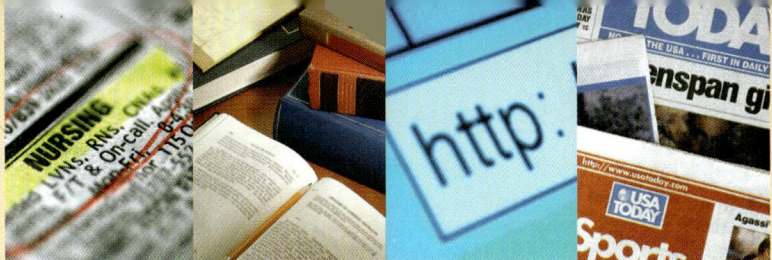

16

Preparing for a Research Project

Your employer asks you to recommend the best software for a particular project. You need to plan a week's stay in Tokyo. Your instructor assigns a term project about a musician. Each of these situations calls for research, for examining various kinds of sources. And each of these situations calls for you to assess the data you collect, to synthesize your findings, and to come up with an original recommendation or conclusion. Many tasks that call for research, such as a research project or a business report, require that your work culminate in a written document that refers to and lists the sources you used. (If the task also requires an oral or multimedia presentation, see Chapter 15.)

16a Analyze the research assignment.

Before you begin any research assignment, make sure you understand the requirements and limits of the assignment. For example, in an introductory writing course, you might receive the following assignment:

> Choose a subject of interest to you, and use it as the basis for a research essay that makes and substantiates a claim.

Your instructor might also explain that the essay should use information from both print and online sources, should be ten to fifteen pages long, and should be written for members of the writing class.

Choosing a topic

If your assignment doesn't specify a topic, consider the following questions:

- What subjects do you already know something about? Which of them would you like to explore more fully?
- What subjects might you like to become an expert on?
- What subjects evoke a strong reaction from you—intense puzzlement, skepticism, affirmation?

Make sure to get some responses to your topic, or to a couple of possible topics, not only from your instructor but from classmates and friends. Ask them whether they would be interested in reading about the topic, whether the topic seems manageable, and whether they can give you any tips on good sources for information on the topic.

Considering the rhetorical situation of the research project

Whether a topic is assigned to you or whether you choose it on your own, be sure to consider the context of any research project. Here are detailed questions to think about:

PURPOSE

If you have been assigned a specific research project, keep in mind the key words in that assignment. Does the assignment ask that you *describe, survey, analyze, persuade, explain, classify, compare,* or *contrast*? What do such words mean in this field (4a)?

AUDIENCE

Who will be the audience for your research project?

- Who will be interested in the information you gather, and why? What will they want to know? What will they already know?
- What do you know about their backgrounds? What assumptions might they hold about the topic?
- What response do you want to elicit from them?
- What kinds of evidence will you need to convince them of your view?
- What will your supervisor or instructor expect?

RHETORICAL STANCE

Think about your attitude toward your topic. Are you curious about it? critical of it? Do you like it? dislike it? find it confusing? What influences have shaped your stance?

SCOPE

How many or what kind(s) of sources should you use? What kind(s) of visuals—charts, maps, photographs, and so on—will you need to include? Will you be doing any field research—interviewing, surveying, or observing? Will the Web be an appropriate place to look?

LENGTH

How long is your project supposed to be? The amount of research and writing time you will need for a five-page essay differs markedly from that for a fifteen-page essay.

DEADLINES

When is the project due? Are any preliminary materials—a working bibliography, a thesis, an outline, a first draft—due before this date? Here is a sample schedule for a research project.

AT A GLANCE

Scheduling a Research Project

Date assigned: _____   Try to do by:

Analyze project; decide on primary purpose and
audience; choose topic.   _____

Develop tentative research question and hypothesis.   _____

Set aside library time; develop search strategy.   _____

Set up a research log.   _____

Do background reading, catalog and online searches;
narrow topic if necessary.   _____

Develop working thesis.   _____

Start working bibliography; track down sources.   _____

Gather or develop necessary visuals.   _____

If necessary, conduct interviews, make observations,
or distribute and collect questionnaires.   _____

Read and evaluate sources; take notes; analyze data
from field research.   _____

Draft explicit thesis and outline, storyboard, or site map.   _____

Prepare draft, including all visuals.   _____

Rough draft due.   _____

Conduct more research if necessary.   _____

Revise draft; prepare final list of works cited or
bibliography.   _____

Edit revised draft; use spell checker.   _____

Prepare final draft.   _____

Do final proofreading.   _____

Final draft due: _____

16b   Formulate a research question and hypothesis.

Once you have analyzed your task, picked a topic, and narrowed it (see 7a), formulate a research question that you can tentatively answer with a hypothesis. The hypothesis, a statement of what you anticipate your research will show, needs to be manageable, interesting, and specific. In addition, it must be a debatable proposition that you can prove or disprove with a reasonable amount of research evidence.

Here is an example of the move from general topic to a narrowed topic and then to a hypothesis:

TOPIC	Movie heroes
NARROWED TOPIC	Images of heroes in U.S. films
ISSUE	Changes in the images of heroes in U.S. films
RESEARCH QUESTION	How have the images of heroes changed since heroes found a home in Hollywood?
HYPOTHESIS	As real-life heroes have been dethroned in popular U.S. culture over the last century, so have film heroes, and current films suggest that the hero may not have a future at all.

16c   Plan your research.

Once you have formulated a hypothesis, determine what you already know about your topic. Tap your memory for sources by listing everything you can remember about *where* you learned about your topic: the Internet, email, books, magazines, courses, conversations, television. What you know comes from somewhere, and "somewhere" can serve as a starting point for your research. (See Chapter 6 for more strategies for exploring ideas and getting your initial thoughts about a topic down on paper.)

After you've considered what you already know about your topic, you can develop a research plan. To do so, answer the following questions:

- What kinds of sources (books, journal articles, videos, government documents, encyclopedias, visuals, and so on) do you think you will need to consult? How many sources should you consult?

- How current do your sources need to be? (For topical issues, especially those related to science, current sources are usually most important. For historical subjects, older sources may offer the best information.)

- Do you know the location and availability of the kinds of sources you need?

One goal of your research plan is to build a strong working bibliography (16f). Carrying out systematic research and keeping careful notes on your sources will make developing your works-cited list, or bibliography, easier later on.

16d Set up a research log.

Keeping a research log—either in print or electronic form—will make the job of writing and documenting your sources more efficient and accurate. You can use your research log to jot down ideas about possible sources and to keep track of print and online materials. Whenever you record an online source in your log, include the URL, especially if you are unable to bookmark Web materials on your computer.

Here are a few guidelines for setting up an electronic research log:

1. Create a folder and label it with a name that will be easy to identify, such as *Research Log for Project on Movie Heroes*.
2. Within this folder, create subfolders that will help you manage your project. These subfolders might include *Notes on Hypothesis and Thesis, Background Information, Visuals, Draft 1, Working Bibliography,* and so on.

You might prefer to begin a Web log (blog) for your research project. You can use it to record your thoughts on the reading you are doing and, especially, add links from there to Web sites, documents, and articles you have found online. You might even find bloggers out there who are writing about your topic. If so, be sure to check them out carefully before citing information from a blog in support of your research project. (For more on blogs, see 12b.)

If you prefer not to keep an electronic research log, set up a binder with dividers similar to the subfolders listed above. Whether your log is electronic or not, be sure to carefully distinguish the notes and comments you make from quoted passages you record.

16e Move from hypothesis to working thesis.

Begin this important stage by searching library catalogs and online databases and consulting general sources related to your narrowed topic, such as encyclopedia entries, bibliographical dictionaries, and so on.

As you gather information and begin reading and evaluating sources, you will probably refine your research question and change your hypothesis significantly. Only after you have explored your hypothesis, tested it, and sharpened it by reading, writing, and talking with others does it become a working thesis. Here's the working thesis developed by the student writing on heroes in U.S. films:

Although a case of mistaken identity dealt a near-fatal blow to the image of the hero in U.S. films, a study of recent movies suggests that the hero lives on—in two startlingly different forms.

16f   Keep a working bibliography.

As you locate research sources—books, articles, Web sites, and so on—you should create a working bibliography, which is a list of the sources that you may ultimately use for your project. You should record source information—such as the call number, author(s) or editor(s), title, publication information, page numbers, URL, and so on—for every source you think you might use. The emphasis here is on *working* because the list will probably include materials that end up not being useful. For this reason, you don't need to put all entries in your working bibliography into one of the documentation styles detailed in Chapters 52–58. If you do style your entries appropriately, however, that part of your work will be done when you prepare your final draft. Use the following lists to help you keep track of the information you should try to find.

FOR A BOOK

Call number
Author(s) or editor(s)
Title (and subtitle, if any)
Place of publication
Publisher
Year of publication
Other information (translator, volume, edition)

FOR PART OF A BOOK

Call number
Author(s) of part
Title of part
Author(s) or editor(s) of book
Title of book
Place of publication
Publisher
Year of publication
Inclusive page numbers for part you are using

FOR A PERIODICAL ARTICLE

Call number of periodical
Author(s) of article
Title of article
Name of periodical
Volume number
Issue number
Date of issue
Inclusive page numbers for article

FOR AN ONLINE SOURCE

Author (if available)
Title of site
Editor or sponsor of site
Title of document
Name of database or online source
Date of electronic publication
Date you accessed the source
Full electronic address (URL)

Sometimes an instructor may ask you to compile an annotated bibliography, one that includes your own description and comments as well as publishing information. Even if annotations aren't required, many students like to create them because they help them understand and remember what's in the source.

ANNOTATED BIBLIOGRAPHY

Gere, Anne Ruggles. "Kitchen Tables and Rented Rooms: The Extracurriculum of
   Composition." <u>Literacy: A Critical Sourcebook</u>. Ed. Ellen Cushman, Eugene R.
   Kintgen, Barry M. Kroll, and Mike Rose. Boston: Bedford, 2001. 275-89.

This history of writing instruction argues that writing instruction takes place--
and has historically taken place--in far less formal venues than the writing
classroom. Gere presents numerous examples and comments on their importance
to the study of writing today.

bedfordstmartins.com/everyday_writer   For research tips, go to **Links** and click on
Reference Resources.

17

Doing Research

A few minutes' thought may bring to mind some piece of everyday research you have done, such as researching the best pizza or ice cream in town and writing an article about it for your school paper. If you have done this kind of analysis, you already know something about "doing" research. Whether you are researching pizza or Picasso, however, you need to be familiar with the kinds of sources you are likely to use, the searches you are likely to perform, and the three main types of research you will most often be called on to conduct: library, Internet, and field research.

17a Understand different kinds of sources.

Before you begin your research project in earnest, take time to consider some important differences among sources.

Print versus Internet sources

Distinguishing between print and Internet sources can be tricky: some Internet sources are electronic versions of printed texts, but most Internet sources do not have a print equivalent. Why is this distinction so important?

- If you use a scholarly book or journal—which probably would have been published first in print and then online—you can be fairly sure that the text was sent out to experts for review before it was published. Many other print publishers—of newspapers, magazines, and books—also obtain reviews or check facts before publication. However, for most materials published only on the Internet, reviewing and editorial oversight depend solely on the author of the text. As a result, you need to know whether a source exists only in electronic form and, if so, how much you can trust it.

- Internet sources are generally less stable than print sources. Since such sources can easily be changed or deleted from the Internet entirely, you need to make a copy (either print or electronic) so that you have a record of the original.

- Since most print sources do not exist online and vice versa, be careful not to limit the type of research you do. If you use only Internet sources, for example, you will miss out on valuable sources available only in print.

Primary versus secondary sources

Another difference in sources is between primary sources, or firsthand knowledge, and secondary sources, information available from the research of others. Primary sources are basic sources of raw information, including experiments, surveys, or interviews you conduct; notes from your own field research; works of art or other objects you examine; literary works you read; and eyewitness accounts, photographs, news reports, and historical documents (such as letters, diaries, and speeches). Secondary sources are descriptions or interpretations of primary sources, such as researchers' reports, reviews of books, and biographies. Most research projects draw on both primary and secondary sources. Often what constitutes a primary or secondary source will depend on your purpose or field. A critic's evaluation of a painting, for example, serves as a secondary work if you are writing an essay on that painting but as a primary work if you are conducting a study of the critic's writing.

Scholarly versus popular sources

While nonacademic sources like popular magazines can help you get started on a research project, you will usually want to depend more on authorities in a particular field, whose work usually appears in scholarly journals. The following lists of features will help you distinguish scholarly journals from popular magazines:

SCHOLARLY

POPULAR

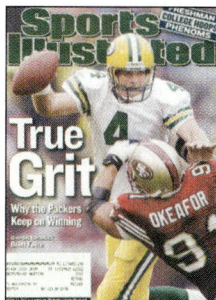

Cover may list contents of issue	Cover features a color picture
Title often contains the word *Journal*	*Journal* usually does not appear in title
Source found at the library	Source found at grocery stores, newsstands, and so on
Few commercial advertisements	Lots of advertisements
Authors identified with academic credentials	Authors are journalists or reporters, not experts
Summary or abstract appears on first page of article; articles are fairly long	No summary or abstract; articles are fairly short
Articles have bibliographies	No bibliographies included

Older versus current sources

Most research projects can benefit from both older, historical sources and more current ones. However, if you are examining a recent scientific discovery, you will want to depend primarily on contemporary sources.

17b Understand different kinds of searches.

Even when you have a general idea of what kinds of sources exist and which kinds you need for your research project, you still have to locate these sources. The library and the Internet give you a variety of options for searching for sources.

Online library resource searches

It is a good idea to work with the electronic sources available to you through your college library before you turn to the Web. Your library's computers hold resources that are either not available on the Web or not accessible to students except through the library's system. Most college libraries subscribe to databases—electronic collections of information, such as indexes to journal and magazine articles, texts of news stories and legal cases, lists of sources on particular topics, and compilations of statistics—that students can access for free. Many of these databases—such as LexisNexis, MLA bibliography, and ERIC—have been screened or compiled by editors, librarians, or other scholars.

Catalog and database searches

Library catalogs and databases usually index their contents not only by author and title but also by subject headings—standardized words and phrases used to classify the subject matter of books and articles. (For books, most U.S. libraries use the Library of Congress Subject Headings, or LCSH.) When you search the catalog by subject, you need to use the exact subject words. When you search using keywords, on the other hand, you can search for any term in any field of the electronic record. Keyword searching is less restrictive, but it requires you to put some thought into choosing your search terms to get the best results.

Internet searches

The Internet offers two ways for you to search for sources: one using subject categories and one using keywords. Most Internet search tools, such as Yahoo! and Google, offer both options. A subject directory

GOOGLE'S SUBJECT DIRECTORY

allows you to choose a broad category like "Art" and then to click on increasingly narrow categories like "Movies" or "Thrillers" until you reach a point where you are given a list of Web sites or the opportunity to do a keyword search. The second option, a search engine, allows you to start right off with a keyword search. Because the Internet contains more material than even the largest library catalog or database, using a search engine requires even more care in the choice of keywords.

17c Start your research, and gather background information.

When you have a working thesis and some idea of the sources you need to look for, you need to consider the logistical challenges of your project. Consider the amount of time you have to do your research. Also think about issues of access: can you get to the materials, people, or other items you need in the time allowed? Finally, consider contacts you may need to make—to set up an interview, to secure materials through interlibrary loan, and so on.

Consulting others

Before you start looking for specific sources, talk with other people about what you're looking for. One valuable resource is your library staff, especially reference librarians. To get the most helpful advice, pose specific questions. Many other people—friends, classmates, experts, and subscribers to electronic discussion lists (or listservs)—can lead you to sources or can serve as sources themselves.

Consulting reference works

Consulting general reference works is is a good way to get an overview of a topic, to identify subtopics, to find more specialized sources, and to identify useful keywords for electronic searches. Researchers often consult general and specialized encyclopedias (such as *Academic American Encyclopedia* and *Encyclopedia of Computer Science and Technology*), biographical resources (such as *Biography Index*), and almanacs, yearbooks, news digests, and atlases (such as *Facts on File Yearbook* and *National Geographic Atlas of the World*). Many of these materials are available either online or on CD-ROM; your librarian can help you access them.

17d Use library resources to gather research material.

The library is one of a researcher's best friends, especially in an age of electronic communication. Your college library houses a great number of print materials and gives you access to electronic catalogs and data-bases. To learn about your library, visit its Web site; make an appointment with a librarian; and participate in a tour, tutorial, or workshop.

Using the library catalog

The library catalog lists all of the library's books as well as its periodical holdings and subscriptions. Most libraries have an electronic catalog you can access easily. Note that many electronic catalogs, like the one the example below comes from, indicate whether a book has been checked out and, if so, when it is due to be returned.

```
AUTHOR        Rushing, Janice Hocker.
TITLE         Projecting the shadow : the cyborg hero in American
              film / Janice Hocker Rushing, Thomas S. Frentz.
PUBLISH INFO  Chicago : University of Chicago Press, 1995.
DESCRIPTION   x, 261 p. : ill. ; 24 cm.
SERIES        New practices of inquiry.
NOTES         Includes bibliographical references (p. 222-244)
              and index.
SUBJECTS      Cyborgs in motion picures.
              Myth in motion pictures.
ADD AUTHORS   Frentz, Thomas S.
OCLC #        32737837.
ISBN          0226731669 (cloth : alk. paper)

    LOCATION          CALL NO.          YEAR       STATUS
1 > JOU Stacks        PN1995.9.C9 R57   1995       DUE 11-05-04
```

Besides identifying a book's author, title, subject, and publication information, each catalog entry also lists a call number—the book's identification number. Once you have printed out the catalog entry for the book or written down the call number, look for a library map or shelving plan to tell you where your book is housed. When you find it, take the time to browse through the books around it. Often you will find other books related to your topic in the immediate area.

Using indexes

Other useful library sources include various indexes, which can help you locate information about books, reviews, or periodicals.

- Book indexes (such as *Books in Print* and *Cumulative Book Index*) can help you locate complete bibliographic information on a book when you know only one piece of it—the author's last name, perhaps, or the title. These sources can also alert you to other works by a particular author or on a particular subject.

- Review indexes (such as *Book Review Digest* and *Index to Book Reviews in the Humanities*) allow you to check the relevance of a source or to get a thumbnail sketch of its contents.

- Periodical indexes are guides to articles published in newspapers, magazines, and scholarly journals, items that will not appear in your library's catalog. Each index covers a specific group of periodicals. General indexes of periodicals list articles from general-interest magazines (such as *Time*), newspapers, or a combination of these. Specialized indexes and abstracts help researchers find detailed information. In general, specialized indexes list articles in scholarly journals, but they may include other publications as well.

Although many of these indexes were originally available only in print form, most are now available as electronic databases.

Using other library resources

Libraries also give you access to many other useful materials that might be appropriate for your research.

- *Bibliographies.* Look at any bibliographies (lists of sources) in books or articles you are using; they can lead you to other valuable resources. In addition, check with a reference librarian to find out whether your library has bibliographies devoted to the area of your research.
- *Special collections and archives.* Your library may house archives (collections of valuable papers) or other special materials that are often available to student researchers.
- *Audio, video, and art collections.* Many libraries have areas devoted to media and art, where they collect films, videos, paintings, and sound recordings.
- *Government documents and statistical sources.* Check the online version of the Catalog of U.S. Government Publications <www.gpoaccess.gov> to identify publications appropriate to your topic, and then see if your library has them. Or ask your reference librarian to recommend other statistical sources you might need.
- *Interlibrary loans.* To borrow books, journals, and video or audio materials from another library, use an interlibrary loan. Such loans can take time, however, so be sure to plan ahead.

17e Use the Internet to gather research material.

The Web is many college students' favorite way of accessing information. Since no one is responsible for regulating information on the Web, it's possible to find anything and everything there, from the most banal statements to outright misinformation. As a result, you need to use information from the Web with great care.

Using Web browsers

Web browsers, such as Netscape Navigator and Internet Explorer, not only give you access to powerful search tools but also can provide help in organizing and keeping track of your research.

- *Tracking your searches.* The address bar shows a list of the Web sites you have accessed during your current session. To track your searches over more than one session, find out how to use the browser's HISTORY function. This function can be valuable if you are trying to retrace your steps to find a source you forgot to take notes on or need more information from.
- *Using "bookmarks" and "favorites."* Save the URLs for sites you want to return to by using the BOOKMARK (in Netscape) or FAVORITES (in Internet Explorer) function.

Using search tools

As noted earlier, most search engines (such as Yahoo! and Google) allow you to conduct keyword searches as well as subject directory searches. The following are some of the most-often-used search engines:

AltaVista <www.altavista.digital.com>   Lycos <www.lycos.com>

Excite <www.excite.com>   Teoma <www.teoma.com>

Google <www.google.com>   Yahoo! <www.yahoo.com>

HotBot <www.hotbot.com>

Using keywords, Boolean operators, and quotation marks

You know that using a search engine can result in millions of "hits" if you don't choose your keywords carefully. To be useful, the keywords—names, titles, concepts—you choose need to lead you to more specific sources. The following tools can help you refine your searches:

- *Do advanced searches.* Most search engines offer options (sometimes on a separate advanced-search page) for narrowing searches. These options let you combine keywords, search for an exact phrase, or exclude items containing particular keywords. Often they let you limit your search in other ways as well—such as by date, language, country of origin, or location of the keyword within a site.
- *Use Boolean operators.* Many library catalogs and some search engines offer a search option using the Boolean operators AND, NOT, and OR as well as parentheses and quotation marks. The Boolean operators work this way:

    AND *limits your search.* If you enter the terms *Hollywood AND heroes,* the search engine will retrieve only those items that contain *both* those terms.

    NOT *also limits your search.* If you enter the terms *Hollywood NOT heroes,* the search engine will retrieve every item that contains *Hollywood* except those that also contain the term *heroes.*

OR *expands your search*. If you enter the terms *Hollywood OR heroes*, the computer will retrieve every item that contains the term *Hollywood* and every item that contains the term *heroes*.

Parentheses customize your search further. Entering *Oscar AND (Denzel Washington OR Will Smith)*, for example, will locate items that mention either of those actors in connection with the Academy Awards.

- *Use quotation marks.* Quotation marks around a phrase can also help you narrow your search because they indicate that all the words in the phrase must appear together in the exact order you have typed them.

Using online libraries, governmental and news sites, and periodicals

The Web enables you to access information in libraries other than your own. These virtual libraries (such as Infomine at <http://infomine.ucr.edu> from the University of California at Riverside) allow you to access part of another library's collection.

You may find online collections housed in governmental sites helpful (such as the Library of Congress at <www.loc.gov> and *Statistical Abstracts of the United States* at <www.census.gov/statab/www>). For current news events, you can consult online versions and archives of newspapers (such as the *New York Times* at <www.nytimes.com>) and news services that are available electronically (such as C-SPAN at <www.c-span.org>).

Some scholarly journals and some general-interest magazines are now published only on the Web, and many other publications make part of their contents available online. To access a wide variety of online articles from many different magazines, try <www.highbeam.com> and <www.newsdirectory.com>.

bedfordstmartins.com/everyday_writer For information, links, and tips, go to **Links** and click on **Reference Resources.**

17f Conduct field research.

For many research projects, particularly those in the social sciences and business, you will need to collect field data. The "field" may be many things—a classroom, a church, a laboratory, or the corner grocery store. As a field researcher, you will need to discover *where* you can find relevant information, *how* to gather it, and *who* might be your best providers of information.

Interviews

Some information is best obtained by asking direct questions of other people. If you can talk with an expert—in person, on the telephone, or via the Internet—you might get information you could not have obtained through any other kind of research. In addition to getting an expert opinion, you might ask for firsthand accounts or suggestions of other places to look or other people to consult.

AT A GLANCE

Conducting an Interview

1. Determine your exact purpose, and be sure it relates to your research question and your hypothesis.

2. Set up the interview well in advance. Specify how long it will take, and if you wish to tape-record the session, ask permission to do so.

3. Prepare a written list of factual and open-ended questions. Brainstorming or freewriting can help you come up with questions. (6a and b) Leave plenty of space for notes after each question. If the interview proceeds in a direction that seems fruitful, do not feel that you have to ask all of your prepared questions.

4. Record the subject, date, time, and place of the interview.

5. Thank those you interview, either in person or in a letter or email.

Observation

Trained observers report that making a faithful record of an observation requires intense concentration and mental agility.

AT A GLANCE

Conducting an Observation

1. Determine the purpose of the observation, and be sure it relates to your research question and hypothesis.
2. Brainstorm about what you are looking for, but don't be rigidly bound to your expectations.
3. Develop an appropriate system for recording data. Consider using a split notebook or page: on one side, record your observations directly; on the other, record your thoughts or interpretations.
4. Record the date, time, and place of observation.

Opinion surveys

Surveys usually depend on questionnaires. On any questionnaire, the questions should be clear and easy to understand and designed so that you can analyze the answers easily. Questions that ask respondents to say *yes* or *no* or to rank items on a scale are particularly easy to tabulate:

The parking facilities on our campus are adequate.

| Strongly agree | Somewhat agree | Unsure | Somewhat disagree | Strongly disagree |

AT A GLANCE

Designing a Questionnaire

1. Write out your purpose, and review your research question and hypothesis to determine the kinds of questions to ask.
2. Figure out how to reach the respondents you need.
3. Draft potential questions, and make sure that each question calls for a short, specific answer.
4. Test the questions on several people, and revise questions that seem unfair, ambiguous, too hard to answer, or too time-consuming.
5. For a questionnaire that is to be mailed, draft a cover letter explaining your purpose. Provide a self-addressed, stamped envelope, and be sure to state a deadline.
6. On the final version of the questionnaire, leave adequate space for answers.
7. Proofread the questionnaire carefully.

Analyzing, synthesizing, and interpreting data from field research

To make sense of your data, find a focus for your analysis, since you can't pay attention to everything. Then synthesize the data by looking for recurring words or ideas that fall into patterns. Establish a system for coding your information, labeling each pattern you identify—a plus sign for every positive response, for example. Finally, interpret your data by summing up the meaning of what you have found. What is the significance of your findings? Be careful not to make big generalizations.

18

Evaluating Sources and Taking Notes

All research builds on the careful and sometimes inspired use of sources—that is, on research done by others. Whether you are doing research to identify the most affordable laptop, to persuade your college administration to improve campus safety, or to prepare a strong academic argument for a class, you will want to make the most of your sources. In other words, you will want to use the insights you gain from your sources to help you create powerful prose of your own.

18a   Understand why you should use sources.

While all research draws on sources, it is worth thinking about why writers decide to use one source rather than another. What specifically can sources provide for your research projects?

- background and contextual information that sets the scene for your project or that your audience will need to follow your argument
- explanations of concepts unfamiliar to your audience
- verbal and visual emphasis for points you are making
- authority for the claims you are making, which in turn helps you create your own authority
- evidence to support your claims

- counter-examples or counter-evidence that you need to reflect on and respond to in your own argument
- varying perspectives on your topic

18b Evaluate the usefulness and credibility of potential sources.

Since you want the information you glean from sources to be reliable and persuasive, you must evaluate each potential source carefully. The following guidelines can help you assess the usefulness of a source:

- *Your purpose.* What will this source add to your research project? Does it help you support a major point, demonstrate that you have thoroughly researched your topic, or help establish your own credibility through its authority?
- *Relevance.* How closely related is the source to the narrowed topic you are pursuing? You may need to read beyond the title and opening paragraph to check for relevance.
- *Publisher's credentials.* What do you know about the publisher of the source you are using? For example, is it a major newspaper that is known for integrity in reporting, or is it a tabloid? Is it a popular magazine or a journal sponsored by a professional or scholarly organization?
- *Author's credentials.* Is the author an expert on the topic? An author's credentials may be presented in the article, book, or Web site, or you can search the Internet for information on the author.
- *Date of publication.* Recent sources are often more useful than older ones, particularly in the sciences or other fields that change rapidly. However, in some fields—such as the humanities—the most authoritative works may be the older ones. The publication dates of Internet sites can often be difficult to pin down. And even for sites that include the dates of posting, remember that the material posted may have been composed some time earlier. Most reliable will be those sites that list the dates of updating regularly.
- *Accuracy of source.* How accurate and complete is the information in the source? How thorough is the bibliography or list of works cited that accompanies the source? Can you find other sources that corroborate what your source is saying?
- *Stance of source.* Identify the source's point of view or rhetorical stance, and scrutinize it carefully. What does the author or sponsoring group want to make happen? to convince you of an idea? sell you something? call you to action in some way?
- *Cross-referencing.* Is the source cited in other works? If you see your source cited by others, looking at how they cite it and what they say about it can provide additional clues to its credibility.

- *Level of specialization.* General sources can be helpful as you begin your research, but you may then need the authority or currentness of more specialized sources. On the other hand, extremely specialized works may be very hard to understand.

- *Audience of source.* Was the source written for the general public? specialists? advocates or opponents?

As you look at potential sources, be sure to evaluate Internet sources with special scrutiny. Remember that much of the material on the Internet does not go through an editorial or review process. You must be the judge of just how accurate and trustworthy the sources are.

FOR MULTILINGUAL WRITERS

Understanding Authority

Who or what holds most authority in your native language and culture? A religious text or leader? A political creed? A set of laws? What counts as an authority in one place may not be considered authoritative in another. You'll want to think carefully about authoritative sources in the community and culture in which you are writing.

18c   Read and interpret your sources.

As you read and take notes on your sources, keep in mind that you will need to present data and sources to other readers so that they can understand the point you are making. To do so, you'll need to interpret your sources, which entails synthesizing—grouping similar pieces of data together, looking for patterns or trends, and identifying the main points of the data—and drawing inferences—making conclusions on your own that follow logically from the data given.

18d   Take notes, and annotate your sources.

While note-taking methods vary from one researcher to another, you should (1) record enough information to help you recall the major points of the source; (2) put the information in the form in which you are most likely to incorporate it into your research essay; and (3) note all the information you will need to cite the source accurately. The following example shows the major items a note should include:

ELEMENTS OF AN ACCURATE NOTE

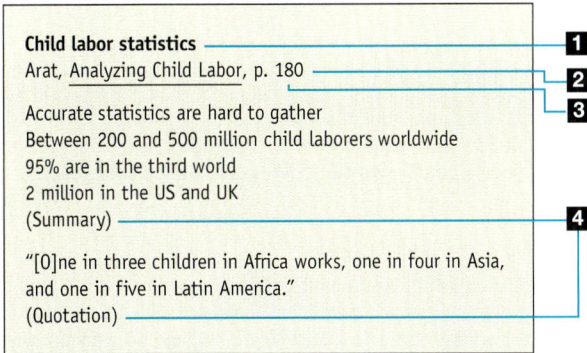

> **Child labor statistics** ──────────────── **1**
> Arat, Analyzing Child Labor, p. 180 ───── **2**
> ──────────── **3**
> Accurate statistics are hard to gather
> Between 200 and 500 million child laborers worldwide
> 95% are in the third world
> 2 million in the US and UK
> (Summary) ──────────────────── **4**
>
> "[O]ne in three children in Africa works, one in four in Asia,
> and one in five in Latin America."
> (Quotation) ────────────────────

1 *Use a subject heading.* Label each note with a brief but descriptive subject heading so you can group similar subtopics together.

2 *Identify the source.* List the author's name and a shortened title of the source. Your working-bibliography entry (16f) for the source will contain the full bibliographic information, so you don't need to repeat it in each note.

3 *Record exact page references (if available).* For online or other sources without page numbers, record the paragraph, screen, or other section number(s) if indicated.

4 *Indicate whether the note is a summary, paraphrase, or direct quotation* (see below). Make sure quotations are copied accurately. Put square brackets around any change you make, and use ellipses if you omit material.

Taking complete notes will help you digest the source information as you read and incorporate the material into your text without inadvertently plagiarizing the source. Be sure to reread each note carefully, and recheck it against the source to make sure quotations, statistics, and specific facts are accurate.

Quoting

Quoting involves bringing a source's exact words into your text. Use an author's exact words when the wording is so memorable or expresses a point so well that you cannot improve or shorten it without weakening it, when the author is a respected authority whose opinion supports your own ideas, or when an author challenges or disagrees profoundly with others in the field. An example of a quotation note is on page 164.

SOURCE MAP: Evaluating Articles

Determine the relevance of the source.

1 Look for an abstract, which provides a summary of the entire article. Is this source directly related to your research? Does it provide useful information and insights? Will your readers consider it persuasive support for your thesis?

Determine the credibility of the publication.

2 Consider the publication's title. Words in the title such as *Journal, Review,* and *Quarterly* may indicate that the periodical is a scholarly source. Most research essays rely on authorities in a particular field, whose work usually appears in scholarly journals. For more on distinguishing between scholarly and popular sources, see 17a.

3 Try to determine the publisher or sponsor. This journal is published by Johns Hopkins University Press. Academic presses such as this one generally review articles carefully before publishing them and bear the authority of their academic sponsors.

Determine the credibility of the author.

4 Evaluate the author's credentials. In this case, they are given in a note, which indicates that the author is a college professor and has written at least two books on related topics.

Determine the currency of the article.

5 Look at the publication date and think about whether your topic and your credibility depend on your use of very current sources.

Determine the accuracy of the article.

6 Look at the sources cited by the author of the article. Here, they are documented in footnotes. Ask yourself whether the works the author has cited seem credible and current. Are any of these works cited in other articles you've considered?

In addition, consider the following questions:

- What is the article's stance or point of view? What are the author's goals? What does the author want you to know or believe?

- How does this source fit in with your other sources? Does any of the information it provides contradict or challenge other sources?

1

HUMAN RIGHTS QUARTERLY

Prisons and Politics in Contemporary Latin America

Mark Ungar*

2

ABSTRACT

Despite democratization throughout Latin America, massive human rights abuses continue in the region's prisons. Conditions have become so bad that most governments have begun to enact improvements, including new criminal codes and facility decongestion. However, once in place, these reforms are undermined by chaotic criminal justice systems, poor policy administration, and rising crime rates leading to greater detention powers for the police. After describing current prison conditions in Latin America and the principal reforms to address them, this article explains how political and administrative limitations hinder the range of agencies and officials responsible for implementing those changes.

I. INTRODUCTION

Prison conditions not only constitute some of the worst human rights violations in contemporary Latin American democracies, but also reveal fundamental weaknesses in those democracies. Unlike most other human rights problems, those in the penitentiary system cannot be easily explained with authoritarian legacies or renegade officials. The systemic killing, overcrowding, disease, torture, rape, corruption, and due process abuses all occur under the state's twenty-four hour watch. Since the mid-1990s,

* *Mark Ungar* is Associate Professor of Political Science at Brooklyn College, City University of New York. Recent publications include the books *Elusive Reform: Democracy and the Rule of Law in Latin America* (Lynne Rienner, 2002) and *Violence and Politics: Globalization's Paradox* (Routledge, 2001) as well as articles and book chapters on democratization, policing, and judicial access. He works with Amnesty International USA and local rights groups in Latin America.

Human Rights Quarterly 25 (2003) 909–934 © 2003 by The Johns Hopkins University Press

3 The Johns Hopkins University Press **5** 2003

10. Inspector General de Cárceles, Informe Anual (Caracas: Ministerio de Justicia 1994).
11. *Overcrowding Main Cause of Riots in Latin American Prisons*, AFP, 30 Dec. 1997.
12. Interviews with inmates, speaking on condition of anonymity in San Pedro prison (19 July 2000); Interviews with inmates, speaking on condition of anonymity in La Paz FELCN Prison (20 July 2000).
13. Typhus, cholera, tuberculosis, and scabies run rampant and the HIV rate may be as high as 25 percent. The warden of Retén de la Planta, where cells built for one inmate house three or four, says the prisons "are collapsing" because of insufficient budgets to train personnel. "Things fall apart and stay that way." Interview, Luis A. Lara Roche, Warden of Retén de la Planta, Caracas, Venezuela, 19 May 1995. At El Dorado prison in Bolívar state, there is one bed for every four inmates, cells are infested with vermin, and inmates lack clean bathing water and eating utensils.
14. *La Crisis Penitenciaria*, El Nacional (Caracas), 2 Sept. 1988, at D2. On file with author.

4

6

Source Map: Evaluating Web Sources

Determine the credibility of the sponsoring organization.

1 Consider the URL, specifically the top-level domain name. (For example, *.edu* may indicate that the sponsor is an accredited college or university; *.org* may indicate it's a nonprofit organization.) Ask yourself whether such a sponsor might be biased about the topic you're researching.

2 Look for an *About* page or a link to the homepage for background information on the sponsor, including a mission statement. What is the sponsoring organization's stance or point of view? Does the mission statement seem biased or balanced? Does the sponsor seem to take other points of view into account? What is the intended purpose of the site? Is this site meant to inform? Or is it trying to persuade, advertise, or accomplish something else?

Determine the credibility of the author.

3 Evaluate the author's credentials. On this Web page, the authors' professional affiliations are listed, but other information about them isn't provided. You will often have to look elsewhere — such as at other sites on the Web — to find out more about an author. When you do, ask yourself if the author seems qualified to write about the topic.

Determine the currency of the Web source.

4 Look for the date that indicates when the information was posted or last updated. Here, the date is given at the beginning of the press release.

5 Check to see if the sources referred to are also up-to-date. These authors cite sources from September and October 2003. Ask yourself if, given your topic, an older source is acceptable or if only the most recent information will do.

Determine the accuracy of the information.

6 How complete is the information in the source? Examine the works cited by the author. Are sources for statistics included? Do the sources cited seem credible? Is a list of additional resources provided? Here, the authors cite the U.S. Navy and the U.S. Air Force, but they do not give enough information to track down these sources. Ask yourself whether you can find a way to corroborate what a source is saying.

1 `http://www.audubon.org/news/press_releases/NC_Navy_Suit.html`

2 About Audubon

3
Chris Canfield
Audubon North Carolina
919/929-3899
ccanfield@audubon.org
Derb Carter
Michelle Nowlin
Southern Environmental
Law Center
919/967-1450
derbc@selcnc.org
mnowlin@selcnc.org

4 January 9, 2004

Audubon News - Microsoft Internet Explorer

File Edit View Favorites Tools Help

Back · · · Search · Favorites · Media · · · ·

Address http://www.audubon.org/news/press_releases/NC_Navy_Suit.html Go

Audubon

About Audubon Take Action
Contact Us Home

Search

Give Now | States, Centers & Chapters | Birds & Science | Issues & Action | Audubon At Home | News

Archives:
Select a month:

News > Audubon Press Releases >

Press Releases:

Audubon President Pens Forward to 'Chicken Soup for the Nature Lover's Soul' (3/3/04)

Birds vs. Windows: A Clear and Present Danger - 03/03/04

Audubon CA Publishes First IBA Book, 3/3/04

Audubon Named Darryl Brown Vice President, Director of Development - 03/02/04

Audubon OH Testimony on Proposed Lake Erie Legislation, 2/19/04

Chris Canfield
Audubon North Carolina
919/929-3899
ccanfield@audubon.org
Derb Carter
Michelle Nowlin
Southern Environmental Law Center
919/967-1450
derbc@selcnc.org
mnowlin@selcnc.org

GROUPS JOIN IN SUIT AGAINST NAVY AIRFIELD PLAN
Plan Imperils Pilots, Migratory Birds, and Communities

Raleigh, NC, January 9, 2004 - The Southern Environmental Law Center (SELC), representing the National Audubon Society, Defenders of Wildlife and the North Carolina Wildlife Federation, will file suit in federal court Friday challenging the Navy's plan to build a military jet landing field in the heart of the Atlantic migratory bird flyway and a few miles from a national wildlife refuge. The groups say the government's environmental impact studies for the landing field downplayed the substantial risk of collisions between jets and the large flocks of tundra swans, snow geese and other birds that winter in the area, and minimized adverse impacts to the wildlife refuge.

Of Interest:

Check out Audubon's National Seafood Wallet Card

Audubon Magazine: Check out the latest issue of our award-winning magazine.

Member of the Global Province Network

Done Internet

Audubon N
File Edit
Back
Address

Plan -

PA Takes Up the Challenge of Deer Overabundance - 12/23/03

Aullwood Director Charity Krueger Receives Top Honor, 12/22/03

Administration Reverses Decision to Remove Federal Wetlands Protection - 12/19/03

Also on Friday, a coalition of landowners and other opponents have schedule a ribbon cutting for a "tent city" near the site of the proposed landing field where they vow to camp out around-the-clock, seven days a week to protest the project. Attorneys and conservation leaders will also hold a briefing for press and the community at the tent city near Plymouth, North Carolina, at 2:30 p.m. on Friday. Directions to the location and other information are available at www.albemarlecommunity.net/SiteIndex.html or by calling 252-927-3792.

On September 10, 2003, the Navy issued a decision to base new squadrons of Super Hornet jets at bases in Virginia and North Carolina, and to share training runs at the proposed new field, which lies in between. Pilots would use the field to practice landing on aircraft carriers. The plaintiff groups, along with dozens of other conservation organizations, federal and state wildlife agencies, political leaders and community groups, have consistently objected to the location as destructive to the environment and dangerous for pilots.

"Siting the landing field near this wildlife refuge puts pilots and birds on a collision course that will be deadly for both," said Derb Carter, SELC senior attorney. "Of all the places to put this kind of facility, the Navy has chosen one of the worst."

"The Navy has had almost two years to listen to the experts, be honest with the public about their intentions, and to find a safe location for this field," said Chris Canfield, executive director of Audubon North Carolina. "They have failed on all accounts, so we have no choice but to launch this legal battle to defend some of the nation's most important natural areas."

Ronald L. Merritt, former head of Bird Aircraft Strike Hazard programs for the U.S. Air Force worldwide, and a consultant to the Navy in its study on the project, wrote to the Navy secretary in October 2003 that

5 September 10, 2003,

6 U.S. Air Force

QUOTATION STYLE

Subject heading ── **Cyborg heroes**

Author and short title of source; page reference of quotation ── Haraway, Simians, p. 178.

"The replicant Rachel in the Ridley Scott film Blade Runner stands as the image of a cyborg culture's fear, love, and confusion."

Label identifies this note as a quotation ── (Quotation)

AT A GLANCE

Quoting Accurately

- Copy quotations carefully, with punctuation, capitalization, and spelling exactly as in the original. (46a)
- Enclose the quotation in quotation marks; don't rely on your memory to distinguish your own words from those of the source. (46a)
- Use brackets if you introduce words of your own into the quotation or make changes in it. (47b)
- Use ellipses if you omit words from the quotation. (47f)
- If you later incorporate the quotation into your research essay, copy it from the note precisely, including brackets and ellipses.
- Record the author's name, shortened title, and page number(s) on which the quotation appeared. For online sources without page numbers, record the paragraph, screen, or other section number(s) if indicated.
- Make sure you have a corresponding working-bibliography entry with complete source information. (16f)
- Label the note with a subject heading, and identify it as a quotation.

Paraphrasing

When you paraphrase, you put an author's material (including major and minor points, usually in the order they are presented) into *your own words and sentence structures.* If you wish to cite some of the author's words within the paraphrase, enclose them in quotation marks. The following examples of paraphrases resemble the original either too little or too much.

ORIGINAL

It is not clear who makes and who is made in the relation between human and machine. It is not clear what is mind and what body in machines that resolve into coding practices. In so far as we know ourselves in both formal discourse (for example, biology) and in daily practice (for example, the home-work economy in the integrated circuit), we find ourselves to be cyborgs, hybrids, mosaics, chimeras. Biological organisms have become biotic systems, communications devices like others. There is no fundamental, ontological separation in our formal knowledge of machine and organism, of technical and organic. The replicant Rachel in the Ridley Scott film *Blade Runner* stands as the image of a cyborg culture's fear, love, and confusion.

— DONNA J. HARAWAY, *Simians, Cyborgs, and Women*

UNACCEPTABLE PARAPHRASE: STRAYING FROM THE AUTHOR'S IDEAS

Haraway's point is that we can no longer be sure of the distinction between humans and machines. In fact, she argues that we are all already combinations — part body, part mind, part machine. On the other hand, Haraway could be completely wrong: the cyborg metaphor doesn't always work.

Note that this paraphrase starts off well enough, but it moves away from paraphrasing the original to inserting the writer's ideas into the paraphrase of Haraway's text.

UNACCEPTABLE PARAPHRASE: USING THE AUTHOR'S WORDS

As Haraway explains, in a high-tech culture like ours, *who makes and who is made, what is mind or body, becomes unclear.* When we look at ourselves in relation to the real or the mechanical world, we must admit we are cyborgs, and even *biological organisms* are now *communications systems.* Thus our beings can't be separated from machines. A fine example of this cyborg image is Rachel in Ridley Scott's *Blade Runner.*

Because the italicized phrases are either borrowed from the original without quotation marks or changed only superficially, this paraphrase plagiarizes.

UNACCEPTABLE PARAPHRASE: USING THE AUTHOR'S SENTENCE STRUCTURES

As Haraway explains, it is unclear who is the maker and who is the made. It is unclear what in the processes of machines might be the mind and what the body. Thus in order to know ourselves at all, we must recognize ourselves to be cyborgs. Biology then becomes just another device for communicating. As beings, we can't separate the bodily from the mechanical anymore. Thus Rachel in Ridley Scott's *Blade Runner* becomes the perfect symbol of cyborg culture.

Although this paraphrase is not overly reliant on the words of the original, it does follow the sentence structures too closely. A paraphrase must represent your own interpretation of the material and thus must show your own thought patterns.

Now look at a paraphrase that expresses the author's ideas accurately and acceptably in the writer's own words.

ACCEPTABLE PARAPHRASE

> **Cyborg heroes**
>
> Haraway, Simians, pp. 177–178.
>
> As Haraway demonstrates, today the line between person and machine is forever blurred, especially in terms of the binary coding systems used by computers to "know." If knowing thyself is still important, we must know ourselves as a mixture of body, mind, and machine. Moviemaker Ridley Scott provides a good example of this mixture in the character of Rachel in Blade Runner.
>
> (Paraphrase)

AT A GLANCE

Paraphrasing Accurately

- Include all main points and any important details from the original source in the same order in which the author presents them.
- State the meaning in your own words and sentence structures. If you want to include especially memorable language from the original, enclose it in quotation marks.
- Save for another use your own comments, elaborations, or reactions.
- Record the author, shortened title, and the page number(s) on which the original material appeared. For online sources without page numbers, record the paragraph, screen, or other section number(s) if indicated.
- Make sure you have a corresponding working-bibliography entry with complete source information. (16f)
- Label the note with a subject heading, and identify it as a paraphrase to avoid confusion with a summary.
- Recheck to be sure that the words and sentence structures are your own and that they express the author's meaning accurately.

Summarizing

A summary is a significantly shortened version of a passage or even a whole chapter or work that captures main ideas *in your own words.* Unlike a paraphrase, a summary uses just enough information to record the points you wish to emphasize. To summarize a short passage, read it carefully and, without looking at the text, write a one- or two-sentence summary. For a long passage or an entire chapter, skim the headings and topic sentences, and make notes of each; then write your summary in a paragraph or two. For a whole book, you may want to refer to the preface and introduction as well as chapter titles, headings, and topic sentences—and your summary may take a page or more.

A summary of the passage by Haraway follows. Notice that it states the author's main points selectively and without using her words.

ACCEPTABLE SUMMARY

> **Cyborg heroes**
>
> Haraway, Simians, pp. 177–78.
>
> Haraway says humans today are already part machine, and she cites the Ridley Scott movie Blade Runner as an example.
>
> (Summary)

AT A GLANCE

Summarizing Accurately

- Include just enough information to recount the main points you want to cite. A summary is usually far shorter than the original.

- Use your own words. If you include any language from the original, enclose it in quotation marks.

- Record the author, shortened title, and page number(s) on which the original material appeared. For online sources without page numbers, record the paragraph, screen, or other section number(s) if indicated.

- Make sure you have a corresponding working-bibliography entry with complete source information. (16f)

- Label the note with a subject heading, and identify it as a summary to avoid confusion with a paraphrase.

- Recheck to be sure you have captured the author's meaning and that the words are entirely your own.

Annotating sources

Sometimes you may photocopy or print out a source you intend to use. In such cases, you can annotate the photocopies or printouts with your thoughts and questions and highlight interesting quotations and key terms.

FOR MULTILINGUAL WRITERS

Identifying Sources

While some language communities and cultures expect audiences to recognize the sources of important documents and texts, thereby eliminating the need to cite them directly, conventions for writing in North America call for careful attribution of any quoted, paraphrased, or summarized material. When in doubt, explicitly identify your sources.

If you take notes in a computer file, you may be able to copy online sources electronically, paste them into the file, and annotate them there, perhaps even using software designed for this purpose. Try not to rely too heavily on copying or printing out whole pieces, however; you still need to read the material very carefully. And resist the temptation to treat copied material as notes, an action that could lead to inadvertent plagiarizing. (In a computer file, using a different color for text pasted from a source will help prevent this problem.)

19

Integrating Sources and Avoiding Plagiarism

In some ways, there really is nothing new under the sun, in writing and research as well as in life. If you think hard, you'll see that whatever writing you do has in some way been influenced by what you have already read and experienced. As you work on your research project, you will need to know how to use, integrate, and acknowledge the work of others. And all writers need to understand current definitions of plagiarism (which have changed over time and differ from culture to culture) as well as the concept of intellectual property—those works protected by copyright and other laws—so they can give credit where credit is due.

FOR MULTILINGUAL WRITERS

Thinking about Plagiarism as a Cultural Concept

Many cultures do not recognize Western notions of plagiarism, which rest on a belief that language and ideas can be owned by writers. Indeed, in many countries other than the United States, and even within some communities in the United States, using the words and ideas of others without attribution is considered a sign of deep respect as well as an indication of knowledge. In academic writing in the United States, however, you should credit all materials except those that are common knowledge, that are available in a wide variety of sources, or that are your own creations (photographs, drawings, and so on) or your own findings from field research.

19a Decide whether to quote, paraphrase, or summarize.

You tentatively decided to quote, paraphrase, or summarize material when you took notes on your sources. As you choose some of these sources for your research project and decide how to use them, however, you may reevaluate those decisions. The following guidelines can help you decide whether to quote, paraphrase, or summarize.

AT A GLANCE

Knowing When to Quote, Paraphrase, or Summarize

QUOTE

- wording that is so memorable or powerful, or expresses a point so perfectly, that you cannot change it without weakening its meaning
- authors' opinions you wish to emphasize
- authors' words that show you are considering varying perspectives
- respected authorities whose opinions support your ideas
- authors whose opinions challenge or vary greatly from those of others in the field

PARAPHRASE

- passages you do not wish to quote but that use details important to your point

SUMMARIZE

- long passages in which the main point is important to your point but the details are not

19b Integrate quotations, paraphrases, and summaries effectively.

Here are some general guidelines for integrating source materials into your writing.

Incorporating quotations

Quotations from respected authorities can help establish your credibility and show that you are considering various perspectives. However, because your essay is primarily your own work, limit your use of quotations.

BRIEF QUOTATIONS

Short quotations should run in with your text, enclosed by quotation marks (46a).

> In Miss Eckhart, Welty recognizes a character who shares with her "the love of her art and the love of giving it, the desire to give it until there is no more left" (10).

LONG QUOTATIONS

If you are writing according to the style of the Modern Language Association (MLA), set off a quotation longer than four lines. If you are writing according to the style of the American Psychological Association (APA) or the *Chicago Manual of Style,* set off a quotation of more than forty words or more than one paragraph. Begin such a quotation on a new line, and indent every line ten spaces (MLA), five to seven spaces (APA), or eight spaces (*Chicago*) from the left margin. This indentation sets off the quotation clearly, so quotation marks are unnecessary. Type the quotation to the right margin, and double-space it. Introduce long quotations by a signal phrase (p. 171) or a sentence followed by a colon. The following example shows MLA style:

> A good seating arrangement can prevent problems; however, *withitness,* as defined by Woolfolk, works even better:
>
>> Withitness is the ability to communicate to students that you are aware of what is happening in the classroom, that you "don't miss anything." With-it teachers seem to have "eyes in the back of their heads." They avoid becoming too absorbed with a few students, since this allows the rest of the class to wander. (359)
>
> This technique works, however, only if students actually believe that their teacher will know everything that goes on.

INTEGRATING QUOTATIONS SMOOTHLY INTO YOUR TEXT

Carefully integrate quotations into your text so that they flow smoothly and clearly into the surrounding sentences. Use a signal phrase or verb, such as those underlined in the following examples and listed below.

As Eudora Welty notes, "learning stamps you with its moments. Childhood's learning," she continues, "is made up of moments. It isn't steady. It's a pulse" (9).

In her essay, Haraway strongly opposes those who condemn technology outright, arguing that we must not indulge in a "demonology of technology" (181).

Notice that the examples alert readers to the quotations by using signal phrases that include the author's name. When you cite a quotation in this way, you need put only the page number in parentheses.

SIGNAL VERBS

acknowledges	concludes	emphasizes	replies
advises	concurs	expresses	reports
agrees	confirms	interprets	responds
allows	criticizes	lists	reveals
answers	declares	objects	says
asserts	describes	observes	states
believes	disagrees	offers	suggests
charges	discusses	opposes	thinks
claims	disputes	remarks	writes

BRACKETS AND ELLIPSES

In direct quotations, enclose in brackets any words you change or add, and indicate any deletions with ellipsis points (47f).

A farmer, Jane Lee, spoke to the Nuclear Regulatory Commission about the occurrences. "There is something wrong in the [Three Mile Island] area. It is happening within nature itself," she said, referring to human miscarriages, stillbirths, and birth defects in farm animals ("Legacy" 33).

Economist John Kenneth Galbraith has pointed out that "large corporations cannot afford to compete with one another. . . . In a truly competitive market someone loses. . . . American big business has finally learned that everybody has to protect everybody else's investment" (Key 17).

Incorporating paraphrases and summaries

Introduce paraphrases and summaries clearly, usually with a signal phrase that includes the author of the source, as the underlined words in this example indicate.

> Professor of linguistics Deborah Tannen says that she offers her book *That's Not What I Meant!* to "women and men everywhere who are trying their best to talk to each other" (19). <u>Tannen goes on to illustrate</u> how communication between women and men breaks down <u>and then to suggest</u> that a full awareness of "genderlects" can improve relationships (297).

19c Integrate visuals effectively.

If you are using visuals (such as graphs, cartoons, maps, photographs, charts, tables, or time lines), integrate them smoothly into your text.

- Make sure the graphic conveys information more efficiently than words alone could do.
- Position the visual immediately after the text it illustrates or refers to—or as close to it as possible.
- Refer to the visual by number in the text *before* it appears. For example: *As Figure 3 demonstrates.*
- Explain or comment on the relevance of the visual. This can be done *after* the visual.
- Label each visual clearly and consistently (*Figure 1: Photograph of the New York Skyline*).
- Check the documentation system you are using to make sure you label visuals appropriately; MLA, for instance, asks that you number and title tables and figures (*Table 1: Average Amount of Rainfall by Region*).
- If you are posting your document or essay on a Web site, make sure you have permission to use any visuals that are covered by copyright.

For more on using visuals, see Chapters 5 and 13.

19d Understand why you should acknowledge your sources.

Acknowledging sources says to your reader that you have done your homework, that you have gained expertise on your topic, and that you are credible. Acknowledging sources can also demonstrate fairness— that you have considered several points of view. In addition, recognizing your sources can help provide background for your research by placing it in the context of other thinking. Most of all, you should acknowledge sources in order to help your readers so that they can follow your thoughts, understand how your ideas relate to the thoughts of others, and know where to go to find more information on your topic.

19e Know which sources to acknowledge.

As you carry out research, it is important to understand the distinction between materials that require acknowledgment (in in-text citations, footnotes, or endnotes; and in the works-cited lists or bibliography) and those that do not.

Materials that don't require acknowledgment

- *Common knowledge.* If most readers already know a fact, you probably do not need to cite a source for it. You do not need to credit a source for the statement that George Bush was inaugurated as president in 2001, for example.
- *Facts available in a wide variety of sources.* If a number of encyclopedias, almanacs, or textbooks include a certain piece of information, you usually need not cite a specific source for it.
- *Your own findings from field research.* If you conduct observations or surveys, simply announce your findings as your own. Do acknowledge people you interview as individuals rather than as part of a survey, however.

Materials that require acknowledgment

Some of the information you use may need to be credited to a source:

- *Quotations, paraphrases, and summaries.* Whenever you use another person's words, ideas, or opinions, credit the source. Even though the wording of a paraphrase or summary is your own, you should still acknowledge the source.
- *Facts not widely known or claims that are arguable.* If your readers would be unlikely to know a fact, or if an author presents as fact a claim that may or may not be true, cite the source. If you are not sure whether a fact will be familiar to your readers or whether a statement is arguable, cite the source.
- *Visuals from any source.* Credit all visual and statistical material not derived from your own field research, even if you yourself create a graph or table from the data provided in a source.
- *Help provided by others.* If an instructor gave you a good idea or if friends responded to your draft or helped you conduct surveys, give credit.

19f Uphold your academic integrity, and avoid plagiarism.

One of the cornerstones of intellectual work is academic integrity. This principle accounts for our being able to trust those sources we use and to demonstrate that our own work is equally trustworthy. While there are many ways to damage academic integrity, two that are especially important are inaccurate or incomplete acknowledgment of sources in citations—sometimes called unintentional plagiarism—and plagiarism that is deliberately intended to pass off one writer's work as another's.

Whether it is intentional or not, plagiarism can result in serious consequences. At some colleges, students who plagiarize fail the course automatically; at others, they are expelled. Instructors who plagiarize, even inadvertently, have had their degrees revoked, their books withdrawn from publication. And outside academic life, eminent political, business, and scientific leaders have been stripped of candidacies, positions, and awards because of plagiarism.

Inaccurate or incomplete citation of sources

If your paraphrase is too close to the wording or sentence structure of a source (even if you identify the source); if after a quotation you do not identify the source (even if you include the quotation marks); or if you fail to indicate clearly the source of an idea that you obviously did not come up with on your own, you may be accused of plagiarism even if your intent was not to plagiarize. This kind of inaccurate or incomplete acknowledgment of sources often results either from carelessness or from not learning how to borrow material properly in the first place. Still, because the costs of even unintentional plagiarism can be severe, it's important to understand how it can happen and how you can guard against it.

As a writer of academic integrity, you will want to take responsibility for your research and for acknowledging all sources accurately. Doing so is considerably easier now because sources can be photocopied and the needed quotations identified right on the copy and because software programs allow writers to insert footnotes or endnotes into the text as they are writing it.

Deliberate plagiarism

Deliberate plagiarism—handing in an essay written by a friend or purchased (or simply downloaded) from an essay-writing company; cutting and pasting passages directly from source materials without marking them with quotation marks and acknowledging their sources; failing to credit the source of an idea or concept in your text—is what most people think of when they hear the word *plagiarism*. This form of plagiarism is particularly troubling because it represents dishonesty and deception: those who intentionally plagiarize present the hard thinking and hard work of someone else as their own, and they claim knowledge they really don't have, thus deceiving their readers.

Deliberate plagiarism is also fairly simple to spot: your instructor will be well acquainted with your writing and likely to notice any sudden shifts in the style or quality of your work. In addition, by typing a few words from an essay into a search engine, your instructor can identify "matches" very easily.

AT A GLANCE

Avoiding Plagiarism

- Maintain an accurate and thorough working bibliography. (16f)

- Establish a consistent note-taking system, listing sources and page numbers and clearly identifying all quotations, paraphrases, summaries, statistics, and visuals. (18d)

- Identify all quotations with quotation marks—both in your notes and in your essay. Be sure your summaries and paraphrases use your own words and sentence structures. (19b)

- Give a citation or note for each quotation, paraphrase, summary, arguable assertion or opinion, statistic, and visual that is from a source. (See Chapter 52, 56a, 57a, and 58a.)

- Prepare an accurate and complete list of sources cited according to the required documentation style. (See Chapter 52, 56c, 57b, and 58b.)

---

bedfordstmartins.com/everyday_writer For additional help, click on **The St. Martin's Tutorial on Avoiding Plagiarism.** For tips on using sources and considering your own intellectual property, click on **Additional Resources.**

20

Writing a Research Project

Everyday decisions often call for research and writing. In trying to choose between two jobs in different towns, for example, one person made a long list of questions to answer: Which job location had the lower cost of living? How did the two locations compare in terms of schools, cultural opportunities, major league sports, and so on? After conducting careful research, he was able to write a letter of acceptance to one place and a letter of regret to the other. In much the same way, when you are working on an academic project, there comes a time to draw the strands of your research together and articulate your conclusions in writing.

20a Refine your writing plans.

For almost all research writing, drafting should begin well before the deadline. There is a good reason for this: as your understanding of the subject grows and as you get responses from others, you may need to gather more information or even refine your original research question—and thus do more drafting. Before you start to write, reconsider your purpose, audience, stance, and working thesis.

- What is your central purpose? What other purposes, if any, do you have?
- What is your stance toward your topic? Are you an advocate, a critic, a reporter, an observer?
- What audience(s) are you addressing?
- How much background information does your audience need?
- What supporting information will your readers find convincing—examples? quotations from authorities? statistics? graphs, charts, or other visuals? data from your own observations or from interviews?
- Should your tone be that of a colleague, an expert, or a friend?
- How can you establish common ground with your audience and show them that you have considered points of view other than your own?
- What is your working thesis trying to establish? Will your audience accept it?

Developing an explicit thesis

At the drafting stage, try to develop your working thesis into an explicit statement, which might take the following form:

> **In this research project, I plan to (explain/argue/demonstrate/analyze, and so on) for an audience of** _____
>
> **that** _____
>
> **because/if** _____ .

For example, one student developed the following explicit thesis statement:

> In this research project, I plan to demonstrate for an audience of classmates from my first-year writing class that current trends in Hollywood films signal not the death of the hero but the evolution of the hero into two very different images.

Testing your thesis

Although writing out an explicit thesis will often confirm your research, you may find that your hypothesis is invalid, inadequately supported, or insufficiently focused. In such cases, you need to rethink your original research question and perhaps do further research. To test your thesis, consider the following questions:

1. How can you state your thesis more precisely or more clearly? Should the wording be more specific?
2. In what ways will your thesis interest your audience? What can you do to increase that interest?
3. Is your thesis going to be manageable, given your limits of time and knowledge? If not, what can you do to make it more manageable?
4. What evidence from your research supports each aspect of your thesis? What additional evidence do you need?

Considering design

As you move toward producing a draft, take some time to think about how you want your research essay or project to *look*. What font size will you use? Will you be using color? Will you be inserting text boxes and visuals? Using headings and subheadings?

20b Organize, outline or map, and draft.

To group the many pieces of information that you have collected, examine your notes for connections. Figure out what might be combined with what, which notes will be more useful and which less useful, which ideas lend support to your thesis and which should be put aside, and which visuals you will definitely use.

You can begin this process by grouping your notes and visuals into subject categories to identify main ideas; then try to order the categories in the most effective way. You may also want to develop a working outline, storyboard, or idea map, from your notes, which you can revise as you go along, or you can plot out a more detailed organization in a formal outline (7e).

Begin drafting wherever you feel most confident. If you have an idea for an introduction, begin there. If you are not sure how you want to introduce the project but do know how you want to approach one point, begin with that, and return to the introduction later.

If you will be doing most of your drafting with a word-processing program, remember to take advantage of its outlining and formatting tools. (See Chapter 12.)

Working title and introduction

The title and introduction play special roles, for they set the stage for what is to come. Ideally, the title announces the subject of the research essay or project in an intriguing or memorable way. The introduction should draw readers in and provide any background they will need to understand your discussion. Here are some tips for drafting an introduction to a research essay:

- It is often effective *to open with a question,* especially your research question. Next, you might explain what you will do to answer the question. Then *end with your explicit thesis statement*—in essence, the answer.
- Help readers get their bearings by *forecasting your main points.*
- *Establish your own credibility* by revealing how you have become knowledgeable about the topic.
- In general, you may *not* want to open with a quotation—though it can be a good attention-getter. Keep in mind that opening with a quotation from one source may give that source too much emphasis.

Conclusion

A good conclusion to a research project helps readers know what they have learned. Its job is not to persuade (the body of the essay or project should already have done that) but to contribute to the overall effectiveness of your argument. Here are some strategies that may help:

- Refer to your thesis, and then expand to a more general conclusion that reminds readers of the significance of your discussion.
- If you have covered several main points, you may want to remind readers of them. Be careful, however, to provide more than a mere summary.
- Try to end with something that will have an impact—a provocative quotation or question, a vivid image, a call for action, or a warning. But guard against sounding preachy.

20c Incorporate source materials.

When you reach the point of drafting your research project, a new task awaits: weaving your source materials into your writing. The challenge is to use your sources yet remain the author—to quote, paraphrase, and summarize other voices while remaining the major voice in your work. (See Chapter 19 for tips on integrating sources.)

20d Review and get responses to your draft.

Once you've completed your draft, reread it slowly. As you do so, answer the following questions, and use them as a starting point for revision:

- What do you now see as its *purpose*? How does this compare with your original purpose? Does the draft do what your assignment requires?
- What *audience* does your essay address?

- What is your *stance* toward the topic?
- What is your *thesis*? Is it clearly stated?
- What *evidence* supports your thesis? Is the evidence sufficient?

Next, ask friends, classmates, and, if possible, your instructor to read and respond to your draft. Asking specific questions of your readers will result in the most helpful advice. If you are unsure about whether to include a particular point, how to use a certain quotation, or where to add more examples, ask readers specifically what they think you should do.

bedfordstmartins.com/everyday_writer   If you're using **Comment** in your course, you and your classmates can take part in peer-reviewing activities online.

20e   Revise and edit your draft.

Once you get feedback, reread your draft very carefully, making notes for necessary changes and additions. Look closely at your support for your thesis, and gather additional verbal or visual information if necessary. Pay particular attention to how you have used both print and visual sources, and make sure you have full documentation for all of them. (For more detailed information on revising and editing, see Chapter 9.)

20f   Prepare a list of sources.

Once you have a final draft with your source materials in place, you are ready to prepare your list of sources. Create an entry for each source used in your essay. Then double-check your essay against your list of sources cited; be sure that you have listed every source mentioned in the in-text citations or notes and that you have not listed any sources not cited in your essay. (For guidelines on documentation styles, see Chapters 52–58.)

20g   Prepare and proofread your final copy.

To make sure that the final version of your essay puts your best foot forward, proofread it carefully. Work with a hard copy, since reading onscreen often leads to inaccuracies and missed typos. Proofread once for typographical and grammatical errors and once again to make sure you haven't introduced new errors. (To locate examples of student writing in this book and on the Web site, see the Student Writing Directory at the back of this book.)

Sentence
STYLE

When you start writing—and I think it's true
for a lot of beginning writers—
you're scared to death that if you don't
get that sentence right that minute it's never
going to show up again.
And it isn't. But it doesn't matter—
another one will, and it'll probably be better.

—TONI MORRISON, *THE SIGHT OF MEMORY*

Sentence Style

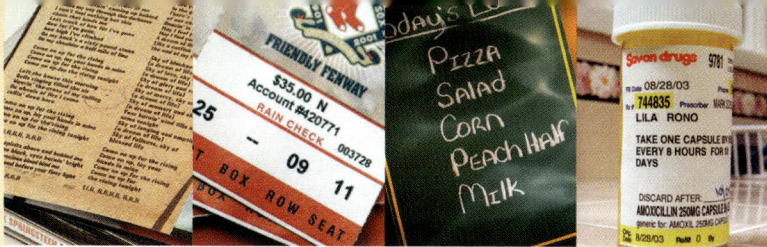

21

Consistency and Completeness

If you listen carefully to the conversations around you, you will hear inconsistent and incomplete structures all the time. For instance, during an interview, Orlando Bloom, who plays the elf Legolas in the film version of *The Lord of the Rings,* was asked whether he had been intimidated when cast in that role. Bloom responded:

> You know, Tolkien created elves to be these perfect beings, to bring the world forward. It's quite a responsibility, trying to take that to the screen. . . . Also, can you imagine for me, coming out of drama school, being thrown into a group of actors like Ian McKellen, Ian Holm, and Christopher Leeyes, it was incredibly daunting.

A couple of Bloom's sentences begin one way but then take off in another direction. The mixed structures posed no problem for the interviewer, but sentences such as these can be confusing to a reader. This chapter provides guidelines for recognizing and editing mixed and incomplete structures.

21a   Make grammatical patterns consistent.

One inconsistency that poses problems for writers and readers is a mixed structure, which results from beginning a sentence with one grammatical pattern and then switching to another one. For example:

> **MIXED**   The fact that I get up at 5:00 AM, a wake-up time that explains why I'm always tired in the evening.

The sentence starts out with a subject (*The fact*) followed by a dependent clause (*that I get up at 5:00 AM*). The sentence needs a predicate to complete the independent clause, but instead it moves to another phrase followed by a dependent clause (*a wake-up time that explains why I'm always tired in the evening*), and what results is a fragment.

REVISED   The fact that I get up at 5:00 AM explains why I'm always tired in the evening.

Deleting *a wake-up time that* changes the rest of the sentence into a predicate.

REVISED   I get up at 5:00 AM, a wake-up time that explains why I'm always tired in the evening.

Deleting *The fact that* turns the beginning of the sentence into an independent clause.

21b   Make subjects and predicates consistent.

Another kind of mixed structure, called faulty predication, occurs when a subject and predicate do not fit together grammatically or simply do not make sense together. Many cases of faulty predication result from using forms of *be* when another verb would be stronger.

▶ A characteristic that I admire is ~~a person who is generous.~~ *generosity.*

A person is not a characteristic.

▶ The rules of the corporation ~~expect~~ employees ~~to~~ be on time. *require that*

Rules cannot expect anything.

AT A GLANCE

Editing for Consistency and Completeness

- If you find an especially confusing sentence, check to see whether it has a subject and a predicate. If not, revise as necessary. (21a) If you find both a subject and a predicate, and you are still confused, see whether the subject and verb make sense together. If not, revise so that they do. (21b)
- Revise any *is when, is where,* and *reason . . . is because* constructions. (21b)

  ▶ Spamming is ~~where~~ companies send electronic junk mail. *a practice in which*

- Check all comparisons for completeness. (21e)

  ▶ We like Lisa better than Margaret. *we like*

Is when, is where, reason . . . is because

Although you will often hear expressions such as *home is where the heart is* in everyday use, these constructions are inappropriate in academic or professional writing.

> *an unfair characterization of*
> ► A stereotype is ~~when someone characterizes~~ a group**.** ~~unfairly.~~
>   *a place*
> ► A confluence is where two rivers join to form one.

> ► ~~The reason~~ I like to play soccer ~~is~~ because it provides aerobic exercise.

21c   Use elliptical structures carefully.

Sometimes writers omit certain words in compound structures. This type of structure, known as an elliptical structure, is appropriate when the word omitted later in the compound is exactly the same as the word earlier in the compound. In the following sentence, the omitted word is in brackets:

> ► **That bell belonged to the figure of Miss Duling as though it grew directly out of her right arm, as wings grew out of an angel or a tail [grew] out of the devil.**   —EUDORA WELTY, *One Writer's Beginnings*

If the omitted word does not match a word in the other part(s) of the compound, readers might be confused, so the omission is inappropriate.

> *is*
> ► **His skills are weak, and his performance only average.**

> The omitted verb *is* does not match the verb in the other part of the compound (*are*), so the writer needs to include it.

21d   Check for missing words.

The best way to catch inadvertent omissions is to proofread carefully.

> *at*
> ► **The new Web site makes it easier to look and choose from the company's inventory.**

21e Make comparisons complete, consistent, and clear.

When you compare two or more things, the comparison must be complete, logically consistent, and clear.

▶ I was embarrassed because my parents were so different/ *from my friends' parents.*

Different from what? Adding *from my friends' parents* tells readers with what the comparison is being made.

▶ Woodberry's biography is better than Fields. *the one by*

This sentence illogically compares a book with a person. The editing makes the comparison logical.

UNCLEAR	Aneil always felt more affection for his brother than his sister.
CLEAR	Aneil always felt more affection for his brother *than his sister did.*
CLEAR	Aneil always felt more affection for his brother *than he did for his sister.*

bedfordstmartins.com/everyday_writer   For exercises, go to **Exercise Central** and click on **Consistency and Completeness.**

22

Coordination and Subordination

If you think about how you build sentences, you may notice a difference between your spoken and your written language. In speech, people tend to use *and* and *so* as all-purpose connectors.

I'm going home now, and I'll see you later.

The meaning of this sentence may be perfectly clear in speech, which provides clues with voice, facial expressions, and gestures. But in writing, the actual meaning might not be clear. The sentence could, for instance, have two rather different meanings.

Because I'm going home now, I'll see you later.

I'm going home now because I'll see you later.

The first sentence links two ideas with *and,* a coordinating conjunction; the other two sentences link ideas with *because,* a subordinating conjunction. These examples show two different ways of combining ideas in a sentence: a coordinating conjunction gives the ideas equal emphasis, and a subordinating conjunction emphasizes one idea more than another.

AT A GLANCE

Editing for Coordination and Subordination

How do your ideas flow from one sentence to another? Do they connect smoothly and clearly? Are the more important ideas given more emphasis than less important ones? These guidelines will help you edit with such questions in mind.

- Look for strings of short sentences that might be combined to join related ideas. (22a)

  ▶ The report was short*,* ~~It~~ was persuasive*;* ~~It~~ changed my mind.
               but it   *i*

- How often do you link ideas with *and*? If you use *and* excessively, decide whether all the ideas are equally important. If they are not equal, edit to subordinate the less important ones. (22b)

- Are the most important ideas in independent clauses? If not, edit so that they are. (22b)

  ▶ *Even though the*
  ~~The~~ report was short, ~~even though~~ it changed my mind.

22a   Use coordination to relate equal ideas.

When you want to give equal emphasis to different ideas in a sentence, link them with a coordinating conjunction (*and, but, for, nor, or, so, yet*) or a semicolon.

▶ They acquired horses, *and* their ancient nomadic spirit was suddenly free of the ground.

▶ There is perfect freedom in the mountains, *but* it belongs to the eagle and the elk, the badger and the bear.

▶ No longer were they slaves to the simple necessity of survival; they were a lordly and dangerous society of fighters and thieves, hunters and priests of the sun. —N. Scott Momaday, *The Way to Rainy Mountain*

Coordination can help make explicit the relationship between two separate ideas.

▶ My son watches *The Simpsons* religiously; Forced to choose, he
would probably choose Homer Simpson over his sister.

Connecting these two sentences with a semicolon strengthens the connection between two closely related ideas.

When you connect ideas in a sentence, make sure that the relationship between the ideas is clear.

                                                        but

▶ Watching television is a common way to spend leisure time, ~~and~~ it
makes viewers apathetic.

The relationship between the two ideas in the original sentence is unclear: what does being a common form of leisure have to do with making viewers apathetic? Changing *and* to *but* better relates the two ideas.

22b Use subordination to distinguish main ideas.

Subordination allows you to distinguish major points from minor points or to bring in supporting details. If, for instance, you put your main idea in an independent clause, you might then put any less significant ideas in dependent clauses, phrases, or even single words. The following sentence shows the subordinated point in italics:

▶ Mrs. Viola Cullinan was a plump woman *who lived in a three-bedroom house somewhere behind the post office.*
—Maya Angelou, "My Name Is Margaret"

The dependent clause adds important information about Mrs. Cullinan, but it is subordinate to the independent clause.

    Notice that the choice of what to subordinate rests with the writer and depends on the intended meaning. Angelou might have given the same basic information differently.

▶ Mrs. Viola Cullinan, *a plump woman,* lived in a three-bedroom house somewhere behind the post office.

Subordinating the information about Mrs. Cullinan's size to that about her house would suggest a slightly different meaning, of course. As a writer, you must think carefully about what you want to emphasize and must subordinate information accordingly.

Subordination also establishes logical relationships among ideas. These relationships are often specified by subordinating conjunctions.

SOME COMMON SUBORDINATING CONJUNCTIONS

after	if	though
although	in order that	unless
as	once	until
as if	since	when
because	so that	where
before	than	while
even though	that	

The following sentence is shown with the subordinate clause italicized and the subordinating word underlined:

▶ **She usually rested her smile until late afternoon *when her women friends dropped in and Miss Glory, the cook, served them cold drinks on the closed-in porch.*** —MAYA ANGELOU, "My Name Is Margaret"

Using too many coordinate structures can be monotonous and can make it hard for readers to recognize the most important ideas. Subordinating lesser ideas can help highlight the main ideas.

▶ **Many people come home tired in the evening, so they turn on the TV to**
Though they
relax. ~~They~~ may intend to watch just the news, ~~but then~~ a game show
         which   *Eventually,*
comes on next, ~~and~~ they decide to watch ~~it~~ for just a short while/. ~~and~~

they get too comfortable to get up, and they end up spending the

whole evening in front of the TV.

By subordinating some of the less important ideas, the editing makes clear to the reader that some of the ideas are more important than others.

Determining what to subordinate

Although our
▶ **~~Our~~ new boss can be difficult, ~~although~~ she has revived and maybe even saved the division.**

The editing puts the more important information—that she has saved part of the company—in an independent clause and subordinates the rest.

Avoiding excessive subordination

When too many subordinate clauses are strung together, readers may have trouble keeping track of the main idea expressed in the independent clause.

TOO MUCH SUBORDINATION

▶ Philip II sent the Spanish Armada to conquer England, which was ruled by Elizabeth, who had executed Mary because she was plotting to overthrow Elizabeth, who was a Protestant, whereas Mary and Philip were Roman Catholics.

REVISED

▶ Philip II sent the Spanish Armada to conquer England, which was ruled by Elizabeth, a Protestant. She had executed Mary, a Roman Catholic like Philip, because Mary was plotting to overthrow her.

Putting the facts about Elizabeth executing Mary into an independent clause makes key information easier to recognize.

A MATTER OF STYLE

Subordination

Carefully used subordination can create powerful effects. Some particularly fine examples come from Martin Luther King Jr.

> Perhaps it is easy for those who have never felt the stinging darts of segregation to say, "Wait." But *when* you have seen vicious mobs lynch your mothers and fathers at will and drown your sisters and brothers at whim; *when* you have seen hate-filled policemen curse, kick, and even kill your black brothers and sisters; . . . *when* you have to concoct an answer for a five-year-old son who is asking: "Daddy, why do white people treat colored people so mean?"; *when* you take a cross-country drive and find it necessary to sleep night after night in the uncomfortable corners of your automobile because no motel will accept you; . . . *when* your first name becomes "nigger," your middle name becomes "boy" (however old you are) and your last name becomes "John," and your wife and mother are never given the respected title "Mrs."; . . . *when* you are forever fighting a degenerating sense of "nobodiness" — then you will understand why we find it difficult to wait.
>
> —MARTIN LUTHER KING JR., "Letter from Birmingham Jail"

---

bedfordstmartins.com/everyday_writer For exercises, go to **Exercise Central** and click on **Coordination and Subordination**.

23

Parallelism

Parallel grammatical structures show up in many of our most familiar phrases: *sink or swim, rise and shine, shape up or ship out.* If you look and listen for these structures, you will see parallelism in everyday use. Bumper stickers often use parallel grammatical structures to make their messages memorable (*Minds are like parachutes; both work best when open*), as do song lyrics and jump-rope rhymes. This chapter will help you use parallel structures to create pleasing rhythmic effects in your own writing.

AT A GLANCE

Editing for Parallelism

- Look for any series of three or more items, and make all of the items parallel in structure. If you want to emphasize one particular item, try putting it at the end of the series. (23a)
- Be sure items in lists are parallel in form. (23a)
- Be sure all headings are parallel in form. (23a)
- Check for places where two ideas are compared, contrasted, or otherwise paired in the same sentence. Often these ideas will appear on either side of *and, but, or, nor, for, so,* or *yet,* or after each part of *both . . . and, either . . . or, neither . . . nor, not only . . . but also, whether . . . or,* or *just as . . . so.* Edit to make the two ideas parallel in structure. (23b)
- Check all parallel structures to be sure that you have included all the necessary words—articles, prepositions, the *to* of the infinitive, and so on. (23c)

23a Make items in a series parallel.

Parallelism makes a series both graceful and easy to follow.

▶ In the eighteenth century, armed forces could fight *in open fields* and *on the high seas.* Today, they can clash *on the ground anywhere, on the sea, under the sea,* and *in the air.*
> —DONALD SNOW AND EUGENE BROWN, *The Contours of Power*

The parallel phrases, as well as the parallel structure of the sentences themselves, highlight the contrast between warfare in the eighteenth century and warfare today.

In the sentences below, note how the revisions make all items in the series parallel.

▶ The quarter horse skipped, pranced, and ~~was sashaying~~ *sashayed* onto the track.

▶ The children ran down the hill, skipped over the lawn, and *jumped* into the swimming pool.

▶ The duties of the job include babysitting, housecleaning, and ~~preparation of~~ *preparing* meals.

Items in a list, on a formal outline, and in headings should be parallel (p. 47).

▶ Kitchen rules: (1) Coffee to be made only by library staff. (2) Coffee service to be closed at 4:00 PM. (3) Doughnuts to be kept in cabinet. (4) ~~No faculty members should handle coffee materials.~~ *Coffee materials not to be handled by faculty.*

23b Use parallel structures to pair ideas.

Parallel structures can help you pair two ideas effectively. The more nearly parallel the two structures are, the stronger the connection between the ideas will be.

▶ History became popular, and historians became alarmed.
— WILL DURANT

▶ I type in one place, but I write all over the house.
— TONI MORRISON

▶ Writers are often more interesting on the page than they are in ~~person.~~ *the flesh.*

In these examples, the parallel structures help readers see an important contrast between two ideas or acts.

With coordinating conjunctions

When you link ideas with *and, but, or, nor, for, so,* or *yet,* try to make the ideas parallel in structure.

▶ Consult a friend in your class or ~~who is~~ good at math.

(editor's insertion above: who is)

▶ The wise politician promises the possible and ~~should accept~~ the inevitable.

(editor's insertion above: accepts)

In both sentences, the editing links the two ideas by making them parallel.

A MATTER OF STYLE

Parallelism

Parallel structures can help a writer emphasize important ideas, as Joan Didion does in the following sentence:

> I would like to promise her that she will grow up with a sense of her cousins and of rivers and of her great-grandmother's teacups, would like to pledge her a picnic on a river with fried chicken and her hair uncombed, would like to give her *home* for her birthday, but we live differently now and I can promise her nothing like that.
> —JOAN DIDION, "On Going Home"

The first two parallel phrases—*would like to promise her, would like to pledge her*—introduce a series of specific concrete details and images that lead up to the general statement in the last phrase, that she *would like to give her* daughter a sense of "home." Although Didion could have stated this general point first and then gone on to illustrate it with concrete details, she achieves greater emphasis by making it the last in a series of parallel structures. (For more on emphasis, see Chapter 25.)

With correlative conjunctions

Use the same structure after both parts of the following correlative conjunctions: *either . . . or, both . . . and, neither . . . nor, not . . . but, not only . . . but also, just as . . . so,* and *whether . . . or.*

▶ I wanted not only to go away to school but also ~~to~~ New England.

(editor's insertion above: live in)

Balancing *to go* with *to live* links the two ideas and makes the sentence easier to read.

23c Include all necessary words.

In addition to making parallel elements grammatically similar, be sure to include any words—prepositions, articles, verb forms, and so on—that are necessary for clarity, grammar, or idiom.

▶ We'll move to a town in the Southwest or ^*in*^ Mexico.

> To a town in Mexico or to Mexico in general? The editing clarifies the meaning.

bedfordstmartins.com/everyday_writer For exercises, go to **Exercise Central** and click on **Parallelism.**

24

Shifts

A shift in writing is an abrupt change of some sort that results in inconsistency. Sometimes a writer will shift deliberately, as Dave Barry does in noting he "would have to say that the greatest single achievement of the American medical establishment is nasal spray." Barry's shift in tone from the serious (the American medical establishment) to the banal (nasal spray) makes us laugh, as Barry wishes us to. Although writers sometimes deliberately make such shifts for good reasons, unintentional shifts can be jolting and confusing to readers. This chapter helps you edit out unintentional shifts in verbs, pronouns, and tone.

24a Check for unnecessary shifts in tense.

If the verbs in a passage refer to actions occurring at different times, they may require different tenses. Be careful, however, not to change tenses for no reason.

▶ A few countries produce almost all of the world's illegal drugs, but addiction ~~affected~~ ^*affects*^ many countries.

AT A GLANCE

Confusing Shifts

- If you shift from one verb tense to another, check to be sure there is a reason for doing so. (24a)
- Do you see any shifts in mood—perhaps from an indicative statement to an imperative—and, if so, are they necessary? (24b)
- Check for shifts from active (*She asks questions*) to passive voice (*Questions are asked*). Are they intentional—and, if so, for what reason? (24c)
- Do you see any shifts in person or number—from *we* to *you*, for example—and, if so, what are the reasons for the shifts? (24d)
- Check your writing for consistency in tone. If your tone is serious, is it consistently so? (24f)

FOR MULTILINGUAL WRITERS

Shifting Tenses in Reported Speech

If Al said to Maria, "I will marry you," why did she then correctly tell her mom, "He said that he *would* marry me"? For guidelines on reporting speech, see 65b.

24b Check for shifts in mood.

Be careful not to shift from one mood to another without good reason. The mood of a verb can be indicative (he *closes* the door), imperative (*close* the door), or subjunctive (if the door *were closed*) (29h).

▶ Keep your eye on the ball, and ~~you should~~ bend your knees.

The sentence shifts from the imperative to the indicative; the editing makes both verbs imperative since the writer's purpose is to give orders.

24c Check for shifts in voice.

Do not shift without reason between the active voice (she *sold* it) and the passive voice (it *was sold*). Sometimes a shift in voice is justified, but often it may only confuse readers (29g).

> ▶ Two youths approached me/ and ~~I was~~ asked for my wallet. *me*

The original sentence shifts from the active (*youths approached*) to the passive (*I was asked*), so it is unclear who asked for the wallet. Making both verbs active clears up the confusion.

24d Check for shifts in person and number.

Unnecessary shifts between first-person point of view (*I, we*), second-person (*you*), and third-person (*he, she, it, one,* or *they*), or between singular and plural subjects can be very confusing to readers.

> ▶ ~~One~~ can do well on this job if you budget your time. *You*

It was not clear whether the writer was making a general statement or giving advice to someone. Eliminating the shift eliminates this confusion.

> ▶ Nurses receive much less pay than doctors, even though ~~a nurse has~~ *nurses have*
>
> the primary responsibility for daily patient care.

The writer had no reason to shift from third-person plural (*nurses*) to third-person singular (*a nurse*).

24e Check for shifts between direct and indirect discourse.

When you quote someone's exact words, you are using direct discourse: *She said, "I'm an editor."* When you report what someone says without repeating the exact words, you are using indirect discourse: *She said she is an editor.* Shifting between direct and indirect discourse in the same sentence can cause problems, especially with questions.

> ▶ Bob asked what could ~~he~~ do to help~~?~~. *he*

The editing eliminates an awkward shift by reporting Bob's question indirectly. It could also be edited to quote Bob directly: *Bob asked, "What can I do to help?"*

24f Check for shifts in tone and diction.

Tone (a writer's attitude toward a topic or audience) is related to diction, or word choice, and to overall formality or informality. Watch out for tone or diction shifts that can confuse readers and leave them wondering what your real attitude is (p. 68).

INCONSISTENT TONE

The question of child care forces a society to make profound decisions about its economic values. Can most families with young children actually live adequately on only one salary? If some conservatives had their way, June Cleaver would still be stuck in the kitchen baking cookies for Wally and the Beaver and waiting for Ward to bring home the bacon, except that, with only one income, the Cleavers would be lucky to afford hot dogs.

In this version, the first two sentences, setting a serious, formal tone, discuss child care in fairly general, abstract terms. But in the third sentence, the writer shifts suddenly to sarcasm, to references to television characters of an earlier era, and to informal language like *stuck* and *bring home the bacon*. Readers cannot tell whether the writer is presenting a serious analysis or preparing for a humorous satire. See how the passage was revised to make the tone consistent.

REVISED

The question of child care forces a society to make profound decisions about its economic values. Can most families with young children actually live adequately on only one salary? Some conservatives believe that women with young children should not work outside the home, but many mothers are forced to do so for financial reasons.

bedfordstmartins.com/everyday_writer   For exercises, go to **Exercise Central** and click on **Shifts**.

25

Emphasis

In speaking, we can easily indicate emphasis by raising our voices, putting extra stress on an important word, or drawing out a phrase. And much of the writing we see around us—in advertisements, on Web sites, and in magazines—gains emphasis in similar fashion by using color, graphics, or bold type, for instance.

Academic or professional writing, however, can't always rely on such graphic devices for emphasis. Luckily, writers have other tools at their disposal. This chapter will help you write emphatic sentences that put the spotlight on main ideas so that readers know which elements are most important.

AT A GLANCE

Editing for Sentence Emphasis

As you revise a draft, follow these steps to make sure that each sentence emphasizes the ideas you *want* emphasized.

- Identify the word or words you want to receive special emphasis. If those words are buried in the middle of a sentence, edit the sentence to change their position. The end and the beginning are generally the most emphatic. (25a)
- Note any sentences that include a series of three or more words, phrases, or clauses. Can the items in the series be arranged in climactic order, with the most important item last? (25b)

25a   Use closing and opening positions for emphasis.

When you read a sentence, what are you likely to remember? Other things being equal, you remember the ending. This is the part of the sentence that should move the writing forward by providing new information, as it does in the following example:

▶ To protect her skin, she took along *plenty of sunblock lotion.*

▶ We hear language through a powerful filter of *social values and stereotypes.*

A less emphatic but still important position in a sentence is the opening, which often associates the new sentence with the meaning of what has come before.

▶ When Rosita went to the beach, she was anxious not to get a sunburn. *So plenty of sunblock lotion* went with her.

If you place relatively unimportant information in the memorable closing position of a sentence, you may undercut what you want to emphasize or give more emphasis to the closing words than you intend.

> *Last month, she*   *$500,000.*
> ▶ She gave $500,000 to the school capital campaign last month.
>   ^   ^

Moving *$500,000* to the end of the sentence emphasizes the amount.

25b Use climactic order to emphasize important ideas.

When you arrange ideas in order of increasing importance, power, or drama, your writing builds to a climax. By saving its most dramatic item for last, the following sentence makes its point forcefully and memorably:

> ▶ After they've finished with the pantry, the medicine cabinet, and the attic, [neat people] will throw out the red geranium (too many leaves), sell the dog (too many fleas), and send the children off to boarding school (too many scuffmarks on the hardwood floors).
> –SUSANNE BRITT, "Neat People vs. Sloppy People"

The original version of the next sentence fails to achieve strong emphasis because its verbs are not sequenced in order of increasing power; the editing provides climactic order.

>   *offend our ears,   and*
> ▶ Soap operas assault our eyes, damage our brains/. and offend our ears.
>   ^   ^   ^

A MATTER OF STYLE

Anticlimax and Humor

Sometimes it's fun to turn the principle of climactic order upside down, opening with grand or exaggerated language only to end anticlimactically, with everyday words.

> He is a writer for the ages—the ages of four to eight.
> –DOROTHY PARKER

Parker builds up high expectations at the beginning of the sentence—only to undercut them unexpectedly by shifting the meaning of *ages*. Having led readers to expect something dramatic, she makes us laugh, or at least smile, with words that are decidedly undramatic.

---

bedfordstmartins.com/everyday_writer   For exercises, go to **Exercise Central** and click on **Emphasis**.

26

Conciseness

You can see the importance of conciseness in directions, particularly those on medicines. Consider the following directions found on one common prescription drug:

> Take one tablet daily. Some nonprescription drugs may aggravate your condition, so read all labels carefully. If any include a warning, check with your doctor.

Squeezing words onto a three-inch label is probably not your ordinary writing situation, but more often than not, you will want to write as concisely as you can.

AT A GLANCE

Editing for Conciseness

- Look for unnecessary or redundant words. If you are unsure about a word, read the sentence without it; if meaning is not affected, leave the word out. (26a and b)
- Take out empty words—words like *aspect* or *factor, definitely* or *very*. (26c)
- Replace wordy phrases with a single word. Instead of *because of the fact that,* try *because.* (26d)
- Reconsider any sentences that begin with *it is* or *there is/are.* Unless they create special emphasis, try recasting the sentences without these words. (26e)

26a Eliminate unnecessary words.

Usually you'll want to make your point in the fewest possible words.

> ▶ Her constant and continual use of vulgar expressions with obscene meanings indicated to her pre-elementary supervisory group that she was rather deficient in terms of her ability to interact in an efficient manner with peers in her potential interaction group.

Why write that sentence when you could instead write the following?

> ▶ Her constant use of four-letter words told the day-care workers she might have trouble getting along with other four-year-olds.

A MATTER OF E-STYLE

Brevity in Email

Make sure your subject line states your purpose as clearly and succinctly as possible.

> Subject: Meeting 10/3/04—apologies for missing

The preceding subject line is much clearer than one such as *Oops* and more succinct than one such as *Apologies for not getting to your meeting the other day.*

In general, keep your emails brief. Readers do not enjoy scrolling through a lot of onscreen text. Set your email format at sixty to seventy characters per line in order to avoid the one- or two-word lines that sometimes occur when one email system downloads to another.

26b Eliminate redundant words.

Sometimes writers add words for emphasis. For example, they say that something is large *in size* or red *in color* or that two ingredients should be *combined together.* The deleted words below, however, are redundant—unnecessary for meaning.

▶ ~~Compulsory~~ Attendance at assemblies is required.

▶ The auction featured ~~contemporary~~ "antiques" made recently.

▶ Many different forms of hazing occur, such as physical ~~abuse~~ and mental abuse.

26c Eliminate empty words.

Empty words are those that contribute no real meaning. In general, delete them.

EMPTY WORDS

> angle, area, aspect, case, character, element, factor, field, kind, nature, scope, situation, thing, type

Many modifiers are so common that they have become empty words, adding no meaning to a statement.

MEANINGLESS MODIFIERS

absolutely, awesome, awfully, central, definitely, fine, great, literally, major, quite, really, very

When you cannot simply delete empty words, try to think of a more specific way to say what you mean.

>   *H*   *strongly influence*
> ▶ The ʰousing ~~situation~~ can ~~have a really significant impact on the~~
>   ^*social*
> ~~social aspect of~~ a student's life.
>   ^

26d   Replace wordy phrases.

Wordy phrases are those that you can reduce to a word or two with no loss in meaning.

WORDY	CONCISE
at all times	always
at the present time	now/today
at that point in time	then
due to the fact that	because
for the purpose of	for
in order to	to
in spite of the fact that	although
in the event that	if

26e   Simplify sentence structure.

Using the simplest grammatical structures possible can tighten and strengthen your sentences considerably.

> ▶ Kennedy, ~~who was~~ only the second Roman Catholic ~~to be~~ nominated
>
> for the presidency by a major party, had to handle the religion issue
> *delicately.*
> ~~in a delicate manner.~~
> ^

Reducing a clause to an appositive, deleting unnecessary words, and replacing four words with one tighten the sentence and make it easier to read.

Using strong verbs

Be verbs (*is, are, was, were, been*) often result in wordiness.

> *harms*
> ▶ A high-fat, high-cholesterol diet ~~is bad for~~ your heart.
>   ^

Avoiding expletives

Sometimes expletive constructions—*there is, there are,* and *it is*—are an effective way to introduce a topic; often, however, your writing will be better without them.

> *M*
> ▶ ~~There are~~ ᴍany people ~~who~~ fear success because they believe they do
>
> not deserve it.

> *P*   *need*
> ▶ ~~It is necessary for~~ ᴘresidential candidates to perform well on
>   ^
> television.

Using active voice

Some writing situations call for the passive voice, but it is always wordier than the active—and often makes for dull or even difficult reading (29g).

> *Gower*
> ▶ ~~In Gower's research, it was~~ found that pythons often dwell in trees.
>   ^

bedfordstmartins.com/everyday_writer   For exercises, go to **Exercise Central** and
click on **Conciseness.**

27

Sentence Variety

Row upon row of trees identical in size and shape may appeal, at some level, to our sense of orderliness, but in spite of that appeal, the rows soon become boring. Constant uniformity in anything, in fact, soon gets tiresome, while its opposite, variation, is usually pleasing to readers.

Variety is important in sentence structures because too much uniformity results in dull, listless prose. This chapter examines ways to revise sentences—by creating variety in length and in openings.

AT A GLANCE

Editing for Sentence Variety

- Count the words in each of your sentences. If the difference between the longest and shortest sentences is fairly small—say, five words or fewer—try revising your sentences to create greater variety. (27a)

- If many sentences have fewer than ten words, consider whether any of them need more detail or should be combined with other sentences.

- How do your sentences open? If all or most of them open with a subject, try recasting some sentences to begin with a transition, a phrase, or a dependent clause. (27b)

27a Vary sentence length.

Deciding how and when to vary sentence length is not always easy. Is there a "just right" length for a particular sentence or idea? The answer depends on, among other things, your purpose, intended audience, and topic. Frequent alternation in sentence length characterizes much memorable writing. After one or more long sentences with complex ideas or images, the punch of a short sentence can be refreshing.

A MATTER OF STYLE

Technical Writing

For some types of writing, varying sentence structure and length is not always appropriate. Many technical writers, particularly those who write manuals that will be translated into other languages, must follow stringent rules for sentence structure and length. Technical writers working for Hewlett-Packard, for example, must adhere to a strict subject-verb-object order and limit all sentences to a maximum length of fifteen words. You will want to understand the style conventions of your field as fully as possible and bring them to bear on your own sentence revisions.

> The fire of, I think, five machine-guns was pouring upon us, and there was a series of heavy crashes caused by the Fascists flinging bombs over their own parapet in the most idiotic manner. It was intensely dark. —GEORGE ORWELL, *Homage to Catalonia*

27b Vary sentence openings.

If sentence after sentence begins with a subject, a passage may become monotonous or even hard to read.

> The way football and basketball are played is as interesting as the
> *Because football*
> players. ~~Football~~ is a game of precision /. ~~E~~ach play is diagrammed to
> *however,*
> accomplish a certain goal. Basketball, is a game of endurance.
> *In fact, a*
> ~~A~~ basketball game looks like a track meet; the team that drops of
> exhaustion first loses. Basketball players are often compared to artists /.
> *their*
> ~~The players~~' moves and slam dunks are their masterpieces.

The editing adds variety by using subordinating words (*Because* in the second line) and a prepositional phrase (*In fact* in the fourth line) and by linking sentences. Varying sentence openings prevents the passage from seeming to jerk or lurch along.

You can add variety to your sentence openings by using transitions, various kinds of phrases, and introductory dependent clauses.

TRANSITIONAL EXPRESSIONS

> *In contrast,* our approach will save time and money.

> *Nevertheless,* the show must go on.

PHRASES

> *At each desk,* a computer printout provides necessary data.

> *Frustrated by the delays,* the drivers started honking their horns.

> *To qualify for flight training,* one must be in good physical condition.

> *Our hopes for snow dashed,* we started home.

DEPENDENT CLAUSES

> *What they want* is a place to call home.

> *Because the hills were dry,* the fire spread rapidly.

A MATTER OF E-STYLE

Style and Grammar Checkers

Editing programs can alert you to style issues such as sentence length, verb voice, and sentence openers. Grammar checkers in word processors such as Microsoft Word can check your drafts for common sentence-level errors such as wordiness and fragments. But these tools give advice out of context and may indicate an error when there isn't any. (For more on grammar, style, and spell checkers, see Chapter 12.)

---

bedfordstmartins.com/everyday_writer   For exercises, go to **Exercise Central** and click on **Sentence Variety.**

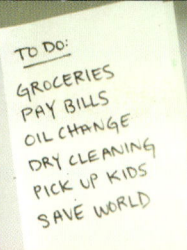

Sentence GRAMMAR

We learn a great deal about grammar from reading—and not grammar books but newspapers, novels, poetry, magazines, even the labels on cereal boxes.

−LYNN Z. BLOOM, *STRATEGIC WRITING*

Sentence Grammar

28

Basic Grammar

The grammar of our first language comes to us almost automatically, without our thinking much about it or even being aware of it. Listen in, for instance, on a conversation between two six-year-olds.

> CHARLOTTE: My new bike that Grandma got me has a red basket and a loud horn, and I love it.
>
> TORIA: Can I ride it?
>
> CHARLOTTE: Sure, as soon as I take a turn.

This simple conversation features sophisticated grammar—the subordination of one clause to another, a compound object, and a number of adjectives—used effortlessly. Though native speakers know the basic grammatical rules, these rules can produce a broad range of sentences, some more effective and artful than others. Understanding the grammatical structures presented in this chapter can help you produce sentences that are grammatical—and appropriate and effective as well.

28a The basic grammar of sentences

A sentence is a grammatically complete group of words that expresses a thought. To be grammatically complete, a group of words must contain a subject, which identifies what the sentence is about, and a predicate, which says or asks something about the subject or tells the subject to do something.

SUBJECT	PREDICATE
I	have a dream.
The rain in Spain	stays mainly in the plain.
Harry Potter, wizard extraordinaire,	lives at Hogwarts.

Some sentences have only a one-word predicate with an implied, or understood, subject (for example, *Stop!*). Most sentences, however, contain additional words that expand the basic subject and predicate. In the preceding example, for instance, the subject might have been simply *Harry Potter;* the words *wizard extraordinaire* tell us more about the subject. Similarly, the predicate of that sentence could grammatically be *lives;* the words *at Hogwarts* expand the predicate by telling us where Harry lives.

PARTS OF SPEECH

All English words belong to one or more of nine grammatical categories called parts of speech: verbs, nouns, pronouns, adjectives, adverbs, prepositions, conjunctions, interjections, and articles. Many English words regularly function as more than one part of speech. Take the word *book,* for example: when you *book a plane flight,* it is a verb; when you *take a good book to the beach,* it is a noun; and when you *have book knowledge,* it is an adjective.

28b Verbs

Verbs are among the most important words because they move the meanings of sentences along. Verbs show actions of body or mind (*skip, speculate*), occurrences (*become, happen*), or states of being (*be, seem*). They can also change form to show *time, person, number, voice,* and *mood.*

TIME	we *work*, we *worked*
PERSON	I *work*, she *works*
NUMBER	one person *works*, two people *work*
VOICE	she *asks*, she *is asked*
MOOD	we *see*, if we *saw*

Auxiliary verbs (also called helping verbs) combine with other verbs (often called main verbs) to create verb phrases. Auxiliaries include the various forms of *be, do,* and *have* (which can also function as main verbs) and the words *can, could, may, might, must, shall, should, will,* and *would.*

▶ You *do need* some sleep tonight!

▶ I *could have danced* all night.

▶ She *would prefer* to learn Italian rather than Spanish.

See Chapters 29 and 30 for a complete discussion of verbs.

28c Nouns

Nouns name persons (*aviator, child*), places (*lake, library*), things (*truck, suitcase*), and concepts (*happiness, balance*). Proper nouns name specific persons, places, things, and concepts: *Bill, Iowa, Supreme Court, Buddhism.* Collective nouns name groups: *team, flock, jury* (30d).

You can change most nouns from singular (one) to plural (more than one) by adding *-s* or *-es: horse, horses; kiss, kisses.* Some nouns, however, have irregular plural forms: *woman, women; alumnus, alumni; mouse, mice; deer, deer.* Noncount nouns—such as *dust, peace,* and *prosperity*—do not have a plural form because they name something that cannot easily be counted (39c and 64a).

To show ownership, nouns take the possessive form by adding an apostrophe plus *-s* to a singular noun or just an apostrophe to a plural noun: *the horse's owner, the boys' dilemma* (45a).

Often the article *a, an,* or *the* precedes a noun: *a rocket, an astronaut, the launch* (28j and 64c and d). Articles are also known as noun markers or determiners.

FOR MULTILINGUAL WRITERS

Using Count and Noncount Nouns

Is the hill covered with grass or grasses? See 64a for a discussion of count and noncount nouns.

28d Pronouns

Pronouns often take the place of nouns, other pronouns, or other words functioning as a noun. The pronouns serve as short forms so that you do not have to repeat a word or group of words you have already mentioned. A word or group of words that a pronoun replaces or refers to is the antecedent of the pronoun. (See Chapter 33.)

ANTECEDENT   PRONOUN
▶ *Caitlin* **refused the invitation even though** *she* **wanted to go.**

Here are the categories of pronouns:

PERSONAL PRONOUNS
Personal pronouns refer to specific persons or things.

I, me, you, he, she, him, it, we, they

▶ After the scouts made camp, *they* ran along the beach.

POSSESSIVE PRONOUNS

Possessive pronouns are personal pronouns that indicate ownership.

my, mine, your, yours, her, hers, his, its, our, ours, their, theirs

▶ My roommate lost *her* keys.

REFLEXIVE PRONOUNS

Reflexive pronouns refer to the subject of the sentence or clause in which they appear. They end in -*self* or -*selves*.

myself, yourself, himself, herself, itself, oneself, ourselves, yourselves, themselves

▶ The seals sunned *themselves* on the warm rocks.

INTENSIVE PRONOUNS

Intensive pronouns have the same form as reflexive pronouns. They emphasize a noun or another pronoun.

▶ He decided to paint the apartment *himself.*

INDEFINITE PRONOUNS

Indefinite pronouns do not refer to specific nouns, although they may refer to identifiable persons or things. The following is a partial list:

all, another, anybody, both, each, either, everything, few, many, most, neither, none, no one, nothing, one, some, something

▶ *Somebody* screamed when the lights went out.

DEMONSTRATIVE PRONOUNS

Demonstrative pronouns identify or point to specific nouns.

this, that, these, those

▶ *These* are Peter's books.

INTERROGATIVE PRONOUNS

Interrogative pronouns are used to ask questions.

who, which, what

▶ *Who* can help set up the chairs for the meeting?

RELATIVE PRONOUNS

Relative pronouns introduce dependent clauses and relate the dependent clause to the rest of the sentence (28n).

> who, which, that, what, whoever, whichever, whatever

▶ **Maya owns the car** *that* **is parked by the corner.**

The interrogative pronoun *who* and the relative pronouns *who* and *whoever* have different forms depending on how they are used in a sentence (33b).

RECIPROCAL PRONOUNS

Reciprocal pronouns refer to individual parts of a plural antecedent.

> each other, one another

▶ **The business failed because the partners distrusted** *each other.*

28e   Adjectives

Adjectives modify (limit the meaning of) nouns and pronouns, usually by describing, identifying, or quantifying those words. Some people refer to the identifying or quantifying adjectives as *determiners* (64c).

▶ **The** *red* **Corvette ran off the road.** [describes]
▶ *That* **Corvette needs to be repaired.** [identifies]
▶ **We saw** *several* **Corvettes race by.** [quantifies]

In addition to their basic forms, most descriptive adjectives have other forms that allow you to make comparisons: *small, smaller, smallest; foolish, more foolish, most foolish, less foolish, least foolish* (31c). Many of the words that function in some sentences as pronouns (28d) can function as identifying adjectives (or determiners) when they are followed by a noun.

▶ *That* **is a dangerous intersection.** [pronoun]
▶ *That* **intersection is dangerous.** [identifying adjective]

Adjectives usually precede the words they modify, though they may follow linking verbs: *The car was* <u>defective</u>.

Other kinds of identifying or quantifying adjectives are articles (*a, an, the*) and numbers (*three, sixty-fifth*).

Proper adjectives are adjectives formed from or related to proper nouns (*British, Emersonian*). Proper adjectives begin with a capital letter (48b).

28f Adverbs

Adverbs modify verbs, adjectives, other adverbs, or entire clauses. Many adverbs have an *-ly* ending, though some do not (*always, never, very, well*), and some words that end in *-ly* are not adverbs but adjectives (*scholarly, lovely*). One of the most common adverbs is *not*.

▶ Jabari *recently* visited his roommate's family in Maine. [modifies the verb *visited*]

▶ It was an *unexpectedly* exciting trip. [modifies the adjective *exciting*]

▶ He *very* soon discovered lobster. [modifies the adverb *soon*]

▶ *Frankly,* he would have liked to stay another month. [modifies the independent clause that makes up the rest of the sentence]

Many adverbs, like many adjectives, have other forms that can be used to make comparisons: *forcefully, more forcefully, most forcefully, less forcefully, least forcefully* (31c).

Conjunctive adverbs modify an entire clause and help connect the meaning between that clause and the preceding clause (or sentence). Examples of conjunctive adverbs include *however, furthermore, therefore,* and *likewise* (28h).

28g Prepositions

Prepositions are important structural words that express relationships—in time, space, or other senses—between nouns or pronouns and other words in a sentence.

▶ We did not want to leave *during* the game.

▶ The contestants waited nervously *for* the announcement.

▶ Drive *across* the bridge, go *down* the avenue *past* three stoplights, and then turn left *before* the Gulf station.

SOME COMMON PREPOSITIONS

about	at	down	near	since
above	before	during	of	through
across	behind	except	off	toward
after	below	for	on	under
against	beneath	from	onto	until
along	beside	in	out	up
among	between	inside	over	upon
around	beyond	into	past	with
as	by	like	regarding	without

SOME COMPOUND PREPOSITIONS

according to	except for	instead of
as well as	in addition to	next to
because of	in front of	out of
by way of	in place of	with regard to
due to	in spite of	

28h   Conjunctions

Conjunctions connect words or groups of words to each other and tell something about the relationship between these words.

Coordinating conjunctions

Coordinating conjunctions join equivalent structures—two or more nouns, pronouns, verbs, adjectives, adverbs, prepositions, conjunctions, phrases, or clauses (22a).

▶ A strong *but* warm breeze blew across the desert.

▶ Please print *or* type the information on the application form.

▶ Taiwo worked two shifts today, *so* she is tired tonight.

COORDINATING CONJUNCTIONS

and	for	or	yet
but	nor	so	

Correlative conjunctions

Correlative conjunctions join equal elements, and they come in pairs.

▶ *Both* Bechtel *and* Kaiser submitted bids on the project.

▶ Jeff *not only* sent a card *but also* visited me in the hospital.

CORRELATIVE CONJUNCTIONS

both . . . and	neither . . . nor
either . . . or	not only . . . but also
just as . . . so	whether . . . or

Subordinating conjunctions

Subordinating conjunctions introduce adverb clauses and signal the relationship between an adverb clause and another clause, usually an independent clause (22b, 28n). For instance, in the following sentence, the subordinating conjunction *while* signals a time relationship between the two events in the sentence, letting us know that they happened simultaneously:

▶ **Sweat ran down my face *while* I frantically searched for my child.**

SOME SUBORDINATING CONJUNCTIONS

after	if	unless
although	in order that	until
as	once	when
as if	since	where
because	so that	whether
before	than	while
even though	though	

Conjunctive adverbs

Conjunctive adverbs signal a logical relationship between parts of a sentence and, when used with a semicolon, can link independent clauses (28n).

▶ **The cider tasted bitter; *however,* each of us drank a tall glass of it.**
▶ **The cider tasted bitter; each of us, *however,* drank a tall glass of it.**

SOME CONJUNCTIVE ADVERBS

also	indeed	now
anyway	instead	otherwise
besides	likewise	similarly
certainly	meanwhile	still
finally	moreover	then
furthermore	namely	therefore
however	nevertheless	thus
incidentally	next	undoubtedly

28i Interjections

Interjections express surprise or emotion: *oh, ouch, ah, hey.* Interjections often stand alone, as fragments. Even when interjections are part of a sentence, they do not relate grammatically to the rest of the sentence.

▶ **The problem suggested, *alas,* no easy solution.**

28j Articles

The indefinite articles *a* and *an* and the definite article *the* sometimes precede nouns or other words that come before a noun.

▶ *The* **problem suggested no easy solution.**

The precedes a noun.

▶ *The* **difficult problem would not go away.**

The precedes another word that comes before a noun.

In this book, we consider articles another part of speech, but some people consider articles a kind of adjective (28e) or a kind of determiner (64c).

FOR MULTILINGUAL WRITERS

Deciding When Articles Are Necessary

Do you say *I'm at university now* or *I'm at* the *university now*? Deciding when to use the articles *a, an,* and *the* can be challenging for multilingual writers since many languages have nothing directly comparable to them. For help on using articles, see 64d.

PARTS OF SENTENCES

Knowing a word's part of speech helps us understand how to use that word. But we also need to look at the way the word functions in a particular sentence. Consider, for instance, the word *description.*

SUBJECT
▶ **This** *description* **evokes the ecology of the Everglades.**

DIRECT OBJECT
▶ **I need a** *description* **of the ecology of the Everglades.**

Description is a noun in both sentences, yet in the first it serves as the subject of the verb *evokes,* while in the second it serves as the direct object of the verb *need.*

Basic sentence patterns

1. SUBJECT/VERB

S   V
▶ **Babies cry.**

2. SUBJECT/VERB/SUBJECT COMPLEMENT

▶ S   V   SC
Babies seem fragile.

3. SUBJECT/VERB/DIRECT OBJECT

▶ S   V   DO
Babies drink milk.

4. SUBJECT/VERB/INDIRECT OBJECT/DIRECT OBJECT

▶ S   V   IO   DO
Babies give grandparents pleasure.

5. SUBJECT/VERB/DIRECT OBJECT/OBJECT COMPLEMENT

▶ S   V   DO   OC
Babies make parents proud.

28k Subjects

The subject of a sentence identifies what the sentence is about. The simple subject consists of one or more nouns or pronouns; the complete subject consists of the simple subject (ss) with all its modifiers.

┌────── COMPLETE SUBJECT ──────┐
                      ss
▶ *Sailing over the fence, the ball* **crashed through Mr. Wilson's window.**

┌───── COMPLETE SUBJECT ─────┐
  ss
▶ *Stadiums with real grass* **are popular once again.**

┌────── COMPLETE SUBJECT ──────┐
ss
▶ *Those who sit in the bleachers* **have the most fun.**

A compound subject contains two or more simple subjects joined with a coordinating conjunction (*and, but, or*) or a correlative conjunction (*both . . . and, either . . . or, neither . . . nor*).

▶ *Baseball and softball* **developed from cricket.**
▶ *Both baseball and softball* **developed from cricket.**

The subject usually comes before the predicate, or verb, but not always. Sometimes writers reverse this order to achieve a particular effect.

▶ **Up to the plate stepped** *Casey.*

In imperative sentences, which express requests or commands, the subject *you* is almost always implied, not stated.

▶ (*You*) **Keep your eye on the ball.**

In questions and certain other constructions, the subject usually appears between the auxiliary verb (28b) and the main verb.

▶ **Did** *Casey* **save the game?**

In sentences beginning with *there* or *here* followed by a form of *be,* the subject always follows the verb. *There* and *here* in such sentences are never the subject.

▶ **There was no** *joy* **in Mudville.**

28l   Predicates

In addition to a subject, every sentence has a predicate, which asserts or asks something about the subject or tells the subject to do something. The hinge, or key word, of a predicate is the verb. The simple predicate (sp) of a sentence consists of the main verb and any auxiliaries (28b); the complete predicate includes the simple predicate plus any modifiers of the verb and any objects or complements and their modifiers.

```
            ┌──── COMPLETE PREDICATE ────┐
            ┌── SP ──┐
```
▶ **Both of us** *are planning to work at home.*

A compound predicate contains two or more verbs that have the same subject, usually joined by a coordinating or a correlative conjunction.

```
      S   ┌──────── COMPOUND PREDICATE ────────┐
```
▶ **Charles** *shut the book, put it back on the shelf, and sighed.*

```
      ┌── S ──┐┌──── COMPOUND PREDICATE ────┐
```
▶ **The Amish** *neither drive cars nor use electricity.*

On the basis of how they function in predicates, verbs can be divided into three categories: linking, transitive, and intransitive.

Linking verbs

A linking verb links, or joins, a subject with a subject complement. A subject complement is a word or group of words that identifies or describes the subject.

```
      S     V   ┌── SC ──┐
```
▶ **Nastassia is a single mother.**

```
      S   V   SC
```
▶ **She is patient.**

If it identifies the subject, the complement is a noun or pronoun (*a single mother*). If it describes the subject, the complement is an adjective (*patient*).

The forms of *be,* when used as main verbs rather than as auxiliary verbs, are linking verbs (like *are* in this sentence). Other verbs—such as *appear, become, feel, grow, look, make, seem, smell,* and *sound*—can also function as linking verbs, depending on the sense of the sentence.

Transitive verbs

A transitive verb expresses action that is directed toward a noun or pronoun. The noun or pronoun that receives the action is called the direct object of the verb.

▶ I will analyze three poems.

In the preceding example, the subject and verb do not express a complete thought. The direct object completes the thought by saying *what* I will analyze.

A direct object may be followed by an object complement, a word or word group that describes or identifies the direct object. Object complements may be adjectives, as in the next example, or nouns, as in the second example.

▶ I consider Marianne Moore's poetry exquisite.

▶ Her poems and personality made Moore a celebrity.

A transitive verb may also be followed by an indirect object, which tells to whom or what, or for whom or what, the verb's action is done. You might say the indirect object is the recipient of the direct object.

▶ Moore's poems about the Dodgers give me considerable pleasure.

Intransitive verbs

An intransitive verb expresses action that is not directed toward an object. Therefore, an intransitive verb does not have a direct object, though it is often followed by an adverb.

▶ The Red Sox persevered.

▶ Their fans watched helplessly.

The verb *persevered* has no object (it makes no sense to ask, *persevered what?* or *persevered whom?*), and the verb *watched* has an object that is implied but not expressed.

Verbs that can be transitive or intransitive

Some verbs that express action can be only transitive or only intransitive, but most can be used either way, with or without a direct object.

► **A maid wearing a uniform opened the door.**

The verb *opened* is transitive here.

► **The door opened silently.**

The verb *opened* is intransitive here.

28m   Phrases

A phrase is a group of words that lacks either a subject or a predicate or both.

Noun phrases

A noun phrase consists of a noun and all its modifiers. In a sentence, a noun phrase can function as a subject, object, or complement.

► *Delicious, gooey peanut butter* **is surprisingly healthful.**

► **Dieters prefer** *green salad.*

► **A tuna sandwich is** *a popular lunch.*

Verb phrases

A main verb and its auxiliary verbs make up a verb phrase, which can function only one way in a sentence: as a predicate.

► **I** *can swim* **for a long time.**

► **His problem** *might have been caused* **by tension between his parents.**

Prepositional phrases

A prepositional phrase includes a preposition, a noun or pronoun (called the object of the preposition), and any modifiers of the object. Prepositional phrases usually function as adjectives or adverbs.

ADJECTIVE   Our house *in Maine* is a cabin.

ADVERB   *From Cadillac Mountain,* you can see the northern lights.

Verbal phrases

Verbals are verb forms that do not function as verbs. Instead, they function as nouns, adjectives, or adverbs. There are three kinds of verbals: participles, gerunds, and infinitives. A verbal phrase is made up of a verbal and any modifiers, objects, or complements.

PARTICIPIAL PHRASES

Participial phrases always function as adjectives. They can include a present participle (the *crying* child) or a past participle (the *spoken* word).

▶ A dog *howling at the moon* kept me awake.

▶ *Irritated by the delay,* Louise complained.

GERUND PHRASES

A gerund has the same form as a present participle, ending in *-ing*. But gerunds and gerund phrases always function as nouns.

SUBJECT
▶ *Opening their eyes to the problem* was not easy.

DIRECT OBJECT
▶ They suddenly heard *a loud wailing from the sandbox.*

INFINITIVE PHRASES

Infinitive phrases can function as nouns, adjectives, or adverbs. The infinitive is the *to-* form of a verb: *to be, to write.*

ADJECTIVE
▶ A vote would be a good way *to end the meeting.*

ADVERB
▶ *To perfect a draft,* always proofread carefully.

NOUN
▶ *To know him* is a pleasure.

Absolute phrases

Absolute phrases usually include a noun or pronoun and a participle. They modify an entire sentence rather than a particular word. Absolutes may appear almost anywhere in a sentence and are usually set off from the rest of the sentence with commas (42a).

▶ I stood on the deck, *the wind whipping my hair.*

▶ *My fears laid to rest,* I climbed into the plane for my first solo flight.

Appositive phrases

A noun phrase that renames the noun or pronoun immediately preceding it is called an appositive phrase.

▶ The report, *a hefty three-volume work,* included forty-five recommendations.

▶ A single desire, *to change the corporation's policies,* guided our actions.

28n Clauses

A clause is a group of words containing a subject and a predicate. There are two kinds of clauses: independent and dependent.

Independent clauses (also known as main clauses) can stand alone as complete sentences: *The window is open.* Pairs of independent clauses may be joined with a comma and a coordinating conjunction (*and, but, for, or, nor, so,* or *yet*).

▶ The window is open, *so* we'd better be quiet.

Like independent clauses, dependent clauses (also known as subordinate clauses) contain a subject and a predicate. They cannot stand alone as complete sentences, however, for they begin with a subordinating word (22b). Dependent clauses function as nouns, adjectives, or adverbs.

▶ *Because the window is open,* the room feels cool.

In this combination, the subordinating conjunction *because* transforms the independent clause *the window is open* into a dependent adverb clause. In doing so, it indicates a causal relationship between the two clauses.

Noun clauses

Noun clauses can function as subjects, direct objects, subject complements, or objects of prepositions. Thus a noun clause does not stand apart but is always contained within another clause. Noun clauses usually begin with a relative pronoun (*that, which, what, who, whom, whose, whatever, whoever, whomever, whichever*) or with *when, where, whether, why,* or *how.*

> ┌────── S ──────┐
> ▶ *That she had a good job* **was important to him.**

> ┌────── DO ──────┐
> ▶ **He asked** *where she went to college.*

> ┌────── SC ──────┐
> ▶ **The real question was** *why he wanted to know.*

> ┌────── OBJ OF PREP ──────┐
> ▶ **He was looking for** *whatever he could dig up.*

Notice that in each of these sentences the noun clause is an integral part of the independent clause that makes up the sentence. For example, in the second sentence, the independent clause is not just *he asked* but *he asked where she went to college.*

Adjective clauses

Adjective clauses modify nouns and pronouns in other clauses. Usually adjective clauses immediately follow the words they modify. Most of these clauses begin with the relative pronoun *who, whom, whose, that,* or *which.* Some begin with *when, where,* or *why.*

> ▶ **The surgery,** *which took three hours,* **was a complete success.**

> ▶ **It was performed by the surgeon** *who had developed the procedure.*

> ▶ **The hospital was the one** *where I was born.*

Sometimes the relative pronoun introducing an adjective clause may be omitted.

> ▶ **That is one book** *[that] I intend to read.*

Adverb clauses

Adverb clauses modify verbs, adjectives, or other adverbs. They begin with a subordinating conjunction (*after, although, as, as if, because, before, even though, if, in order that, once, since, so that, than, though, unless, until, when, where, whether, while*).

▶ We hiked *where there were few other hikers.*

▶ My backpack felt heavier *than it ever had.*

▶ I climbed as swiftly *as I could under the weight of my backpack.*

TYPES OF SENTENCES

Like words, sentences can be classified in different ways: grammatically and functionally.

28o   Classifying sentences grammatically

Grammatically, sentences may be classified as simple, compound, complex, and compound-complex.

Simple sentences

A simple sentence consists of one independent clause and no dependent clause.

┌────────────INDEPENDENT CLAUSE────────────┐
▶ **The trailer is surrounded by a wooden deck.**

Compound sentences

A compound sentence consists of two or more independent clauses and no dependent clause. The clauses may be joined by a comma and a coordinating conjunction (*and, but, or, nor, for, so, yet*) or by a semicolon.

┌──────────IND CLAUSE──────────┐ ┌──────────IND CLAUSE──────────┐
▶ **Occasionally, a car goes up the dirt trail, and dust flies everywhere.**

┌──────────IND CLAUSE──────────┐ ┌──────────IND CLAUSE──────────┐
▶ **Angelo is obsessed with soccer; he eats, breathes, and lives the game.**

Complex sentences

A complex sentence consists of one independent clause and at least one dependent clause.

┌──────IND CLAUSE──────┐ ┌──────DEP CLAUSE──────┐
▶ **Many people believe that anyone can earn a living.**

Compound-complex sentences

A compound-complex sentence consists of two or more independent clauses and at least one dependent clause.

⌐——IND CLAUSE——⌐——DEP CLAUSE——⌐——IND CLAUSE——⌐
▶ **I complimented Luis when he finished the job, and he seemed pleased.**

⌐————IND CLAUSE————⌐ ⌐————IND CLAUSE————⌐
▶ **Sister Lucy tried her best to help Martin, but he was an undisciplined**
⌐————DEP CLAUSE————⌐
boy who drove many teachers to despair.

28p Classifying sentences functionally

In terms of function, sentences can be classified as declarative (making a statement), interrogative (asking a question), imperative (giving a command), or exclamatory (expressing strong feeling).

DECLARATIVE	He sings with the Grace Church Boys Choir.
INTERROGATIVE	How long has he sung with them?
IMPERATIVE	Comb his hair before the performance starts.
EXCLAMATORY	What voices those boys have!

bedfordstmartins.com/everyday_writer For exercises, go to **Exercise Central** and click on **Basic Grammar.**

29

Verbs

Restaurant menus are often a good source of verbs in action. One famous place in Boston, for instance, offers to bake, broil, pan-fry, deep-fry, poach, sauté, fricassee, blacken, or scallop any of the fish entrees on its menu. To someone ordering—or cooking—at this restaurant, the important distinctions lie entirely in the verbs.

When used skillfully, verbs can be the heartbeat of prose, moving it along, enlivening it, carrying its action. This chapter will help you use verbs in all these ways. (See Chapter 30 for advice on subject-verb agreement and Chapter 65 for more about verbs for multilingual writers.)

Editing the Verbs in Your Own Writing

- If you have trouble with verb endings, review the rules for using them in 29a and c.
- Double-check forms of *lie* and *lay, sit* and *set, rise* and *raise.* See that the words you use are appropriate for your meaning. (29d)
- If you are writing about a literary work, remember to refer to the action in the work in the present tense. (29e)
- If you have problems with verb tenses, use the guidelines on p. 236 to check your verbs.
- Check all uses of the passive voice for appropriateness. (29g)
- Check all verbs used to introduce quotations, paraphrases, and summaries. If you rely on *say, write,* and other very general verbs, try substituting more vivid, specific verbs (*claim, insist,* and *wonder,* for instance).

29a The five forms of verbs

Except for *be,* all English verbs have five forms.

BASE FORM	PAST TENSE	PAST PARTICIPLE	PRESENT PARTICIPLE	-S FORM
talk	talked	talked	talking	talks
adore	adored	adored	adoring	adores

BASE FORM	We often *go* to Legal Sea Foods.
PAST TENSE	Grandpa always *ordered* bluefish.
PAST PARTICIPLE	Grandma has *tried* the oyster stew.
PRESENT PARTICIPLE	Juanita is *getting* the shrimp platter.
-S FORM	The chowder *needs* salt and pepper.

-s *and* -es *endings*

Except with *be* and *have,* the *-s* form consists of the base form plus *-s* or *-es.* This form indicates action in the present for third-person singular subjects. All singular nouns; the personal pronouns *he, she,* and *it;* and many other pronouns (such as *this, anyone, everything,* or *someone*) are third-person singular.

	SINGULAR	PLURAL
FIRST PERSON	I *wish*	we *wish*
SECOND PERSON	you *wish*	you *wish*
THIRD PERSON	he/she/it *wishes*	they *wish*
	Joe *wishes*	children *wish*
	someone *wishes*	many *wish*

Forms of be

Be has three forms in the present tense and two in the past tense.

BASE FORM	be
PAST PARTICIPLE	been
PRESENT PARTICIPLE	being
PRESENT TENSE	I *am,* he/she/it *is,* we/you/they *are*
PAST TENSE	I/he/she/it *was,* we/you/they *were*

A MATTER OF STYLE

Everyday Use of *Be*

My sister at work. She be there every day 'til five.

The first sentence shows the absence of *be;* the second shows the use of "habitual *be,*" indicating that something is usually the case. In academic English, these sentences would read *My sister is at work. She is there every day until five.*

You may well have occasion to quote dialogue featuring such usages of *be* in your own writing; doing so can be a good way to evoke particular regions or communities. (For help on using varieties of English appropriately, see Chapter 38.)

29b Use the appropriate auxiliary verbs.

Auxiliary verbs are used with a base form, present participle, or past participle to form verb tenses, questions, and negatives. The most common auxiliaries are forms of *be, do,* and *have.*

▶ We *have considered* all viewpoints.

▶ The problem *is ranking* them fairly.

▶ Do you *know* the answer? No, I *do* not *know* it.

Modal auxiliaries—*can, could, might, may, must, ought to, shall, will, should, would*—indicate future actions, possibility, necessity, obligation, and so on.

▶ You *can see* three states from the top of the mountain.

▶ She *should visit* this spot more often.

FOR MULTILINGUAL WRITERS

Using Modal Auxiliaries

Why do we not say "Alice can to read Latin"? For a discussion of *can* and other modal auxiliaries, see 65a.

29c Regular and irregular verb forms

A verb is regular when its past tense and past participle are formed by adding *-ed* or *-d* to the base form.

BASE FORM	PAST TENSE	PAST PARTICIPLE
love	loved	loved
honor	honored	honored
obey	obeyed	obeyed

A verb is irregular when it does not follow the *-ed* or *-d* pattern. If you are unsure about whether a verb form is regular or irregular, or what the correct form is, consult the following list or a dictionary. Dictionaries list any irregular forms under the entry for the base form.

Some common irregular verbs

BASE FORM	PAST TENSE	PAST PARTICIPLE
arise	arose	arisen
be	was/were	been
beat	beat	beaten
become	became	become
begin	began	begun

BASE FORM	PAST TENSE	PAST PARTICIPLE
bite	bit	bitten, bit
blow	blew	blown
break	broke	broken
bring	brought	brought
build	built	built
burn	burned, burnt	burned, burnt
burst	burst	burst
buy	bought	bought
catch	caught	caught
choose	chose	chosen
come	came	come
cost	cost	cost
dig	dug	dug
dive	dived, dove	dived
do	did	done
draw	drew	drawn
dream	dreamed, dreamt	dreamed, dreamt
drink	drank	drunk
drive	drove	driven
eat	ate	eaten
fall	fell	fallen
fight	fought	fought
find	found	found
fly	flew	flown
forget	forgot	forgotten, forgot
freeze	froze	frozen
get	got	gotten, got
give	gave	given
go	went	gone
grow	grew	grown
hang (suspend)[1]	hung	hung
have	had	had
hear	heard	heard
hide	hid	hidden

---

[1]*Hang* meaning "execute by hanging" is regular: *hang, hanged, hanged.*

BASE FORM	PAST TENSE	PAST PARTICIPLE
hit	hit	hit
keep	kept	kept
know	knew	known
lay	laid	laid
lead	led	led
lend	lent	lent
let	let	let
lie (recline)[2]	lay	lain
lose	lost	lost
make	made	made
mean	meant	meant
meet	met	met
prove	proved	proved, proven
read	read	read
ride	rode	ridden
ring	rang	rung
rise	rose	risen
run	ran	run
say	said	said
see	saw	seen
send	sent	sent
set	set	set
shake	shook	shaken
shoot	shot	shot
show	showed	showed, shown
shrink	shrank	shrunk
sing	sang	sung
sink	sank	sunk
sit	sat	sat
sleep	slept	slept
speak	spoke	spoken
spring	sprang, sprung	sprung
stand	stood	stood

---

[2] *Lie* meaning "tell a falsehood" is regular: *lie, lied, lied.*

BASE FORM	PAST TENSE	PAST PARTICIPLE
steal	stole	stolen
strike	struck	struck, stricken
swim	swam	swum
swing	swung	swung
take	took	taken
tear	tore	torn
throw	threw	thrown
wake	woke, waked	waked, woken
wear	wore	worn
write	wrote	written

29d Distinguish between *lie* and *lay, sit* and *set, rise* and *raise.*

These pairs of verbs cause confusion because both verbs in each pair have similar-sounding forms and somewhat related meanings. In each pair, one of the verbs is transitive, meaning that it is followed by a direct object (*I lay the package on the counter*). The other is intransitive, meaning that it does not have an object (*He lies on the floor unable to move*). The best way to avoid confusing these verbs is to memorize their forms and meanings.

BASE FORM	PAST TENSE	PAST PARTICIPLE	PRESENT PARTICIPLE	-S FORM
lie (recline)	lay	lain	lying	lies
lay (put)	laid	laid	laying	lays
sit (be seated)	sat	sat	sitting	sits
set (put)	set	set	setting	sets
rise (get up)	rose	risen	rising	rises
raise (lift)	raised	raised	raising	raises

▶ The doctor asked the patient to ~~lay~~ *lie* on his side.

▶ She ~~sat~~ *set* the vase on the table.

▶ He ~~rose~~ *raised* himself to a sitting position.

29e   Verb tenses

Tenses show when the action expressed by a verb takes place. The three simple tenses are the present tense, the past tense, and the future tense.

PRESENT TENSE	I *ask, write*
PAST TENSE	I *asked, wrote*
FUTURE TENSE	I *will ask, will write*

More complex aspects of time are expressed through progressive, perfect, and perfect progressive forms of the simple tenses.

PRESENT PROGRESSIVE	she *is asking, is writing*
PAST PROGRESSIVE	she *was asking, was writing*
FUTURE PROGRESSIVE	she *will be asking, will be writing*
PRESENT PERFECT	she *has asked, has written*
PAST PERFECT	she *had asked, had written*
FUTURE PERFECT	she *will have asked, will have written*
PRESENT PERFECT PROGRESSIVE	she *has been asking, has been writing*
PAST PERFECT PROGRESSIVE	she *had been asking, had been writing*
FUTURE PERFECT PROGRESSIVE	she *will have been asking, will have been writing*

The simple tenses locate an action only within the three basic time frames of present, past, and future. Progressive forms express *continuing* actions; perfect forms express actions *completed* before another action or time in the present, past, or future; perfect progressive forms express actions that *continue up to some point* in the present, past, or future.

Present tense

SIMPLE PRESENT

Use the simple present to indicate actions occurring now and those occurring habitually.

▶ I *eat* breakfast every day at 8:00 AM.

▶ Love *conquers* all.

When writing about action in literary works, use the simple present.

▶ Ishmael slowly ~~came~~ comes to realize all that ~~was~~ is at stake in the search for the white whale.

General truths or scientific facts should be in the simple present, even when the predicate of the sentence is in the past tense.

▶ Pasteur demonstrated that his boiling process ~~made~~ *makes* milk safe.

When you are quoting, summarizing, or paraphrasing a work, in general use the present tense.

▶ Keith Walters ~~wrote~~ *writes* that the "reputed consequences and promised blessings of literacy are legion."

But in an essay using APA (American Psychological Association) style, the reporting of your experiments or another researcher's work should be in the past tense (*wrote, noted*) or the present perfect (*has reported*). (See Chapter 56.)

▶ Comer (1995) ~~notes~~ *noted* that protesters who deprive themselves of food (for example, Gandhi) are seen not as dysfunctional but rather as "caring, sacrificing, even heroic" (p. 5).

PRESENT PROGRESSIVE

Use the present progressive to indicate actions that are ongoing in the present: *You are driving too fast.*

PRESENT PERFECT

Use the present perfect to indicate actions begun in the past and either completed at some unspecified time in the past or continuing into the present: *Uncontrolled logging has destroyed many forests.*

PRESENT PERFECT PROGRESSIVE

Use the present perfect progressive to indicate an ongoing action begun in the past and continuing into the present: *The two sides have been trying to settle the case out of court.*

Past tense

SIMPLE PAST

Use the simple past to indicate actions that occurred at a specific time and do not extend into the present: *Germany invaded Poland on September 1, 1939.*

PAST PROGRESSIVE

Use the past progressive to indicate continuing actions in the past: *Lenin was living in exile in Zurich when the tsar was overthrown.*

PAST PERFECT

Use the past perfect to indicate actions that were completed by a specific time in the past or before some other past action occurred: *By the fourth century, Christianity had become the state religion.*

PAST PERFECT PROGRESSIVE

Use the past perfect progressive to indicate continuing actions in the past that began before a specific time or before some other past action began: *Carter had been planning a naval career until his father died.*

Future tense

SIMPLE FUTURE

Use the simple future to indicate actions that have yet to begin: *The Vermeer show will come to Washington in September.*

FUTURE PROGRESSIVE

Use the future progressive to indicate continuing actions in the future: *The loans will be coming due in the next two years.*

FUTURE PERFECT

Use the future perfect to indicate actions that will be completed by a specified time in the future: *In ten years, your investment will have doubled.*

AT A GLANCE

Editing Verb Tenses

If you have trouble with verb tenses, make a point of checking for these common errors as you proofread.

- Errors of verb form: writing *seen* for *saw,* for example, which is an instance of confusing the past-participle and past-tense forms. (29c)
- Errors in tense: using the simple past (*Uncle Charlie arrived*) when meaning requires the present perfect (*Uncle Charlie has arrived*). (29e)
- Other errors result from using a regional or ethnic variety of English (*she nervous*) in situations calling for standard academic English (*she is nervous*). (See Chapter 38.)

FUTURE PERFECT PROGRESSIVE

Use the future perfect progressive to indicate continuing actions that will be completed by some specified time in the future: *In May, I will* <u>have been working</u> *at IBM for five years.*

29f Sequence verb tenses accurately.

Careful and accurate use of tenses is important for clear writing. Even the simplest narrative describes actions that take place at different times. When you use the appropriate tense for each action, readers can follow such time changes easily.

> *had*
> ▶ By the time he lent her the money, she ^ declared bankruptcy.

The original sentence suggests that the two events occurred at the same time; the revised sentence makes clear that the bankruptcy occurred before the loan.

Use an infinitive (*to* plus a base form: *to go*) to indicate actions occurring at the same time as or later than the action of the predicate verb.

> *to plant*
> ▶ We had hoped ~~to have planted~~ our garden by now.
> ^

The action of the infinitive *to plant* follows that of the sentence's main verb (*had hoped*).

Use a present participle (base form plus *-ing*) to indicate actions occurring at the same time as that of the predicate verb.

> ▶ Seeking to relieve unemployment, Roosevelt established several public works programs.

The seeking and establishment of the programs occurred simultaneously.

A past participle or a present-perfect participle (*having* plus a past participle) indicates actions occurring before that of the predicate verb.

> *Flown*
> ▶ ~~Flying~~ to the front, the troops joined their hard-pressed comrades.
> ^

The past participle *flown* shows that the flying occurred before the joining.

> *Having crushed*
> ▶ ~~Crushing~~ all opposition at home, he launched a war of conquest.
> ^

He launched the war after he crushed the opposition.

One common error is to use *would* in both clauses of a sentence with an *if* clause. Use *would* only in one clause.

>   *had*
> ▶ If I ~~would have~~ played harder, I would have won.
>   ^

29g   Use active voice and passive voice appropriately.

Voice tells whether a subject is acting (*He questions us*) or being acted upon (*He is questioned*). When the subject is acting, the verb is in the active voice; when the subject is being acted upon, the verb is in the passive voice. Most contemporary writers use the active voice as much as possible because it livens up their prose.

> PASSIVE   Huge pine trees *were uprooted* by the storm.
>
> ACTIVE   The storm *uprooted* huge pine trees.

The passive voice can work to good advantage in some situations. Newspaper reporters often use the passive voice to protect the confidentiality of their sources, as in the familiar expression *it is reported that.* You can also use the passive voice when you want to emphasize the recipient of an action rather than the performer of the action.

> DALLAS, NOV. 22—President John Fitzgerald Kennedy was shot and killed by an assassin today.   —TOM WICKER, *New York Times*

Wicker uses the passive voice with good reason: to focus on Kennedy, not on who killed him.

To shift a sentence from passive to active voice, make the performer of the action the subject of the sentence.

>   *Researchers told the*
> ▶ ~~The~~ test administrator ~~was told~~ to give students an electric shock
>   ^
>   *they gave*
> each time a wrong answer • ~~was given.~~
>   ^   ^

A MATTER OF STYLE

Technical and Scientific Writing

Much technical and scientific writing uses the passive voice effectively to highlight what is being studied rather than who is doing the studying. Look at the following example, from a description of geological movement:

> The Earth's plates are created where they separate and are recycled where they collide, in a continuous process of creation and destruction.
>   —FRANK PRESS AND RAYMOND SIEVER, *Understanding Earth*

29h Select the appropriate mood.

The mood of a verb indicates the attitude of the writer toward what he or she is saying. The indicative mood states facts or opinions and asks questions: *I did the right thing.* The imperative mood gives commands and instructions: *Do the right thing.* The subjunctive mood (used primarily in dependent clauses beginning with *that* or *if*) expresses wishes and conditions that are contrary to fact: *If I were doing the right thing, I'd know it.*

Forming and using the subjunctive

The present subjunctive uses the base form of the verb with all subjects.

▶ It is important that children *be* psychologically ready for a new sibling.

The past subjunctive is the same as the simple past except for the verb *be,* which uses *were* for all subjects.

▶ He spent money as if he *had* infinite credit.
▶ If the store *were* better located, it would attract more customers.

Because the subjunctive creates a rather formal tone, many people today tend to substitute the indicative mood in informal conversation.

▶ If the store *was* better located, it would attract more customers.

For academic or professional writing, use the subjunctive in the following contexts:

CLAUSES EXPRESSING A WISH

▶ He wished that his mother ~~was~~ still living nearby.
                                were

THAT CLAUSES EXPRESSING A REQUEST OR DEMAND

▶ The job demands that employees ~~are~~ in good physical condition.
                                   be

IF CLAUSES EXPRESSING A CONDITION THAT DOES NOT EXIST

▶ If the federal government ~~was~~ to ban the sale of tobacco, tobacco
                             were
companies and distributors would suffer a great loss.

FOR MULTILINGUAL WRITERS

Using the Subjunctive

"If you were to practice writing every day, it would eventually seem much easier to you." For a discussion of this and other uses of the subjunctive, see 67g.

---

bedfordstmartins.com/everyday_writer For exercises, go to **Exercise Central** and click on **Verbs.**

30

Subject-Verb Agreement

In everyday terms, the word *agreement* refers to an accord of some sort: you reach an agreement with your boss about salary; friends agree to go to a movie; the members of a family agree to share household chores. This meaning covers grammatical agreement as well. In the present tense, verbs agree with their subjects in number (singular or plural) and in person (first, second, or third). This chapter will take a closer look at subject-verb agreement.

30a Make verbs agree with third-person singular subjects.

To make a verb in the present tense agree with a third-person singular subject, add *-s* or *-es* to the base form.

▶ A vegetarian diet *lowers* the risk of heart disease.

▶ What you eat *affects* your health.

> In the preceding example, the subject is the noun clause *what you eat*. The clause is singular, so the base form of the verb *affect* takes an *-s*.

To make a verb in the present tense agree with any other subject, use the base form of the verb.

▶ I *miss* my family.

▶ They *live* in another state.

AT A GLANCE

Editing for Subject-Verb Agreement

- Check your drafts verb by verb, and identify the subject that goes with each verb.

  are
▶ **The players on our side is sure to win.**
     ^

  Because the simple subject here is plural—*players*—the verb needs to be *are*. When you take away the words between the subject and the verb, it is easier to identify agreement problems. (30b)

- Check compound subjects. Those joined by *and* usually take a plural verb. With those subjects joined by *or* or *nor*, however, the verb agrees with the part of the subject closer or closest to the verb. *Neither Claire's parents nor Claire plans to vote.* (30c)

- Check collective-noun subjects. These nouns take a singular verb when they refer to a group as a single unit, but they take a plural verb when they refer to the multiple members of a group. *The crowd screams its support.* (30d)

- Check indefinite-pronoun subjects. Most take a singular verb. (*Both, few, many, others,* and *several* take a plural verb.) *Each of the singers rehearses for three hours daily.* (30e)

Have and *be* do not follow the *-s* or *-es* pattern with third-person singular subjects. *Have* changes to *has; be* has irregular forms in both the present and past tenses (29a).

▶ **War *is* hell.**

▶ **The soldier *was* brave beyond the call of duty.**

30b Make subjects and verbs agree when separated by other words.

Make sure the verb agrees with the subject and not with another noun that falls in between.

▶ **A vase of flowers *makes* a room attractive.**

  have
▶ **Many books on the best-seller list has little literary value.**
                                      ^

  The simple subject is *books,* not *list.*

The phrases as well as, along with, in addition to, together with

Be careful when you use these and other similar phrases. They do not make a singular subject plural.

> *was*
> ▶ A passenger, as well as the driver, ~~were~~ injured in the accident.
>   ^

> Though this sentence has a grammatically singular subject, it suggests the idea of a plural subject. The sentence makes better sense with a compound subject: *The driver and a passenger were injured in the accident.*

30c   Make verbs agree with compound subjects.

> *were*
> ▶ A backpack, a canteen, and a rifle ~~was~~ issued to each recruit.
>   ^

When subjects joined by *and* are considered a single unit or refer to the same person or thing, they take a singular verb form.

> ▶ George W. Bush's close friend and political ally *is* his brother.

> *remains*
> ▶ Drinking and driving ~~remain~~ a major cause of highway accidents
>   ^
> and fatalities.

> In this sentence, *drinking and driving* is considered a single activity, and a singular verb is used.

If the word *each* or *every* precedes subjects joined by *and,* the verb form is singular.

> ▶ Each boy and girl *chooses* one gift to take home.

With subjects joined by *or* or *nor,* the verb agrees with the part closer or closest to the verb.

> ▶ Neither my roommate nor my neighbors *like* my loud music.

> ▶ Either the witnesses or the defendant *is* lying.

> If you find this sentence awkward, put the plural noun closer to the verb: *Either the defendant or the witnesses are lying.*

30d Make verbs agree with subjects that are collective nouns.

Collective nouns—such as *family, team, audience, group, jury, crowd, band, class,* and *committee*—refer to a group. Collective nouns can take either singular or plural verbs, depending on whether they refer to the group as a single unit or to the multiple members of the group. The meaning of a sentence as a whole is your guide to whether a collective noun refers to a unit or to the multiple parts of a unit.

▶ After deliberating, the jury *reports* its verdict.

  The jury acts as a single unit.

▶ The jury still *disagree* on a number of counts.

  The members of the jury act as multiple individuals.

  scatter
▶ The family of ducklings ~~scatters~~ when the cat approaches.

  Family here refers to the many ducks; they cannot scatter as one.

Numerical subjects

When the subject is a quantity, treat it as singular if you are thinking about it as a single unit or amount.

▶ A million years *is* nothing, geologically speaking.
▶ The million dollars *has* earned a handsome interest.
▶ Five miles *is* more than I can run.
▶ Two-thirds of the park *has* burned.

  Two-thirds refers to the single portion of the park that burned.

▶ Two-thirds of the students *were* commuters.

  Two-thirds here refers to the students who commuted as many individuals.

Pairs

Even though eyeglasses, scissors, pants, and other such words refer to single items, they take plural verbs because they are made up of pairs.

▶ My jeans *need* washing.
▶ Where *are* my reading glasses?

The phrases the number of, a number of

Treat phrases starting with *the number of* as singular and with *a number of* as plural.

SINGULAR   The number of applicants for the internship *was* unbelievable.

PLURAL   A number of applicants *were* put on the waiting list.

30e Make verbs agree with indefinite-pronoun subjects.

Indefinite pronouns are those that do not refer to specific persons or things. Most take singular verb forms.

SOME COMMON INDEFINITE PRONOUNS

another	each	much	one
any	either	neither	other
anybody	everybody	nobody	somebody
anyone	everyone	no one	someone
anything	everything	nothing	something

▶ Of the two jobs, neither *holds* much appeal.

depicts
▶ Each of the plays ~~depict~~ a hero undone by a tragic flaw.

Both, few, many, others, and *several* are plural.

▶ Though many *apply*, few *are* chosen.

All, any, enough, more, most, none, and *some* can be singular or plural, depending on the noun they refer to.

▶ All of the cake *was* eaten.

▶ All of the candidates *promise* to improve the schools.

30f Make verbs agree with the antecedents of *who, which,* and *that.*

When the relative pronouns *who, which,* and *that* are used as a subject, the verb agrees with the antecedent of the pronoun.

▶ Fear is an ingredient that *goes* into creating stereotypes.

▶ Guilt and fear are ingredients that *go* into creating stereotypes.

Problems often occur with the words *one of the.* In general, *one of the* takes a plural verb, while *the only one of the* takes a singular verb.

               work
▶ Carla is one of the employees who always ~~works~~ overtime.

    Some employees always work overtime. Carla is among them. Thus *who* refers to *employees,* and the verb is plural.

                   works
▶ Ming is the only one of the employees who always ~~work~~ overtime.

    Only one employee always works overtime, and that employee is Ming. Thus *one,* and not *employees,* is the antecedent of *who,* and the verb form must be singular.

30g Make linking verbs agree with their subjects, not with their complements.

A linking verb should agree with its subject, which usually precedes the verb, not with the subject complement, that follows it.

             are
▶ The signings of three key treaties ~~is~~ the topic of my talk.

    The subject is *signings,* not *topic.*

          was
▶ Nero Wolfe's passion ~~were~~ orchids.

    The subject is *passion,* not *orchids.*

30h Make verbs agree with subjects that are plural in form but singular in meaning.

Some words that end in *-s* seem to be plural but are singular in meaning and thus take singular verbs.

     strikes
▶ Measles still ~~strike~~ many Americans.

Some nouns of this kind (such as *statistics* and *politics*) may be either singular or plural, depending on context.

    SINGULAR   Statistics *is* a course I really dread.

    PLURAL   The statistics in that study *are* highly questionable.

30i Make verbs agree with subjects that follow them.

In English, verbs usually follow subjects. When this order is reversed, make the verb agree with the subject, not with a noun that happens to precede it.

▶ Beside the barn ~~stands~~ silos filled with grain.
stand

The subject is *silos;* it is plural, so the verb must be *stand.*

In sentences beginning with *there is* or *there are* (or *there was* or *were*), *there* serves only as an introductory word; the subject follows the verb.

▶ There *are* five basic positions in classical ballet.

The subject, *positions,* is plural, so the verb must also be plural.

30j Make verbs agree with titles and words used as words.

▶ *One Writer's Beginnings* ~~describe~~ Eudora Welty's childhood.
describes

▶ *Steroids* ~~are~~ a little word that packs a big punch in the world of sports.
is

bedfordstmartins.com/everyday_writer For exercises, go to **Exercise Central** and click on **Subject-Verb Agreement**.

31

Adjectives and Adverbs

Adjectives and adverbs often bring indispensable differences in meaning to the words they modify. In basketball, for example, there is an important difference between a *flagrant* foul and a *technical* foul, a layup and a *reverse* layup, and an *angry* coach and an *out-of-control* coach. In each instance, the modifiers are crucial to accurate communication.

Adjectives modify nouns and pronouns; they answer the questions *which? how many?* and *what kind?* Adverbs modify verbs, adjectives, and other adverbs; they answer the questions *how? when? where?* and *to what extent?* Many adverbs are formed by adding *-ly* to adjectives (*slight, slightly*), but many adverbs are formed in other ways (*outdoors*) or have forms of their own (*very*).

AT A GLANCE

Editing Adjectives and Adverbs

- Carefully scrutinize each adjective and adverb in your writing to see whether it's the best word possible. Considering one or two synonyms for each adjective or adverb should help you decide.

- Is each adjective necessary? Would a more specific noun eliminate the need for an adjective (*mansion* rather than *enormous house*, for instance)? Follow this same line of inquiry with the verbs and adverbs in your writing.

- Look for places where you might make your writing more specific or vivid by adding an adjective or adverb.

- Check that adjectives modify only nouns and pronouns and that adverbs modify only verbs, adjectives, and other adverbs. (31b) Check especially for proper use of *good* and *well*, *bad* and *badly*, *real* and *really*. (31b and c)

- Are all comparisons complete? (31c)

- If English is not your first language, check that adjectives are in the right order. (64e)

31a Use adjectives after linking verbs.

When adjectives come after linking verbs, they usually serve as a subject complement, to describe the subject: *I am patient.* Note that in specific sentences, some verbs may or may not be linking verbs—*appear, become, feel, grow, look, make, prove, seem, smell, sound,* and *taste,* for instance. When a word following one of these verbs modifies the subject, use an adjective; when it modifies the verb, use an adverb.

ADJECTIVE   Otis Thorpe looked *angry.*

ADVERB   He looked *angrily* at the referee.

Linking verbs suggest a state of being, not an action. In the preceding examples, *looked angry* suggests the state of being angry; *looked angrily* suggests an angry action.

FOR MULTILINGUAL WRITERS

Using Adjectives with Plural Nouns

In Spanish, Russian, and many other languages, adjectives agree in number with the nouns they modify. In English, adjectives do not change number this way: *her dogs are small* (not *smalls*). However, there is an exception; before a noun, the adjectives *this, that, those,* and *these* change from singular to plural depending on the noun that follows: *this dog, these dogs.*

31b   Use adverbs to modify verbs, adjectives, and adverbs.

In everyday conversation, you will often hear (and perhaps use) adjectives in place of adverbs. For example, people often say *go quick* instead of *go quickly.* When you write in standard academic English, however, use adverbs to modify verbs, adjectives, and other adverbs.

▶ You can feel the song's meter if you listen ~~careful~~.
                                                         carefully.

▶ The audience was ~~real~~ disappointed by the show.
                    really

Good, well, bad, *and* badly

The modifiers *good, well, bad,* and *badly* cause problems for many writers because the distinctions between *good* and *well* and between *bad* and *badly* are often not observed in conversation. Problems also arise because *well* can function as either an adjective or an adverb. Furthermore, *well* appears in sentences about physical health, but *good* and *bad* show up in sentences about emotional health.

Good *and* well

▶ I look ~~well~~ in blue.
         good

This sentence contains a linking verb, so it requires an adjective. But the adjective *well* refers to physical health, which is not the context of this sentence.

well
▶ Now that the fever has broken, I feel ~~good~~ again.
  ^

  As an adjective, *well* means "in good physical health," so the sentence calls for *well*, not *good.*

good
▶ I'm feeling ~~well~~ about the math final.
  ^

  This sentence is about an emotional state, so it requires the adjective *good.*

well
▶ He plays the trumpet ~~good~~.
  ^

Bad *and* badly

bad   *badly.*
▶ I feel ~~badly~~ for the Toronto fans. Their team played ~~bad.~~
  ^   ^

  The first of the two sentences is about the speaker's emotional health, so it requires the adjective *bad.*

FOR MULTILINGUAL WRITERS

Determining Adjective Sequence

Should you write *these beautiful blue kitchen tiles* or *these blue beautiful kitchen tiles*? See 64e for guidelines on adjective sequence.

31c Comparatives and superlatives

Most adjectives and adverbs have three forms: positive, comparative, and superlative.

POSITIVE	COMPARATIVE	SUPERLATIVE
large	larger	largest
early	earlier	earliest
careful	more careful	most careful
happily	more happily	most happily

▶ Canada is *larger* than the United States.
▶ My son needs to be *more careful* with his money.
▶ They are the *most happily* married couple I know.

As these examples show, you usually form the comparative and superlative of one- or two-syllable adjectives by adding *-er* and *-est*: *short, shorter, shortest.* With some two-syllable adjectives, with longer adjectives, and with most adverbs, use *more* and *most*: *scientific, more scientific, most scientific; elegantly, more elegantly, most elegantly.*

Irregular adjectives and adverbs

Some short adjectives and adverbs have irregular comparative and superlative forms.

POSITIVE	COMPARATIVE	SUPERLATIVE
good	better	best
well	better	best
bad, badly	worse	worst
little (quantity)	less	least
many, much	more	most

Comparatives vs. superlatives

Use the comparative to compare two things; use the superlative to compare three or more things.

▶ Rome is a much *older* city than New York.

　　　　　　　　　　　　　oldest
▶ Damascus is one of the ~~older~~ cities in the world.
　　　　　　　　　　　　　　 ^

Double comparatives and superlatives

Double comparatives and superlatives are those that unnecessarily use both the *-er* or *-est* ending and *more* or *most*. Occasionally, these forms can act to build a special emphasis, as in the title of Spike Lee's movie *Mo' Better Blues.* In academic and professional writing, however, do not use *more* or *most* before adjectives or adverbs ending in *-er* or *-est*.

▶ Paris is the ~~most~~ loveliest city in the world.

　　　　　　　 much
▶ Rome lasted ~~more~~ longer than Carthage.
　　　　　　　　 ^

Incomplete comparisons

In speaking, we sometimes state only part of a comparison because the context makes the meaning clear. For example, after comparing your car with a friend's, you might say "Yours is better," but the context makes it clear that you mean "Yours is better *than mine.*" In writing, such a context may not exist. So, when editing, take the time to check for incomplete comparisons—and to complete them if they are unclear.

▶ The patients taking the drug appeared healthier. *than those receiving a placebo.*

Absolute concepts

Some adjectives and adverbs—such as *perfect, final,* and *unique*—are absolute concepts, so it is illogical to form comparatives or superlatives of these words.

▶ The patient felt compelled to have ~~more~~ perfect control over his thoughts.

▶ Anne has ~~the most~~ *a* unique sense of humor.

A MATTER OF STYLE

Multiple Negation

Speakers of English sometimes use more than one negative at a time— saying, for instance, "I can't hardly see you." Multiple negatives, in fact, have a long history in English and can be found in the works of Chaucer and Shakespeare. It was only in the eighteenth century, in an effort to make English more uniform, that double negatives came to be seen as incorrect.

The use of double negatives for emphasis is very popular in many areas of the South. Someone might say, for example, "Can't nothing be done." Emphatic double negatives—and triple, quadruple, and more— are used by many speakers of African American vernacular English, who may say, for instance, "Don't none of my people come from up North."

Even though they occur in many varieties of English (and in many other languages, including French and Russian), multiple negatives are not characteristic of academic English. In academic or professional writing, you may well have reason to quote passages that include multiple negatives—whether you're quoting Shakespeare, Toni Morrison, or your grandmother—but you will play it safe if you avoid other uses of multiple negatives.

---

bedfordstmartins.com/everyday_writer For exercises, go to **Exercise Central** and click on **Adjectives and Adverbs.**

32

Modifier Placement

Modifiers enrich writing by making it more concrete or vivid, often adding important or even essential details. To be effective, modifiers should refer clearly to the words they modify and be positioned close to those words. Consider, for example, a sign seen recently in a hotel:

> DO NOT USE THE ELEVATORS IN CASE OF FIRE.

Should we really avoid the elevators altogether for fear of causing a fire? Repositioning the modifier *in case of fire* eliminates such confusion—and makes clear that we are to avoid the elevators only if there is a fire: IN CASE OF FIRE, DO NOT USE THE ELEVATORS. This chapter reviews the conventions of accurate modifier placement.

AT A GLANCE

Editing Misplaced or Dangling Modifiers

1. Identify all the modifiers in each sentence, and draw an arrow from each modifier to the word it modifies.

2. If a modifier is far from the word it modifies, try to move the two closer together. (32a)

3. Does any modifier seem to refer to a word other than the one it is intended to modify? If so, move the modifier so that it refers clearly to only the intended word. (32a and c)

4. If you cannot find the word to which a modifier refers, revise the sentence: supply such a word, or revise the modifier itself so that it clearly refers to a word already in the sentence. (32d)

32a Position modifiers close to the words they modify.

Modifiers can cause confusion or ambiguity if they are not close enough to the words they modify or if they seem to modify more than one word in the sentence.

▶ She teaches a seminar this term ~~on voodoo~~ at Skyline College.
　　　　　　　　　　　　　　　　　　　　on voodoo
　　　　　　　　　　　　　　　　^

The voodoo was not at the college; the seminar is.

> ~~Billowing from every window, he~~ saw clouds of smoke.
> *He* *billowing from every window.*

People cannot billow from windows.

> *After he lost the 1962 gubernatorial race,*
> Nixon told reporters that he planned to get out of politics. ~~after he lost the 1962 gubernatorial race.~~

The unedited sentence implies that Nixon planned to lose the race.

Limiting modifiers

Be especially careful with the placement of limiting modifiers such as *almost, even, just, merely,* and *only.* In general, these modifiers should be placed right before or after the words they modify. Putting them in other positions may produce not just ambiguity but a completely different meaning.

AMBIGUOUS	The court *only* hears civil cases on Tuesdays.
CLEAR	The court hears *only* civil cases on Tuesdays.
CLEAR	The court hears civil cases on Tuesdays *only*.

Placing *only* before *hears* makes the meaning ambiguous. Does the writer mean that civil cases are the only cases heard on Tuesdays or that those are the only days when civil cases are heard?

> The city ~~almost~~ spent $20 million on the new stadium.
> *almost*

The original sentence suggests the money was almost spent; moving *almost* makes clear that the amount spent was almost $20 million.

Squinting modifiers

If a modifier can refer to *either* the word before it *or* the word after it, it is a squinting modifier. Put the modifier where it clearly relates to only a single word.

SQUINTING	Students who practice writing *often* will benefit.
REVISED	Students who *often* practice writing will benefit.
REVISED	Students who practice writing will *often* benefit.

32b Move disruptive modifiers.

Disruptive modifiers interrupt the connections between parts of a grammatical structure or a sentence; they make it hard for readers to follow the progress of the thought.

▶ ~~Vegetables will, if they are cooked too long,~~ lose most of their
  If they are cooked too long, vegetables will
  ⌃
  nutritional value.

32c Move modifiers that unnecessarily split an infinitive.

In general, do not place a modifier between the *to* and the verb of an infinitive (*to often complain*). Doing so makes it hard for readers to recognize that the two go together.

▶ Hitler expected the British to fairly quickly . ~~surrender.~~
                                          ⌃   ⌃
                                     surrender

In some sentences, however, a modifier sounds awkward if it does not split the infinitive. In such cases, it may be best to reword the sentence to eliminate the infinitive altogether.

SPLIT   I hope *to* almost *equal* my last year's income.

REVISED   I hope that I will earn almost as much as I did last year.

32d Revise dangling modifiers.

Dangling modifiers are words that modify nothing in particular in the rest of a sentence. They often *seem* to modify something that is implied but not actually present in the sentence. Dangling modifiers frequently appear at the beginnings or ends of sentences.

DANGLING   Driving nonstop, Salishan Lodge is located two hours from
           Portland.

REVISED   Driving nonstop from Portland, you can reach Salishan
           Lodge in two hours.

To revise a dangling modifier, often you need to add a subject that the modifier clearly refers to; sometimes you have to revise the modifier itself, turning it into a phrase or a clause.

▶ Reluctantly, the hound ~~was given away~~ to a neighbor.
                         ⌃
                    our family gave away

In the original sentence, was the dog reluctant, or was someone else who is not mentioned reluctant?

When he was
▶ ~~As~~ a young boy, his grandmother told stories of her years as a country
  ^
schoolteacher.

His grandmother was never a young boy.

                                    My
▶ ~~Thumbing through the magazine, my~~ eyes automatically noticed the
                                 ^
           as I was thumbing through the magazine.
perfume ads.
           ^

Eyes cannot thumb through a magazine.

bedfordstmartins.com/everyday_writer For exercises, go to **Exercise Central** and
click on **Modifier Placement.**

33

Pronouns

As words that stand in for nouns, pronouns carry a lot of weight in
everyday discourse. For example:

> Take the Interstate until you come to Exit 3 and Route 313. Go past it, and
> take the next exit, which will be Broadway.

These directions, intended to lead an out-of-towner to her friend's
house, provide a good example of why it's important for a pronoun to
refer clearly to a specific noun or pronoun antecedent. The little word *it*
in this example can mean either Exit 3 or Route 313. Or does *it* mean that
Exit 3 *is* Route 313? This chapter aims to help you use pronouns accurately.

33a Pronoun case

Most speakers of English know intuitively when to use *I, me,* and *my.*
Our choices reflect differences in case, the form a pronoun takes to indicate its function in a sentence. Pronouns functioning as subjects are in the
subjective case (*I*); those functioning as objects are in the objective case
(*me*); those functioning as possessives are in the possessive case (*my*).

Editing Pronouns

- Are all pronouns after forms of the verb *be* in the subjective case? *It's me* is common in spoken English, but in writing it should be *It is I.* (33a)

- To check for correct use of *who* and *whom* (and *whoever* and *whomever*), try substituting *he* or *him*. If *he* is correct, use *who* (or *whoever*); if *him*, use *whom* or *whomever.* (33b)

- In compound structures, make sure any pronouns are in the same case they would be in if used alone (*She and Jake were living in Spain*). (33c)

- When a pronoun follows *than* or *as,* complete the sentence mentally. If the pronoun is the subject of an unstated verb, it should be subjective (*I like her better than he [likes her]*). If it is the object of an unstated verb, make it objective (*I like her better than [I like] him*). (33d)

- Check your treatment of *everyone* and other singular indefinite pronouns. If you have used *he, his,* or *him* to refer to *everyone* when *everyone* includes both males and females, revise the sentence. (33f)

- For each pronoun, identify a specific word that it refers to. If you cannot find one specific word, supply one. If the pronoun refers to more than one word, revise the sentence. (33g)

- Check each use of *it, this, that,* and *which* to be sure the pronoun refers to a specific word elsewhere in the sentence or prior sentence. (33g)

- Be sure that any use of *you* refers to your specific reader or readers.

SUBJECTIVE PRONOUNS	OBJECTIVE PRONOUNS	POSSESSIVE PRONOUNS
I	me	my/mine
we	us	our/ours
you	you	your/yours
he/she/it	him/her/it	his/her/hers/its
they	them	their/theirs
who/whoever	whom/whomever	whose

Subjective case

A pronoun should be in the subjective case (*I, we, you, he/she/it, they, who, whoever*) when it is a subject, a subject complement, or an appositive renaming a subject or subject complement.

SUBJECT

She was passionate about recycling.

SUBJECT COMPLEMENT

The main supporter of the recycling program was *she.*

APPOSITIVE RENAMING A SUBJECT OR SUBJECT COMPLEMENT

Three colleagues—Peter, John, and *she*—worked on the program.

Many Americans routinely use the objective case for subject comple-ments, especially in conversation: *Who's there? It's me.* If the subjective case for a subject complement sounds stilted or awkward (*It's I*), try rewriting the sentence using the pronoun as the subject (*I'm here*).

She was the
▶ ~~The~~ first person to see Kishore after the awards. ~~was she.~~
   ^   ^

Objective case

A pronoun should be in the objective case (*me, us, you, him/her/it, them*) when it functions as a direct or indirect object, an object of a preposition, an appositive renaming an object, or a subject of an infinitive.

DIRECT OBJECT

The boss surprised *her* with a big raise.

INDIRECT OBJECT

The owner gave *him* a reward.

OBJECT OF A PREPOSITION

Several friends went with *me.*

APPOSITIVE RENAMING AN OBJECT

We elected two representatives, Joan and *me.*

SUBJECT OF AN INFINITIVE

The students convinced *him* to vote for the school bond.

Possessive case

A pronoun should be in the possessive case when it shows possession or ownership. Notice that there are two forms of possessive pronouns: adjective forms, which are used before nouns or gerunds (*my, our, your, his/her/its, their, whose*), and noun forms, which take the place of a pos-sessive noun (*mine, ours, yours, his/hers/its, theirs, whose*).

BEFORE A NOUN

The sound of *her* voice came right through the walls.

IN PLACE OF A POSSESSIVE NOUN

The responsibility is *hers.*

Pronouns before a gerund should be in the possessive case.

his
▶ I remember ~~him~~ singing.
    ^

His modifies the gerund *singing.*

33b Use *who, whoever, whom,* and *whomever* appropriately.

A common problem with pronoun case is deciding whether to use *who* or *whom.* Use *who* and *whoever,* which are subjective-case pronouns, for subjects or subject complements. Use *whom* and *whomever,* which are objective-case pronouns, for objects. Two particular situations lead to confusion with *who* and *whom:* when they begin a question and when they introduce a dependent clause.

In questions

You can determine whether to use *who* or *whom* at the beginning of a question by answering the question using a personal pronoun. If the answer is in the subjective case, use *who;* if it is in the objective case, use *whom.*

Whom
▶ ~~Who~~ did you visit?
    ^

I visited *them. Them* is objective; thus *whom* is correct.

Who
▶ ~~Whom~~ do you think wrote the story?
    ^

I think *she* wrote the story. *She* is subjective; thus *who* is correct.

In dependent clauses

The case of a pronoun in a dependent clause is determined by its function in the clause, no matter how that clause functions in the sentence. If the pronoun acts as a subject or subject complement in the clause, use *who* or *whoever.* If the pronoun acts as an object in the clause, use *whom* or *whomever.*

▶ Anyone can hypnotize someone ~~whom~~ *who* wants to be hypnotized.

> The verb of the clause is *wants,* and its subject is *who.*

▶ ~~Whoever~~ *Whomever* the party suspected of disloyalty was executed.

> *Whomever* is the object of *suspected* in the clause *whomever the party suspected of disloyalty.*

If you are not sure which case to use, try separating the dependent clause from the rest of the sentence and looking at it in isolation. Then rewrite the clause as a new sentence, and substitute a personal pronoun for *who(ever)* or *whom(ever).* If the personal pronoun you substitute is in the subjective case, use *who* or *whoever;* if it is in the objective case, use *whom* or *whomever.*

▶ The minister grimaced at (*whoever/whomever*) made any noise.

> Isolate the clause *whoever/whomever made any noise.* Substituting a personal pronoun gives you *they made any noise. They* is in the subjective case; therefore, *The minister grimaced at <u>whoever</u> made any noise.*

▶ The minister smiled at (*whoever/whomever*) she greeted.

> Isolate and transpose the clause to get *she greeted whoever/whomever.* Substituting a personal pronoun gives you *she greeted them. Them* is in the objective case; therefore, *The minister smiled at <u>whomever</u> she greeted.*

▶ The minister grimaced at *whoever* she thought made the noise.

> Ignore such expressions as *he thinks* and *she says* when you isolate the clause.

33c Use the appropriate case in compound structures.

When a pronoun is part of a compound subject, complement, object, or appositive, put it in the same case you would use if the pronoun were alone.

▶ When ~~him~~ *he* and Zelda were first married, they lived in New York.

▶ The boss invited ~~she~~ *her* and her family to dinner.

▶ This morning saw yet another conflict between my sister and ~~I.~~ *me.*

▶ Both panelists, Javonne and ~~me,~~ *I*, were stumped.

To decide whether to use the subjective or objective case in a compound structure, use each part of the compound alone in the sentence.

▶   **Come to the park with Anh and ~~I.~~**
                                          me.
                                          ^

>   Separating the compound structure gives you *Come to the park with Anh* and *Come to the park with me;* thus *Come to the park with Anh and* <u>me</u>.

33d   Use the correct case in elliptical constructions.

Elliptical constructions are those in which some words are understood but left out. When an elliptical construction ends in a pronoun, put the pronoun in the case it would be in if the construction were complete.

▶   **His sister has always been more athletic than** *he* **[is].**

In some elliptical constructions, the case of the pronoun depends on the meaning intended.

▶   **Willie likes Lily more than** *she* **[likes Lily].**

>   *She* is the subject of the omitted verb *likes.*

▶   **Willie likes Lily more than [he likes]** *her.*

>   *Her* is the object of the omitted verb *likes.*

33e   Use *we* and *us* appropriately before a noun.

If you are unsure about whether to use *we* or *us* before a noun, recasting the sentence without the noun will give you the answer. Use whichever pronoun would be correct if the noun were omitted.

      We
▶   **~~Us~~ fans never give up hope.**
     ^

>   Without *fans, we* would be the subject.

                           us
▶   **The Rangers depend on ~~we~~ fans.**
                            ^

>   Without *fans, us* would be the object of a preposition.

33f   Make pronouns agree with their antecedents.

The antecedent of a pronoun is the word the pronoun refers to. The antecedent usually appears before the pronoun—earlier in the sentence or in the prior sentence. Pronouns and antecedents are said to agree when they match up in person, number, and gender.

SINGULAR   The *choirmaster* raised *his* baton.

PLURAL   The *boys* picked up *their* music.

Compound antecedents

Compound antecedents joined by *and* require plural pronouns.

▶ **My parents and I tried to resolve *our* disagreement.**

When *each* or *every* precedes a compound antecedent, however, it takes a singular pronoun.

▶ **Every *plant* and *animal* has *its* own ecological niche.**

With a compound antecedent joined by *or* or *nor,* the pronoun agrees with the nearer or nearest antecedent. If the parts of the antecedent are of different genders or persons, however, this kind of sentence can be awkward or ambiguous and may need to be revised.

AWKWARD   Neither Annie nor Barry got *his* work done.

REVISED   Annie didn't get *her* work done, and neither did Barry.

When a compound antecedent contains both singular and plural parts, the sentence may sound awkward unless the plural part comes last.

▶ **Neither the newspaper nor the radio stations would reveal *their* sources.**

Collective-noun antecedents

A collective noun that refers to a single unit (*herd, team, audience*) requires a singular pronoun.

▶ **The *audience* fixed *its* attention on center stage.**

When such an antecedent refers to the multiple parts of a unit, however, it requires a plural pronoun.

▶ **The director chose this *cast* for the play because *they* had experience in the roles.**

Indefinite-pronoun antecedents

Indefinite pronouns are those that do not refer to specific persons or things. Most indefinite pronouns are always singular; a few are always plural. Some can be singular or plural depending on the context.

▶ *One* of the ballerinas lost *her* balance.

▶ *Many* in the audience jumped to *their* feet.

SINGULAR   *Some* of the furniture was showing *its* age.

PLURAL   *Some* of the farmers abandoned *their* land.

Sexist pronouns

Indefinite pronouns often serve as antecedents that may be either male or female. Writers used to use a masculine pronoun, known as the generic *he,* to refer to such indefinite pronouns. In recent decades, however, many people have pointed out that such wording ignores or even excludes females—and thus should not be used.

AT A GLANCE

Editing Out Sexist Pronouns

Everyone should know his *legal rights.*

Here are three ways to express the same idea without *his:*

1. Revise to make the antecedent a plural noun.
   All citizens should know their *legal rights.*

2. Revise the sentence altogether.
   Everyone should have some knowledge of basic legal rights.

3. Use both masculine and feminine pronouns.
   Everyone should know his *or* her *legal rights.*

   This third option, using both masculine and feminine pronouns, can be awkward, especially when repeated several times in a passage.

When the antecedent is *anybody, each,* or *everyone,* some people avoid the generic *he* by using a plural pronoun.

▶ *Everyone* should know *their* legal rights.

You will hear such sentences in conversation and even see them in writing, but many people in academic contexts still consider *anybody, each,* and *everyone* singular, and they think using *their* with singular antecedents is too informal. They prefer one of the solutions in the box.

33g Maintain clear pronoun reference.

The antecedent of a pronoun is the word the pronoun substitutes for. If a pronoun is too far from its antecedent, readers will have trouble making the connection between the two.

Ambiguous antecedents

Readers have trouble when a pronoun can refer to more than one antecedent.

▶ The meeting between Bowman and Sonny makes ~~him~~ compare his **Bowman**
 own unsatisfying domestic life with one that is emotionally secure.

Who is the antecedent of *him* and *his:* Bowman or Sonny? The revision makes the reference clear by replacing a pronoun (*him*) with a noun (*Bowman*).

▶ Kerry told Ellen**,** ~~she~~ should be ready soon.**"** **"I**

Reporting Kerry's words directly, in quotation marks, eliminates the ambiguity.

Vague use of *it*, *this*, *that*, *and* which

The words *it, this, that,* and *which* often function as a shortcut for referring to something mentioned earlier. But such shortcuts can cause confusion. Like other pronouns, each must refer to a specific antecedent.

▶ When the senators realized the bill would be defeated, they tried to
 postpone the vote but failed. ~~It~~ was a fiasco. **The entire effort**

▶ Nancy just found out that she won the lottery, ~~which~~ explains her **and that news**
 sudden resignation from her job.

Indefinite use of *you*, *it*, *and* they

In conversation, we frequently use *you, it,* and *they* in an indefinite sense in such expressions as *you never know; in the paper, it said;* and *on television, they said.* In academic and professional writing, however, use *you* only to mean "you, the reader," and *they* or *it* only to refer to a clear antecedent.

> *people*
▶ Commercials try to make ~~you~~ buy without thinking.
  ^

> *one*   *hears*
▶ In Texas, ~~you~~ often ~~hear~~ about the influence of big oil corporations.
  ^   ^

> *The*
▶ ~~On the~~ Weather Channel, ~~it~~ reported that Hurricane Fran will hit
  ^
  Virginia Beach tomorrow morning.

> *Many restaurants in France*
▶ ~~In France, they~~ allow dogs. ~~in many restaurants.~~
  ^   ^

Possessive antecedents

A possessive may *suggest* a noun antecedent but does not serve as a clear antecedent. To get rid of a possessive, you might revise the following sentence as shown:

> *her*   *Welty*
▶ In ~~Welty's~~ story, ~~she~~ characterizes Bowman as a man unaware of his
  ^   ^
  own isolation.

In the original sentence, some people would claim that the only antecedent is the possessive noun phrase *Welty's story,* which should not be referred to by *she.* However, nowadays, sentences such as the original one are widely accepted.

▶ Detention centers routinely blocked efforts by *detainees'* families and lawyers to locate *them.*

It is clear from the context that *them* refers to *detainees,* even though only the possessive form appears before the pronoun.

FOR MULTILINGUAL WRITERS

Using Pronoun Subjects

In Arabic and some other languages, personal pronouns are added to the verbs as suffixes or prefixes. Native speakers of these languages sometimes overcorrect in English by doubling the subject: *Shahid he lives next door.* If you are using a pronoun subject, make sure that you have not used a proper noun subject as well: *He lives next door.*

34

Comma Splices and Fused Sentences

A comma splice results from placing only a comma between clauses. We often see comma splices in advertising, where they can give slogans a catchy rhythm.

> It's not just a job, it's an adventure.
> —U.S. ARMY RECRUITING SLOGAN

Another common error is a fused, or run-on, sentence, which results from joining two independent clauses with no punctuation or connecting word between them. The army slogan as a fused sentence would be "It's not just a job it's an adventure."

You will seldom if ever profit from using comma splices or fused sentences in academic or professional writing. In fact, doing so will almost always draw an instructor's criticism. This chapter will guide you in revising comma splices and fused sentences.

34a Separate the clauses into two sentences.

The simplest way to revise comma splices or fused sentences is to separate them into two sentences.

COMMA
SPLICE   My mother spends long hours every spring tilling the
           soil and moving manure, this part of gardening is
           nauseating.

FUSED
SENTENCE   My mother spends long hours every spring tilling the
           soil and moving manure. this part of gardening is
           nauseating.

If the two clauses are very short, making them two sentences may sound abrupt and terse, so some other method of revision is probably preferable.

AT A GLANCE

Editing for Comma Splices and Fused Sentences

Look for independent clauses—groups of words that can stand alone as a sentence—coming one after another. If you find no punctuation between two independent clauses, you have identified a fused sentence. If you find two such clauses joined only by a comma, you have identified a comma splice. Here are six methods of editing comma splices and fused sentences:

1. Separate the clauses into two sentences. (34a)

   ▶ *Education* is an elusive word~~/. it~~ *It* often means different things to different people.

2. Link the clauses with a comma and a coordinating conjunction (*and, but, or, nor, for, so,* or *yet*). (34b)

   ▶ *Education* is an elusive word, *for* it often means different things to different people.

3. Link the clauses with a semicolon. (34c)

   ▶ *Education* is an elusive word/**;** it often means different things to different people.

   If the clauses are linked with only a comma and a conjunctive adverb—a word like *however, then, therefore*—add a semicolon.

   ▶ *Education* is an elusive word/**;** indeed, it often means different things to different people.

4. Recast the two clauses as one independent clause. (34d)

   An elusive word, education
   ▶ ~~*Education* is an elusive word, it~~ often means different things to different people.

5. Recast one independent clause as a dependent clause. (34e)

   ▶ *Education* is an elusive word/ *because* it often means different things to different people.

6. In informal writing, link the clauses with a dash. (34f)

▶ *Education* is an elusive word/ it often means different
things to different people.

Look at the sentences before and after the ones you are revising. Doing so will help you determine how a particular method will affect the rhythm of the passage.

34b Link the clauses with a comma and a coordinating conjunction.

If the two clauses are closely related and equally important, join them with a comma and a coordinating conjunction (*and, but, or, nor, for, so,* or *yet*).

COMMA SPLICE
and
I got up feeling bad, I feel even worse now.

FUSED SENTENCE
but
I should pay my tuition, I need a new car.

34c Link the clauses with a semicolon.

If the ideas in the two clauses are closely related, and you want to give them equal emphasis, link them with a semicolon.

COMMA SPLICE
This photograph is not at all realistic; it even uses dreamlike images to convey its message.

FUSED SENTENCE
The practice of journalism is changing dramatically; advances in technology have sped up news cycles.

Be careful when you link clauses with a conjunctive adverb or a transitional phrase. You must use such words and phrases with a semicolon, with a period, or with a comma combined with a coordinating conjunction.

COMMA
SPLICE

Many Third World countries have very high birthrates/**;**

therefore**,** most of their citizens are young.

FUSED
SENTENCE

Many Third World countries have very high birthrates**.**

T

/therefore**,** most of their citizens are young.

and,

FUSED
SENTENCE

Many Third World countries have very high birthrates**,**

therefore**,** most of their citizens are young.

SOME CONJUNCTIVE ADVERBS AND TRANSITIONAL PHRASES

also	in contrast	next
anyway	indeed	now
besides	in fact	otherwise
certainly	instead	similarly
finally	likewise	still
furthermore	meanwhile	then
however	moreover	therefore
in addition	namely	thus
incidentally	nevertheless	undoubtedly

FOR MULTILINGUAL WRITERS

Judging Sentence Length

If you speak a language that tends to use long sentences—Arabic, Farsi, or Chinese, for instance—be careful not to join English sentences in a way that results in comma-splice errors. Note that in standard academic and professional English, a sentence should contain only one independent clause *unless* the clauses are joined by a comma and a coordinating conjunction or by a semicolon. (See Chapter 67.)

34d **Recast the two clauses as one independent clause.**

Sometimes you can reduce two spliced or fused independent clauses to a single independent clause.

	Most	*and*
COMMA SPLICE	~~A large part~~ of my mail is advertisements, ~~most of the rest is~~ bills.	

	Most	*and*
FUSED SENTENCE	~~A large part~~ of my mail is advertisements ~~most of the rest is~~ bills.	

A MATTER OF STYLE

Comma Splices

Spliced and fused sentences appear frequently in literary and journalistic writing, for, like many other structures we commonly identify as errors, each can produce a powerful effect. See how comma splices create momentum with a rush of details:

> Golden eagles sit in every tree and watch us watch them watch us, although there are bird experts who will tell you in all seriousness that there are no golden eagles here. Bald eagles are common, ospreys abound, we have herons and mergansers and kingfishers, we have logging with percherons and belgians, we have park land and nature trails, we have enough oddballs, weirdos, and loons to satisfy anybody. — ANNE CAMERON

Suppose that Cameron were writing this description for a college class. Then she might well decide to omit the comma splices altogether, yielding a passage like the following:

> Golden eagles sit in every tree and watch us watch them watch us, although there are bird experts who will tell you in all seriousness that there are no golden eagles here. Bald eagles are common; ospreys abound. We have herons and mergansers and kingfishers; we have logging with percherons and belgians; we have park land and nature trails. We have enough oddballs, weirdos, and loons to satisfy anybody.

Neither of these passages is right or wrong out of context: depending on the audience, purpose, and situation, either can be appropriate and effective.

34e Recast one independent clause as a dependent clause.

When one independent clause is more important than the other, try converting the less important one to a dependent clause.

COMMA
SPLICE
> *Although*
> Zora Neale Hurston is regarded as one of America's
> ^
> major novelists, she died in obscurity.

FUSED
SENTENCE
> *Although*
> Zora Neale Hurston is regarded as one of America's
> ^
> major novelists**,** she died in obscurity.
> ^

In the revision, the writer chooses to emphasize the second clause and to make the first one into a dependent clause by adding the subordinating conjunction *although.*

COMMA
SPLICE
> *, which reacted against mass production,*
> The arts and crafts movement called for handmade
> ^
> objects/. ~~it reacted against mass production.~~
> ^

In the revision, the writer chooses to emphasize the first clause, the one describing what the movement advocated, and to make the second clause, the one describing what it reacted against, into a dependent clause.

34f   Link the two clauses with a dash.

In informal writing, you can use a dash to join the two clauses, especially when the second clause elaborates on the first clause.

COMMA
SPLICE
> —
> Exercise trends come and go/this year yoga is hot.
> ^

A MATTER OF E-STYLE

Comma Splices and Fused Sentences

Much email and other forms of electronic communication are appropriately informal; they are like conversation in their use of fragments, comma splices, and fused sentences: *Long time, no see—gimme some news, will you?* But if you're emailing your boss in response to a request, you will want to be more formal and to observe conventions: *I am responding to your request for an update on sales in the northern region.*

---

bedfordstmartins.com/everyday_writer   For exercises, go to **Exercise Central** and click on **Comma Splices and Fused Sentences.**

35

Sentence Fragments

If you pay close attention to advertisements, you will find sentence fragments in frequent use. For example:

> Our Lifetime Guarantee may come as a shock.
> *Or a strut. Or a muffler.* Because once you pay to replace them, Toyota's Lifetime Guarantee covers parts and labor on any dealer-installed muffler, shock, or strut for as long as you own your Toyota! So if anything should ever go wrong, your Toyota dealer will fix it. *Absolutely free.*
> —TOYOTA ADVERTISEMENT

The three fragments (italicized here) grab our attention, the first two by creating a play on words and the third by emphasizing that something is absolutely free. As complete sentences, the information would be less clever and far less memorable.

As this ad illustrates, sentence fragments are groups of words that are punctuated as sentences but lack either a subject or a verb or form only a dependent clause. Although you will find fragments in literature, hear them in conversation, and see them in journalism and in advertising, you will seldom, if ever, want to use them in academic or professional writing (where some readers might regard them as errors).

35a Combine phrase fragments with an independent clause, or make them into sentences.

Phrases are groups of words that lack a subject, a verb, or both. When verbal phrases, prepositional phrases, noun phrases, and appositive phrases are punctuated like sentences, they become fragments. To revise these fragments, attach them to an independent clause, or make them a separate sentence.

▶ NBC is broadcasting the debates. *with* ~~With~~ discussions afterward.

> The second word group is a prepositional phrase, not a sentence. The editing combines the phrase with an independent clause.

▶ The town's growth is controlled by zoning laws. *a* ~~A~~ strict set of regulations for builders and corporations.

> *A strict set of regulations for builders and corporations* is an appositive phrase renaming the noun *zoning laws*. The editing attaches the fragment to the sentence containing that noun.

AT A GLANCE

Editing for Sentence Fragments

A group of words must meet three criteria to form a complete sentence. If it does not meet all three, it is a fragment. Revise a fragment by combining it with a nearby sentence or by rewriting it as a complete sentence.

1. A sentence must have a subject. (28k)

2. A sentence must have a verb, not just a verbal. A verbal cannot function as a sentence's verb without an auxiliary verb. (28l and m)

   VERB   **The terrier** *is barking.*

   VERBAL   **The terrier** *barking.*

3. Unless it is a question, a sentence must have at least one clause that does not begin with a subordinating word. (35c) Following are some common subordinating words:

although	if	when
as	since	where
because	that	whether
before	though	which
how	unless	who

▶ **Kamika stayed out of school for three months after Linda was born.**

She did so to
~~To~~ **recuperate and to take care of her.**
  ^

To recuperate and to take care of her includes verbals, not verbs. The revision—adding a subject (*she*) and a verb (*did*)—turns the fragment into a separate sentence.

Fragments beginning with transitions

If you introduce an example or explanation with one of the following transitions, be certain you write a sentence, not a fragment.

also	for example	like
as a result	for instance	such as
besides	instead	that is

> Joan Didion has written on many subjects/, ~~Such~~ *such* as the Hoover Dam and migraine headaches.

The second word group is a phrase, not a sentence. The editing combines it with an independent clause.

35b Combine compound-predicate fragments with independent clauses.

A compound predicate consists of two or more verbs, along with their modifiers and objects, that have the same subject. Fragments occur when one part of a compound predicate lacks a subject but is punctuated as a separate sentence. These fragments usually begin with *and, but,* or *or.* You can revise them by attaching them to the independent clause that contains the rest of the predicate.

> They sold their house/, ~~And~~ *and* moved into an apartment.

35c Combine dependent-clause fragments with independent clauses, or delete opening words.

Dependent clauses contain both a subject and a verb, but they cannot stand alone as sentences; they depend on an independent clause to complete their meaning. Dependent clauses usually begin with words such as *after, because, before, if, since, though, unless, until, when, where, while, who, which,* and *that.* You can usually combine dependent-clause fragments with a nearby independent clause.

> When I decided to work part-time/, I gave up a lot of my earning potential.

If you cannot smoothly attach a clause to a nearby independent clause, try deleting the opening subordinating word and turning the dependent clause into a sentence.

> The majority of injuries in automobile accidents occur in two ways. ~~When~~ *A*n occupant either is hurt by something inside the car or is thrown from the car.

A MATTER OF STYLE

Fragments

We often find sentence fragments in narrative writing, where they call up the rhythms of speech. For example:

> On Sundays, for religion, we went up on the hill. Skipping along the hexagon-shaped tile in Colonial Park. Darting up the steps to Edgecomb Avenue. Stopping in the candy store on St. Nicholas to load up. Leaning forward for leverage to finish the climb up to the church. I was always impressed by this particular house of the Lord.
>
> —KEITH GILYARD, *Voices of the Self*

Here Gilyard uses fragments to move the narrative—and the reader—up the hill. He could have strung the fragments together into one long sentence, but the series of fragments (as well as the parallelism of *skipping, darting, stopping,* and *leaning*) is more effective: he creates a rhythm and a sense of movement.

bedfordstmartins.com/everyday_writer　For exercises, go to **Exercise Central** and click on **Sentence Fragments.**

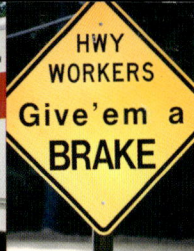

LANGUAGE/
Glossary of Usage

A word is dead
When it is said,
Some say.
I say it just
Begins to live
That day.
—EMILY DICKINSON

Language/Glossary of Usage

36

Writing to the World

In 1967, when media guru Marshall McLuhan referred to the world as a global village, the phrase seemed unfamiliar and highly exaggerated. Almost four decades later, his words are practically a cliché, part of our everyday language. People today often communicate instantaneously across vast distances and cultures. Businesspeople complete multinational transactions with ease, students take classes at distant universities via the Web, and grandmothers check in with family members across four or five—or six—time zones.

In this era of extreme communication, you might find yourself writing to (or with) students throughout the country or even across the globe—and you may well be in classes with people from other cultures, language groups, and countries. In business, government, and education, writers increasingly operate on an international stage and must become *world writers,* able to communicate across cultures.

AT A GLANCE

Communicating across Cultures

- Recognize what you consider "normal." Examine your own customary behaviors and assumptions, and think about how they may affect what you think and say (and write). (36a)
- When writing to someone from another culture, define your terms. (36b)
- Think about your audience's expectations. How explicit does your writing need to be? (36d)
- What kind of evidence will count most with your audience? (36e)
- Organize your writing with your audience's expectations in mind. (36f)
- If in doubt, use formal style. (36g)

36a Think about what you consider "normal."

How do you decide what is "normal" in a given situation? More than likely, your judgment is based on assumptions that you are not even aware of.

Remember that behavior that is considered out of place in one community may appear perfectly normal in another. If you want to communicate with people across cultures, try to learn something about the norms in those cultures and, even more important, be aware of the norms that guide your own behavior.

- Remember that most of us tend to see our own way as the "normal" or right way to do things. How do your own values and assumptions guide your thinking and behavior? Keep in mind that if your ways seem inherently right, then—even without thinking about it—you may assume that other ways are somehow less than right.
- Know that most ways of communicating are influenced by cultural contexts and differ widely from one culture to the next.
- Pay close attention to the ways that people from cultures other than your own communicate, and be flexible and open to their ways.
- Pay attention to and respect the differences among individual people *within* a given culture. Do not assume that all members of a community behave in just the same way or value exactly the same things.

Don't overgeneralize. For example, just because empathy—as opposed to explicit criticism—is a preferred method of persuasion for some Asians does not mean this cultural pattern holds true for all Asians. As a world writer, you need to be aware of and sensitive to differences within—as well as across—cultures.

Overgeneralizations result from *stereotypes*—standardized or fixed ideas about a group. Because stereotypes are often based on half-truths, misunderstandings, and hand-me-down prejudices, they can lead to bias, bigotry, and intolerance. Most stereotypes are negative—for example, *women drivers are lousy.* But even positive stereotypes—for example, *Jewish doctors are the best*—or neutral ones—for example, *all children like to play*—can hurt, for they inevitably ignore the uniqueness of an individual. Careful writers make sure that their language doesn't stereotype any group *or* individual.

36b Define your terms.

When an instructor called for "originality" in his students' essays, what did he mean? A Filipina student thought *originality* meant going to an original source and explaining it; a student from Massachusetts took *originality* to mean an idea entirely her own. The professor, however, expected students to read sources and develop a critical point of their own about the sources. In subsequent classes, this professor defined *originality* in class and gave examples of student work he judged original.

This brief example points to the challenges all writers face in trying to communicate across space, across languages, across cultures. While there are no foolproof rules, here are some tips for writing to people from cultures other than your own:

- Don't hesitate to ask people to explain a point if you're not absolutely sure you understand.
- Take care to be explicit about the meanings of the words you use.
- Invite response—ask whether you're making yourself clear. This kind of back-and-forth is particularly easy (and necessary) in email.

36c   Consider your own authority as a writer.

How should you sound to your readers—like an expert? a beginner? a subordinate? an angry employee or customer? a boss? The answer often depends on how much authority you as a writer have and how that authority relates to others. In the United States, students are often asked to establish authority in their writing—by drawing on certain kinds of personal experience, by reporting on research they or others have conducted, or by taking a position for which they can offer strong evidence and support. But this expectation about writerly authority is by no means universal. Indeed, some cultures position student writers as novices whose job is to reflect what they learn from their teachers—those who hold the most important knowledge, wisdom, and, hence, authority. One Japanese student, for example, said he was taught that it's rude to challenge a teacher: "Are you ever so smart that you should challenge the wisdom of the ages?"

As this student's comment reveals, a writer's tone also depends on his or her relationship with listeners and readers. As a world writer, you need to remember that those you're addressing may hold very different attitudes about authority.

- Whom are you addressing, and what is your relationship to him or her?
- What knowledge are you expected to have? Is it appropriate for or expected of you to demonstrate that knowledge—and if so, how?
- What is your goal—to answer a question? to make a point? to agree? something else?
- What tone is appropriate? If in doubt, show respect: politeness is rarely if ever inappropriate.

36d Consider your responsibility to your audience.

In the United States and Great Britain, many audiences (and especially those in the academic and business worlds) expect a writer to "get to the point" as directly as possible and to take on the major responsibility of articulating that point efficiently and unambiguously. But not all audiences have such expectations. Thus, world writers must think carefully about whether audience members expect the writer to make the meaning of a text explicitly clear or, rather, expect to do some of the work themselves, supplying some of the information necessary to the meaning. A typical news report on British radio or television, for example, puts the overwhelming responsibility on the writer to present an unambiguous message. Such a report begins with a clear overview of all the major points to be covered, follows with an orderly discussion of each point, and ends with a brief summary. In many other cultures, however, writers organize information differently because they expect the audience to take more responsibility for figuring out what is being said. In fact, readers or listeners from some cultures may be insulted if they think they are being led by the hand through a report. Here are tips for thinking about reader and writer responsibility:

- What general knowledge do members of your audience have about your topic? What information do they expect—or need—you to provide?
- Do members of your audience tend to be very direct, saying explicitly what they mean? Or are they more subtle—are they less likely to call a spade a spade? Look for cues to determine how much responsibility you have as the writer.

36e Consider what counts as evidence.

How do you decide what evidence will best support your ideas? The answer depends, in large part, on how you define *evidence.* Americans generally give great weight to factual evidence.

Every writer must think carefully about how he or she uses evidence in writing and pay attention to what counts as evidence to members of other cultures.

- Do you rely on facts? concrete examples? firsthand experience?
- Do you include the testimony of experts? Which experts are valued most, and why?
- Do you cite religious or philosophical texts? proverbs or everyday wisdom? other sources?
- Do you use analogies as support? How much do they count?

- Once you determine what counts as evidence in your own thinking and writing, think about where you learned to use and value this kind of evidence. You can ask these same questions about the use of evidence by members of other cultures.

36f Consider organization.

As you make choices about how to organize your writing, remember that cultural influences are at work here as well: the patterns that you find pleasing are likely to be ones that are deeply embedded in your own culture. Many U.S. students, for example, know American professors who value the following structure: introduction and thesis, necessary background, overview of the parts to follow, systematic presentation of evidence, consideration of other viewpoints, and conclusion. If a piece of writing follows this pattern, Anglo-American readers ordinarily find it "well organized" or "coherent."

However, in cultures that value indirection and subtlety, writers tend to organize materials differently. One common pattern in Korean writing, for example, includes an introduction; a topic with development; a tangential topic, again with development; and then a conclusion—with the thesis appearing only at the end.

Some cultures value repetition. Arabic listeners, for example, expect a speaker to reiterate a major point from several different perspectives as a way of making that point.

When writing for world audiences, think about how you can organize material to get your message across effectively. One expert in international business communication recommends, for example, that businesspeople writing to others in Japan should state their requests indirectly—and only after a formal and respectful opening. There are no hard-and-fast rules to help you organize your writing for effectiveness across cultures, but here are a couple of things for you to consider:

- Determine when to state your thesis—at the beginning? at the end? somewhere else? not at all?
- Consider whether digressions are a good idea, a requirement, or best avoided with your intended audience.

36g Consider style.

As with beauty, good style is most definitely in the eye of the beholder—and thus is always affected by language, culture, and rhetorical tradition. In fact, what constitutes effective style varies broadly across cultures and depends on the rhetorical situation—purpose, audience, and so on (see Chapter 4). Even so, there is one important style question to consider when writing across cultures: what level of formality is most appropriate? In most writing to a general audience in the United States, a fairly informal style is often acceptable, even appreciated. Many cultures, however, tend to value a more formal approach. When in doubt, it may be wise to err on the side of formality in writing to people from other cultures, especially to elders or to those in authority.

- Be careful to use proper titles:

  Dr. Beverly Moss   Professor Jaime Mejía

- Avoid slang and informal structures such as fragments.

- Do not use first names in correspondence (even in email) unless invited to do so. Note, however, that an invitation to use a first name could come indirectly; if someone signs an email message or letter to you with his or her first name, you are implicitly invited to do the same.

- For international business email, use complete sentences and words; avoid contractions. Open with the salutation "Dear Mr./Ms. _____." Write dates by listing the day before the month and spelling out the name of the month rather than using a numeral (*7 June 2004*).

Beyond formality, other stylistic preferences vary widely. World writers take nothing about language for granted. To be an effective world writer, you will want to work to recognize and respect those differences as you move from culture to culture.

37

Language That Builds Common Ground

As a child, you may have learned to "do to others what you would have them do to you." To that golden rule, we could add, "Say to others what you would have them say to you." For the words we select have power: they can praise, delight, inspire—and also hurt, offend, or even destroy. Words that offend break the golden rule of language use, preventing others from identifying with you and thus damaging your credibility.

Few absolute guidelines exist for using words that respect differences and build common ground. Two rules, however, can help: consider carefully the sensitivities and preferences of others, and watch for words that betray your assumptions, even though you have not directly stated them.

AT A GLANCE

Using Language That Builds Common Ground

- What unstated assumptions might come between you and your readers? Look, for instance, for language implying approval or disapproval and for the ways you use *we, you,* and *they.* (37a)
- Have you eliminated potentially sexist language? (37b)
- Are your references to race, religion, gender, sexual orientation, and so on relevant or necessary to your discussion? If not, consider leaving them out. (37c and d)
- Are the terms you use to refer to groups accurate and acceptable? (37c and d)

37a Watch for unstated assumptions.

Unstated assumptions that enter into thinking and writing can destroy common ground by ignoring the differences between others and ourselves. For example, a student in a religion seminar who uses *we* to refer to Christians and *they* to refer to members of other religions had better be sure that everyone in the class is Christian, or some students may feel left out of the discussion.

Sometimes assumptions even lead writers to call special attention to a group affiliation when it is not relevant to the point, as in *a woman bus driver* or *a Jewish doctor.*

A MATTER OF E-STYLE

Online Etiquette

In online exchanges, help build common ground by putting yourself in your readers' shoes: How will they interpret your message? Might they interpret it as a flame, an attack of some kind? Remember that online readers don't have your facial expression or gestures to help them know if you are teasing. On the other hand, if you feel you have been flamed, try never to respond in kind: what you think is a flame may not have been intended as one at all.

37b Consider assumptions about gender.

Powerful and often invisible gender-related words affect our thinking and our behavior. Consider the traditional use of *man* and *mankind* to refer to people of both sexes and the use of *he, him, his,* and *himself* to refer to people of unknown sex. Because such usage ignores half the human race, it hardly helps a writer build common ground.

Sexist language, those words and phrases that stereotype or ignore members of either sex or that unnecessarily call attention to gender, can usually be revised fairly easily. There are several alternatives to using masculine pronouns to refer to persons of unknown sex. One option is to recast the sentence using plural forms.

▶ A lawyer must pass the bar exam before he can begin to practice.
    Lawyers   *they*

Another option is to substitute pairs of pronouns such as *he or she, him or her,* and so on.

▶ A lawyer must pass the bar exam before he *or she* can begin to practice.

Yet another way to revise the sentence is to eliminate the pronouns.

▶ A lawyer must pass the bar exam before he can begin to practice. *beginning*

Beyond the pronoun issue, try to eliminate sexist nouns from your writing.

INSTEAD OF	TRY USING
anchorman, anchorwoman	anchor
businessman	businessperson, business executive
chairman, chairwoman	chair, chairperson
congressman	member of Congress, representative
fireman	firefighter
mailman	mail carrier
male nurse	nurse
man, mankind	humans, human beings, humanity, the human race, humankind
manpower	workers, personnel
mothering	parenting
policeman, policewoman	police officer
salesman	salesperson, sales associate
woman engineer	engineer

37c Consider assumptions about race and ethnicity.

In building common ground, writers must watch for any words that ignore differences not only among individual members of a race or ethnic group but also among subgroups. Writers must be aware, for instance, of the many nations to which American Indians belong and of the diverse places from which Americans of Spanish-speaking ancestry have emigrated.

Preferred terms

Identifying preferred terms is sometimes not an easy task, for they can change often and even vary widely.

The word *colored,* for example, was once widely used in the United States to refer to Americans of African ancestry. By the 1950s, the preferred term had become *Negro.* This changed in the 1960s, however, as *black* came to be preferred by most, though certainly not all, members of that community. Then, in the late 1980s, some leaders of the American black community urged that *black* be replaced by *African American.*

The word *Oriental,* once used to refer to people of East Asian descent, is now often considered offensive. At the University of California at Berkeley, the Oriental Languages Department is now known as the East Asian Languages Department. One advocate of the change explained that *Oriental* is appropriate for objects like rugs but not for people.

Once widely preferred, the term *Native American* is being challenged by those who argue that the most appropriate way to refer to indigenous people is by the specific name of the tribe or pueblo, such as *Chippewa, Crow,* or *Diné.* In Alaska and parts of Canada, many indigenous peoples once referred to as *Eskimos* now prefer *Inuit* or a specific term such as *Tlinget, Haida,* or *Tsimshian.* If you do not know a specific term, it's probably wise to use the term *American Indian* or *Indigenous Peoples.*

Among Americans of Spanish-speaking descent, the preferred terms of reference are many: *Chicano/Chicana, Hispanic, Latin American, Latino/Latina, Mexican American, Dominican,* and *Puerto Rican,* to name but a few.

Clearly, then, ethnic terminology changes often enough to challenge even the most careful writers. The best advice may be to consider your words carefully, to *listen* for the way members of groups refer to themselves (or *ask* them their preferences), and to check any term you're unsure of in a current dictionary.

37d Consider other kinds of difference.

Age

Mention age if it is relevant, but be aware that age-related terms can carry derogatory connotations (*matronly, well-preserved,* and so on). Describing Mr. Fry as *elderly but still active* may sound polite to you, but chances are Mr. Fry would prefer being called *an active seventy-eight-year-old*—or just *a seventy-eight-year-old,* which eliminates the unstated assumption of surprise that he is active at his age.

Class

Take special care to examine your words for assumptions about class. As a writer, you should not assume that all your readers share your background or values—that the members of your audience are all homeowners, for instance. And avoid using any words—*redneck, blue blood,* and the like—that might alienate members of an audience.

Geographical areas

You should not assume that geography determines personality or lifestyle. New Englanders are not all thrifty and tight-lipped; Florida offers more than retirement and tourism; midwesterners are not all hardworking; not all Californians care about the latest trends. Be careful not to make these kinds of simplistic assumptions.

Check also that you use geographical terms accurately.

AMERICA, AMERICAN Although many people use these words to refer to the United States *alone,* such usage will not necessarily be acceptable to people from Canada, Mexico, and Central or South America.

BRITISH, ENGLISH Use *British* to refer to the island of Great Britain, which includes England, Scotland, and Wales, or to the United Kingdom of Great Britain and Northern Ireland. In general, do not use *English* for these broader senses.

ARAB This term refers only to people of Arabic-speaking descent. Note that Iran is not an Arab nation; its people speak Farsi, not Arabic. Note also that *Arab* is not synonymous with *Muslim* or *Moslem* (a believer in Islam). Most (but not all) Arabs are Muslim, but many Muslims (those in Pakistan, for example) are not Arab.

Physical ability or health

When writing about a person with a serious illness or physical disability, ask yourself whether mentioning the disability is relevant to your discussion and whether the words you use carry negative connotations. You might choose, for example, to say someone *uses* a wheelchair rather than to say he or she *is confined to* one. Similarly, you might note a subtle but meaningful difference in calling someone a *person with AIDS* rather than an *AIDS victim.* Mentioning the person first and the disability second, such as referring to a *child with diabetes* rather than a *diabetic child* or a *diabetic,* is always a good idea.

CONSIDERING DISABILITIES

Know Your Readers

Nearly 10 percent of first-year college students—about 155,000—say they have one or more disabilities. That's no small number. Effective writers consider their own and their readers' disabilities so that they can find ways to build common ground.

Religion

Assumptions about religious groups are very often inaccurate and unfair. For example, Roman Catholics hold a wide spectrum of views on abortion, Muslim women do not all wear veils, and many Baptists are not fundamentalists. In fact, many people do not believe in or practice a religion at all, so be careful of such assumptions. As in other cases, do not use religious labels without considering their relevance to your point.

Sexual orientation

If you wish to build common ground, do not assume that readers all share one sexual orientation. As with any label, reference to sexual orientation should be governed by context. Someone writing about Representative Barney Frank's economic views would probably have little if any reason to refer to his sexual orientation. On the other hand, someone writing about diversity in U.S. government might find it important to note that Frank is a representative who has long made his homosexuality public.

---

bedfordstmartins.com/everyday_writer For information on learning disabilities and inclusive writing, go to **Links** and click on **Language**. For exercises, go to **Exercise Central** and click on **Language That Builds Common Ground**.

38

Language Variety

English comes in many varieties that differ from one another in pronunciation, vocabulary, rhetoric, and grammar. Whether you order a hero, a poor boy, a hoagie, a submarine, a grinder, or a *cubano* reflects such differences. In addition to numerous varieties of English, many other languages are spoken in the United States. Linguist Dell Hymes suggests that perhaps this multilingualism is what the Founders meant by choosing the Latin motto "E pluribus unum" (out of many, one): "E pluribus unum—bilingualism is . . . only as far away as the nearest nickel."

AT A GLANCE

Language Variety

You can use different varieties of language to good effect for the following purposes:

- to repeat someone's exact words
- to evoke a person, place, or activity
- to establish your credibility and build common ground
- to make a strong point
- to get your audience's attention

38a Standard varieties of English

One variety of English, often referred to as the "standard" or "standard academic," is that taught prescriptively in schools, represented in this and all other textbooks, used in the national media, and written and spoken widely by those wielding the most social and economic power. As the language used in business and most public institutions, standard English is a variety you will want to be completely familiar with. Standard English, however, is only one of many effective varieties of English and itself varies according to purpose and audience, from the very formal style used in academic writing to the informal style characteristic of casual conversation.

38b Ethnic varieties of English

Whether you are an American Indian or trace your ancestry to Europe, Asia, Africa, Latin America, or elsewhere, you have an ethnic heritage that probably lives on in the English language. See how one Hawaiian writer uses an ethnic variety of English to paint a picture of young teens hearing a scary "chicken skin" story about sharks from their grandmother.

> "—So, rather dan being rid of da shark, da people were stuck with many little ones, for dere mistake."
> Then Grandma Wong wen' pause, for dramatic effect, I guess, and she wen' add, "Dis is one of dose times. . . . Da time of da sharks."
> Those words ended another of Grandma's chicken skin stories. The stories she told us had been passed on to her by her grandmother, who had heard them from her grandmother. Always skipping a generation.
> —RODNEY MORALES, "When the Shark Bites"

Notice how the narrator uses both standard and ethnic varieties of English—presenting information necessary to the story line mostly in standard English and using a local, ethnic variety to represent spoken language, which helps us hear the characters talk.

Zora Neale Hurston often mixes African American vernacular (sometimes referred to as Ebonics) with standard English:

> My grandmother worried about my forward ways a great deal. She had known slavery and to her my brazenness was unthinkable.
> "Git down offa dat gate-post! You li'l sow, you! Git down! Setting up dere looking dem white folks right in de face! They's gowine to lynch you, yet. And don't stand in dat doorway gazing out at 'em neither. Youse too brazen to live long."
> Nevertheless, I kept right on gazing at them, and "going a piece of the way" whenever I could make it.
> —ZORA NEALE HURSTON, *Dust Tracks on a Road*

In each of these examples, one important reason for the shift from standard English is to demonstrate that the writer is a member of the community whose language he or she is representing and thus to build credibility with others in the community.

Take care, however, in using the language of communities other than your own. When used inappropriately, such language can have an opposite effect, perhaps destroying credibility and alienating your audience.

bedfordstmartins.com/everyday_writer For links to articles and Web sites on language policy issues, go to **Links** and click on **Language.**

38c Occupational varieties of English

From the fast-food business to taxi driving, every job has its own special variety of English. Here is an example from the computer world about how Extensible Markup Language (XML) is changing the way databases are created and making them more sophisticated:

> Most database servers are on a collision course with XML. The move to XML is a natural tie-in with a new approach to computing—deploying database-enabled Web applications running on application servers in place of stand-alone Windows programs. XML is causing database vendors to rethink their direction from the ground up, and the SQL language itself could well be on the way out in a few years, potentially to be replaced by an XML-based language called XML Query, now in development.
>
> —TIMOTHY DYCK, "Clash of the Titans"

The writer here uses technical abbreviations (*XML, SQL*) as well as ordinary words that have special meanings, such as *database-enabled.*

38d Regional varieties of English

Using regional language is an effective way to evoke a character or place. Look at the following piece of dialogue from an essay about Vermont:

> "There'll be some fine music on the green tonight, don't ya know?"
> "Well, I sure do want to go."
> "So don't I!"

Here the regional English creates a homespun effect and captures some of the language used in a particular place.

See how an anthropologist weaves together regional and standard academic English in writing about one Carolina community.

> For Roadville, schooling is something most folks have not gotten enough of, but everybody believes will do something toward helping an individual "get on." In the words of one oldtime resident, "Folks that ain't got no schooling don't get to be nobody nowadays."
>
> —SHIRLEY BRICE HEATH, *Ways with Words*

Notice that the researcher takes care to let a resident of Roadville speak her mind—and in her own words.

38e Other languages

You might use a language other than English for the same reasons you might use different varieties of English: to represent the actual words of

---

FOR MULTILINGUAL WRITERS

Recognizing Varieties of English

English is used in many countries around the world, resulting in many global varieties. You may, for example, have learned a British variety. British English differs somewhat from U.S. English in certain vocabulary (*bonnet* for *hood* of a car), syntax (*to hospital* rather than *to the hospital*), spelling (*centre* rather than *center*), and, of course, pronunciation. If you have learned a British variety of English, you will want to recognize the ways in which it differs from the U.S. standard.

---

a speaker, to make a point, to connect with your audience, or to get their attention. See how Gerald Haslam uses Spanish to capture his great-grandmother's words and to make a point about his relationship to her.

> *"Expectoran su sangre!"* exclaimed Great-grandma when I showed her the small horned toad I had removed from my breast pocket. I turned toward my mother, who translated: "They spit blood."
>
> *"De los ojos,"* Grandma added. "From their eyes," mother explained, herself uncomfortable in the presence of the small beast.
>
> I grinned, "Awwwwwww."
>
> But my Great-grandmother did not smile. *"Son muy toxicos,"* she nodded with finality. Mother moved back an involuntary step, her hands suddenly busy at her breast. "Put that thing down," she ordered.
>
> "His name's John," I said.
>
> —GERALD HASLAM, *California Childhood*

39

Diction

One restaurant's *down-home beef stew with spuds* may be similar to another restaurant's *boeuf bourguignon with butter-creamed potatoes*. Both describe beef dishes, but in each case the words say something about how the beef is prepared as well as something about the restaurant serving it. This chapter will help you with diction—choosing words that are clear and appropriate for your purpose, topic, and audience.

AT A GLANCE

Editing for Appropriate and Precise Language

- Check to see that your language reflects the appropriate level of formality and courtesy for your audience, purpose, and topic. (39a)

- Unless you are writing for a specialized audience that will understand jargon, either define the jargon or replace it with words that will be understood. (39a)

- Consider the connotations of words carefully. If you say someone is *pushy*, be sure you mean to be critical; otherwise, use a word like *assertive*. (39b)

- Be sure to use both general and specific words. If you are writing about the general category of "beds," for example, do you give enough concrete detail (*an antique four-poster bed*)? (39c)

- Look for clichés. Are they effective or stale? If the latter, try to replace them with fresher language. (39d)

39a   Use the appropriate level of formality.

You need to choose a level of formality that matches your audience and purpose. In an email or letter to a friend or close associate, informal language is often appropriate. For most academic and professional writing, however, more formal language is appropriate, since you are addressing people you do not know well. Compare the following responses to a request for information about a job candidate:

EMAIL TO SOMEONE YOU KNOW WELL

Myisha is great—hire her if you can!

LETTER OF RECOMMENDATION TO SOMEONE YOU DO NOT KNOW

I am pleased to recommend Myisha Fisher. She will bring good ideas and extraordinary energy to your organization.

Slang and colloquial language

Slang, or extremely informal language, is often confined to a relatively small group and usually becomes obsolete rather quickly, though some slang gains wide use (*yuppie, bummer*). Colloquial language, such as *a lot, in a bind,* or *snooze,* is less informal, more widely used, and longer lasting than most slang.

A MATTER OF E-STYLE

Online Jargon

Frequently used terms such as *asynchronous communication* and *email* are examples of the jargon online writers should know. Other terms, like the jargon in this sentence—*Savvy wavelet compression is the fiber signpost of the virtual chillout room*—may be appropriate for techies talking to one another, but they are not useful to those trying to communicate with a nontechnical or general audience. Before you use technical online jargon, remember your readers: if they will not understand the terms, or if you don't know your audience well enough to judge, then say what you need to say in everyday language.

Writers who use slang and colloquial language run the risk of not being understood or of not being taken seriously. If you are writing for a general audience about arms-control negotiations, for example, and you use the term *nukes* to refer to nuclear missiles, some readers may not know what you mean, and others may be irritated by what they see as a frivolous reference to a deadly serious subject.

Jargon

Jargon is the special vocabulary of—or special meanings given to common words by members of—a trade, profession, or field. Reserve such technical language as much as possible for an audience that will understand your terms, and replace or define terms that they will not.

Jargon can be useful for technical audiences. Here is an example from the computer world about a problem plaguing the World Wide Web:

> Right now, even if you're using a fully stocked Pentium and have a T1 line running into your bedroom, the Web can seem overloaded and painfully slow. Conventional wisdom says the solution lies in new network technologies like ATM and fiber optics. But researchers are investigating how to change the way computers communicate to minimize pauses, stutters, and false starts. After all, using the Internet isn't just a matter of shouting, "Hey, hotwired.com, shoot me that GIF!"
>
> –STEVE G. STEINBERG, *Wired*

Since this piece was written for a specialized audience (readers of *Wired* magazine), its use of jargon is appropriate. If Steinberg were writing for the general public, however, other language would be called for.

Recently, a number of business and industry firms have begun making attempts at getting rid of unnecessary jargon, often with the help of new software programs. Deloitte Consulting, for example, offers a free software program, Bullfighter, that will point out jargon and suggest substitute language. Of course, you can act as your own "bullfighter" by asking yourself whether each word you choose will be widely understood.

Pompous language, euphemisms, and doublespeak

Stuffy or pompous language is unnecessarily formal for the purpose, audience, or topic. It often gives writing an insincere or unintentionally humorous tone, making a writer's ideas seem insignificant or even unbelievable.

POMPOUS

Pursuant to the August 9 memorandum regarding petroleum supply exigencies, it is incumbent upon us to endeavor to make maximal utilization of telephonic communication in lieu of personal visitation.

REVISED

As of August 9, petroleum shortages require us to use the telephone whenever possible rather than make personal visits.

As these examples illustrate, some writers use words in an attempt to sound expert, and these puffed-up words can easily backfire.

INSTEAD OF	TRY USING	INSTEAD OF	TRY USING
ascertain	find out	operationalize	start, put into
commence	begin		operation
factor	cause	optimal	best
finalize	finish or	parameters	boundaries
	complete	peruse	look at
functionality	function	prioritize	rank
impact (as verb)	affect	ramp up	increase
methodology	method	utilize	use

Euphemisms are words and phrases that make unpleasant ideas seem less harsh. *Your position is being eliminated* seeks to soften the blow of being fired or laid off. Other euphemisms include *pass on* for *die* and *sanitation engineer* for *garbage collector*. Although euphemisms can sometimes appeal to an audience by showing that you are considerate of people's feelings, they can also sound insincere or evasive.

Doublespeak, a word coined from the *Newspeak* and *doublethink* of George Orwell's novel *1984,* is language used to hide or distort the

FOR MULTILINGUAL WRITERS

Avoiding Fancy Diction

In writing standard academic English, which is fairly formal, you may be inclined to use the biggest and newest words that you know in English. Though your intention is good—to put new words to good use—resist the temptation to use flowery or high-flown diction in your college writing. Academic writing calls first of all for clear, concise prose.

truth. During massive layoffs and cutbacks in the business world, companies speak of firings as *work reengineering, employee repositioning, proactive downsizing, deverticalization, smartsizing,* and *special reprogramming.* The public—and particularly those who lose their jobs—recognize these terms as doublespeak.

39b Be alert to a word's denotation and connotation.

Think of a stone tossed into a pool, and imagine the ripples spreading out from it. This image can help you understand the distinction between denotation, the stone, and connotation, the ripples. That is, denotation refers to the general, or dictionary, meaning of a word, whereas connotation refers to the associations that accompany the word. The words *maxim, epigram, proverb, saw, saying,* and *motto* all carry roughly the same denotation. Because of their different connotations, however, *proverb* would be the appropriate word to use in reference to a saying from the Bible, *saw* in reference to wisdom handed down anonymously, *epigram* in reference to a witty statement by a particular person.

Note the differences in connotation among the following three statements:

▶ Students Against Racism (SAR) erected a temporary barrier on the campus oval. They say it symbolizes "the many barriers to those discriminated against by university policies."

▶ Left-wing agitators threw up an eyesore right on the oval to try to stampede the university into giving in to their demands.

▶ Supporters of human rights for all students challenged the university's investment in racism by erecting a protest barrier on campus.

The first statement is the most neutral, merely stating facts (and quoting the assertion about university policy to represent it as someone's words

---

FOR MULTILINGUAL WRITERS

Learning Idioms

Why do you wear a diamond *on* your finger but *in* your ear (or nose)?
See 66a.

---

rather than as facts); the second, by using words with negative connotations (*agitators, eyesore, stampede*), is strongly critical; the third, by using words with positive connotations (*supporters of human rights*) and presenting assertions as facts (*the university's investment in racism*), gives a favorable slant to the story.

39c   Balance general and specific diction.

Effective writers balance general words (those that name groups or classes) with specific words (those that identify individual and particular things). Abstractions, which are types of general words, refer to things we cannot perceive through our five senses. Specific words are often concrete, naming things we can see, hear, touch, taste, or smell. Rarely can we draw a clear-cut line between general or abstract words on the one hand and specific or concrete ones on the other. Instead, most words fall somewhere between these two extremes.

GENERAL	LESS GENERAL	SPECIFIC	MORE SPECIFIC
book	dictionary	abridged dictionary	my 2002 edition of the *American Heritage College Dictionary*

ABSTRACT	LESS ABSTRACT	CONCRETE	MORE CONCRETE
culture	visual art	painting	Van Gogh's *Starry Night*

Strong writing must usually provide readers both with a general idea or overall picture and with specific examples or concrete details to fill in that picture. In the following passage, the author might have simply made a general statement—*their breakfast was always liberal and good*—or simply given the details of the breakfast. Instead, he is both general and specific.

> There would be a brisk fire crackling in the hearth, the old smoke-gold of morning and the smell of fog, the crisp cheerful voices of the people and their ruddy competent morning look, and the cheerful smells of breakfast, which was always liberal and good, the best meal that they had: kidneys and ham and eggs and sausages and toast and marmalade and tea.
>
> —THOMAS WOLFE, *Of Time and the River*

39d Use figurative language to create vivid pictures.

Figurative language, or figures of speech, paints pictures in readers' minds, allowing readers to "see" a point readily and clearly. Far from being a frill, such language is crucial to understanding.

Similes, metaphors, and analogies

Similes use *like, as, as if,* or *as though* to make explicit the comparison between two seemingly different things.

▶ One reviewer says that the characters in Don DeLillo's *Cosmopolis* drone on and on and on, "like palm pilots with lips."
— WALTER KIRN, "Cosmopolis"

▶ The comb felt as if it was raking my skin off.
— MALCOLM X, "My First Conk"

Metaphors are implicit comparisons, omitting the *like, as, as if,* or *as though* of similes.

▶ Today, America Online might be called the Carnival Cruise Lines of interactivity, but in the spring of 1985 it was a tiny start-up called Quantum Computer Services, Inc. — *Wired Style*

Mixed metaphors make comparisons that are inconsistent.

▶ The lectures were like brilliant comets streaking through the night sky, *dazzling* *flashes* ~~showering~~ listeners with ~~a torrential rain~~ of insights.

The images of streaking light and heavy precipitation are inconsistent; in the revised sentence, all of the images relate to light.

Analogies compare similar features of two dissimilar things; they explain something unfamiliar by relating it to something familiar.

▶ The mouse genome . . . [is] the Rosetta Stone for understanding the language of life. — TOM FRIEND

▶ One Hundred and Twenty-fifth Street was to Harlem what the Mississippi was to the South, a long traveling river always going somewhere, carrying something. — MAYA ANGELOU, *The Heart of a Woman*

Clichés

A cliché is a frequently used expression such as *busy as a bee.* By definition, we use clichés all the time, especially in speech, and many serve usefully as shorthand for familiar ideas or as a way of connecting to an audience. In addition, one person's cliché can be another's fresh and vivid image. But if you depend on clichés to excess in your writing, readers may conclude that what you are saying is not very new or is even insincere. To check your writing for clichés, use this rule of thumb: if you can predict exactly what the upcoming word or words in a phrase will be, the phrase stands a very good chance of being a cliché.

A MATTER OF STYLE

Signifying

One distinctive use of figurative language found extensively in African American English is signifying, in which a speaker cleverly and often humorously needles or insults the listener. In the following passage, two African American men (Grave Digger and Coffin Ed) signify on their white supervisor (Anderson), who ordered them to find the originators of a riot:

> "I take it you've discovered who started the riot," Anderson said.
> "We knew who he was all along," Grave Digger said.
> "It's just nothing we can do to him," Coffin Ed echoed.
> "Why not, for God's sake?"
> "He's dead," Coffin Ed said.
> "Who?"
> "Lincoln," Grave Digger said.
> "He hadn't ought to have freed us if he didn't want to make provisions to feed us," Coffin Ed said. "Anyone could have told him that."
> —CHESTER HIMES, *Hot Day, Hot Night*

Coffin Ed and Grave Digger demonstrate the major characteristics of effective signifying: indirection, ironic humor, fluid rhythm—and a surprising twist at the end. Rather than insulting Anderson directly by pointing out that he's asked a dumb question, they criticize the question indirectly by ultimately blaming a white man (and one they're all supposed to revere). This twist leaves the supervisor speechless, teaching him something *and* giving Grave Digger and Coffin Ed the last word.

bedfordstmartins.com/everyday_writer For exercises, go to **Exercise Central** and click on **Diction**.

40

Spelling

Drive down any commercial street, and you are sure to see many words intentionally misspelled or spelled in a shorthand way—from a Krispy Kreme doughnut shop to an ad promising to XCLR8 your online experience. Such fanciful or playful spelling will get you no points, however, in academic or professional writing. This chapter provides some fairly straightforward rules and guidelines about English spelling.

40a Learn the most commonly misspelled words.

The thousands of first-year essays used in the research for this book revealed a fairly small number of persistently misspelled words. Look over the fifty words most commonly misspelled. If you have trouble with any of them, take a moment to create a special memory device, such as the following, to help you remember them correctly: *They're certain their coats were over there.*

The fifty most commonly misspelled words

1. their/there/they're
2. too/to
3. a lot
4. noticeable
5. receive/-d/-s
6. lose
7. you're/your
8. an/and
9. develop/-s
10. definitely
11. than/then
12. believe/-d/-s
13. occurred
14. affect/-s
15. cannot
16. separate
17. success
18. through
19. until
20. where
21. successful/-ly
22. truly
23. argument/-s
24. experience/-s
25. environment
26. exercise/-s/-ing
27. necessary
28. sense
29. therefore
30. accept/-ed
31. heroes
32. professor
33. whether
34. without
35. business/-es
36. dependent
37. every day
38. may be
39. occasion/-s
40. occurrences
41. woman
42. all right
43. apparent/-ly
44. categories
45. final/-ly
46. immediate/-ly
47. roommate/-s
48. against
49. before
50. beginning

AT A GLANCE

Using a Spell Checker

• Unless you are part of a speedy electronic conversation, proofread and spell-check your messages before you send them. The more important the message, the more careful you should be about its accuracy and clarity.

• Keep a dictionary near your computer, and look up any word the spell checker highlights, but that you are not absolutely sure of.

• If your program has a LEARN option, enter into your spell-checker dictionary any proper names, non-English words, or specialized language you use regularly and have trouble spelling.

• Remember that spell checkers do not recognize homonym errors (misspelling *there* as *their,* for example). If you know that you mix up certain words, check for them after running your spell checker. Use the SEARCH function to identify words you need to check—every *their, there,* and *they're,* for instance.

• Remember that spell checkers are not sensitive to capitalization. If you write "president bush," the spell checker won't question it. (See 48b for InterCaps.)

• Always proofread carefully, even after you have used the spell checker.

40b Learn to distinguish among homonyms.

English has many homonyms—words that sound alike but have different spellings and meanings. But a relatively small number of them—just eight groups—cause writers frequent trouble.

The most troublesome homonyms

accept (to take or receive)
except (to leave out)

affect (an emotion; to have an
 influence)
effect (a result; to cause to
 happen)

its (possessive of *it*)
it's (contraction of *it is* or *it has*)

their (possessive of *they*)
there (in that place)
they're (contraction of *they are*)

to (in the direction of)
too (in addition; excessive)
two (number between *one* and *three*)

weather (climatic conditions)
whether (introducing a choice)

who's (contraction of *who is* or *who
 has*)
whose (possessive of *who*)

your (possessive of *you*)
you're (contraction of *you are*)

Other homonyms and frequently confused words

advice (suggestion)
advise (suggest [to])

all ready (fully prepared)
already (previously)

allude (refer indirectly [to])
elude (avoid or escape)

allusion (indirect reference)
illusion (false idea or appearance)

all ways (by every means)
always (at all times)

altar (sacred platform or table)
alter (change)

bare (uncovered; to uncover)
bear (animal; to carry or endure)

brake (device for stopping; to
    stop)
break (fracture; to fragment)

buy (purchase)
by (near; beside; through)

capital (principal city)
capitol (legislators' building)

cite (refer to)
sight (seeing; something seen)
site (location)

coarse (rough or crude)
course (plan of study; path)

complement (something that
    completes; to complete)
compliment (praise; to praise)

conscience (moral sense)
conscious (mentally aware)

council (leadership group)
counsel (advice; to advise)

desert (dry area; to abandon)
dessert (course at end of a meal)

elicit (draw forth)
illicit (illegal)

eminent (distinguished)
imminent (expected immediately)

every day (each day)
everyday (daily, ordinary)

forth (forward)
fourth (between *third* and *fifth*)

gorilla (ape)
guerrilla (irregular soldier)

hear (perceive with the ears)
here (in this place)

hoarse (sounding rough)
horse (animal)

know (understand)
no (opposite of *yes*)

lead (a metal; to go before)
led (past tense of *lead*)

loose (not tight; not confined)
lose (misplace; fail to win)

may be (might be)
maybe (perhaps)

passed (went by; received a
    passing grade)
past (beyond; events that have
    already occurred)

patience (quality of being patient)
patients (persons under medical
    care)

personal (private or individual)
personnel (employees)

plain (simple, not fancy; flat land)
plane (airplane; tool; flat surface)

presence (condition of being)
presents (gifts; gives)

principal (most important; head of
    a school)
principle (fundamental truth)

rain (precipitation)
reign (period of rule; to rule)
rein (strap; to control)

right (correct; opposite of *left*)
rite (ceremony)
write (produce words on a
    surface)

scene (setting; view)
seen (past participle of *see*)

stationary (unmoving)
stationery (writing paper)

than (as compared with)
then (at that time; therefore)

(continued on next page)

thorough (complete)
threw (past tense of *throw*)
through (in one side and out the
   other; by means of)
waist (part of the body)
waste (trash; to squander)

weak (feeble)
week (seven days)
which (what; that)
witch (woman with supernatural
   power)

FOR MULTILINGUAL WRITERS

Recognizing British Spellings

The following are some words that are spelled differently in American
and British English:

AMERICAN	BRITISH
center	centre
check	cheque
civilization	civilisation
color	colour
connection	connexion
criticize	criticise
judgment	judgement
realize	realise
theater	theatre

40c   Take advantage of spelling rules.

i *before* e *except after* c

Here is a slightly expanded version of the "*i* before *e*" rule:

I BEFORE E	achieve, brief, field, friend
EXCEPT AFTER C	ceiling, receipt, perceive
OR WHEN PRONOUNCED "AY"	eighth, neighbor, reign, weigh
OR IN WEIRD EXCEPTIONS	either, foreign, height, leisure, neither, seize

Prefixes

A prefix does not change the spelling of the word it is added to. (See 51e
on using hyphens with some prefixes and suffixes.)

dis- + service = disservice   over- + rate = overrate

Suffixes

A suffix may change the spelling of the word it is added to.

FINAL SILENT *E*

Drop the final silent *e* on a word when you add a suffix that starts with a vowel.

    imagine + -able = imaginable   exercise + -ing = exercising

Keep the final *e* if the suffix starts with a consonant.

    force + -ful = forceful   state + -ly = stately

    EXCEPTIONS argument, changeable, judgment, noticeable, truly

FINAL *Y*

If adding a suffix to a word that ends in *y*, change the *y* to an *i* if it is preceded by a consonant.

    try, tried   busy, busily

Keep the *y* if it follows a vowel, if it is part of a proper name, or if the suffix begins with *i*.

    employ, employed   Kennedy, Kennedyesque   dry, drying

FINAL CONSONANTS

When adding a suffix to a word that ends in a vowel and a consonant, double the final consonant if the word contains only one syllable or ends in an accented syllable.

    stop, stopped   begin, beginner   occur, occurrence

Do not double the final consonant if it is preceded by more than one vowel or by a vowel and another consonant or if the new word is not accented on the last syllable.

    bait, baiting   start, started   refer, reference
    benefit, benefiting   infer, inference   fight, fighter

Plurals

ADDING *-S* OR *-ES*

For most words, add *-s*. For words ending in *s, ch, sh, x,* or *z,* add *-es*.

    pencil, pencils   church, churches   bus, buses

Add *-s* to words ending in *o* if the *o* is preceded by a vowel. Add *-es* if the *o* is preceded by a consonant.

rodeo, rodeos	patio, patios	zoo, zoos
potato, potatoes	hero, heroes	veto, vetoes

EXCEPTIONS memo, memos; piano, pianos; solo, solos

For some words ending in *f* or *fe,* change *f* to *v,* and add *-s* or *-es.*

calf, calves	life, lives	hoof, hooves

OTHER PLURALS

For words ending in *y,* change *y* to *i* and add *-es* if the *y* is preceded by a consonant. Keep the *y* and add *-s* if the *y* is preceded by a vowel or if it ends a proper name.

theory, theories	eighty, eighties	Kennedy, Kennedys
attorney, attorneys	guy, guys	

Memorize irregular plurals.

bacterium, bacteria	criterion, criteria	ox, oxen

For compound nouns written as separate or hyphenated words, make the most important part plural.

brothers-in-law	lieutenant governors

For plurals of numbers, letters, symbols, and words used as terms, see 45c.

CONSIDERING DISABILITIES

Spelling

Spelling is especially difficult for people who have trouble processing letters and sounds in sequence. Technology can help, including "talking pens," which scan words and read them aloud, and voice-recognition programs, which transcribe dictated text.

---

bedfordstmartins.com/everyday_writer For exercises, go to **Exercise Central** and click on **Spelling.** For information on programs that transcribe dictated text, go to **Links** and click on **Considering Disabilities.**

41

Glossary of Usage

This glossary provides usage guidelines for some commonly confused words and phrases, such as *imply* and *infer*. Some confusing pairs are homonyms or near homonyms, such as *censor* and *censure*. (For some homonyms not in this glossary, see 40b.) The list here also contains items considered too informal (for example, *being as*) or wordy (for example, *owing to the fact that*) for academic or professional writing.

a, an   Use *a* with a word that begins with a consonant (*a book*), with a consonant sound such as "*y*" or "*w*" (*a euphoric moment, a one-sided match*), and with a sounded *h* (*a hemisphere*). Use *an* with a word that begins with a vowel (*an umbrella*), with a vowel sound (*an X-ray*), and with a silent *h* (*an honor*).

adapt, adopt   *Adapt* means "make fit or become accustomed" and usually takes the preposition *to*. *Adopt* means "take by choice." *We adopted the dog because we knew he'd adapt to our home.*

aggravate   The formal meaning is "make worse." *Having another mouth to feed aggravated their poverty.* In academic and professional writing, avoid using *aggravate* to mean "irritate" or "annoy."

all right   Avoid the spelling *alright.*

all together, altogether   *All together* means "all in a group" or "gathered in one place." *Altogether* means "completely" or "everything considered." *When the union members were all together in the room, their consensus was altogether obvious.*

a lot, lots, lots of   *A lot* is spelled as two words. Avoid these informal expressions meaning "much" or "many" in academic or professional writing.

alright   See *all right.*

altogether   See *all together, altogether.*

among, between   In referring to two things or people, use *between*. In referring to three or more, generally use *among*. *The relationship between the twins is different from that among the other three children.*

amount, number   Use *amount* with quantities you cannot count; use *number* for quantities you can count. *A small number of volunteers cleared a large amount of brush within a few hours.*

an   See *a, an.*

and/or   Avoid this term except in business or legal writing, where it is a short way of saying that one or both of two terms apply.

any body, anybody; any one, anyone   *Anybody* and *anyone* are pronouns meaning "any person." *Anyone [or anybody] would enjoy this film. Any body* is an adjective (*any*) modifying a noun (*body*). *Any body of water has its own ecology. Any one* is two adjectives or a pronoun modified by an adjective. *Customers could buy only two sale items at any one time.*

any more, anymore *Anymore* means "now." *Any more* means "no more" in a sentence that already has a negative. *Popular movies don't have <u>any more</u> violence than they used to, but I can't watch them <u>anymore</u>.*

anyplace In academic and professional writing, use *anywhere* instead.

anyway, anyways In writing, use *anyway*, not *anyways*.

apt, liable, likely *Likely to* means "probably will," and *apt to* means "inclines or tends to." Either will do in many instances. *Liable to* often carries a more negative sense, and *liable* is also a legal term meaning "obligated" or "responsible for."

as, as if, like Use *as* to identify equivalent terms in a description. *Gary served <u>as</u> moderator at the meeting.* Use *like* as a preposition to indicate similarity but not equivalency. *Hugo, <u>like</u> Jane, was a detailed observer. Like* cannot act as a conjunction introducing a clause. *The dog howled like a wolf, just <u>as if</u>* [not *like*] *she were a wild animal.*

as regards, in regard to Use one expression or the other; do not use the mixed expression *in regards to*.

assure, ensure, insure *Assure* means "convince" or "promise"; its direct object is usually a person or persons. *She <u>assured</u> voters she would not raise taxes. Ensure* and *insure* both mean "make certain," but *insure* usually refers to protection against financial loss. *When the city rationed water to <u>ensure</u> that the supply would last, the Browns could no longer afford to <u>insure</u> their car-wash business.*

as to Do not use *as to* as a substitute for *about. Karen was unsure <u>about</u>* [not *as to*] *Bruce's intentions.*

at, where See *where*.

awful, awfully *Awful* and *awfully* mean "awe-inspiring" and "in an awe-inspiring way." In academic and professional writing, avoid using *awful* to mean "bad" (*I had an <u>awful</u> day*) and *awfully* to mean "very" (*It was <u>awfully</u> cold*).

a while, awhile Always use *a while* after a preposition such as *for, in,* or *after. We drove <u>awhile</u> and then stopped for <u>a while</u>.*

bad, badly Use *bad* after a linking verb such as *be, feel,* or *seem*. Use *badly* to modify an action verb, an adjective, or another verb. *The hostess felt <u>bad</u> because the dinner was <u>badly</u> prepared.*

because of, due to Use *due to* when the effect, stated as a noun, appears before a form of the verb *be. His illness was <u>due to</u> malnutrition.* (*Illness,* a noun, is the effect.) Use *because of* when the effect is stated as a clause. *He was sick <u>because of</u> malnutrition.* (*He was sick,* a clause, is the effect.)

being as, being that In academic and professional writing, use *because* or *since* instead of these expressions. *<u>Because</u>* [not *<u>being as</u>*] *Romeo killed Tybalt, he was banished to Padua.*

beside, besides *Beside* is only a preposition, meaning "next to." *Besides* can be a preposition meaning "other than" or an adverb meaning "in addition." *No one <u>besides</u> Francesca would sit <u>beside</u> him.*

between See *among, between*.

breath, breathe *Breath* is a noun; *breathe*, a verb. *"<u>Breathe</u>," said the nurse, so June took a deep <u>breath</u> of laughing gas.*

bring, take   Use *bring* when an object is moved from a farther to a nearer place; use *take* when the opposite is true. *Take this box to the post office; bring back my mail.*

but, yet   Don't use these words together. *He is strong but* [not *but yet*] *gentle.*

but that, but what   Avoid using these as substitutes for *that* in expressions of doubt. *He never doubted that* [not *but that*] *he would solve the case.*

can, may   *Can* refers to ability and *may* to possibility or permission. *Since I can ski the slalom well, I may win the race.*

can't hardly, can't scarcely   *Hardly* and *scarcely* are negatives; therefore, *can't hardly* and *can't scarcely* are double negatives. These expressions are commonly used in some regional and ethnic varieties of English but are not used in standard academic English. *Tim can* [not *can't*] *hardly wait.*

can't help but   This expression is redundant. Use the more formal *I cannot but go* or the less formal *I can't help going* rather than *I can't help but go.*

can't scarcely   See *can't hardly, can't scarcely.*

censor, censure   *Censor* means "remove that which is considered offensive." *Censure* means "formally reprimand." *The public censured the newspaper for censoring letters to the editor.*

compare to, compare with   *Compare to* means "regard as similar." *Anna compared the loss to a kick in the head. Compare with* means "to examine to find differences or similarities." *The article compares Tim Burton's films with David Lynch's.*

comprise, compose   *Comprise* means "contain." *Compose* means "make up." *The class comprises twenty students. Twenty students compose the class.*

consensus of opinion   Use *consensus* instead of this redundant phrase. *The family consensus was to sell the old house.*

continual, continuous   *Continual* means "repeated at regular or frequent intervals." *Continuous* means "ongoing or connected without a break." *The damage done by continuous erosion was increased by the continual storms.*

could care less   Logically, *could care less* means the opposite of what speakers and writers intend. They mean and should say or write, *could not* [or *couldn't*] *care less.*

could of   Use *could have* instead. *We could have* [not *could of*] *gone to the concert.* Similarly, avoid *might of, should of,* and *would of.*

criteria, criterion   *Criterion* means "standard of judgment" or "necessary qualification." *Criteria* is the plural form. *Image is the wrong criterion for choosing a president.*

data   *Data* is the plural form of the Latin word *datum,* meaning "fact." Although *data* is used informally as either singular or plural, in academic or professional writing, treat *data* as plural. *These data indicate that fewer people smoke today than ten years ago.*

different from, different than   *Different from* is generally preferred in academic and professional writing, although both phrases are used widely. *Her lab results were no different from* [not *than*] *his.*

discreet, discrete   *Discreet* means "tactful" or "prudent." *Discrete* means "separate" or "distinct." *The manager's discreet words calmed all the discrete factions.*

disinterested, uninterested   *Disinterested* means "unbiased." *Uninterested* means "indifferent." *Finding disinterested jurors was difficult. She was uninterested in the verdict.*

distinct, distinctive   *Distinct* means "separate" or "well defined." *Distinctive* means "indicating a special quality." *Germany includes many distinct regions, each with a distinctive accent.*

doesn't, don't   *Doesn't* is the contraction for *does not*. Use it with *he, she, it,* and singular nouns. *Don't* stands for *do not*; use it with *I, you, we, they,* and plural nouns.

due to   See *because of, due to.*

each other, one another   Use *each other* in sentences involving two subjects and *one another* in sentences involving more than two.

emigrate from, immigrate to   *Emigrate from* means "move away from one's country." *Immigrate to* means "move to another country and settle there." *We emigrated from Norway in 1957. We immigrated to the United States.*

ensure   See *assure, ensure, insure.*

enthused   Use *enthusiastic* instead in academic and professional writing.

every day, everyday   *Everyday* is an adjective meaning "ordinary." *Every day* is an adjective and a noun, specifying a particular day. *I wore everyday clothes. I wore a dress every day.*

every one, everyone   *Everyone* is a pronoun. *Every one* is an adjective and a pronoun referring to each member of a group. *Because he began the assignment after everyone else, David knew he could not finish every one of the problems.*

explicit, implicit   *Explicit* means "directly or openly expressed." *Implicit* means "indirectly expressed or implied." *The explicit message of the ad urged consumers to buy the product, while the implicit message promised popularity if they did so.*

farther, further   *Farther* refers to physical distance. *How much farther is it to Munich? Further* refers to time or degree. *I want to avoid further delays.*

fewer, less   Use *fewer* with nouns that can be counted. Use *less* with general amounts that you cannot count. *The world will be safer with fewer bombs and less hostility.*

finalize   *Finalize* is a pretentious way of saying "end" or "make final." *We closed* [not *finalized*] *the deal.*

firstly, secondly, thirdly   These are common in British English; *first, second,* and *third* are preferred in U.S. English.

flaunt, flout   *Flaunt* means "show off." *Flout* means "mock" or "scorn." *The teens flouted convention by flaunting their multicolored wigs.*

former, latter   *Former* refers to the first and *latter* to the second of two things previously introduced. *Rap and jazz remain popular; the former, which has been around for a few decades, sometimes shows the influence of the latter, which goes back much further.*

fun, funner, funnest   Do not use these words as adjectives in academic or professional writing. For *fun,* substitute a word such as *amusing, enjoyable, genial, pleasant;* for *funner* or *funnest,* write *more* or *most* with one of the preceding adjectives.

further See *farther, further.*

good, well *Good* is an adjective and should not be used as a substitute for the adverb *well. Gabriel is a good host who cooks well.*

good and *Good and* is colloquial for "very"; avoid it in academic and professional writing.

hanged, hung *Hanged* refers to executions; *hung* is used for all other meanings. *The old woman hung her head as she passed the tree where the murderer was hanged.*

hardly See *can't hardly, can't scarcely.*

herself, himself, myself, yourself Do not use these reflexive pronouns as subjects or as objects unless they are necessary. Compare *John cut him* and *John cut himself. Jane and I* [not *myself*] *agree. They invited John and me* [not *myself*].

he/she, his/her Better solutions for avoiding sexist language are to write out *he or she,* to eliminate pronouns entirely, or to make the subject plural (*they*). Instead of writing *Everyone should carry his/her driver's license,* try *Drivers should carry driver's licenses* or *People should carry their driver's licenses.*

himself See *herself, himself, myself, yourself.*

his/her See *he/she, his/her.*

hisself Use *himself* instead in academic or professional writing.

hopefully *Hopefully* is often misused to mean "it is hoped," but its correct meaning is "with hope." *Sam watched the roulette wheel hopefully* [not *Hopefully, Sam will win*].

hung See *hanged, hung.*

if, whether Use *whether* or *whether or not* for alternatives. *She was considering whether or not to go.* Reserve *if* for the conditional. *If it rains tomorrow, we will meet inside.*

immigrate to See *emigrate from, immigrate to.*

impact Avoid the colloquial use of *impact* or *impact on* as a verb meaning "affect." *Population control may reduce* [not *impact*] *world hunger.*

implicit See *explicit, implicit.*

imply, infer To *imply* is to suggest indirectly. To *infer* is to make an educated guess. *The note implied they were planning a small wedding; we inferred we would not be invited.*

in regards to Do not use this expression. See *as regards, in regard to.*

inside of, outside of Use *inside* and *outside* instead. *The class regularly met outside* [not *outside of*] *the building.*

insure See *assure, ensure, insure.*

interact with, interface with *Interact with* is a vague phrase meaning "do something that somehow involves another person." *Interface with* is computer jargon for "discuss" or "communicate." Avoid both expressions in academic and professional writing.

irregardless, regardless *Irregardless* is a double negative. Use *regardless.*

is when, is where These vague expressions are often incorrectly used in definitions. *Schizophrenia is a psychotic condition in which* [not *Schizophrenia is when* or *is where*] *a person withdraws from reality.*

its, it's *Its* is the possessive form of *it*. *It's* is a contraction for *it is* or *it has*. *It's important to observe the rat before it eats its meal.*

kind, sort, type Modify these singular nouns with *this* or *that,* and follow them with other singular nouns. *Wear this kind of dress* [not *those kind* of *dresses*]. *Wear these kinds of hats.*

kind of, sort of Avoid these colloquialisms. *Amy was somewhat* [not *kind of*] *tired.*

later, latter *Later* means "after some time." *Latter* refers to the last of two items named. *Juan and Chad won all their early matches, but the latter was injured later in the season.*

latter See *former, latter* and *later, latter.*

lay, lie *Lay* means "place" or "put." Its main forms are *lay, laid, laid.* It generally has a direct object, specifying what has been placed. *She laid her books on the desk. Lie* means "recline" or "be positioned" and does not take a direct object. Its main forms are *lie, lay, lain. She lay awake until two.*

leave, let *Leave* means "go away." *Let* means "allow." *Leave alone* and *let alone* are interchangeable. *Let me leave now, and leave* [or *let*] *me alone from now on!*

lend, loan *Loan* is a noun, and *lend* is a verb. *Please lend me your pen so that I may fill out this application for a loan.*

less See *fewer, less.*

let See *leave, let.*

liable See *apt, liable, likely.*

lie See *lay, lie.*

like See *as, as if, like.*

like, such as *Like* means "similar to"; use *like* when comparing a subject with examples. *A hurricane, like a flood or any other major disaster, may strain emergency resources.* Use *such as* when examples represent a general category; *such as* is often an alternative to *for example. A destructive hurricane, such as Floyd in 1999, may drastically alter an area's economy.*

likely See *apt, liable, likely.*

literally *Literally* means "actually" or "exactly as stated." Use it to stress the truth of a statement that might otherwise be understood as figurative. Do not use *literally* as an intensifier in a figurative statement. *Mirna was literally at the edge of her seat* may be accurate, but *Mirna is so hungry that she could literally eat a horse* is not.

loan See *lend, loan.*

loose, lose *Lose* is a verb meaning "misplace." *Loose* is an adjective that means "not securely attached." *Sew on that loose button before you lose it.*

lots, lots of See *a lot, lots, lots of.*

man, mankind Many people consider these terms sexist because they do not mention women. Replace such words with *people, humans, humankind, men and women,* or similar phrases.

may See *can, may.*

media *Media* is the plural form of the noun *medium* and takes a plural verb. *The media are* [not *is*] *being consolidated.*

moral, morale A *moral* is a succinct lesson. *The moral of the story is that generosity is rewarded. Morale* means "spirit" or "mood." *Office morale was low.*

myself See *herself, himself, myself, yourself.*

nor, or Use *either* with *or* and *neither* with *nor.*

nowhere In academic or professional writing, use *nowhere,* not *nowheres.*

number See *amount, number.*

off of Use *off* without *of. The spaghetti slipped off* [not *off of*] *the plate.*

OK, O.K., okay All are acceptable spellings, but avoid this expression in academic and professional writing.

on account of Use this substitute for *because of* sparingly or not at all.

one another See *each other, one another.*

or See *nor, or.*

outside of See *inside of, outside of.*

owing to the fact that Avoid this and other wordy expressions for *because.*

people, persons In general, use *people* as the plural of *person.* An exception is established expressions such as *displaced persons.*

per Use the Latin *per* only in standard technical phrases such as *miles per hour.* Otherwise, find English equivalents. *As mentioned in* [not *as per*] *the latest report, our town's average food expenses every week* [not *per week*] *are $40 per capita.*

percent, percentage Use *percent* with a specific number; use *percentage* with an adjective such as *large* or *small. Last year, 80 percent of the club's members were female. A large percentage of the club's members are women.*

plenty *Plenty* means "enough" or "a great abundance." *They told us America was a land of plenty.* Colloquially, it is used to mean "very," a usage you should avoid in academic and professional writing. *He was very* [not *plenty*] *tired.*

plus *Plus* means "in addition to." *Your salary plus mine will cover our expenses.* Do not use *plus* to mean "besides" or "moreover." *That dress does not fit me. Besides* [not *Plus*], *it is the wrong color.*

precede, proceed *Precede* means "come before"; *proceed* means "go forward." *Despite the storm that preceded the flooding of the parking lot, we proceeded to our cars.*

pretty Avoid using *pretty* as a substitute for "rather," "somewhat," or "quite." *Bill was quite* [not *pretty*] *disagreeable.*

proceed See *precede, proceed.*

quotation, quote *Quote* is a verb, and *quotation* is a noun. *He quoted the president, and the quotation* [not *quote*] *was preserved in history books.*

raise, rise *Raise* means "lift" or "move upward." (Referring to children, it means "bring up.") It takes a direct object; someone raises something. *The guests raised their glasses to toast their host. Rise* means "go upward." It does not take a direct object; something rises by itself. *She saw the steam rise from the pan.*

rarely ever Use *rarely* by itself, or use *hardly ever. When we were poor, we rarely went to the movies.*

real, really *Real* is an adjective, and *really* is an adverb. Do not substitute *real* for *really*. In academic and profesional writing, do not use *real* or *really* to mean "very." *The injured man walked <u>very</u>* [not *real* or *really*] *slowly.*

reason . . . is because Use either *the reason . . . is that* or the word *because*—not both. *The <u>reason</u> the copier stopped <u>is that</u>* [not *is because*] *the paper jammed* or *The copier stopped <u>because</u> the paper jammed.*

reason why This expression is redundant. *The <u>reason</u>* [not *reason why*] *this book is short is market demand.*

regardless See *irregardless, regardless.*

respectfully, respectively *Respectfully* means "with respect." *Respectively* means "in the order given." *Aden and Anya are, <u>respectively</u>, a singer and a clown. Jaime treated his aunt <u>respectfully</u>.*

rise See *raise, rise.*

scarcely See *can't hardly, can't scarcely.*

secondly See *firstly, secondly, thirdly.*

set, sit *Set* means "put" or "place" and takes a direct object. *Sit* refers to taking a seat but does not take an object. *<u>Set</u> your cup on the table, and <u>sit</u> down.*

since *Since* has two uses: (1) to show passage of time, as in *I have been home <u>since</u> Tuesday;* (2) to mean "because," as in *<u>Since</u> you are in a bad mood, I will leave.* Be careful not to use *since* ambiguously. In *<u>Since</u> I broke my leg, I've stayed home, since* might be understood to mean either "because" or "ever since."

sit See *set, sit.*

so In academic and professional writing, follow *so* with *that* to show how the intensified condition leads to a result. *Aaron was <u>so</u> tired <u>that</u> he fell asleep at the wheel.*

someplace Use *somewhere* instead in academic and professional writing.

some time, sometime, sometimes *Some time* refers to a length of time. *Please leave me <u>some time</u> to dress. Sometime* means "at some indefinite later time." *<u>Sometime</u> I will take you to London. Sometimes* means "occasionally." *<u>Sometimes</u> I eat sushi.*

sort See *kind, sort, type.*

sort of See *kind of, sort of.*

so that See *so.*

such as See *like, such as.*

supposed to, used to Both expressions require the final *-d*. *He is <u>supposed to</u> sing.*

sure, surely Avoid using *sure* as an intensifier. Instead, use *surely* (or *certainly* or *without a doubt*). *<u>Surely</u>, the doctor will prescribe an antibiotic.*

take See *bring, take.*

than, then Use *than* in comparative statements. *The cat was bigger <u>than</u> the dog.* Use *then* when referring to a sequence of events. *I won, and <u>then</u> I cried.*

that, which A clause beginning with *that* singles out the item being described. *The book <u>that</u> is on the table is a good one* specifies the book on the table as opposed to some other book. A clause beginning with *which* may or may not single out the object, although some writers use *which* clauses only to add more information about an object being described. *The book, which is on the table, is a good one* contains a *which* clause between the commas. The clause simply adds extra, nonessential information about the book; it does not specify which book.

that, which, who   Use *that* when referring to things or to a group of people. *A band that tours frequently will please its fans.* Use *which* only when referring to things. *The new album, which is the band's first in years, appeals to new listeners.* Use *who* to refer to people. *Alex is the band member who plays drums.* In conversation, *that* can be used to refer to an individual (*the man that plays drums*), but in academic and professional writing, use *who* (*the man who plays drums*).

theirselves   Use *themselves* instead in academic and professional writing.

thirdly   See *firstly, secondly, thirdly.*

to, too, two   *To* generally shows direction. *Too* means "also." *Two* is the number. *We, too, are going to the meeting in two hours.* Avoid using *to* after *where*. *Where are you flying* [not *flying to*]?

to, where   See *where.*

try and   In academic and professional writing, use *try to* followed by another verb. *We try to* [not *try and*] *review our class notes each evening.*

type   See *kind, sort, type.*

uninterested   See *disinterested, uninterested.*

unique   *Unique* means "the one and only." Do not use it with an adverb that suggests degree, such as *very* or *most*. *Mel's hands are unique* [not *very unique*].

used to   See *supposed to, used to.*

very   Avoid using *very* to intensify a weak adjective or adverb; instead, replace the adjective or adverb with a stronger, more precise, or more colorful word. Instead of *very nice*, for example, use *kind, warm, sensitive, endearing,* or *friendly.*

way, ways   When referring to extent, use *way. Graduation was a long way* [not *ways*] *off.*

well   See *good, well.*

when, where   See *is when, is where.*

where   Use *where* alone, not with words such as *at* and *to*. *Where are you going?* [not *Where are you going to?*]

whether   See *if, whether.*

which   See *that, which* and *that, which, who.*

who   See *that, which, who* and *who, whom.*

who, whom   In adjective clauses, use *who* if the following word is a verb. *Liv, who smokes incessantly, is my godmother.* Use *whom* if the following word is a noun or pronoun. *I heard that Liv, whom I have not seen for years, wears only purple.* Exception: ignore an expression such as *I think* within the clause. *Liv, who I think wears nothing but purple, is my godmother.* [Ignore *I think*; use *who* because the next word is a verb, *wears.*]

yet   See *but, yet.*

yourself   See *herself, himself, myself, yourself.*

PUNCTUATION/
Mechanics

You can show a lot with a look. . . . It's punctuation.

—CLINT EASTWOOD

Punctuation/Mechanics

42

Commas

It's hard to go through a day without encountering directions of some kind, and commas often play a crucial role in how you interpret instructions. See how important the comma is in the following directions for making hot cereal:

> Add Cream of Wheat slowly, stirring constantly.

That sentence tells the cook to *add the cereal slowly*. If the comma came before the word *slowly*, however, the cook might add all of the cereal at once and *stir slowly*. This chapter aims to help you use commas correctly and effectively.

42a Use commas to set off introductory words, phrases, and clauses.

▶ Slowly, she became conscious of her predicament.

▶ In fact, only you can decide.

▶ Eventually, John wondered whether he should change careers.

▶ In Fitzgerald's novel, the color green takes on great symbolic qualities.

▶ Sporting a pair of specially made running shoes, Brendan prepared for the race.

▶ To win the game, Connor needed skill and luck.

▶ Pen poised in anticipation, Logan waited for the test to be distributed.

AT A GLANCE

Editing for Commas

Research has shown that five of the most common errors in college writing involve commas. Check your writing for these five errors.

1. Check every sentence that doesn't begin with the subject to see whether it opens with an introductory element (a word, phrase, or clause that describes the subject or tells when, where, how, or why the main action of the sentence occurs). Use a comma to separate an introductory element from the main part of the sentence. (42a)

2. Look at every sentence that contains one of the conjunctions *and, but, or, nor, for, so,* and *yet*. If the groups of words before and after the conjunction both function as complete sentences, you have a compound sentence. Make sure to use a comma before the conjunction. (42b)

3. Look at each adjective clause beginning with *which, who, whom, whose, when,* or *where* and at each phrase and appositive. (28m) Decide whether the element is essential to the meaning of the sentence. If the rest of the sentence would be unclear without it, you should not set off the element with commas. (42c)

4. Identify all adjective clauses beginning with *that,* and make sure they are *not* set off with commas. (42c and j)

5. Check every *and* and *or* to see whether it comes before the last item in a series of three or more words, phrases, or clauses. Be sure that each item in a series (except the last) is followed by a comma. (42d)

▶ Since her mind was not getting enough stimulation, Liz decided to read some good literature.

Note that some writers omit the comma after an introductory element if it is short and does not seem to require a pause after it. However, you will never be wrong if you use a comma. (See also 42i.)

42b Use commas to separate clauses in compound sentences.

A comma usually precedes a coordinating conjunction (*and, but, or, nor, for, so,* or *yet*) that joins two independent clauses in a compound sentence (28n).

▶ The title may sound important, but *administrative clerk* is only a euphemism for *photocopier.*

▶ The climbers have to reach the summit today**,** or they must turn back.

▶ The show started at last**,** and the crowd grew quiet.

With very short clauses, you can sometimes omit the comma.

▶ She saw her chance and she took it.

Always use the comma if there is any chance the sentence will be misread without it.

▶ I opened the junk drawer**,** and the cabinet door jammed.

Use a semicolon rather than a comma when the clauses are long and complex or contain their own commas.

▶ When these early migrations took place, the ice was still confined to the lands in the far north; but eight hundred thousand years ago, when man was already established in the temperate latitudes, the ice moved southward until it covered large parts of Europe and Asia.
—ROBERT JASTROW, *Until the Sun Dies*

42c Use commas to set off nonrestrictive elements.

Nonrestrictive elements are clauses, phrases, and words that do not limit, or restrict, the meaning of the words they modify. Since such elements are not essential to the meaning of a sentence, they should be set off from the rest of the sentence with commas. Restrictive elements, on the other hand, *do* limit meaning; they should *not* be set off with commas.

RESTRICTIVE Drivers *who have been convicted of drunken driving* should lose their licenses.

In the preceding sentence, the clause *who have been convicted of drunken driving* is essential to the meaning because it limits the word it modifies, *Drivers,* to only those drivers who have been convicted of drunken driving. Therefore, it is *not* set off with commas.

NONRESTRICTIVE The two drivers involved in the accident, *who have been convicted of drunken driving,* should lose their licenses.

In the second sentence, however, the clause *who have been convicted of drunken driving* is not essential to the meaning because it does not limit what it modifies, *The two drivers involved in the accident,* but merely provides additional information about these drivers. Therefore, the clause is set off with commas.

To decide whether an element is restrictive or nonrestrictive, mentally delete the element, and see if the deletion changes the meaning of the rest of the sentence or makes it unclear. If the deletion does change the meaning, the element is probably restrictive, and you should not set it off with commas. If it does not change the meaning, the element is probably nonrestrictive and requires commas.

Adjective and adverb clauses

An adjective clause that begins with *that* is always restrictive; do not set it off with commas. An adjective clause beginning with *which* may be either restrictive or nonrestrictive; however, some writers prefer to use *which* only for nonrestrictive clauses, which they set off with commas.

NONRESTRICTIVE CLAUSES

▶ **I borrowed books from the rental library of Shakespeare and Company,** *which was the library and bookstore of Sylvia Beach at 12 rue de l'Odeon.* —ERNEST HEMINGWAY, *A Moveable Feast*

The adjective clause describing Shakespeare and Company is not necessary to the meaning of the independent clause and therefore is set off with a comma.

In general, set off an adverb clause that follows a main clause only if it begins with *although, even though, while,* or another subordinating conjunction expressing the idea of contrast.

▶ **He uses semicolons frequently, while she prefers periods and short sentences.**

The adverb clause *while she prefers periods and short sentences* expresses the idea of contrast; therefore, it is set off with a comma.

RESTRICTIVE CLAUSES

▶ **The claim** *that men like seriously to battle one another to some sort of finish* **is a myth.** —JOHN MCMURTRY, "Kill 'Em! Crush 'Em! Eat 'Em Raw!"

The adjective clause is necessary to the meaning of the sentence because it explains which claim is a myth; therefore, the clause is not set off with commas.

▶ **The man/who rescued Jana's puppy/won her eternal gratitude.**

The adjective clause *who rescued Jana's puppy* is necessary to the meaning because only the man who rescued the puppy won the gratitude; the clause is restrictive and so takes no commas.

With the exceptions noted above, do *not* set off an adverb clause that follows a main clause.

▶ Remember to check your calculations/before you submit the form.

Phrases

Participial phrases may be restrictive or nonrestrictive. Prepositional phrases are usually restrictive, but sometimes they are not essential to the meaning of a sentence and are set off with commas (28m).

NONRESTRICTIVE PHRASES

▶ The bus drivers, rejecting the management offer, remained on strike.

Using commas around the participial phrase makes it nonrestrictive, telling us that all of the drivers remained on strike.

▶ Frédéric Chopin, in spite of poor health, composed prolifically.

The phrase *in spite of poor health* does not limit the meaning of *Frédéric Chopin* and so is set off with commas.

RESTRICTIVE PHRASES

▶ The bus drivers/rejecting the management offer/remained on strike.

If the phrase *rejecting the management offer* limits the meaning of *The bus drivers,* the commas should be deleted. The revised sentence says that only some of the bus drivers, the ones who rejected the offer, remained on strike, implying that the other drivers went back to work.

Appositives

An appositive is a noun or noun phrase that renames a nearby noun. When an appositive is not essential to identify what it renames, it is set off with commas.

NONRESTRICTIVE APPOSITIVES

▶ Savion Glover, the MacArthur Award–winning dancer, taps like poetry in motion.

Savion Glover's name identifies him; the appositive *the MacArthur Award– winning tap dancer* provides extra information.

RESTRICTIVE APPOSITIVES

▶ Mozart's opera/*The Marriage of Figaro*/ was considered revolutionary.

The phrase *The Marriage of Figaro* is essential to the meaning of the sentence because Mozart wrote more than one opera. Therefore, it is *not* set off with commas.

42d Use commas to separate items in a series.

▶ He has plundered our seas, ravaged our coasts, burnt our towns, and destroy the lives of our people.   –Declaration of Independence

You may see a series with no comma after the next-to-last item, particularly in newspaper writing. Occasionally, however, omitting the comma can cause confusion, and you will never be wrong if you include it.

▶ Diners had a choice of broccoli, green beans, peas, and carrots.

Without the comma after *peas,* you wouldn't know if there were three choices (the third being a *mixture* of peas and carrots) or four.

When the items in a series contain commas of their own or other punctuation, separate them with semicolons rather than commas.

▶ Should I serve kidney beans, which are red; cranberry beans, which are white and red; or chickpeas, which are tan?

Coordinate adjectives, those that relate equally to the noun they modify, should be separated by commas.

▶ The long, twisting, muddy road led to a shack in the woods.

In a sentence like *The cracked bathroom mirror reflected his face,* however, *cracked* and *bathroom* are not coordinate because *bathroom mirror* is the equivalent of a single word, which is modified by cracked. Hence, they are *not* separated by commas.

You can usually determine whether adjectives are coordinate by inserting *and* between them. If the sentence makes sense with the *and,* the adjectives are coordinate and should be separated by commas.

▶ They are sincere *and* talented *and* inquisitive researchers.

The sentence makes sense with the *and*'s, so the adjectives *sincere, talented,* and *inquisitive* should be separated by commas: *They are sincere, talented, inquisitive researchers.*

▶ **Byron carried an elegant *and* gold *and* pocket watch.**

The sentence does not make sense with the *and*'s, so the adjectives *elegant, gold,* and *pocket* should not be separated by commas: *Byron carried an elegant gold pocket watch.*

A MATTER OF STYLE

Series Commas

Comma conventions are quite often a matter of style—and of what is called, in the publishing industry, "house style." Many newspapers, for example, follow the style of omitting the comma after the next-to-last item in a series of three or more. Here is such an example from the *New York Times:*

> Current alternative rockers like Courtney Love, P. J. Harvey and Alanis Morisette owe Patti Smith no small debt.
> —JON PARELES, "Return of the Godmother of Punk"

You may be required (by an instructor or by your company's house style) to follow this convention. But, ordinarily, you will never be wrong if you put a comma after each item in a series except the last: *Current alternative rockers like Courtney Love, P. J. Harvey, and Alanis Morisette owe Patti Smith no small debt.*

42e ### Use commas to set off parenthetical and transitional expressions and conjunctive adverbs.

Parenthetical expressions add comments or information. Because they often interrupt the flow of a sentence or digress, they are usually set off with commas.

▶ **Some studies, incidentally, have shown that chocolate, of all things, helps to prevent tooth decay.**

▶ **Roald Dahl's stories, it turns out, were often inspired by his own childhood.**

Transitional expressions, conjunctive adverbs (words such as *however* and *furthermore*), and other words and phrases used to connect parts of sentences are usually set off with commas.

▶ Ozone is a by-product of dry cleaning, for example.

▶ Ceiling fans are, moreover, less expensive than air conditioners.

42f Use commas to set off contrasting elements, interjections, direct address, and tag questions.

CONTRASTING ELEMENTS

▶ On official business it was she, *not my father,* one would usually hear on the phone or in stores.
> —RICHARD RODRIGUEZ, "Aria: A Memoir of a Bilingual Childhood"

INTERJECTIONS

▶ *My God,* who wouldn't want a wife?   —JUDY BRADY, "I Want a Wife"

DIRECT ADDRESS

▶ Remember, *sir,* that you are under oath.

TAG QUESTIONS

▶ The governor did not veto the unemployment bill, *did she?*

42g Use commas to set off parts of dates, addresses, titles, and numbers.

Dates

Use a comma between the day of the week and the month, between the day of the month and the year, and between the year and the rest of the sentence, if any.

▶ The attacks on the morning of Tuesday, September 11, 2001, took the United States by surprise.

Do not use commas with dates in inverted order or with dates consisting of only the month and the year.

▶ She dated the letter *26 August 2004.*
▶ Thousands of Germans swarmed over the wall in *November 1989.*

Addresses and place names

Use a comma after each part of an address or place name, including the state if there is no zip code. Do not precede a zip code with a comma.

▶ Forward my mail to the Department of English, The Ohio State
University, Columbus, Ohio 43210.

▶ Portland, Oregon, is much larger than Portland, Maine.

Titles

Use commas to set off a title such as *MD* and *PhD* from the name preceding it and from the rest of the sentence. The titles *Jr.* and *Sr.,* however,
often appear without commas.

▶ Oliver Sacks, MD, has written about the way the mind works.

▶ Martin Luther King Jr. was one of the twentieth century's greatest
orators.

Numbers

In numerals of five digits or more, use a comma between each group of
three, starting from the right.

▶ The city's population rose to *65,585* in the 2000 census.

The comma is optional within numerals of four digits but never occurs
in four-digit dates, street addresses, or page numbers.

▶ The college had an enrollment of *1,789* [or *1789*] in the fall of 2003.
▶ My grandparents live at *2428* Loring Place.
▶ Turn to page *1566.*

42h Use commas to set off most quotations.

Commas set off a quotation from words used to introduce or identify
the source of the quotation. A comma following a quotation goes inside
the closing quotation mark. (See 47d for advice about using colons
instead of commas to introduce quotations.)

▶ A German proverb warns, "Go to law for a sheep, and lose your cow."

▶ "All I know about grammar," said Joan Didion, "is its infinite power."

Do not use a comma after a question mark or exclamation point.

▶ "What's a thousand dollars?/" asks Groucho Marx in *Cocoanuts.* "Mere chicken feed. A poultry matter."

▶ "Out, damned spot!/" cries Lady Macbeth.

Do not use a comma when you introduce a quotation with *that.*

▶ The writer of Ecclesiastes concludes that/ "all is vanity."

Do not use a comma before an indirect quotation—one that does not use the speaker's exact words.

▶ Patrick Henry declared/ that he wanted either liberty or death.

42i Use commas to prevent confusion.

Sometimes commas are necessary to make sentences easier to read or understand.

▶ The members of the dance troupe strutted in, in matching costumes.

▶ Before, I had planned to major in biology.

42j Eliminate unnecessary commas.

Excessive use of commas can spoil an otherwise fine sentence.

Around restrictive elements

Do not use commas to set off restrictive elements—elements that limit, or define, the meaning of the words they modify or refer to (42c).

▶ I don't let my children watch TV shows/ that are violent.

The *that* clause restricts the meaning of *TV shows,* so the comma should be omitted.

▶ A law/ requiring the use of seat belts/ was passed in 1987.

▶ My only defense/ against my allergies/ is to stay indoors.

▶ The actor/ Russell Crowe/ might win the award.

Between subjects and verbs, verbs and objects or complements, and prepositions and objects

Do not use a comma between a subject and its verb, a verb and its object or complement, or a preposition and its object. This rule holds true even if the subject, object, or complement is a long phrase or clause.

▶ Watching movies late at night/ is a way for me to relax.

▶ Parents must decide/ how much TV their children may watch.

▶ The winner of/ the trophy for community service stepped forward.

In compound constructions

In compound constructions (other than compound sentences), do not use a comma before or after a coordinating conjunction that joins the two parts (42b).

▶ Improved health care/ and more free trade were two goals of the Clinton administration.

The *and* here joins parts of a compound subject, which should not be separated by a comma.

▶ Mark Twain trained as a printer/ and worked as a steamboat pilot.

The *and* here joins parts of a compound predicate, which should not be separated by a comma.

Before the first or after the last item in a series

▶ The auction included/ furniture, paintings, and china.

▶ The swimmer took slow, elegant, powerful/ strokes.

bedfordstmartins.com/everyday_writer   For exercises, go to **Exercise Central** and click on **Commas.**

43

Semicolons

If you've ever pored over the fine print at the bottom of an ad for a big sale, looking for the opening hours or the address of the store nearest you, then you've seen plenty of semicolons in action. Here's an example from a Bloomingdale's ad:

> Stores & Hours—
> *Short Hills:* SUN., 12–6; MON., 10–9:30; TUES., 10–5; WED. through FRI., 10–9:30; SAT., 10–8.

The semicolons separate the information for one day's hours from the next. Semicolons have the effect of creating a pause stronger than that of a comma but not as strong as the full pause of a period.

AT A GLANCE

Editing for Semicolons

- If you use semicolons, be sure they appear only between independent clauses—groups of words that can stand alone as sentences (43a and b)—or between items in a series. (43c)
- If you find few or no semicolons in your writing, ask yourself whether you should add some. Would any closely related ideas in two sentences be better expressed in one sentence with a semicolon? (43a)

43a Use semicolons to link closely related independent clauses.

Though a comma and a coordinating conjunction often join independent clauses, semicolons provide writers with subtler ways of signaling closely related clauses. The clause following a semicolon often restates an idea expressed in the first clause; it sometimes expands on or presents a contrast to the first.

▶ **Immigration acts were passed; newcomers had to prove, besides moral correctness and financial solvency, their ability to read.**
> —MARY GORDON, "More than Just a Shrine"

Gordon uses a semicolon to join the two clauses, giving the sentence an abrupt rhythm that suits the topic: laws that imposed strict requirements.

If two independent clauses joined by a coordinating conjunction contain commas, you may use a semicolon instead of a comma before the conjunction to make the sentence easier to read.

▶ **Every year, whether the Republican or the Democratic party is in office, more and more power drains away from the individual to feed vast reservoirs in far-off places; and we have less and less say about the shape of events which shape our future.**
— WILLIAM F. BUCKLEY JR., "Why Don't We Complain?"

43b Use semicolons to link independent clauses joined by conjunctive adverbs or transitional phrases.

A semicolon should link independent clauses joined by conjunctive adverbs (see list in 28h) or transitional phrases.

▶ **Every kid should have access to a computer; furthermore, access to the Internet should be free.**

▶ **The circus comes as close to being the world in microcosm as anything I know; in a way, it puts all the rest of show business in the shade.**
— E. B. WHITE, "The Ring of Time"

SOME TRANSITIONAL PHRASES

as a result	in addition	in the meantime
as soon as	in conclusion	of course
for example	in fact	on the other hand
for instance	in other words	on the whole
granted that	in short	to summarize

When linking clauses with conjunctive adverbs or transitional phrases, be careful not to write fused sentences or comma splices (34c).

43c Use semicolons to separate items in a series containing other punctuation.

Ordinarily, commas separate items in a series (42d). But when the items themselves contain commas or other marks of punctuation, using semicolons to separate the items will make the sentence clearer and easier to read.

▶ **Anthropology encompasses archaeology, the study of ancient civilizations through artifacts; linguistics, the study of the structure**

and development of language; and cultural anthropology, the study of
language, customs, and behavior.

43d   Eliminate misused semicolons.

A comma, not a semicolon, should separate an independent clause from
a dependent clause or phrase.

▶ The police found fingerprints; which they used to identify the thief.

▶ The new system would encourage students to register for courses
online; thus streamlining registration.

A colon, not a semicolon, should introduce a series or list.

▶ The tour includes visits to the following art museums; the Prado, in
Madrid; the Louvre, in Paris; and the Van Gogh, in Amsterdam.

bedfordstmartins.com/everyday_writer   For exercises, go to **Exercise Central** and
click on **Semicolons.**

44

End Punctuation

Periods, question marks, and exclamation points often appear in advertising to create special effects or draw readers along from line to line.
For example:

> The experts say America Online is a well-designed, easy-to-use service.
>   So what are you waiting for?
>   Get your hands on America Online today!

End punctuation tells us how to read each sentence—as a matter-of-fact
statement, an ironic query, or an emphatic order. This chapter will guide
you in using appropriate end punctuation in your own writing.

44a Periods

Use a period to close sentences that make statements, give mild commands, or make polite requests.

▶ **All books are either dreams or swords.** —AMY LOWELL

▶ **Don't use a fancy word if a simpler word will do.**
—GEORGE ORWELL, "Politics and the English Language"

▶ **Would you please close the door.**

A period also closes indirect questions, which report rather than ask questions.

▶ **I asked how old the child was.**
▶ **We all wonder who will win the election.**

Until recently, periods have been used with most abbreviations in American English. However, more and more abbreviations are appearing without periods.

Mr.	MD	BC *or* B.C.
Ms.	PhD	BCE *or* B.C.E.
Mrs.	MBA	AD *or* A.D.
Jr.	RN	AM *or* a.m.
Dr.	Sen.	PM *or* p.m.

Many of the abbreviations in the third column are in small caps, a typographical option in word-processing programs. You may also use full-size capital letters for these abbreviations.

Ms. is not an abbreviation, but it takes a period in keeping with other titles used before names.

Some abbreviations rarely if ever appear with periods. These include the postal abbreviations of state names, such as *FL* and *TN* (though the traditional abbreviations, such as *Fla.* and *Tenn.*, do call for periods), and most groups of initials (*GE, CIA, DOS, AIDS, YMCA, UNICEF*). If you are not sure whether a particular abbreviation should include periods, check a dictionary, or follow the style guidelines (such as those of the Modern Library Association) you are using in a research paper. (For more about abbreviations, see Chapter 49.)

Do not use an additional period when a sentence ends with an abbreviation that has its own period.

▶ The social worker referred me to John Pintz, Jr./

44b Question marks

Use question marks to close sentences that ask direct questions.

▶ How is the human mind like a computer, and how is it different?
　　　　　　　　　　　　–KATHLEEN STASSEN BERGER AND ROSS A. THOMPSON,
　　　　　　　　　　　　The Developing Person through Childhood and Adolescence

Question marks do not close *indirect* questions, which report rather than ask questions.

▶ She asked whether I opposed his nomination.

Do not use a comma or a period immediately after a question mark that ends a direct quotation.

▶ "Am I my brother's keeper?/" Cain asked.

▶ Cain asked, "Am I my brother's keeper?/"

Questions in a series may have question marks even when they are not separate sentences.

▶ I often confront a difficult choice: should I go to practice? finish my homework? spend time with my friends?

A question mark in parentheses indicates that a writer is unsure of a date, a figure, or a word.

▶ Quintilian died in AD 96 (?).

▶ Gaius Julius Caesar (100?–44 BC) was a Roman statesman and general.

44c Exclamation points

Use an exclamation point to show surprise or strong emotion.

▶ **In those few moments of geologic time will be the story of all that has happened since we became a nation. And what a story it will be!**

—JAMES RETTIE, "But a Watch in the Night"

Use exclamation points very sparingly because they can distract your readers or suggest that you are exaggerating.

▶ **This university is so large, so varied, that attempting to tell someone everything about it would take three years!.**

Do not use a comma or a period immediately after an exclamation point that ends a direct quotation.

▶ **On my last visit, I looked out the sliding glass doors and ran breathlessly to Connor in the kitchen: "There's a *huge* black pig in the backyard!",**

—ELLEN ASHDOWN, "Living by the Dead"

bedfordstmartins.com/everyday_writer   For exercises, go to **Exercise Central** and click on **End Punctuation.**

45

Apostrophes

The little apostrophe can sometimes make a big difference in meaning. One man found that out when he agreed to look after a neighbor's apartment for a few days. "I'll leave instructions on the kitchen counter," the neighbor said as she gave him her key. Here are the instructions he found: "The cat's food is on the counter. Once a day on the patio. Thanks. I'll see you Friday."

Because the note said *cat's,* the man expected one cat—and when he saw one, he put it and the food outside on the patio. When the neighbor returned, she found one healthy cat—and a second, very weak one that had hidden under the bed. The difference between *cat's* and *cats'* in this instance almost cost the neighbor a cat.

AT A GLANCE

Editing for Apostrophes

- Check all nouns and indefinite pronouns that show ownership or possession to be sure they end with an apostrophe in the right place: an apostrophe and -*s* for most singular nouns, including those that end in -*s*; an apostrophe and -*s* for plural nouns not ending in -*s*; and an apostrophe only for plural nouns ending in -*s*. (45a)
- Check all contractions to make sure the apostrophe is used correctly. (45b)
- Check plural forms of numbers, letters, and symbols to ensure that the apostrophe is used correctly. (45c)

45a Use apostrophes to signal possessive case.

The possessive case denotes ownership or possession of one thing by another.

Singular nouns and indefinite pronouns

Add an apostrophe and -*s* to form the possessive of most singular nouns, including those that end in -*s*, and of indefinite pronouns. The possessive forms of personal pronouns do not take apostrophes: *yours, his, hers, its, ours, theirs.*

▶ The *bus's* fumes overpowered her.
▶ George *Lucas's* movies are among the most popular and successful films.
▶ *Anyone's* guess is as good as mine.

Plural nouns

To form the possessive case of plural nouns not ending in -*s*, add an apostrophe and -*s*.

▶ Robert Bly helped to popularize the *men's* movement.

For plural nouns ending in -*s*, add only the apostrophe.

▶ The *clowns'* costumes were bright green and orange.

Compound nouns

For compound nouns, make the last word in the group possessive.

▶ The *secretary of state's* speech was televised.

▶ Both her *daughters-in-law's* birthdays fall in July.

▶ My *in-laws'* disapproval dampened our enthusiasm for the new house.

Two or more nouns

To signal individual possession by two or more owners, make each noun possessive.

▶ Great differences exist between *Angela Bassett's* and *Oprah Winfrey's* films.

> Bassett and Winfrey appeared in different films.

To signal joint possession, make only the last noun possessive.

▶ *MacNeil and Lehrer's* television program focused on current issues.

> MacNeil *and* Lehrer participated in the same program.

45b   Use apostrophes to signal contractions.

Contractions are two-word combinations formed by leaving out certain letters, which are indicated by an apostrophe.

it is, it has/it's	I would, I had/I'd	will not/won't
was not/wasn't	he would, he had/he'd	let us/let's
I am/I'm	would not/wouldn't	who is, who has/who's
he is, he has/he's	do not/don't	cannot/can't
you will/you'll	does not/doesn't	

Contractions such as the preceding ones are common in conversation and informal writing. Academic and professional work, however, often calls for greater formality.

Apostrophes signal omissions in some common phrases.

rock and roll	class of 1997
rock 'n' roll	class of '97

Distinguishing it's *and* its

Its is the possessive form of *it*. *It's* is a contraction for *it is* or *it has*.

▶ This disease is unusual; *its* symptoms vary from person to person.

▶ *It's* a difficult disease to diagnose.

45c Use apostrophes to form certain plurals.

Use an apostrophe and *-s* to form the plural of numbers, letters, symbols, and words referred to as terms.

▶ The gymnasts need marks of *8's* and *9's* to qualify for the finals.
▶ The computer prints *e's* whenever there is an error in the program.
▶ I marked special passages with a series of three *'s.
▶ The five *Shakespeare's* in the essay were spelled five different ways.

As in the above examples, italicize numbers, letters, symbols, and words referred to as terms, but do not italicize the plural ending.

You can omit the apostrophe before the *-s* for the plural of years (*2020s, fashion of the '80s*).

bedfordstmartins.com/everyday_writer For exercises, go to **Exercise Central** and click on **Apostrophes.**

46

Quotation Marks

"Hilarious!" "A great family movie!" "A must see!" Claims of this kind leap out from most movie ads, always set off by quotation marks. In fact, the quotation marks are a key component of such statements; they indicate that the praise comes from people other than the movie promoter. In other words, it is praise that we should believe. This chapter provides tips for using quotation marks for many purposes.

46a Use quotation marks to signal direct quotation.

▶ President Bush referred to an "axis of evil" in his speech.
▶ She smiled and said, "Son, this is one incident that I will never forget."

Use quotation marks to enclose the words of each speaker within running dialogue. Mark each shift in speaker with a new paragraph.

AT A GLANCE

Editing for Quotation Marks

- Use quotation marks around direct quotations and titles of short works. (46a and c)
- In general, do not use quotation marks around set-off quotations of more than four lines of prose or more than three lines of poetry, or around titles of long works. Consult a style guide, such as that of the Modern Language Association (MLA) for guidelines. (46b and c)
- Use quotation marks to signal irony and coinages, but do so sparingly. (46e)
- Check other punctuation used with closing quotation marks. (46f)

  Periods and commas should be *inside* the quotation marks.

  Colons, semicolons, and footnote numbers should be *outside*.

  Question marks, exclamation points, and dashes should be *inside* if they are part of the quoted material, *outside* if they are not.
- Never use quotation marks around indirect quotations. (46g)

  ▶ **Keith said that ⁄he was sorry.⁄**
- Do not use quotation marks just to add emphasis to words. (46g)

"But I can see you're bound to come," said the father. "Only we ain't going to catch us no fish, because there ain't no water left to catch 'em in."

"The river!"

"All but dry."

–EUDORA WELTY, "Ladies in Spring"

Single quotation marks

Single quotation marks enclose a quotation within a quotation. Open and close the quoted passage with double quotation marks, and change any quotation marks that appear *within* the quotation to single quotation marks.

▶ Baldwin says, "The title 'The Uses of the Blues' does not refer to music; I don't know anything about music."

▶ "You know what Eddie said," my [horse] trainer recalled, referring to the late, great trainer Eddie Gregson. "He said about some guy: 'He's the best kind of owner. He's dead.'"

–JANE SMILEY, "Playing the Horses (and the Horse People, Too)"

For information about the brackets in the quotation, see 47b.

46b Use quotation marks to quote fewer than four lines of prose or poetry.

If the prose passage you wish to quote is more than four typed lines, set the quotation off by starting it on a new line and indenting it one inch (or ten spaces) from the left margin. This format, known as block quotation, does not require quotation marks.

> In "Suspended," Joy Harjo tells of her first awareness of jazz as a child:
>> My rite of passage into the world of humanity occurred then, via jazz. The music made a startling bridge between the familiar and strange lands, an appropriate vehicle, for though the music is predominantly west African in concept, with European associations, jazz was influenced by the Creek (or Muscogee) people, for we were there when jazz was born. I recognized it, that humid afternoon in my formative years, as a way to speak beyond the confines of ordinary language. I still hear it. (84)

The page number in parentheses at the end of the quotation is a citation in the style of the Modern Language Association (MLA). The American Psychological Association (APA) has different guidelines for setting off block quotations. (See Chapters 52 and 56.)

When quoting poetry, if the quotation is brief (fewer than four lines), MLA tells you to include it within your text. Separate the lines of the poem with slashes, each preceded and followed by a space, in order to tell the reader where one line of the poem ends and the next begins.

> In one of his best-known poems, Robert Frost remarks, "Two roads diverged in a yellow wood, and I— / I took the one less traveled by / And that has made all the difference."

To quote more than three lines of poetry, indent the block one inch (or ten spaces) from the left margin. Do not use quotation marks. Take care to follow the spacing, capitalization, punctuation, and other features of the original poem.

> The duke in Robert Browning's poem "My Last Duchess" is clearly a jealous, vain person, whose arrogance is illustrated through this statement:
>> She thanked men,—good! but thanked
>> Somehow—I know not how—as if she ranked
>> My gift of a nine-hundred-years-old name
>> With anybody's gift.

46c Use quotation marks around titles of short works.

Quotation marks are used to enclose the titles of short poems, short stories, articles, essays, songs, sections of books, and episodes of television and radio programs.

- "Dover Beach" moves from calmness to sadness. [poem]
- Alice Walker's "Everyday Use" is about more than just quilts. [short story]
- The *Atlantic* published an article entitled "Illiberal Education." [article]
- In "Photography," Susan Sontag considers the role of photography in our society. [essay]
- The *Nature* episode "Echo of the Elephants" portrays ivory hunters unfavorably. [episode of a television program]

Use italics rather than quotation marks for the titles of television series, magazines, movies, and other long works (see 50a).

46d Use quotation marks around definitions.

- In social science, the term *sample size* means "the number of individuals being studied in a research project."
  –KATHLEEN STASSEN BERGER AND ROSS A. THOMPSON,
  The Developing Person through Childhood and Adolescence

Use italics for words used as a term, like *sample size* above (see 50b).

46e Use quotation marks to signal irony and coinages.

To show readers that you are using a word or phrase ironically or that you made it up, enclose it in quotation marks.

- The "banquet" consisted of dried-out chicken and canned vegetables.

  The quotation marks suggest that the meal was anything but a banquet.

- Your whole first paragraph or first page may have to be guillotined in any case after your piece is finished: it is a kind of "forebirth."
  –JACQUES BARZUN, "A Writer's Discipline"

  The writer made up the term *forebirth.*

46f Check other punctuation used with quotation marks.

Periods and commas go *inside* closing quotation marks.

- "Don't compromise yourself," said Janis Joplin. "You are all you've got."

  EXCEPTION When you follow MLA style for documenting a short quotation, place the period *after* the parentheses with source information (see 19b).

▶ **In places, de Beauvoir "sees Marxists as believing in subjectivity" (Whitmarsh 63).**

For more information on using a comma before or after a quotation, see 42h.

Colons, semicolons, and footnote numbers go *outside* closing quotation marks.

▶ **I felt one emotion after finishing "Eveline": sorrow.**

▶ **Everything is dark, and "a visionary light settles in her eyes"; this vision, this light, is her salvation.**

▶ **Tragedy is defined by Aristotle as "an imitation of an action that is serious and of a certain magnitude."[1]**

Question marks, exclamation points, and dashes go *inside* if they are part of the quoted material, *outside* if they are not.

PART OF THE QUOTATION

▶ **Gently shake the injured person while asking, "Are you all right?"**

▶ **"Jump!" one of the firefighters shouted.**

NOT PART OF THE QUOTATION

▶ **What is the theme of "The Birth-Mark"?**

▶ **"Break a leg"—that phrase is supposed to bring good luck.**

A MATTER OF STYLE

Direct Quotation

As a way of bringing other people's words into our own, direct quotation can be a powerful writing tool. For example:

> Mrs. Macken urges parents to get books for their children, to read to them when they are "li'l," and when they start school to make certain they attend regularly. She holds herself up as an example of a "mill-hand's daughter who wanted to be a schoolteacher and did it through sheer hard work."
> —SHIRLEY BRICE HEATH, *Ways with Words*

The writer could have paraphrased—and said, for example, that parents should read to their children when they are young. By quoting, however, she lets her subject speak for herself—and lets us as readers hear that person's voice. In fact, this writer is reporting from field research, which calls for the use of direct quotations. Thus the choice to quote directly is effective and appropriate for both the intended audience and the conventions of the field.

46g Check for misused quotation marks.

Do not use quotation marks for indirect quotations—those that do not use someone's exact words.

▶ Mother smiled and said that ⁀she was sure she would never forget the incident.⁀

Do not use quotation marks just to add emphasis to particular words or phrases.

▶ Michael said that his views may not be ⁀politically correct⁀ but that he wasn't going to change them for anything.

▶ Much time was spent speculating about their ⁀relationship.⁀

Do not use quotation marks around slang or colloquial language; they create the impression that you are apologizing for using those words. If you have a good reason to use slang or a colloquial term, use it without quotation marks.

▶ After our twenty-mile hike, we were completely exhausted and ready to ⁀turn in.⁀

FOR MULTILINGUAL WRITERS

Quoting in American English

Remember that the way you mark quotations in American English (" ") may not be the same as in other languages. In French, for example, quotations are marked with *guillemets* (« »), while in German, quotations take split-level marks („ "). American English and British English offer opposite conventions for double and single quotation marks. Writers of British English use single quotation marks first and, when necessary, double quotation marks for quotations within quotations. If you are writing for an American audience, be careful to follow the U.S. conventions governing quotation marks: double quotation marks first and, when necessary, single quotation marks within double.

47

Other Punctuation

Parentheses, brackets, dashes, colons, slashes, and ellipses are all around us. Pick up the television listings, for instance, and you will find these punctuation marks in abundance, helping viewers preview programs in a clear and efficient way.

⑦⑧ **College Football** *3:30* 501019/592361—Northwestern Wildcats at Ohio State Buckeyes. The Buckeyes are looking for their 20th straight win over Northwestern. (Live) [Time approximate.]

This chapter will guide you in deciding when you can use these marks of punctuation to signal relationships among sentence parts, to create particular rhythms, and to help readers follow your thoughts.

AT A GLANCE

Editing for Effective Use of Punctuation

- Be sure that any material enclosed in parentheses or set off with dashes requires special treatment. Then check to see that the parentheses or dashes don't make the sentence difficult to follow. (47a and c)

- Decide whether the punctuation you have chosen creates the proper effect: parentheses tend to de-emphasize material they enclose; dashes add emphasis. (47a and c)

- Check to see that you use brackets to enclose parenthetical elements in material that is already within parentheses and to enclose words or comments inserted into a quotation. (47b)

- Use dashes to mark off comments or to emphasize material at the end of a sentence. Check to see that you use colons to introduce explanations, series, lists, and some quotations. (47c and d)

- Check to be sure you've used slashes to mark line divisions in poetry quoted within your own text and to separate alternative terms. (47e)

- Make sure you've used ellipses (three equally spaced dots) to indicate omissions from quoted passages. (47f)

- If you are writing an online communication, check your use of asterisks to mark emphasis, underscore symbols before and after the titles of full-length works, and angle brackets to enclose email and World Wide Web addresses. Don't use emoticons—combinations of keyboard characters to express mood, such as the sideways smiley face—in professional communication. (47g)

47a Parentheses

Use parentheses to enclose material that is of minor or secondary importance in a sentence—material that supplements, clarifies, comments on, or illustrates what precedes or follows it.

▶ **Inventors and men of genius have almost always been regarded as fools at the beginning (and very often at the end) of their careers.**
—FYODOR DOSTOYEVSKY

▶ **During my research, I found problems with the flat-rate income tax (a single-rate tax with no deductions).**

Enclosing textual citations

▶ **Freud and his followers have had a most significant impact on the ways abnormal functioning is understood and treated (Joseph, 1991).**
—RONALD J. COMER, *Abnormal Psychology*

▶ **Zamora notes that Kahlo referred to her first self-portrait, given to a close friend, as "your Botticelli" (110).**

The first in-text citation shows the style of the American Psychological Association (APA); the second, the style of the Modern Language Association (MLA).

Enclosing numbers or letters in a list

▶ **Five distinct styles can be distinguished: (1) Old New England, (2) Deep South, (3) Middle American, (4) Wild West, and (5) Far West or Californian.**
—ALISON LURIE, *The Language of Clothes*

With other marks of punctuation

A period may be placed either inside or outside a closing parenthesis, depending on whether the parenthetical text is part of a larger sentence. A comma, if needed, is always placed *outside* a closing parenthesis (and never before an opening one).

▶ **Gene Tunney's single defeat in an eleven-year career was to a flamboyant and dangerous fighter named Harry Greb ("The Human Windmill"), who seems to have been, judging from boxing literature, the dirtiest fighter in history.**
—JOYCE CAROL OATES, "On Boxing"

Choosing among parentheses, commas, and dashes

In general, use commas when the material to be set off is least interruptive (42c, e, and f), parentheses when it is more interruptive, and dashes when it is the most interruptive (47c).

47b Brackets

Use brackets to enclose parenthetical elements in material that is itself within parentheses. Use brackets to enclose explanatory words or comments that you are inserting into a quotation. According to the Modern Language Association (MLA), if you use ellipses to mark a deletion you have made in a quotation that already had another set of ellipses, you should put brackets around your own ellipses; however, some instructors expect brackets around *every* set of ellipses you introduce.

Setting off material within parentheses

▶ Eventually the investigation had to examine the major agencies (including the previously sacrosanct National Security Agency [NSA]) that were conducting covert operations.

Inserting material within quotations

▶ As Tam argues, "He [Johnson] saw it [the war] as a game or wrestling match in which he would make Ho Chi Minh cry 'uncle.' "

The bracketed words clarify the words *he* and *it* in the original quotation.

In the quotation in the following sentence, the artist Gauguin's name is misspelled. The bracketed word *sic,* which means "so," tells readers that the person being quoted—not the writer who has picked up the quotation—made the mistake.

▶ One admirer wrote, "She was the most striking woman I'd ever seen—a sort of wonderful combination of Mia Farrow and one of Gaugin's [*sic*] Polynesian nymphs."

See 47g for information on using angle brackets.

47c Dashes

Use dashes to insert a comment or to highlight material in a sentence. Dashes give more emphasis than parentheses to the material they enclose. On most typewriters and with some word-processing software, a dash is made with two hyphens (--) with no spaces before, between, or after. In some software, a solid dash can be typed as it is in this book (—). Many word-processing programs automatically convert two typed hyphens into a solid dash.

▶ The pleasures of reading itself—who doesn't remember?—were like those of Christmas cake, a sweet devouring.
                                —EUDORA WELTY, "A Sweet Devouring"

▶ Mr. Angell is addicted to dashes and parentheses—small pauses or digressions in a narrative like those moments when the umpire dusts off home plate or a pitcher rubs up a new ball—that serve to slow an already deliberate movement almost to a standstill.

—JOEL CONARROE, *New York Times Book Review*

Emphasizing material at the end of a sentence

▶ In the twentieth century it has become almost impossible to moralize about epidemics—except those which are transmitted sexually.

—SUSAN SONTAG, *AIDS and Its Metaphors*

Marking a sudden change in tone

▶ New York is a catastrophe—but a magnificent catastrophe.

—LE CORBUSIER

Indicating hesitation in speech

▶ As the officer approached his car, the driver stammered, "What—what have I done?"

Introducing a summary or explanation

▶ In walking, the average adult person employs a motor mechanism that weighs about eighty pounds—sixty pounds of muscle and twenty pounds of bone. —EDWIN WAY TEALE

Use dashes carefully, not only because they are somewhat informal but also because they can cause an abrupt break in reading. Too many of them create a jerky, disconnected effect that can make it hard for readers to follow your thought.

47d Colons

Use a colon to introduce explanations or examples and to separate some elements from one another.

Introducing an explanation, an example, or an appositive

▶ The men may also wear the getup known as Sun Belt Cool: a pale beige suit, open-collared shirt (often in a darker shade than the suit), cream-colored loafers and aviator sunglasses.

—ALISON LURIE, *The Language of Clothes*

Introducing a series, a list, or a quotation

▶ At the baby's one-month birthday party, Ah Po gave him the Four Valuable Things: ink, inkslab, paper, and brush.
—MAXINE HONG KINGSTON, *China Men*

▶ We began a series of workshops on nonviolence, and we repeatedly asked ourselves: "Are you able to accept blows without retaliation?"
—MARTIN LUTHER KING JR., "Letter from Birmingham Jail"

The example by King could have taken a comma instead of a colon (see 42h). Use a colon rather than a comma to introduce a quotation when the lead-in is a complete sentence on its own.

▶ President Kennedy's inaugural address included two sentences often quoted: "Let us never negotiate out of fear. But let us never fear to negotiate."

Separating elements

SALUTATIONS IN FORMAL LETTERS

▶ Dear Dr. Chapman:

HOURS, MINUTES, AND SECONDS

▶ 4:59 PM
▶ 2:15:06

RATIOS

▶ a ratio of 5:1

BIBLICAL CHAPTERS AND VERSES

▶ I Corinthians 3:3–5

TITLES AND SUBTITLES

▶ *The Joy of Insight: Passions of a Physicist*

CITIES AND PUBLISHERS IN BIBLIOGRAPHIC ENTRIES

▶ Boston: Bedford, 2004

Editing for colons

Do not put a colon between a verb and its object or complement— unless the object is a quotation.

▶ Some natural fibers are: cotton, wool, silk, and linen.

Do not put a colon between a preposition and its object or after such expressions as *such as, especially,* and *including.*

▶ In poetry, additional power may come from devices such as: simile, metaphor, and alliteration.

47e   Slashes

Use slashes to mark line divisions between two or three lines of poetry quoted within running text. When using a slash to separate lines of poetry, precede and follow it with a space (46b).

▶ **In Sonnet 29, the persona states, "For thy sweet love rememb'red such wealth brings / That then I scorn to change my state with kings."**

Use a slash to separate alternatives.

▶ **Then there was Daryl, the cabdriver/bartender.**
                                    –JOHN L'HEUREUX, *The Handmaid of Desire*

Use slashes to separate parts of fractions and Internet addresses.

▶ **138$\frac{1}{2}$**

▶ **http://www.bedfordstmartins.com/everyday_writer/**

47f   Ellipses

Ellipses, or ellipsis points, are three equally spaced dots. Ellipses are usually used to indicate that something has been omitted from a quoted passage. Just as you should carefully use quotation marks around any material that you quote directly from a source, so you should carefully use ellipses to indicate that you have left out part of a quotation that otherwise appears to be a complete sentence. Ellipses have been used in the following example to indicate two omissions—one in the middle of the first sentence and one at the end of the second sentence.

ORIGINAL TEXT

Much male fear of feminism is the fear that, in becoming whole human beings, women will cease to mother men, to provide the breast, the lullaby, the continuous attention associated by the infant with the mother. Much male fear of feminism is infantilism—the longing to remain the mother's son, to possess a woman who exists purely for him.

                                    –ADRIENNE RICH

WITH ELLIPSES

As Adrienne Rich argues, "Much male fear of feminism is the fear that . . . women will cease to mother men, to provide the breast, the lullaby, the continuous attention associated by the infant with the mother. Much male fear of feminism is infantilism—the longing to remain the mother's son. . . ."

When you omit the last part of a quoted sentence, add a period after the ellipses—for a total of four dots. Be sure a complete sentence comes before and after the four dots.

If you are adding your own ellipses to a quotation that already has other ellipses, enclose yours in brackets. Some instructors call for brackets around all ellipses you add even if the quotation does *not* have other ellipses.

If your shortened quotation ends with a source citation (such as a page number, a name, or a title), follow these steps:

1. Use three ellipsis points but no period after the quotation.
2. Add the closing quotation mark, closed up to the third ellipsis point.
3. Add the source of documentation in parentheses.
4. Use a period to indicate the end of the sentence.

▶ Hawthorne writes, "My friend, whom I shall call Oberon—it was a name of fancy and friendship between him and me . . ." (575).

You can also use ellipses to indicate a pause or a hesitation in speech in the same way that you can use a dash for that purpose (47c).

▶ Then the voice, husky and familiar, came to wash over us—"The winnah, and still heavyweight champeen of the world . . . Joe Louis."
—MAYA ANGELOU, *I Know Why the Caged Bird Sings*

47g   Online punctuation

If you participate in computer bulletin boards, discussion groups, or other electronic communication, you are already familiar with some fairly new uses of punctuation marks and other keyboard characters. These marks can add emphasis, set off the titles of works, and express something about the sender's mood. Limited by formatting constraints, online punctuation and mechanics reflect the informality of the Internet. (See Chapter 12.)

When italics and underlining are unavailable in online communication, use asterisks to help create special emphasis.

▶ Her homepage *must* be updated.

Use the underscore symbol before and after the title of a full-length work.

▶ Have you read Bill Gates's _The Road Ahead_?

You may want to use angle brackets to set off email addresses and addresses on the World Wide Web from the rest of your text.

▶ Visit us on the Web at <www.bedfordstmartins.com>.

bedfordstmartins.com/everyday_writer   For exercises, go to **Exercise Central** and click on **Other Punctuation.**

48

Capitalization

Capital letters are a key signal in everyday life. Look around any store to see their importance: you can shop for Levi's or *any* blue jeans, for Coca-Cola or *any* cola, for Kleenex or *any* house brand. In each of these instances, the capital letter indicates a particular brand. This chapter will help you use capitals appropriately.

AT A GLANCE

Editing for Capitalization

- Usually, capitalize the first letter of each sentence. If you quote a poem, follow its original capitalization. (48a)

- Check to make sure you have appropriately capitalized proper nouns and proper adjectives. (48b)

- If you have used titles of people or of works, make sure that you have capitalized them correctly. (48c and d)

- Double-check the capitalization of geographical directions (*north* or *North*?), family relationships (*dad* or *Dad*?), and seasons of the year (*spring*, never *Spring*). (48e, f, and g)

- Check to make sure your word-processing program has not automatically capitalized words inappropriately. Many programs insert capitals after periods even when a period signals an abbreviation, not the end of a sentence.

48a   Capitalize the first word of a sentence.

With very few exceptions, capitalize the first word of a sentence. If you are quoting a full sentence, capitalize its first word unless the original does not begin with a capital.

▶ Kennedy said, "Let us never negotiate out of fear."

▶ Alison noted that Kennedy did not use a capital letter when he wrote, "ask not what your country can do for you . . . ." So she felt justified in not using one either.

Capitalization of a nonquoted sentence following a colon is optional.

▶ Gould cites the work of Darwin: The [*or* the] theory of natural selection incorporates the principle of evolutionary ties among all animals.

Capitalize a sentence within parentheses unless the parenthetical sentence is inserted into another sentence.

▶ **Gould cites the work of Darwin. (Other researchers cite more recent evolutionary theorists.)**

▶ **Gould cites the work of Darwin (see page 150).**

When citing poetry, follow the capitalization of the original poem. Though most poets capitalize the first word of each line in a poem, some poets do not.

▶ **Morning sun heats up the young beech tree**
  leaves and almost lights them into fireflies

  —JUNE JORDAN, "Aftermath"

48b Capitalize proper nouns and proper adjectives.

Capitalize proper nouns (those naming specific persons, places, and things) and most adjectives formed from proper nouns. All other nouns are common nouns and are not capitalized unless they are used as part of a proper noun: *a street,* but *Elm Street.*

PROPER	COMMON
Alfred Hitchcock, Hitchcockian	a director
Brazil, Brazilian	a nation
World Wide Web	a homepage, a site

Some contemporary companies use capitals called *InterCaps* in the middle of their own or their product's names. In effect, they turn two words into one. Leave the capitals in, following the style you see in company advertising or on the product itself—*eBay, FedEx.*

Some commonly capitalized terms

GEOGRAPHICAL NAMES

Pacific Ocean	an ocean
Africa, African sculpture	a beautiful sculpture

STRUCTURES AND MONUMENTS

| Washington Monument | a monument |

SHIPS, TRAINS, AIRCRAFT, AND SPACECRAFT

S.S. Titanic	a luxury liner
Challenger	a spaceship

ORGANIZATIONS, BUSINESSES, AND GOVERNMENT INSTITUTIONS

Library of Congress	a federal agency
General Motors Corporation	a blue-chip company

ACADEMIC INSTITUTIONS AND COURSES

University of California	a state university
Political Science 102	a political science course

HISTORICAL EVENTS AND ERAS

Shays's Rebellion	a rebellion
the Renaissance in fifteenth-century Europe	a renaissance of sorts

RELIGIONS AND RELIGIOUS TERMS

God	a god
the Qur'an	a prayer book
Catholicism, Catholics	a religion

ETHNIC GROUPS, NATIONALITIES, AND THEIR LANGUAGES

Russian	a language
African American	a group

MOST TRADE NAMES

Nike shoes	sneakers
Levi's	jeans
Cheerios	cereal

FOR MULTILINGUAL WRITERS

Learning English Capitalization

English capitalization may pose challenges for speakers of other languages because capitalization systems vary considerably among languages. Arabic, Chinese, and Hebrew, for example, do not use capital letters at all. English may be the only language to capitalize the first-person singular pronoun (*I*), but Dutch and German capitalize some forms of the second-person pronoun (*you*). German capitalizes all nouns; and, in fact, English used to capitalize more nouns than it does now.

48c Capitalize titles before proper names.

When used alone or following a proper name, most titles are not capitalized. One common exception is the word *president,* which many writers capitalize whenever it refers to the President of the United States.

Justice O'Connor	Sandra Day O'Connor, the justice
Professor Lisa Ede	my history professor
Dr. R. Whisler	R. Whisler, our doctor

48d Capitalize titles of works.

Capitalize most words in titles of books, articles, speeches, stories, essays, plays, poems, documents, films, paintings, and musical compositions. Do not capitalize articles (*a, an, the*), short prepositions, conjunctions, and the *to* in an infinitive unless they are the first or last words in a title or subtitle.

Walt Whitman: A Life	Declaration of Independence
"As Time Goes By"	*The Producers*
"Oops, I Did It Again"	*Harry Potter and the Sorcerer's Stone*

A MATTER OF E-STYLE

Using Capitals Online

Some writers capitalize words or even passages to add special emphasis. Although you may see this use of capitals for emphasis in print, many listservs and newsgroups on the Internet ask participants to practice good netiquette by resisting the urge to use all capital letters, which can be irritating to readers who feel as if they are being SHOUTED AT. (Remember that using all lowercase letters can also be annoying and hard to read.)

48e Capitalize compass directions only if the word designates a specific geographical region.

▶ John Muir headed west, motivated by the desire to explore.

▶ Kobi divided the map into sections: the Northeast, the South, and the West.

48f   Capitalize family relationship words only when used as part of a name or when substituted for a name.

▶ When she was a child, my mother shared a room with her aunt.

▶ I could always tell when Mother was annoyed with Aunt Rose.

48g   Do not capitalize seasons of the year or parts of the academic or financial year.

spring	fall semester
winter	winter term
autumn	third-quarter earnings

bedfordstmartins.com/everyday_writer   For exercises, go to **Exercise Central** and click on **Capitalization.**

49

Abbreviations and Numbers

Any time you open up a telephone book, you see an abundance of abbreviations and numbers, as in the following movie theater listing from the Berkeley, California, telephone book:

Oaks Theater   1875 Solano Av   Brk

AT A GLANCE

Editing Abbreviations and Numbers

- Make sure you use abbreviations and numbers according to the conventions of a specific field (see p. 357): *57%* might be acceptable in a math paper, but *57 percent* may be more appropriate in a sociology essay.
- If you use an abbreviation readers might not understand, make sure you spell out the term the first time you use it and give the abbreviation in parentheses. (49c)

Abbreviations and numbers allow writers to present detailed information in a small amount of space. This chapter explains the conventions for using abbreviations and figures in academic and professional writing.

49a Abbreviate some titles used before and all titles used after proper names.

Ms. Susanna Moller	Henry Louis Gates Jr.
Mr. Aaron Oforlea	Karen Lancry, MD
Dr. Edward Davies	Samuel Cohen, PhD

Other titles—including religious, academic, and government titles—should be spelled out in academic writing. In other writing, they can be abbreviated before a full name but should be written out when used with only a last name.

Rev. Fleming Rutledge	Reverend Rutledge
Prof. Jaime Mejía	Professor Mejía
Gen. Colin Powell	General Powell

Do not use both a title and an academic degree with a person's name. Use one or the other. Instead of *Dr. Beverly Moss, PhD,* write *Dr. Beverly Moss* or *Beverly Moss, PhD.* (Note that academic degrees such as *RN* and *PhD* often appear without periods; see 44a.)

49b Use abbreviations with years and hours.

399 BC ("before Christ")

AD 49 (*anno Domini,* Latin for "year of our Lord")

210 BCE ("before the common era")

11:15 AM (*or* a.m.)

9:00 PM (*or* p.m.)

The abbreviations BCE and CE ("common era") are often preferred with dates; both follow the year. These abbreviations and most of the abbreviations in the preceding list are in small caps, a typographical option in word-processing programs. You may also continue to use full-size capital letters for these abbreviations.

49c Use abbreviations for familiar business, government, and science terms.

As long as you can be sure your readers will understand them, use common abbreviations such as *PBS, NASA, DNA,* and *CIA.* If an abbreviation may be unfamiliar, however, spell out the full term the first time you use it, and give the abbreviation in parentheses. After that, you can use the abbreviation by itself.

▶ **The Comprehensive Test Ban (CTB) Treaty was first proposed in the 1950s. For those nations signing it, the CTB would bring to a halt all nuclear weapons testing.**

bedfordstmartins.com/everyday_writer   For links to lists of popular Internet acronyms, go to **Links** and click on **Language.**

49d Use abbreviations in official company names.

Use such abbreviations as *Co., Inc., Corp.,* and *&* if they are part of a company's official name. Do not, however, use these abbreviations in most other contexts.

▶ **Sears, Roebuck & Co. was the only large ~~corp.~~ in town.**
    corporation

▶ **Paola has a part-time job at the Warner ~~Brothers~~ store in the mall.**
    Bros.

49e Use abbreviations in notes and source citations.

cf.	compare (*confer*)
e.g.	for example (*exempli gratia*)
et al.	and others (*et alia*)
etc.	and so forth (*et cetera*)
i.e.	that is (*id est*)
N.B.	note well (*nota bene*)
P.S.	postscript (*postscriptum*)

These abbreviations are not generally appropriate except in notes and citations in most academic and professional writing.

▶ **Many firms have policies to help working parents—~~e.g.,~~ flexible hours,**
    for example,
    parental leave, and day care.

▶ **Before the conference began, Haivan unpacked the name tags,**
    programs, pens, ~~etc.~~
    and so forth.

A MATTER OF STYLE

Abbreviations and Numbers in Different Fields

Use of abbreviations and numbers varies in different fields. See a typical example from a biochemistry textbook:

> The energy of a green photon ... is 57 kilocalories per mole (kcal/mol). An alternative unit of energy is the joule (J), which is equal to 0.239 calorie; 1 kcal/mol is equal to 4.184 kJ/mol.
> —LUBERT STRYER, *Biochemistry*

These two sentences demonstrate how useful figures and abbreviations can be; reading the same sentences would be very difficult if the numbers and units of measurement were all written out.

You should become familiar with the conventions governing abbreviations and numbers in your field. The following reference books provide guidelines:

MLA Handbook for Writers of Research Papers for literature and the humanities

Publication Manual of the American Psychological Association for the social sciences

Scientific Style and Format: The CSE Manual for Authors, Editors, and Publishers for the natural sciences

The Chicago Manual of Style for the humanities

AIP Style Manual for physics and the applied sciences

49f Abbreviate units of measurement, and use symbols in charts and graphs.

Symbols such as %, +, $, and = are acceptable in charts and graphs. Dollar signs are acceptable with figures: $11 (but not with words: *eleven dollars*). Units of measurement can be abbreviated in charts and graphs (*4 in.*) but not in the body of a paper (*four inches*).

49g Use other abbreviations according to convention.

Some abbreviations required in notes and in source citations are not appropriate in the body of a paper.

CHAPTER AND PAGES	chapter, page, pages (*not* ch., p., pp.)
MONTHS	January, February (*not* Jan., Feb.)
STATES AND NATIONS	California, Mexico (*not* Calif., Mex.)
	Two exceptions are Washington, D.C., and U.S.

49h   Spell out numbers expressed in one or two words.

If you can write out a number in one or two words, do so. Use figures for longer numbers.

▶ Her screams were heard by ~~38~~ people, none of whom called the police.

thirty-eight

▶ A baseball is held together by ~~two hundred sixteen~~ red stitches.

216

If one of several numbers *of the same kind* in the same sentence requires a figure, you should use figures for all the numbers in that sentence.

▶ An audio system can range in cost from ~~one hundred dollars~~ to $2,599.

$100

49i   Spell out numbers that begin sentences.

When a sentence begins with a number, either spell out the number or rewrite the sentence.

▶ ~~119~~ years of CIA labor cost taxpayers sixteen million dollars.

One hundred nineteen

Most readers find it easier to read figures than three-word numbers; thus the best solution may be to rewrite this sentence: *Taxpayers spent sixteen million dollars for 119 years of CIA labor.*

49j   Use figures according to convention.

ADDRESSES	23 Main Street; 175 Fifth Avenue
DATES	September 17, 1951; 6 June 1983; 4 BCE; the 1860s
DECIMALS AND FRACTIONS	65.34; $8^1/_2$
PERCENTAGES	77 percent (*or* 77%)
EXACT AMOUNTS OF MONEY	$7,348; $1.46 trillion; $2.50; thirty-five (*or* 35) cents
SCORES AND STATISTICS	an 8–3 Red Sox victory; a verbal score of 600; an average age of 22; a mean of 53
TIME OF DAY	6:00 AM (*or* a.m.)

Using the Term *Hundred*

The term *hundred* is used idiomatically in English. When it is linked with numbers like two, eight, and so on, the word *hundred* remains singular: *Eight hundred years have passed and still old animosities run deep.* Add the plural *-s* to *hundred* only when no number precedes the term: *Hundreds of priceless books were lost in the fire.*

bedfordstmartins.com/everyday_writer For exercises, go to **Exercise Central** and click on **Abbreviations and Numbers.**

50

Italics

The slanted type known as *italics* is more than just a pretty typeface. Indeed, italics give words special meaning or emphasis. In the sentence "Many people read *People* on the subway every day," the italics (and the capital letter) tell us that *People* is a publication. You may use your computer to produce italic type; if not, underline words that you would otherwise italicize.

AT A GLANCE

Editing for Italics

- Check that all titles of long works are italicized. (50a)
- If you use any words, letters, or numbers as terms, make sure they are in italics. (50b)
- Italicize any non-English words or phrases that are not in an English dictionary. (50c)
- When you use italics to emphasize words, check to be sure you use the italics sparingly. (50e)

50a   Italicize titles of long works.

In general, use italics for titles of long works; use quotation marks for shorter works (46c).

BOOKS	*Paradise*
CHOREOGRAPHIC WORKS	Agnes de Mille's *Rodeo*
FILMS AND VIDEOS	*The Return of the King*
LONG MUSICAL WORKS	*Brandenburg Concertos*
LONG POEMS	*The Bhagavadgita*
MAGAZINES AND JOURNALS	*Ebony, New England Journal of Medicine*
NEWSPAPERS	the Cleveland *Plain Dealer*
PAINTINGS AND SCULPTURE	Georgia O'Keeffe's *Black Iris*
PAMPHLETS	Thomas Paine's *Common Sense*
PLAYS	*The Producers*
RADIO SERIES	*All Things Considered*
RECORDINGS	*The Miseducation of Lauryn Hill*
SOFTWARE	*Quicken*
TELEVISION SERIES	*The Simpsons, Sex and the City*
WEB SITES	*Salon, Voice of the Shuttle*

Do not use italics for sacred books, such as the Bible and the Qur'an; for public documents, such as the Constitution and the Magna Carta; or for the titles of your own papers.

50b   Italicize words, letters, and numbers used as terms.

▶ On the back of his jersey was the famous *24*.

▶ One characteristic of some New York speech is the absence of postvocalic *r*—for example, pronouncing the word *four* as "fouh."

50c   Italicize non-English words and phrases.

Italicize words from other languages unless they have become part of English—like the French "bourgeois" or the Italian "pasta," for example. If a word is in an English dictionary, it does not need italics.

▶ At last one of the phantom sleighs gliding along the street would come to a stop, and with gawky haste Mr. Burness in his fox-furred *shapka* would make for our door.   —VLADIMIR NABOKOV, *Speak, Memory*

Always italicize Latin genus and species names.

▶ The caterpillars of *Hapalia,* when attacked by the wasp *Apanteles machaeralis,* drop suddenly from their leaves and suspend themselves in air by a silken thread. —STEPHEN JAY GOULD, "Nonmoral Nature"

50d Italicize names of aircraft, spacecraft, ships, and trains.

Spirit of St. Louis	Amtrak's *Silver Star*
Discovery	U.S.S. *Iowa*

50e Use italics for emphasis.

Italics can help to create emphasis in writing, but use them sparingly for this purpose. It is usually better to create emphasis with sentence structure and word choice.

▶ Great literature and a class of literate readers are nothing new in India. What is new is the emergence of a gifted generation of Indian writers *working in English.* —SALMAN RUSHDIE

bedfordstmartins.com/everyday_writer For exercises, go to **Exercise Central** and click on **Italics.**

51

Hyphens

Hyphens show up every time you make a left-hand turn, wear a Chicago Bulls T-shirt, buy gasoline at a self-service station, visit a writing center for one-on-one tutoring, worry about a long-term relationship, listen to hip-hop, or eat Tex-Mex food. Sometimes the dictionary will tell you whether to hyphenate a word. Other times, you will have to apply some general rules, which you will find in this chapter.

Editing for Hyphens

- Check that a word that is broken at the end of a line is divided at an appropriate point. (51a)
- Double-check compound words to be sure they are properly closed up, separated, or hyphenated. If in doubt, consult a dictionary. (51b, c, and d)
- Check all terms that have prefixes or suffixes to see whether you need hyphens. (51e)

51a Use a hyphen to divide a word at the end of a line.

Break words between syllables. The word *metaphor,* for instance, contains three syllables (*met-a-phor*), and you can break the word after either the *t* or the *a.* All dictionaries show syllable breaks, so the best advice for dividing words correctly is simply to look them up. In addition, you should follow certain other conventions.

- Never divide one-syllable words or abbreviations, contractions, or figures.
- Leave at least two letters on each line when dividing a word. Do not divide words such as *acorn* (*a-corn*) and *scratchy* (*scratch-y*) at all, and break a word such as *Americana* (*A-mer-i-can-a*) only after the *r* or the *i.*
- Divide compound words, such as *anklebone* and *mother-in-law,* only between their parts (*ankle-bone*) or after their hyphens.
- Divide words with prefixes or suffixes between the parts. Break the word *disappearance,* then, after its prefix (*dis-appearance*) or before its suffix (*disappear-ance*). Divide prefixed words that include a hyphen, such as *self-righteous,* only after the hyphen.

51b Check a dictionary for hyphens in compound nouns and verbs.

Some compound nouns and verbs are one word, some are separate words, and some require hyphens. You should consult a dictionary to be sure.

ONE WORD	rowboat, textbook, flowerpot, homepage
SEPARATE WORDS	high school, parking meter, shut up
WITH HYPHENS	city-state, sister-in-law, cross-fertilize

A MATTER OF E-STYLE

When in Doubt, Close It Up

New compound words associated with technology are quickly becoming part of our everyday language. What should you do when many of these words are not yet in dictionaries? Helpful advice comes from the editors of *Wired* magazine:

> From computer commands like *whois* and onscreen nouns like *logon,* we have evolved this commandment: "When in doubt, close it up." Words spelled solid—like *startup* or *homepage* or *videogame*—may seem odd at first, but . . . we know from experience that new terms often start separated, then become hyphenated, and eventually end up as one word. Go there now.
>
> —*Wired Style*

51c Use a hyphen with compound adjectives before a noun.

Hyphenate most compound adjectives before a noun. Do not hyphenate compound adjectives that follow a noun.

a *well-liked* boss	Our boss is *well liked.*
a *six-foot* plank	The plank is *six feet* long.

In general, the reason for hyphenating compound adjectives is to facilitate reading.

▶ Designers often use potted palms as living-room dividers.

Without the hyphen, *living* may seem to modify *room dividers.*

Never hyphenate an *-ly* adverb and an adjective.

▶ They used a widely distributed mailing list.

Use suspended hyphens in a series of compound adjectives.

▶ Each student did the work him- or herself.

51d Hyphenate fractions and compound numbers from *twenty-one* to *ninety-nine.*

two-sevenths	one and five-eighths
thirty-five	four hundred sixty-two

51e Use a hyphen with some prefixes and suffixes.

Most words containing prefixes or suffixes are written without hyphens: *antiwar, gorillalike.* Here are some exceptions:

BEFORE CAPITALIZED WORDS	pro-Democratic, non-Catholic
WITH FIGURES	pre-1960, post-1945
WITH *ALL-*, *EX-*, AND *SELF-*	all-state, ex-partner, self-possessed
WITH *-ELECT*	mayor-elect
FOR CLARITY	re-cover, anti-inflation, troll-like

Re-cover means "cover again"; the hyphen distinguishes it from *recover,* meaning "get well." In *anti-inflation* and *troll-like,* the hyphens separate double and triple letters.

bedfordstmartins.com/everyday_writer   For exercises, go to **Exercise Central** and click on **Hyphens.**

MLA
Documentation

Learning the rules the *MLA Handbook* outlines will help you **become a writer** whose work deserves serious consideration. Similarly, your study of these rules can make you a more discerning reader: knowing how an author is supposed to use sources is essential to judging a text's reliability.

–PHYLLIS FRANKLIN,
MLA HANDBOOK FOR WRITERS OF RESEARCH PAPERS

MLA Documentation

This part of *The Everyday Writer* discusses the basic format for the Modern Language Association (MLA) style and provides examples of various kinds of sources. MLA style is widely used to document sources in writing that deals with literature, languages, and other fields in the humanities. For further reference, consult the *MLA Handbook for Writers of Research Papers,* Sixth Edition, 2003.

bedfordstmartins.com/everyday_writer   To access this advice online, click on **Documenting Sources.**

DIRECTORY TO MLA STYLE

MLA style for in-text citations (Chapter 52)

MLA style for a list of works cited (Chapter 54)

BOOKS

52

MLA Style for In-Text Citations

MLA style requires documentation in the text of an essay for every quotation, paraphrase, and summary as well as other material requiring documentation (see 19e). In-text citations document material from other sources with both signal phrases and parenthetical references. Signal phrases introduce the material, often including the author's name. Keep your parenthetical references short, but include the information your readers need to locate the full reference in the list of works cited at the end of the text. Place a parenthetical reference as near the relevant material as possible without disrupting the flow of the sentence. Note in the following examples *where* punctuation is placed in relation to the parentheses.

1. AUTHOR NAMED IN A SIGNAL PHRASE

Ordinarily, you can use the author's name in a signal phrase—to introduce the material—and cite the page number(s) in parentheses.

> Herrera indicates that Kahlo believed in a "vitalistic form of pantheism" (328).

2. AUTHOR NAMED IN A PARENTHETICAL REFERENCE

When you do not mention the author in a signal phrase, include the author's last name before the page number(s) in the parentheses. Use no punctuation between the author's name and the page number(s).

> In places, Beauvoir "sees Marxists as believing in subjectivity" (Whitmarsh 63).

3. TWO OR THREE AUTHORS

Use all the authors' last names in a phrase or in parentheses.

> Gortner, Hebrun, and Nicolson maintain that "opinion leaders" influence other people in an organization because they are respected, not because they hold high positions (175).

4. FOUR OR MORE AUTHORS

Use the first author's name and *et al.* ("and others"), or name all the authors in a phrase or in parentheses.

> Similarly, as Belenky et al. assert, examining the lives of women expands our understanding of human development (7).

5. ORGANIZATION AS AUTHOR

Give the group's full name or a shortened form of it in a phrase or in parentheses.

> Any study of social welfare involves a close analysis of "the impacts, the benefits, and the costs" of its policies (Social Research Corporation iii).

6. UNKNOWN AUTHOR

Use the full title, if it is brief, in your text—or a shortened version of the title in parentheses.

> "Hype," by one analysis, is "an artificially engendered atmosphere of hysteria" ("Today's Marketplace" 51).

7. AUTHOR OF TWO OR MORE WORKS

If your list of works cited has more than one work by the same author, include a shortened version of the title of the work you are citing in a phrase or in parentheses.

> Gardner shows readers their own silliness in his description of a "pointless, ridiculous monster, crouched in the shadows, stinking of dead men, murdered children, and martyred cows" (Grendel 2).

8. TWO OR MORE AUTHORS WITH THE SAME LAST NAME

Include the author's first *and* last names in a signal phrase or first initial and last name in a parenthetical reference.

> Children will learn to write if they are allowed to choose their own subjects, James Britton asserts, citing the Schools Council study of the 1960s (37–42).

9. MULTIVOLUME WORK

In a parenthetical reference, note the volume number first and then the page number(s), with a colon and one space between them.

> Modernist writers prized experimentation and gradually even sought to blur the line between poetry and prose, according to Forster (3: 150).

If you name only one volume of the work in your list of works cited, you need include only the page number in the parentheses.

10. LITERARY WORK

Because literary works are often available in many different editions, cite the page number(s) from the edition you used followed by a semi-colon, and then give other identifying information that will lead readers to the passage in any edition. Indicate the act and/or scene in a play (*37; sc. 1*). For a novel, indicate the part or chapter (*175; ch. 4*).

> In utter despair, Dostoyevsky's character Mitya wonders aloud about the "terrible tragedies realism inflicts on people" (376; bk. 8, ch. 2).

For a poem, cite the part (if there is one) and line(s), separated by a period. If you are citing only line numbers, use the word *line(s)* in the first reference (*lines 33–34*).

> On dying, Whitman speculates, "All goes onward and outward, nothing collapses, / And to die is different from what anyone supposed, and luckier" (6.129–30).

For a verse play, give only the act, scene, and line numbers, separated by periods.

As <u>Macbeth</u> begins, the witches greet Banquo as "Lesser than Macbeth, and
greater" (1.3.65).

11. WORK IN AN ANTHOLOGY

For an essay, short story, or other piece of prose reprinted in an anthology,
use the name of the author of the work, not the editor of the anthology,
but use the page number(s) from the anthology.

Narratives of captivity play a major role in early writing by women in the United
States, as demonstrated by Silko (219).

12. SACRED TEXT

To cite a sacred text such as the Qur'an or the Bible, give the title of the
edition you used, the book, and the chapter and verse (or their equivalent) separated by a period. In your text, spell out the names of books.
In parenthetical references, use abbreviations for books with names of
five or more letters (*Gen.* for *Genesis*).

He ignored the admonition "Pride goes before destruction, and a haughty spirit
before a fall" (<u>New Oxford Annotated Bible</u>, Prov. 16.18).

13. INDIRECT SOURCE

Use the abbreviation *qtd. in* to indicate that you are quoting from someone else's report of a conversation, interview, letter, or the like.

As Arthur Miller says, "When somebody is destroyed everybody finally
contributes to it, but in Willy's case, the end product would be virtually the
same" (qtd. in Martin and Meyer 375).

14. TWO OR MORE SOURCES IN ONE PARENTHETICAL REFERENCE

Separate the information with semicolons.

Economists recommend that <u>employment</u> be redefined to include unpaid
domestic labor (Clark 148; Nevins 39).

15. ENTIRE WORK OR ONE-PAGE ARTICLE

Include the reference in the text without any page numbers or parentheses.

Michael Ondaatje's poetic sensibility transfers beautifully to prose in <u>The English
Patient</u>.

16. WORK WITHOUT PAGE NUMBERS

If a work has no page numbers or is only one page long, you may omit the page number. If a work uses paragraph numbers instead, use the abbreviation *par.* (or *pars.*).

> Whitman considered their speech "a source of a native grand opera," in the words of Ellison (par. 13).

17. ELECTRONIC OR NONPRINT SOURCE

Give enough information in a signal phrase or parenthetical reference for readers to locate the source in the list of works cited. Usually give the author or title under which you list the source. Specify a source's page, section, paragraph, or screen numbers, if numbered, in parentheses.

> Describing children's language acquisition, Pinker explains that "what's innate about language is just a way of paying attention to parental speech" (Johnson, sec. 1).

53

MLA Style for Explanatory and Bibliographic Notes

MLA style recommends explanatory notes for information or commentary that does not readily fit into your text but is needed for clarification or further explanation. In addition, MLA style permits bibliographic notes for citing several sources for one point and for offering thanks to, information about, or evaluation of a source. Use superscript numbers in the text to refer readers to the notes, which may appear as endnotes (typed under the heading *Notes* on a separate page after the text but before the list of works cited) or as footnotes at the bottom of the page.

1. SUPERSCRIPT NUMBER IN TEXT

> Stewart emphasizes the existence of social contacts in Hawthorne's life so that the audience will accept a different Hawthorne, one more attuned to modern times than the figure in Woodberry.[3]

2. NOTE

3 Woodberry does, however, show that Hawthorne <u>was</u> often an unsociable individual. He emphasizes the seclusion of Hawthorne's mother, who separated herself from her family after the death of her husband, often even taking meals alone (28). Woodberry seems to imply that Mrs. Hawthorne's isolation rubbed off onto her son.

54

MLA Style for a List of Works Cited

A list of works cited is an alphabetical list of the sources you have referred to in your essay. (If your instructor asks you to list everything you have read as background, call the list *Works Consulted.*) Here are some guidelines for preparing such a list:

- Start your list on a separate page after the text of your essay and any notes.
- Continue the consecutive numbering of pages.
- Type the heading *Works Cited,* not underlined, italicized, or in quotation marks, centered one inch from the top of the page.
- Start each entry flush with the left margin; indent subsequent lines one-half inch or five spaces. Double-space the entire list.
- List sources alphabetically by author's (or editor's) last name. If the author is unknown, alphabetize the source by the first major word of the title.

The sample works-cited entries that follow observe MLA's advice to underline words that are often italicized in print. If you wish to use italics instead, check with your instructor first.

Books

1. ONE AUTHOR

Winchester, Simon. <u>The Meaning of Everything: The Story of the Oxford English Dictionary</u>. Oxford: Oxford UP, 2003.

2. TWO OR THREE AUTHORS

Give the first author listed on the title page, last name first; then list the name(s) of the other author(s) in regular order, with a comma between authors and the word *and* before the last one.

> Martineau, Jane, Desmond Shawe-Taylor, and Jonathan Bate. Shakespeare in Art.
>
> London: Merrell, 2003.

3. FOUR OR MORE AUTHORS

Give the first author listed on the title page, last name first, followed by a comma and *et al.* ("and others"), or list all the names, since the use of *et al.* diminishes the importance of the other contributors.

> Lupton, Ellen, Jennifer Tobias, Alicia Imperiale, Grace Jeffers, and Randi Mates.
>
> Skin: Surface, Substance, and Design. New York: Princeton Architectural,
>
> 2002.

4. ORGANIZATION AS AUTHOR

Give the name of the group listed on the title page as the author, even if the same group published the book.

> Getty Trust Publications. Seeing the Getty Center/Seeing the Getty Gardens. Los
>
> Angeles: Getty Trust Publications, 2000.

5. UNKNOWN AUTHOR

Begin the entry with the title, and list the work alphabetically by the first word of the title after any initial *A, An,* or *The.*

> New Concise World Atlas. Oxford: Oxford UP, 2003.

6. TWO OR MORE BOOKS BY THE SAME AUTHOR(S)

Arrange the entries alphabetically by title. Include the name(s) of the author(s) in the first entry, but in subsequent entries, use three hyphens followed by a period.

> Lorde, Audre. A Burst of Light. Ithaca: Firebrand, 1988.
>
> - - -. Sister Outsider. Trumansburg: Crossing, 1984.

If you cite a work by one author who is also listed as the first coauthor of another work you cite, list the single-author work first, and repeat the author's name in the entry for the coauthored work. Also repeat the author's name if you cite a work in which that author is listed as the first of a different set of coauthors. In other words, use three hyphens only when the work is by *exactly* the same author(s) as the previous entry.

Source Map: Citing Books

When using MLA style to cite a book by one author, include the following elements. Get this information from the book's title page and copyright page (on the reverse side of the title page), not from the book's cover or a library catalog.

1 *Author.* List the last name first, followed by a comma, the first name, and the middle initial (if given). Omit titles such as *MD, PhD,* or *Sir;* include suffixes after the name and a comma (*O'Driscoll, Gerald P., Jr.*). End with a period.

2 *Title.* Underline or (if your instructor permits) italicize the title and any subtitle; capitalize all major words. End with a period. (See 48d for more on capitalizing titles.)

3 *City of publication.* If more than one city is given, use the first one listed. For foreign cities that may be unfamiliar to your readers, add an abbreviation of the country or province (*Cork, Ire.*). Follow it with a colon.

4 *Publisher.* Give a shortened version of the publisher's name (*Harper* for *HarperCollins Publishers; Harcourt* for *Harcourt Brace; Oxford UP* for *Oxford University Press*). Follow it with a comma.

5 *Year of publication.* Consult the copyright page. If more than one copyright date is given, use the most recent one. End with a period.

For a book by one author, use the following format

Last name, First name. Title of book. City: Publisher, Year.

A citation for the book on p. 377 would look like this:

author, last name first   title and subtitle, underlined

Twitchell, James B. Living It Up: America's Love Affair with Luxury. New York:

Simon, 2002. ◄──────── publisher's city and name,
                        year of publication
double-space;
indent one-half inch
or five spaces

For more on using MLA style to cite books, see pp. 374-381. (For guidelines and models for using APA style, see pp. 421-423; for CSE style, see pp. 438-440; for *Chicago* style, see pp. 450-452.)

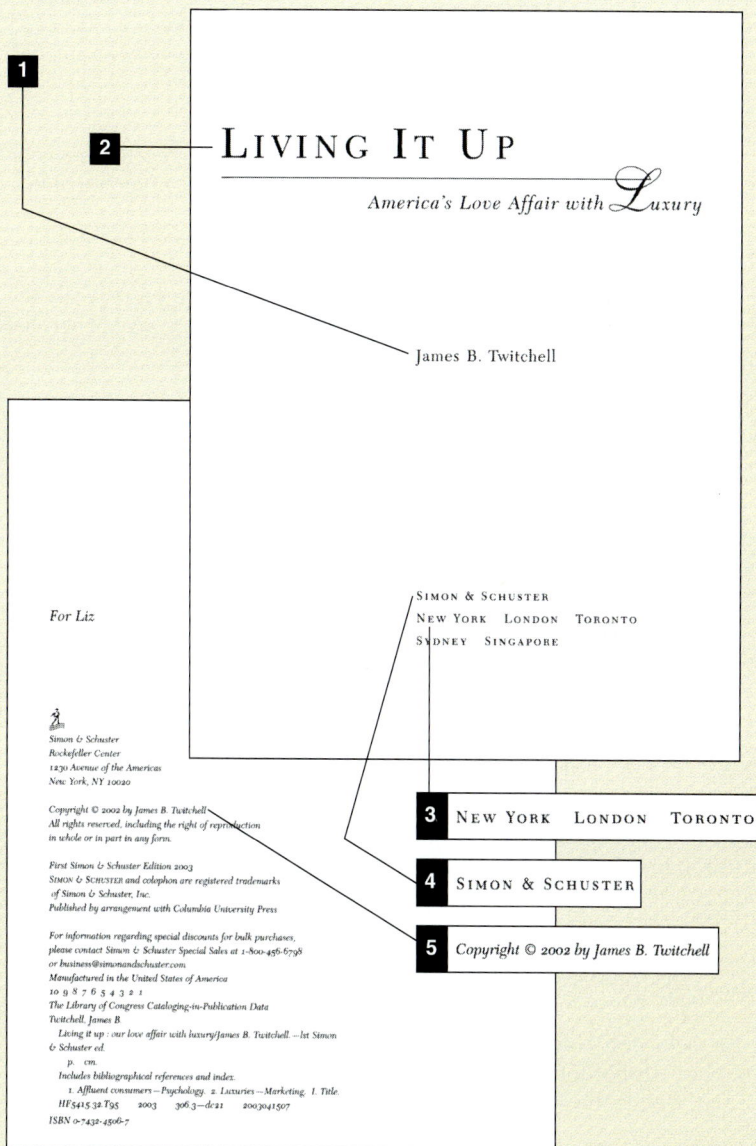

1

2 LIVING IT UP

America's Love Affair with *Luxury*

James B. Twitchell

SIMON & SCHUSTER
NEW YORK   LONDON   TORONTO
SYDNEY   SINGAPORE

For Liz

Simon & Schuster
Rockefeller Center
1230 Avenue of the Americas
New York, NY 10020

Copyright © 2002 by James B. Twitchell
All rights reserved, including the right of reproduction
in whole or in part in any form.

First Simon & Schuster Edition 2003

SIMON & SCHUSTER and colophon are registered trademarks
of Simon & Schuster, Inc.
Published by arrangement with Columbia University Press

For information regarding special discounts for bulk purchases,
please contact Simon & Schuster Special Sales at 1-800-456-6798
or business@simonandschuster.com
Manufactured in the United States of America
10 9 8 7 6 5 4 3 2 1
The Library of Congress Cataloging-in-Publication Data
Twitchell, James B.
    Living it up : our love affair with luxury/James B. Twitchell. — 1st Simon
& Schuster ed.
        p.   cm.
    Includes bibliographical references and index.
        1. Affluent consumers — Psychology. 2. Luxuries — Marketing. I. Title.
    HF5415.32.T95   2003   306.3—dc21   2003041507
ISBN 0-7432-4506-7

3 NEW YORK   LONDON   TORONTO

4 SIMON & SCHUSTER

5 Copyright © 2002 by James B. Twitchell

7. EDITOR(S)

Treat an editor as an author, but add a comma and *ed.* (or *eds.*).

> Wall, Cheryl A., ed. <u>Changing Our Own Words: Essays on Criticism, Theory, and</u>
> <u>Writing by Black Women</u>. New Brunswick: Rutgers UP, 1989.

8. AUTHOR AND EDITOR

If you have cited the body of the text, begin with the author's name. Then list the editor(s), introduced by *Ed.* ("Edited by"), after the title.

> James, Henry. <u>Portrait of a Lady</u>. Ed. Leon Edel. Boston: Houghton, 1963.

If you have cited the editor's contribution, begin the entry with the name of the editor(s), followed by a comma and *ed.* (or *eds.*). Then list the author's name, introduced by *By*, after the title.

> Edel, Leon, ed. <u>Portrait of a Lady</u>. By Henry James. Boston: Houghton, 1963.

9. ANTHOLOGY

Begin with the name of the editor(s) or compiler(s), followed by the abbreviation *ed.* (or *eds.*) or *comp.* (or *comps.*). Then list the title of the anthology, city of publication, name of the publisher, and year of publication.

> Walker, Dale L., ed. <u>Westward: A Fictional History of the American West</u>. New
> York: Forge, 2003.

10. WORK IN AN ANTHOLOGY OR CHAPTER IN A BOOK WITH AN EDITOR

List the author(s) of the selection or chapter; its title; the title of the book in which the selection or chapter appears; *Ed.* and the name(s) of the editor(s) in regular order; the publication information; and the inclusive page numbers of the selection.

> Komunyakaa, Yusef. "Facing It." <u>The Seagull Reader</u>. Ed. Joseph Kelly. New York:
> Norton, 2000. 126-27.

If the selection was originally published in a periodical and you are asked to supply information for this original source, use the following format. *Rpt.* is the abbreviation for *Reprinted.*

> Byatt, A. S. "The Thing in the Forest." <u>New Yorker</u> 3 June 2002: 80-89. Rpt. in
> <u>The O. Henry Prize Stories 2003</u>. Ed. Laura Furman. New York: Anchor, 2003.
> 3-22.

For inclusive page numbers up to 99, note all digits in the second number. For numbers above 99, note only the last two digits and any others that change in the second number (*115–18, 1378–79, 296–301*).

11. TWO OR MORE ITEMS FROM AN ANTHOLOGY

Include the anthology itself in your list of works cited (see model 9, above). Also list each selection separately by its author and title, followed by a cross-reference to the anthology.

> Estleman, Loren D. "Big Tim Magoon and the Wild West." Walker 391-404.

> Salzer, Susan K. "Miss Libbie Tells All." Walker 199-212.

12. TRANSLATION

Begin the entry with the author's name, and give the translator's name, preceded by *Trans.* ("Translated by"), after the title.

> Hietamies, Laila. Red Moon over White Sea. Trans. Borje Vahamaki. Beaverton,
> ON: Aspasia, 2000.

13. BOOK IN A LANGUAGE OTHER THAN ENGLISH

If necessary, you may provide a translation of the book's title in brackets. You may also choose to give the English name of a foreign city in brackets.

> Benedetti, Mario. La borra del café [The Coffee Grind]. Buenos Aires:
> Sudamericana, 2000.

14. EDITION OTHER THAN THE FIRST

Add the information, in abbreviated form, after the title.

> Walker, John A. Art in the Age of Mass Media. 3rd ed. London: Pluto, 2001.

15. MULTIVOLUME WORK

If you cite only one volume, give the volume number after the title. You have the option of giving the number of volumes in the complete work after the date, using the abbreviation *vols.*

> Ch'oe, Yong-Ho, Peter Lee, and William Theodore De Barry, eds. Sources of
> Korean Tradition. Vol. 2. New York: Columbia UP, 2000. 2 vols.

If you cite two or more volumes, give the number of volumes in the complete work after the title.

> Ch'oe, Yong-Ho, Peter Lee, and William Theodore De Barry, eds. Sources of
> Korean Tradition. 2 vols. New York: Columbia UP, 2000.

16. PREFACE, FOREWORD, INTRODUCTION, OR AFTERWORD

List the author of the item, the item title, the title of the book, and the book's author (preceded by *By*) or editor (preceded by *Ed.*). List the inclusive page numbers of the item at the end of the entry.

> Atwan, Robert. Foreword. The Best American Essays 2002. Ed. Stephen Jay
>
> Gould. Boston: Houghton, 2002. viii-xii.

17. ENTRY IN A REFERENCE WORK

List the author of the entry, if known. If no author is identified, begin with the title. For a well-known encyclopedia, just note the edition and year of publication or designate the edition by its year of publication. If the entries in the reference work are in alphabetical order, you need not give volume or page numbers.

> Kettering, Alison McNeil. "Art Nouveau." World Book Encyclopedia. 2002 ed.

18. BOOK THAT IS PART OF A SERIES

Cite the series name as it appears on the title page, followed by any series number.

> Nichanian, Marc, and Vartan Matiossian, eds. Yeghishe Charents: Poet of the
>
> Revolution. Armenian Studies Ser. 5. Costa Mesa: Mazda, 2003.

19. REPUBLICATION

To cite a modern edition of an older book, add the original publication date, followed by a period, after the title.

> Scott, Walter. Kenilworth. 1821. New York: Dodd, 1956.

20. PUBLISHER'S IMPRINT

If a book is published under a publisher's imprint (indicated on the title page), hyphenate the imprint and the publisher's name.

> Gilligan, Carol. The Birth of Pleasure: A New Map of Love. New York: Vintage-
>
> Random, 2003.

21. BOOK WITH A TITLE WITHIN THE TITLE

Do not underline or italicize the title of a book within the title of a book you are citing. Underline or italicize and enclose in quotation marks the title of a short work within a book title.

> Mullaney, Julie. Arundhati Roy's The God of Small Things: A Reader's Guide. New
>
> York: Continuum, 2002.

Rhynes, Martha. "I, Too, Sing America": The Story of Langston Hughes.

Greensboro: Morgan, 2002.

22. GOVERNMENT PUBLICATION

Begin with the author, if identified. Otherwise, start with the name of the government, followed by the agency and any subdivision. Use abbreviations if they can be readily understood. Then give the title. For congressional documents, cite the number and session plus chamber; the type (*Report, Resolution, Document*), in abbreviated form; and the number of the material. If you cite the *Congressional Record*, give only the date and page number. Otherwise, end with the publication information; the publisher is often the Government Printing Office (GPO).

Gregg, Judd. Report to Accompany the Genetic Information Act of 2003. US

108th Cong., 1st sess. S. Rept. 108-22. 2003. Washington: GPO, 2003.

Kinsella, Kevin, and Victoria Velkoff. An Aging World: 2001. U.S. Bureau of the

Census. Population Division. Washington: GPO, 2001.

United States. Natl. Council on Disability. Reconstructing Fair Housing.

Washington: Natl. Council on Disability, 2001.

23. SACRED TEXT

To cite individual published editions of sacred books, begin the entry with the title. For versions of the Bible in which the version is not part of the title, list the version after the title. If you are not citing a particular edition, sacred texts should not appear in the works-cited list.

Quran: The Final Testament (Authorized English Version) with Arabic Text. Trans.

Rashad Khalifa. Fremont: Universal Unity, 2000.

Periodicals

24. ARTICLE IN A JOURNAL PAGINATED BY VOLUME

Follow the journal title with the volume number in arabic numerals.

Gigante, Denise. "The Monster in the Rainbow: Keats and the Science of Life."

PMLA 117 (2002): 433-48.

25. ARTICLE IN A JOURNAL PAGINATED BY ISSUE

If each issue begins with page 1, follow the volume number with a period and the issue number.

Zivley, Sherry Lutz. "Sylvia Plath's Transformations of Modernist Paintings."

College Literature 29.3 (2002): 35-56.

SOURCE MAP: *Citing Articles from Periodicals*

When using MLA style to cite an article in a periodical, include the following elements:

1 *Author.* List the last name first, followed by a comma, the first name, and the middle initial (if given) Omit titles such as *MD, PhD,* or *Sir;* include suffixes after the name and a comma (*O'Driscoll, Gerald P., Jr.*). End with a period.

2 *Article title.* Enclose the title and any subtitle in quotation marks, and capitalize all major words. The closing period goes inside the closing quotation mark. (See 48d for more on capitalizing titles.)

3 *Periodical title.* Underline or italicize the periodical title (excluding any initial *A, An,* or *The*), and capitalize all major words. For journals, give the volume number; if each issue starts with page 1, include the issue number as well.

4 *Date of publication.* For journals, list the year in parentheses followed by a colon. For monthly magazines, list the month and year. For weekly magazines and newspapers, list the day, month, and year.

5 *Inclusive page number(s).* For page numbers up to 99, note all digits in the second number. For numbers above 99, note only the last two digits and any others that change in the second number (115-18, 1378-79, 296-301). Include section letters for newspapers, if relevant. End with a period.

For a journal article, use the following format:

Last name, First name. "Title of article." Journal Volume number (year): Page number(s).

For a newspaper article, use the following format:

Last name, First name. "Title." Newspaper Date, Edition (if any): Section number (if any):
    Page number(s) (including section letter, if any).

For a magazine article, use the following format:

Last name, First name. "Title of article." Magazine Date: Page number(s).

A citation for the magazine article on p. 383 would look like this:

author,   article title and subtitle,
last name first   in quotation marks

Hamilton, Anita. "All the Right Questions: Discussion Groups Based on

the Teachings of Socrates Are Reviving the Art of Conversation." Time

    5 Apr. 2004: 65-66. ◄—— inclusive page   periodical
        date   numbers   title,
                                                        underlined

double-space; indent one-half inch or five spaces

For more on using MLA style to cite periodical articles, see pp. 381-385. (For guidelines and models for using APA style, see pp. 423-424; for CSE style, see pp. 440-441; for *Chicago* style, see pp. 452-453.)

1 By ANITA HAMILTON

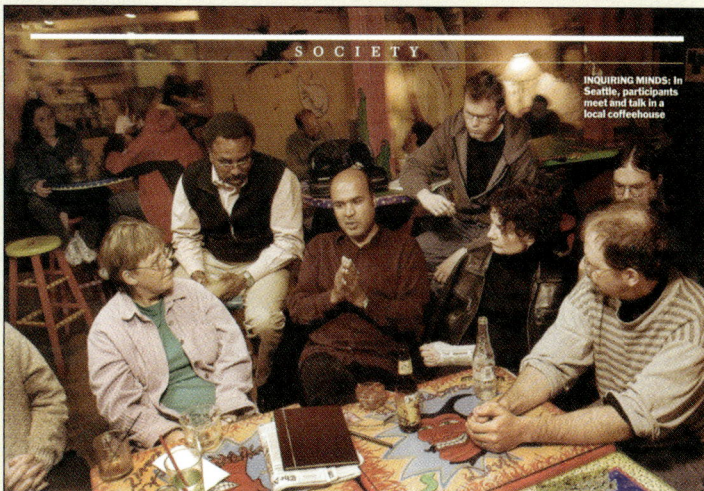

SOCIETY

INQUIRING MINDS: In Seattle, participants meet and talk in a local coffeehouse

2 # All the Right Questions

Discussion groups based on the teachings of Socrates are reviving the art of conversation

By ANITA HAMILTON

THERE'S A BUZZ IN THE AIR AT THE El Diablo Coffee Co. in Seattle, and it's not just coming from the aroma of the shop's Cuban-style espresso drinks. On a recent Wednesday evening, as most patrons sat quietly reading books or tapping away on their laptop computers, about 15 people gathered in a circle discussing philosophy. "When is violence necessary?" asked one. "What is a well-lived life?" asked another, as the group enjoyed a well-caffeinated, intellectual high.

Known as a Socrates Café, the group at El Diablo is just one of 150 or so that meet in coffee shops, bookstores, libraries, churches and community centers across the country. Founded by Christopher Phil-

lips, a former journalist and teacher, the cafés are designed to get people talking about philosophical issues. Using a kind of Socratic method, they encourage people to develop their views by posing questions, being open to challenges and considering alternative answers. Adhering to Socrates' belief that the unexamined life is not worth living, the cafés focus on exchanging ideas, not using them to pummel other participants.

"Instead of just yelling back and forth, we take a few steps back and examine people's underlying values. People can ask why to their heart's content," says Phillips, whose most recent book, *Six Questions of Socrates* (Norton; 320 pages), came out earlier this year.

While a modern-day discussion group based on the teachings of a thinker from

the 5th century B.C. may seem quaintly outdated, Socrates Cafés have found a surprisingly large and diverse following. Meetings have been held everywhere from a Navajo Nation reservation in Ganado, Ariz., to an airplane terminal in Providence, R.I. Ongoing groups have formed in prisons, senior centers and homeless shelters. In recent months, international groups have popped up in Afghanistan, Finland and Spain. The common denominator? "People who get off on ideas come to this," says Fred Korn, 65, a retired philosophy professor, who attends the Wednesday-night meetings at El Diablo. "Outside of college, there's not a lot of opportunity to get together with people who want to talk about ideas," he says.

For Phillips, the dialogue groups are about much more than good conversation. "It's grass-roots democracy," he says. "It's only in a group setting that people can hash out their ideas about how we should act not just as an individual but as a society." To

3 TIME,   **4** APRIL 5, 2004   **5** 65

26. ARTICLE THAT SKIPS PAGES

When an article skips pages, give only the first page number and a plus sign.

> Tyrnauer, Matthew. "Empire by Martha." Vanity Fair Sept. 2002: 364+.

27. ARTICLE WITH A TITLE WITHIN THE TITLE

Enclose in single quotation marks the title of a short work within an article title.

> Frey, Leonard H. "Irony and Point of View in 'That Evening Sun.'" Faulkner
>   Studies 2 (1953): 33-40.

Underline or italicize the title of a book within an article title.

28. ARTICLE IN A MONTHLY MAGAZINE

Put the month (or months, hyphenated) before the year. Separate the date and page number(s) with a colon.

> Fonda, Daren. "Saving the Dead." Life Apr. 2000: 69-72.

29. ARTICLE IN A WEEKLY MAGAZINE

Include the day, month, and year in that order, with no commas between them. Separate the date and page number(s) with a colon.

> Gilgoff, Dan. "Unusual Suspects." US News and World Report 26 Nov. 2001: 51.

30. ARTICLE IN A NEWSPAPER

After the author and title of the article, give the name of the newspaper, underlined or italicized, as it appears on the front page but without any initial *A, An,* or *The.* Add the city in brackets after the name if it is not part of the title. Then give the date and the edition (if listed), followed by a colon, a space, the section number or letter (if listed), and the page number(s). If the article does not appear on consecutive pages, give only the first page number and a plus sign.

> Vogel, Carol. "With Huge Gift, the Whitney Is No Longer a Poor Cousin." New
>   York Times 3 Aug. 2002, late ed.: A1+.

31. ARTICLE IN A COLLECTION OF REPRINTED ARTICLES

First give the citation for the original publication. Then give the citation for the collection in which the article is reprinted. Insert *Rpt. in* ("Reprinted in") between the two citations. *Comp.* stands for "compiled by." *Ed.* and *Trans.* are other common abbreviations used in citing a collection.

Quindlen, Anna. "Playing God on No Sleep." Newsweek 2 July 2001: 64. Rpt. in

The Best American Magazine Writing 2002. Comp. Amer. Soc. of Magazine

Eds. New York: Perennial, 2002. 458-62.

32. EDITORIAL OR LETTER TO THE EDITOR

Use the label *Editorial* or *Letter,* not underlined, italicized, or in quotation marks, after the title or, if there is no title, after the author's name.

Magee, Doug. "Soldier's Home." Editorial. Nation 26 Mar. 1988: 400-01.

33. REVIEW

List the reviewer's name and the title of the review, if any, followed by *Rev. of* and the title and author or director of the work reviewed. Then add the publication information for the periodical in which the review appears.

Schwarz, Benjamin. Rev. of The Second World War: A Short History, by R. A. C.

Parker. Atlantic Monthly May 2002: 110-11.

34. UNSIGNED ARTICLE

Begin with the article title, alphabetizing the entry according to the first word after any initial *A, An,* or *The.*

"Performance of the Week." Time 6 Oct. 2003: 18.

Electronic sources

Electronic sources such as CD-ROMs, Web sites, and email differ from print sources in the ease with which they can be—and frequently are—changed, updated, or even eliminated. In addition, as the *MLA Handbook for Writers of Research Papers* notes, electronic media "so far lack agreed-on means of organizing works"; as a result, it is often difficult for readers to find electronic sources. As the *Handbook* adds, "References to electronic works therefore must provide more information than print citations generally offer."

The most commonly cited electronic sources are documents from an Internet site, such as essays, articles, poems, and other short works within a reference database, a professional site, or an online periodical. The entry for such a source may include up to five basic elements, as in the following list, but must always include the last two.

- *Author.* List the last name first, followed by a comma and the first name, and end with a period. If no author is given, begin the entry with the title. For variations on authors, see models 2–8 in Chapter 52.

- *Title.* Enclose the title and subtitle of the document in quotation marks unless you are citing an entire site or an online book, both of which should be underlined or italicized. Capitalize all major words, and end with a period inside the closing quotation marks. (See 48d for more on capitalizing titles.)
- *Print publication information.* Give any information the document provides about any previous or simultaneous publication in print.
- *Electronic publication information.* List the following items, with a period after each one: the title of the site, underlined or italicized, with all major words capitalized; the editor(s) of the site, preceded by *Ed.*; the version number of the site, preceded by *Vers.*; the date of electronic publication or of the latest update, with the month, if any, abbreviated except for May, June, and July; and the name of any institution or organization that sponsors the site. (The sponsor's name usually appears at the bottom of the site's home page.)
- *Access information.* Give the most recent date you accessed the document and its URL, enclosed in angle brackets; put a period after the closing bracket. In general, give the complete URL, including the opening *http, ftp, gopher, telnet,* or *news.* If the URL is very long and complicated, however, give the URL of the site's search page, if there is one, instead. If the site does not provide a usable URL for individual documents and citing the search page is inappropriate, give the URL of the site's home page, if you know it. In this situation, if a user can reach the document from the home page by clicking on a sequence of links, do the following: after the URL, give the word *Path* followed by a colon, and then give the sequence of links. Use semicolons between the links and a period at the end. Whenever a URL will not fit on one line, break it only after a slash, and do not add a hyphen at the break or allow your word-processing program to add one.

Further guidelines for citing electronic sources can be found in the *MLA Handbook for Writers of Research Papers* and online at <http://www.mla.org>.

35. ARTICLE FROM AN ONLINE DATABASE OR SUBSCRIPTION SERVICE

For a work from an online database, begin by giving the author's name (unless no author is given), the title of the work in quotation marks, as well as the date and place of publication if it is a book (if applicable). Next, give the name of the online database (underlined or italicized), the name of its editor (if any), preceded by *Ed.*, the date of the most recent revision, and the name of any organization or institution with which the database is affiliated. End with the date of access and the URL, in angle brackets.

"Bolivia: Elecciones Presidenciales de 2002." Political Database of the Americas.

1999. Georgetown U and Organization of Amer. States. 12 Nov. 2003

<http://www.georgetown.edu/pdba/Elecdata/Bolivia /pres02B.html>.

If you accessed a work through a library's subscription to a service, after the information about the work give the name of the database, underlined or italicized, if you know it; the name of the service; the library; the date of access; and the URL of the service's home page, in angle brackets, if you know it.

> Gordon, Andrew. "It's Not Such a Wonderful Life: The Neurotic George Bailey."
>
> American Journal of Psychoanalysis 54.3 (1994): 219-33. PsycINFO.
>
> EBSCO. Graduate Center Lib., City U of New York. 26 Oct. 2003
>
> <http://www.epnet.com>.

To cite a work from a personal online subscription service such as America Online, follow the guidelines throughout this chapter for the appropriate type of work, such as an online book or an article in an online periodical. If possible, end the entry with the URL of the specific work or, if it is very long and complicated, the URL of the service's search page. If, however, the service supplies no URL or one that is not accessible to other subscribers, you will need to provide other access information. Specifically, after the date, depending on the service's retrieval system, give either the word *Keyword* followed by a colon and the keyword you used or the word *Path* followed by a colon and the sequence of links you followed, with semicolons between the links.

> "Steps in Reading a Poem." AOL's Academic Assistance Center. 11 Feb. 2004.
>
> Path: Reading & Learning; Poetry; Analysis and Interpreting Poetry.
>
> Weeks, W. William. "Beyond the Ark." Nature Conservancy Mar.-Apr. 1999.
>
> America Online. 2 Apr. 1999. Keyword: Ecology.

36. WORK FROM A PERSONAL WEB SITE

Include the name of the person who created the site; the title, underlined or italicized, or (if there is no title) a description such as *Home page*; the date of the last update, if given; the access information; and the site's URL.

> Lunsford, Andrea A. Home page. 15 Mar. 2003. 17 May 2004 <http://
>
> www.stanford.edu/~lunsfor1/>.

37. WORK FROM A PROFESSIONAL WEB SITE

Include the author (if available) and title of the document, followed by the name of the Web site, underlined or italicized; the date of publication or latest update; and the name of the institution or organization associated with the site. Be sure to include the name of the editor (if applicable); the date of access; and the document's URL, in angle brackets.

SOURCE MAP: *Citing Articles from Databases*

Libraries pay for services—such as InfoTrac, EBSCOhost, ProQuest, and LexisNexis—that provide access to huge databases of electronic articles.

When using MLA style to cite articles from databases, include the following elements:

1 *Author.* List the last name first.

2 *Article title.* Enclose the title and any subtitle in quotation marks.

3 *Periodical title.* Underline or italicize it. Exclude any initial *A, An,* or *The.*

4 *Volume number.* Also list the issue number if appropriate.

5 *Date of publication.* Give the year for journals; the month and year for monthly magazines; the day, month, and year for weekly magazines and newspapers.

6 *Inclusive page number(s).* Include section letters for newspapers, if relevant. If only the first page number is given, follow it with a hyphen, a space, and a period.

7 *Name of the database.* Like the periodical title, it should be underlined or italicized.

8 *Name of the subscription service, if available.* Here, it is InfoTrac.

9 *Name of the library where you accessed the article.* Also list the city and, if necessary, an abbreviation for the state (*Burnt Hills, NY*).

✱ End with the date you accessed the article and a brief URL for the database.

For an article from a database, use the following format:

[Citation format for the journal, magazine, or newspaper article—see p. 382]. Name of Database. Name of Service. Library Name, Location. Date accessed <Brief Web address>.

A citation for the article on p. 389 would look like this:

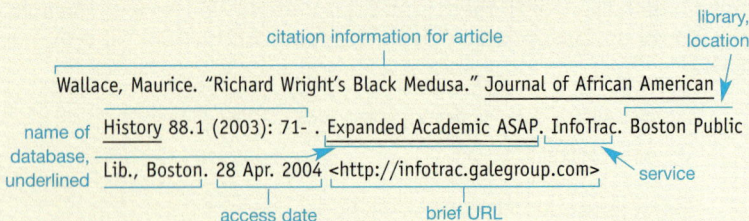

citation information for article   library, location

Wallace, Maurice. "Richard Wright's Black Medusa." Journal of African American

name of database, underlined   History 88.1 (2003): 71- . Expanded Academic ASAP. InfoTrac. Boston Public

Lib., Boston. 28 Apr. 2004 <http://infotrac.galegroup.com>   service

access date   brief URL

For more on using MLA style to cite articles from databases, see pp. 386-387. (For guidelines and models for using APA style, see pp. 425-426; for CSE style, see p. 444; for *Chicago* style, see p. 454.)

6 p71(7)

7 Expanded Academic ASAP

8 I N F O T R A C

9 Boston Public Library

Article 1 - Microsoft Internet Explorer

File   Edit   View   Favorites   Tools   Help

Back

Search   Favorites   Media

Address   http://web2.infotrac.galegroup.com/itw/infomark/108/539/50958947w2/purl=rc1_EAIM_0_A1011737078dyn=18!xrn_1_0_A1   Go

INFOTRAC

- Help - Article
- Dictionary
- Title List

- Print
- E-mail or Retrieval
- Links
- View mark list

Back to ...
- Citations
- Search
- Gale Group Databases
- Library

Boston Public Library
Expanded Academic ASAP

—— Article 1 of 1 ——

☐ *The Journal of African American History*, Wntr 2003 v88 i1 p71(7)
Mark

Richard Wright's Black Medusa. *Maurice Wallace.*

Full Text: COPYRIGHT 2003 Association for the Study of Afro-American Life and History, Inc.

I'm honored to have been invited to participate in this brilliant event, and to have been thought of alongside such a great a company of teachers and scholars as those with whom I am sharing today's panels. As much as I have long adored Claudia Tate, I must admit that had I known who'd also speak this afternoon when I eagerly and rather adolescently accepted the invitation to Princeton (without so much as asking who else had been invited), another mind, that of an untried neophyte, might well have prevailed. I revere every one of this symposium's participants. Among my venerated colleagues today, I would like to single out, briefly, Professor Hazel Carby, the panelist I know best because I formerly held an

1 *Maurice Wallace.*

2 Richard Wright's Black Medusa.

3 *The Journal of African American History,*

4 v88 i1

5 Wntr 2003

Source Map: *Citing Works from Web Sites*

When using MLA style to cite a work from a Web site, include the following elements. You may need to browse other parts of a site to find some of these elements, and on some sites, details may be missing. Uncover as much information as you can.

1 *Author of the work.* List the last name first, followed by a comma, the first name, and the middle initial (if given). End with a period. If no author is given, begin with the title.

2 *Title of the work.* Enclose the title and any subtitle of the work in quotation marks.

3 *Title of the Web site.* Give the title of the entire site, underlined or italicized. Where there is no clear title, use *Home page* without underlining or italicizing it.

4 *Date of publication or last update.*

5 *Name of the sponsoring organization.* The sponsor's name often appears at the bottom of the site's home page.

6 *Access information.* Give the most recent date you accessed the work. Give the complete URL, enclosed in angle brackets. If the URL is very long and complicated, however, you can give the URL of the site's search page instead. If the URL will not fit on one line, break it only after a slash, and do not add a hyphen.

For a work from a Web site, use the following format:

Last name, First name. "Title of work." Title of Web site. Date of publication or latest
    update. Sponsoring organization. Date accessed <Web address>.

A citation for the work on p. 391 would look like this:

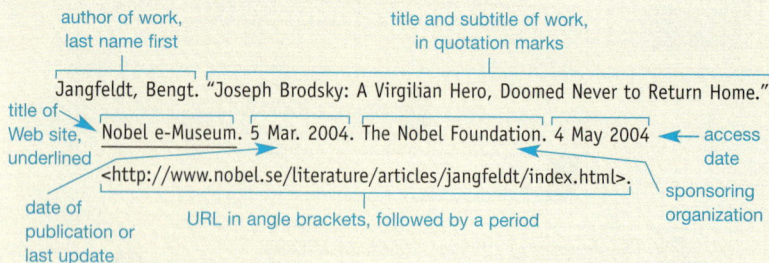

author of work,
last name first

title and subtitle of work,
in quotation marks

Jangfeldt, Bengt. "Joseph Brodsky: A Virgilian Hero, Doomed Never to Return Home."

title of
Web site,   Nobel e-Museum. 5 Mar. 2004. The Nobel Foundation. 4 May 2004 ← access
underlined   date

<http://www.nobel.se/literature/articles/jangfeldt/index.html>.
                                                                          sponsoring
date of   organization
publication or   URL in angle brackets, followed by a period
last update

For more on using MLA style to cite Web documents, see pp. 385-397. (For guidelines and models for using APA style, see pp. 424-426; for CSE style, see pp. 441-444; for *Chicago* style, see pp. 453-454.)

1 by Bengt Jangfeldt

2

3 NOBEL *e*-MUSEUM

Joseph Brodsky: A Virgilian Hero, Doomed Never to Return Home - Microsoft Internet Explorer

File   Edit   View   Favorites   Tools   Help

Back ▾   ⬤ ▾   ⬤   ⬤   ⬤   🔍 Search   ⭐ Favorites   Media   ⬤   ⬤ ▾   ⬤   ⬤   ⬤

Address http://www.nobel.se/literature/articles/jangfeldt/index.html   ➜ Go

HOME   SITE HELP   ABOUT   SEARCH

NOBEL   PHYSICS   CHEMISTRY   MEDICINE   **LITERATURE**   PEACE   ECONOMICS
NOBEL *e*-MUSEUM   LAUREATES   ▶**ARTICLES**   EDUCATIONAL

Joseph Brodsky: A Virgilian Hero, Doomed Never to Return Home

by Bengt Jangfeldt

"All my poems are more or less about the same thing — about Time. About what time does to Man." - Joseph Brodsky

Contents of this article:
Rebel Poet
Time Is Greater than Space
Language Is Greater than Time
Poetry Is Greater than Prose
Linear Thinking

Rebel Poet

It is impossible to speak about Russian literature without taking into account the society in which it was written. This is especially true for the 20th century, when five Russian writers were awarded the Nobel Prize. When the émigré writer Ivan Bunin got it in 1933, the Swedish Academy was reproached for not having awarded the prize to the pro-Soviet Maxim Gorki; Boris Pasternak's prize, in 1958, was fiercely attacked by the Soviet authorities as a political, anti-Soviet act; Mikhail Sholokhov's, seven years later, was criticized for being, in its turn, a conciliatory gesture toward the Soviet regime; and Aleksandr Solzhenitsyn's award (1970) was conceived in the same vein as the prize to Pasternak.

Joseph Brodsky

File   Edit   View   F

Back ▾

Address http://www

Brodsky
Novemb
Photo by

One consequenc
in one direction
homeland. His th
age of thirty-two
never to return h

When asked why he did not want to go back, Brodsky answered that he didn't want to visit his home country as a tourist. Or that he didn't want to go on an invitation from official institutions. His final argument was: "The best part of me is already there: my poetry."

SITE FEEDBACK   CONTACT   RATE THIS   TELL A FRIEND   PRINTER-FRIENDLY PAGE   BACK TO TOP

First published December 12, 2003   The Official Web Site of The Nobel Foundation
Last modified March 5, 2004   Copyright© 2004 The Nobel Foundation

4 First published December 12, 2003

5 Copyright© 2004 The Nobel Foundation

6 http://www.nobel.se/literature/articles/jangfeldt/index.html

"Important Dates in the Women's Rights Movement." <u>HistoryChannel.com</u>. 2003.
    History Channel. 13 Mar. 2003 <http://historychannel.com>. Path: Women's
    History; Special Feature--Women's Suffrage; The History of Women's Suffrage
    in America; Timeline.

Stauder, Ellen Keck. "Darkness Audible: Negative Capability and Mark Doty's
    'Nocturne in Black and Gold.'" <u>Romantic Circles Praxis Series</u>. Ed. Orrin
    Wang. 2003. 28 Sept. 2003 <http://www.rc.umd.edu/praxis/poetics/
    stauder/stauder.html>.

38. ENTIRE WEB SITE

Follow the guidelines for a specific work from the Web, but begin with
the title of the entire site and the name of the editor(s), if any.

<u>Electronic Poetry Center</u>. Ed. Charles Bernstein, Kenneth Goldsmith, Martin
    Spinelli, and Patrick Durgin. 2003. Poetics Program/Dept. of Media Study,
    SUNY Buffalo. 26 Sept. 2003 <http://wings.buffalo.edu/epc/>.

<u>Weather.com</u>. 2003. Weather Channel Interactive. 13 Mar. 2003 <http://
    www.weather.com>.

39. ACADEMIC COURSE OR DEPARTMENT WEB SITE

For the site of an academic course, give the name of the instructor, the
title of the course, a description such as *Course home page*, the dates of
the course, the name of the department, the name of the institution, the
date of access, and the URL.

Lunsford, Andrea A. Memory and Media. Course home page. Sept.-Dec. 2002.
    Dept. of English, Stanford U. 13 Mar. 2003 <http://www.stanford.edu/
    class/english12sc>.

For the site of an academic department, give the name of the department, such as *English*; a description such as *Dept. home page*; the name of
the institution; and the access information.

English. Dept. home page. Amherst Coll. 4 Nov. 2003 <http://www.amherst.edu/
    ~english/>.

40. ONLINE BOOK

Cite an online book as you would a print book. After the print publication information (city, publisher, and year), if any, give the date of access
and the URL, in angle brackets.

Euripides. The Trojan Women. Trans. Gilbert Murray. New York: Oxford UP, 1915.
12 Oct. 2003 <http://www.sacred-texts.com/cla/eurip/trojan.htm>.

41. ONLINE POEM

Include the poet's name and the title of the poem, followed by the print
publication information for the poem (if applicable). End with the online
access information, including the name of the Web site, the name of the
organization or institution that sponsors the site (if any), the date of electronic publication, the date of access, and the URL in angle brackets.

Muench, Simone. "The Melos of Medusa." Notebook. Knife. Mentholatum. Grand
Rapids: New Michigan Press, 2003. Verse Daily. 23 July 2003. 9 Nov. 2003
<http://www.versedaily.org/melosmedusa.shtml>.

42. ARTICLE IN AN ONLINE JOURNAL, MAGAZINE, OR NEWSPAPER

Cite the article as you would an article from a print journal (see models
24 and 25), magazine (see models 28 and 29), or newspaper (see model
30). End with the range or total number of pages, paragraphs, parts, or
other sections, if numbered; the date of access; and the URL, in angle
brackets.

Burt, Stephen. "The True Legacy of Marianne Moore, Modernist Monument." Slate
11 Nov. 2003. 12 Nov. 2003 <http://slate.msn.com/id/2091081/>.

Gallagher, Brian. "Greta Garbo Is Sad: Some Historical Reflections on the
Paradoxes of Stardom in the American Film Industry, 1910-1960." Images:
A Journal of Film and Popular Culture 3 (1997): 7 pts. 7 Aug. 2002
<http://imagesjournal.com/issue03/infocus.htm>.

Shea, Christopher. "Five Truths about Tuition." New York Times on the Web
9 Nov. 2003. 11 Nov. 2003 <http://www.nytimes.com/2003/11/09/edlife/
1109SHT.html>.

43. ENTRY IN AN ONLINE REFERENCE WORK

Cite the entry as you would an entry from a print reference work (see
model 17). End with the online access information, including the sponsor, date of access, and the URL in angle brackets.

"France." Encyclopaedia Britannica Online. 2003. Encyclopaedia Britannica. 13
Mar. 2003 <http://search.eb.com>.

44. ONLINE EDITORIAL OR LETTER TO THE EDITOR

Include the word *Editorial* or *Letter* following the title. If the letter is untitled, insert *Letter* after the author's name. End with the online access information, including the name of the Web site, the date of electronic publication, the date of access, and the URL, in angle brackets.

> "The Funding Gap." Editorial. Washingtonpost.com 5 Nov. 2003. 9 Nov. 2003
>
>   <http://www.washingtonpost.com/wp-dyn/articles/A1087-2003Nov5.html>.

> Piccato, Pablo. Letter. New York Times on the Web 9 Nov. 2003. 9 Nov. 2003
>
>   <http://www.nytimes.com/2003/11/09/opinion/L09IMMI.html>.

45. ONLINE REVIEW

Begin with the author's name and the title of the review (if any), followed by *Rev. of*, the title of the reviewed work, and the name of the work's author, editor, or director. End with the online access information, including the name of the Web site, the date of electronic publication, the date of access, and the URL, in angle brackets.

> Kryah, Joshua. Rev. of Eating in the Underworld, by Rachel Zucker. Electronic
>
>   Poetry Review 6 (2003). 9 Nov. 2003 <http://www.poetry.org/issues/
>
>   issue6/text/prose/kryah1.htm>.

46. ONLINE FILM OR FILM CLIP

In general, start with the name of the director; then give the title of the film, underlined or italicized, and the date of its release. End with the online access information, including the name of the Web site, the date of access, and the URL, in angle brackets.

> Moore, Michael, dir. Bowling for Columbine. 2002. BowlingforColumbine.com. 30
>
>   Sept. 2003 <http://www.bowlingforcolumbine.com/media/clips/index.php>.

47. ONLINE WORK OF ART

Include the name of the artist; the work's title, underlined or italicized; date the work was created; the name of the museum or other location; and the city. End with the online access information, including the name of the Web site, the date of access, and the URL in angle brackets.

> Chagall, Marc. The Poet with the Birds. 1911. Minneapolis Inst. of Arts. 6 Oct.
>
>   2003 <http://www.artsmia.org/collection/search/art.cfm?id=1427>.

48. ONLINE MAP OR CHART

Begin with the title, and add the label *Map* or *Chart*. End with the online access information, including the name of the Web site, the date of access, and the URL, in angle brackets.

> Australia. Map. Perry-Castañeda Library Map Collection. 4 Nov. 2003 <http://
>
> www.lib.utexas.edu/maps/australia/australia_rel99.jpg>.

49. ONLINE ADVERTISEMENT

Name the item or organization being advertised, add the word *Advertisement*, and then supply the online access information, including the name of the Web site, date of online publication, date of online access, and the URL, in angle brackets.

> Microsoft. Advertisement. New York Times on the Web 11 Nov. 2003. 11 Nov.
>
> 2003 <http://www.nytimes.com/>.

50. POSTING TO A DISCUSSION GROUP

To cite a posting to an online discussion group such as a listserv or Usenet newsgroup, begin with the author's name; the title of the posting, in quotation marks; the description *Online posting*; and the date of posting. For a listserv posting, then give the name of the listserv; the date of access; and the URL of the listserv or the email address of its moderator. Always cite an archival version of the posting if one is available.

> Daly, Catherine. "Poetry Slams." Online posting. 29 Aug. 2003. SUNY Buffalo
>
> Poetics Discussion List. 1 Oct. 2003 <http://listserv.acsu.buffalo.edu/
>
> archives/poetics.html>.

For a newsgroup posting, end with the date of access and the name of the newsgroup, in angle brackets, with the prefix *news*.

> Stonehouse, Robert. "Repeated Words in Shakespeare's Sonnets." Online posting.
>
> 27 July 2003. 24 Sept. 2003 <news:humanities.lit.authors.shakespeare>.

51. EMAIL

Include the writer's name; the subject line of the message, in quotation marks; a description of the message that mentions the recipient; and the date of the message.

> Harris, J. "Thoughts on Impromptu Stage Productions." Email to Sarah Eitzel. 16
>
> July 2003.

52. REAL-TIME COMMUNICATION

In citing a posting in a forum such as a MUD, a MOO, or an IRC, include the name(s) of any specific speaker(s) you are citing; a description of the event; its date; the name of the forum; the date of access; and the URL. Always cite an archival version of the posting if one is available.

> Hong, Billy. Billy's Final Draft: Homeless Essay. 14 Oct. 2003. LinguaMOO. 12
>
> Nov. 2003 <http://lingua.utdallas.edu:7000/25871/>.

53. OTHER ONLINE SOURCES

In citing other kinds of online sources, follow the guidelines given on pp. 385-386, but adapt them as necessary to the electronic medium. Here are examples of citations for a radio program and an interview, accessed online.

> Komando, Kim. "E-mail Hacking and the Law." WCBS Radio. WCBS, New York.
>
> 28 Oct. 2003. 11 Nov. 2003 <http://wcbs880.com/komando/
>
> local_story_309135535.html>.

> Ebert, Roger. Interview with Matthew Rothschild. Progressive. Aug. 2003. 5 Oct.
>
> 2003 <http://www.progressive.org/aug03/intv0803.html>.

54. COMPUTER SOFTWARE OR VIDEO GAME

Include the title, underlined or italicized, version number (if given), and publication information. If you are citing software that was downloaded, replace the publication information with the date of access and the URL, in angle brackets.

> The Sims 2. Redwood City: Electronic Arts, 2004.

> Web Cache Illuminator. Vers. 4.02. 12 Nov. 2003 <http://www.tucows.com/
>
> adnload/332309_126245.html>.

55. PERIODICALLY REVISED CD-ROM

After the publication information for the print version, if any, of the text, give the medium (*CD-ROM*); the name of the company or group producing it; and the electronic publication date (month and year, if possible).

> Ashenfelter, Orley, and Kathryn Graddy. "Auctions and the Price of Art." Journal
>
> of Economic Literature 41.3 (2003): 763-87. CD-ROM. Amer. Economic Assn.
>
> Sept. 2003.

56. SINGLE-ISSUE CD-ROM

Cite this kind of electronic source, which is *not* regularly updated, much like a book, but add the medium and, if appropriate, the number of the electronic edition, release, or version. If you are citing only a part of the source, indicate which part and end with the numbers of the part (*pp. 78–83, 8 screens*) if provided.

> Cambridge Advanced Learner's Dictionary. CD-ROM. Cambridge: Cambridge UP,
>
> 2003.

57. MULTIDISC CD-ROM

After indicating the medium, give either the total number of discs (*3 discs*) or, if you used material from only one, the number of that disc.

> IRIS: Immigration Research Information Service, LawDesk. CD-ROM. Disc 2.
>
> Eagan, MN: West, 2003.

Other sources

58. REPORT OR PAMPHLET

Cite the report or pamphlet as you would a book.

> Allen, Katherine, and Lee Rainie. Parents Online. Washington: Pew Internet and
>
> Amer. Life Project, 2002.

> Murray, Alasdair. Corporate Social Responsibility in the EU. London: Centre for
>
> European Reform, 2003.

59. PUBLISHED PROCEEDINGS OF A CONFERENCE

Cite proceedings as you would a book. Add any necessary information about the conference after the title if the title itself doesn't include enough information.

> Cleary, John, and Gary Gurtler, eds. Proceedings of the Boston Area Colloquium
>
> in Ancient Philosophy 2002. Boston: Brill Academic, 2003.

60. UNPUBLISHED DISSERTATION OR THESIS

Enclose the title in quotation marks. Add the identification *Diss.* or *MA thesis, MS thesis,* and so on; the name of the university or professional school; a comma; and the year the dissertation or thesis was accepted.

> LeCourt, Donna. "The Self in Motion: The Status of the (Student) Subject in
>
> Composition Studies." Diss. Ohio State U, 1993.

61. PUBLISHED DISSERTATION

Cite a published dissertation as you would a book, adding the identification *Diss.,* the name of the university, and the year the dissertation was accepted. Then give the publication information. If the dissertation was published by University Microfilms International, add *Ann Arbor: UMI* and the year, and list the UMI number at the end of the entry.

> Yau, Rittchell Ann. The Portrayal of Immigration in a Selection of Picture Books
>
> Published since 1970. Diss. U of San Francisco, 2003. Ann Arbor: UMI,
>
> 2003. 3103491.

62. DISSERTATION ABSTRACT

Begin with the author's name and the title of the dissertation, followed by *Diss.;* then give the name of the institution granting the author's degree and the date of the dissertation. If you use *Dissertation Abstracts International (DAI),* include the *DAI* volume, year (in parentheses), and page number. If you cite a dissertation service that uses item numbers, replace the page number with *item* followed by the item number.

> Huang-Tiller, Gillian C. "The Power of the Meta-Genre: Cultural, Sexual, and
>
> Racial Politics of the American Modernist Sonnet." Diss. U of Notre Dame,
>
> 2000. DAI 61 (2000): 1401.

63. UNPUBLISHED OR PERSONAL INTERVIEW

List the person interviewed, and then use the label *Telephone interview, Personal interview,* or *Email interview.* End with the date(s) the interview took place.

> Freedman, Sasha. Personal interview. 10 Nov. 2003.

64. PUBLISHED INTERVIEW

List the person interviewed and then the title of the interview. If the interview has no title, use the label *Interview* (not underlined, italicized, or in quotation marks), and identify the source.

> Taylor, Max. "Max Taylor on Winning." Time 13 Nov. 2000: 66.

65. BROADCAST INTERVIEW

List the person interviewed and then the title of the interview. If the interview has no title, use the label *Interview* (not underlined, italicized, or in quotation marks) and the name of the interviewer, if pertinent. End with information about the program and the date(s) the interview took place.

Gyllenhaal, Maggie. Interview with Terry Gross. <u>Fresh Air</u>. Natl. Public Radio.

    WBUR, Boston. 30 Sept. 2003.

66. UNPUBLISHED LETTER

If the letter was sent to you, follow this form:

Lanois, Sophia. Letter to the author. 25 Aug. 2003.

67. MANUSCRIPT OR OTHER UNPUBLISHED WORK

Begin with the author's name (if applicable) and the title or, if there is no title, a description of the material. Then note the form of the material (such as *ms.* for manuscript or *ts.* for typescript) and any identifying numbers assigned to it. End by giving the name and location of the library or research institution housing the material (if applicable).

Woolf, Virginia. "The Searchlight." Ts. Ser. III, Box 4, Item 184. Papers of

    Virginia Woolf, 1902-1956. Smith College, Northampton, MA.

68. LEGAL SOURCE

To cite a legal case, give the name of the case with no underlining or quotation marks, followed by *No.* and the number of the case. End with the name of the court deciding the case and the year of the decision.

Eldred v. Ashcroft. No. 01-618. Supreme Ct. of the US. 15 Jan. 2003.

To cite an act, give the name of the act with no underlining or quotation marks, followed by *Pub. L.* (for "Public Law") and the Public Law number of the act. Then list the date it was enacted, followed by *Stat.* (for "Statutes at Large") and the Statutes at Large cataloging number of the act.

Museum and Library Services Act of 2003. Pub. L. 108-81. 25 Sept. 2003. Stat.

    117.991.

69. FILM, VIDEO, OR DVD

In general, start with the title, underlined or italicized; then name the director, the distributor, and the year of release. Other contributors, such as writers or actors, may follow the director. If you cite a particular person's work, start the entry with that person's name. For a videocassette or DVD, include the original film release date (if relevant) and the label *Videocassette* or *DVD*.

<u>The Hours</u>. Dir. Stephen Daldry. Perf. Meryl Streep, Julianne Moore, and Nicole

    Kidman. Paramount and Miramax, 2002.

Damon, Matt, perf. <u>The Bourne Identity</u>. Dir. Doug Limon. Universal, 2003.

<u>Jungle Fever</u>. Dir. Spike Lee. 1991. DVD. Universal, 2003.

70. TELEVISION OR RADIO PROGRAM

In general, begin with the title of the program, underlined or italicized. Then list the narrator, writer, director, actors, or other contributors, as necessary; the network; the local station and city, if any; and the broadcast date. If you cite a particular person's work, begin the entry with that person's name. If you cite a particular episode, include any title, in quotation marks, before the program's title. If the program is part of a series, include the series title (not underlined, italicized, or in quotation marks) before the network.

"Los Angeles: Silenced Partner." <u>City Confidential</u>. Narr. Paul Winfield. Arts and Entertainment Network. 25 Sept. 2003.

Newman, Paul, perf. <u>Our Town</u>. By Thornton Wilder. Masterpiece Theatre. PBS. WNET, New York. 5 Oct. 2003.

71. SOUND RECORDING

Begin with the name of the composer, performer, or conductor, depending on whose work you are citing. Next give the title of the recording, underlined or italicized. End with the manufacturer, a comma, and the year of issue. If you are not citing a compact disc, give the medium (such as *Audiocassette* or *LP*) before the manufacturer. If you are citing a particular song, include its title, in quotation marks, before the title of the recording.

Bach, Johann Sebastian. <u>Bach: Violin Concertos</u>. Perf. Itzhak Perlman and Pinchas Zukerman. English Chamber Orchestra. EMI, 2002.

Massive Attack. "Future Proof." <u>100th Window</u>. Virgin, 2003.

72. MUSICAL COMPOSITION

When you are *not* citing a specific published version, first give the composer's name, followed by the title. Underline or italicize the title of an opera, a ballet, or a piece of instrumental music that is identified by name (such as *Don Giovanni* or *Pastoral Symphony*). However, do not underline, italicize, or enclose in quotation marks the form, number, and key when used to identify an instrumental composition (e.g., Symphony no. 95 in C minor).

Mozart, Wolfgang Amadeus. <u>Don Giovanni</u>, K527.

Mozart, Wolfgang Amadeus. Symphony no. 41 in C major, K551.

To cite a published score, first list the composer's name, followed by the title, underlined or italicized. Be sure to capitalize the abbreviations *No.* and *Op.* If you wish to include the date when the musical composition was written, do so immediately following the title. End with the publication information.

> Schoenberg, Arnold. <u>Chamber Symphony No. 1 for 15 Solo Instruments, Op. 9.</u>
>
> 1906. New York: Dover, 2002.

73. LECTURE OR SPEECH

List the speaker, the title in quotation marks, the name of the sponsoring institution or group, the place, and the date. If the speech is untitled, use a label such as *Lecture* or *Keynote speech.*

> Eugenides, Jeffrey. Lecture. Portland Arts and Lectures. Arlene Schnitzer Concert
>
> Hall, Portland, OR. 30 Sept. 2003.

74. LIVE PERFORMANCE

List the title, other appropriate details (such as composer, writer, performer, or director), the place, and the date. If you cite a particular person's work, begin the entry with that person's name.

> <u>Anything Goes.</u> By Cole Porter. Perf. Klea Blackhurst. Shubert Theater, New
>
> Haven. 7 Oct. 2003.

75. WORK OF ART OR PHOTOGRAPH

List the artist; the work's title, underlined or italicized; the name of the museum or other location; and the city. If you want to include the date the work was created, add it after the title.

> Kahlo, Frida. <u>Self-Portrait with Cropped Hair.</u> 1940. Museum of Mod. Art, New
>
> York.

76. MAP OR CHART

Cite a map or chart as you would a book with an unknown author, adding the label *Map* or *Chart.*

> <u>California.</u> Map. Chicago: Rand, 2002.

77. ADVERTISEMENT

Name the item or organization being advertised, add the word *Advertisement,* and then supply the standard information about the source in which the ad appears.

> Microsoft. Advertisement. <u>Harper's</u> Oct. 2003: 2-3.

78. CARTOON OR COMIC STRIP

List the artist's name; the title (if any) of the cartoon or comic strip, in quotation marks; the label *Cartoon* or *Comic strip*; and the usual publication information.

Lewis, Eric. "The Unpublished Freud." Cartoon. New Yorker 11 Mar. 2002: 80.

55

A Student Research Essay, MLA Style

A brief research essay by David Craig appears on the following pages. David followed the MLA guidelines described in the preceding chapters. Note that this essay has been reproduced in a narrow format to allow for annotation.

Student Writer

David Craig

Craig 1

David Craig

Professor Turkman

English 219

8 December 2003

Instant Messaging: The Language of Youth Literacy

The English language is under attack. At least, that is what many people would have you believe. From concerned parents to local librarians, everybody seems to have a negative comment on the state of youth literacy today, and many pin the blame on new technology. They say that the current generation of grade school students will graduate with an extremely low level of literacy and, worse yet, that although language education hasn't changed much, kids are having more trouble reading and writing. Slang is more pervasive than ever, and teachers often must struggle with students who refuse to learn the conventionally correct way to use language.

In the Chronicle of Higher Education, for instance, Wendy Leibowitz quotes Sven Birkerts of Mount Holyoke College as saying "[Students] read more casually. They strip-mine what they read" on the Internet. Those casual reading habits, in turn, produce "quickly generated, casual prose." When asked about the causes of this situation, many point directly to new inventions, such as email and cell phones, and to the instant messaging (IM), which coincides with the new technology.

Instant messaging allows two individuals who are separated by any distance to engage in real-time, written communication. Although IM relies on the written word to transmit meaning, many messengers disregard standard writing conventions. For example, here is a snippet from an IM conversation between two teenage girls:[1]

---

[1] This transcript of an IM conversation was collected on 20 Nov. 2003. The teenagers' names are concealed to protect privacy.

Writer's name, instructor's name, course number, and date aligned at left margin and double-spaced

Title centered; announces topic and engages readers' interest

Opens with a short, attention-getting statement

First paragraph provides background on the problem of youth literacy

Quotation from educator used as evidence

Instant messaging introduced as focus of critics

Definition and example of IM provided

Superscript refers readers to explanatory note; see Chapter 53

Craig 2

Teen One: sorry im talkinto like 10 ppl at a time

Teen Two: u izzyful person

Teen Two: kwel

Teen One: hey i g2g

As this brief conversation shows, participants must use words to communicate via IM, but their words do not have to be in standard English.

Overview of the criticism of IM

Instant messaging, according to many, threatens youth literacy because it creates and compounds undesirable reading and writing habits and discourages students from learning standard literacy skills. Passionate or not, however, the critics' arguments don't hold up. In

Explicit thesis stated

fact, IM seems to be a beneficial force in the development of youth literacy because it promotes regular contact with words, the use of a written medium for communication, and the development of an alternative form of literacy. Perhaps most important, IM can actually

Transition to discussion of background information

help students learn conventional English. Before turning to the pros and cons of IM, however, I wish to look more closely at two background issues: the current state of literacy and the prevalence of IM.

Writer considers argument that youth literacy is in decline

Regardless of one's views on IM, the issue of youth literacy does demand attention because standardized test scores for language assessments, such as the verbal section of the College Board's SAT, have declined in recent years. This trend is illustrated in a chart distributed by the College Board as part of its 2002 analysis of

Figure explained in text and cited in parenthetical reference

aggregate SAT data (see Fig. 1).

The trend lines, which I added to the original chart, illustrate a significant pattern that may lead to the conclusion that youth literacy is on the decline. These lines display the seven-year paths (from 1995 to 2002) of math and verbal scores, respectively. Within this time period, the average SAT math score jumped more than ten

Discussion of Figure 1

points. The average verbal score, however, actually dropped a few points--and appears to be headed toward a further decline in the

Craig 3

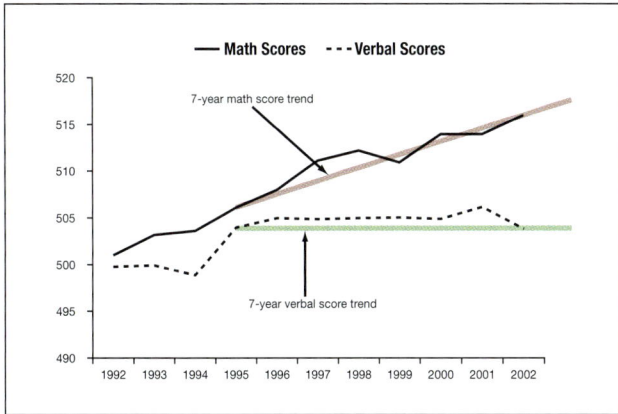

Fig. 1. Comparison of SAT math and verbal scores (1992-2002), from Kristin Carnahan and Chiara Coletti, Ten-Year Trend in SAT Scores Indicates Increased Emphasis on Math Is Yielding Results; Reading and Writing Are Causes for Concern (New York: College Board, 2002) 9. Trend lines added.

future. Corroborating this evidence is a report from the United States Department of Education's National Center for Education Statistics. According to this agency's study, the percentage of twelfth graders whose writing ability was "at or above the basic level" of performance dropped from 78 to 74 percent between 1998 and 2002 (Persky, Daane, and Jin 21).

Based on the preceding statistics, parents and educators appear to be right about the decline in youth literacy. And this trend is occurring while IM usage is on the rise. According to the Pew Internet and American Life Project, 54 percent of American youths aged twelve to seventeen have used IM (qtd. in Lenhart and Lewis 20). This figure translates to a pool of some thirteen million young instant messagers. Of this group, Pew reports, half send instant messages every time they go online, with 46 percent spending between thirty and sixty minutes messaging and another 21 percent

Figure labeled (as Fig. 1), titled, and credited to source. Figure uses MLA style and is inserted at appropriate point in text.

Government source cited for statistical evidence

Writer acknowledges part of critics' argument; transition to next point-- frequency of IM use

Statistical evidence cited

Craig 4

spending more than an hour. The most conservative estimate indicates that American youths spend, at a minimum, nearly three million hours per day on IM. What's more, they seem to be using a new vocabulary, and this is one of the things that bothers IM's critics. In order to have an effect on youth literacy, however, this new vocabulary must actually exist, so I set out to determine if it did.

Writer's field research introduced

In the interest of establishing the existence of an IM language, I analyzed 11,341 lines of text from IM conversations between youths in my target demographic: US residents aged twelve to seventeen. Young messagers voluntarily sent me chat logs, but they were unaware of the exact nature of my research. Once all of the logs had been gathered, I went through them, recording the number of times IM language was used in place of conventional words and phrases. Then I generated graphs to display how often these replacements were used.

Findings of field research presented

During the course of my study, I identified four types of IM language: phonetic replacements, acronyms, abbreviations, and inanities. An example of phonetic replacement is using ur for you are. Another popular type of IM language is the acronym; for a majority of the people in my study, the most common acronym was lol, a construction that means laughing out loud. Abbreviations are also common in IM, but I discovered that IM's typical abbreviations, such as etc., are not new to the English language. Finally, I found a class of words that I call "inanities." These words include completely new words or expressions, combinations of several slang categories, or simply nonsensical variations of other words. My favorite from this category is lolz, an inanity that translates directly to lol yet includes a terminating z for no obvious reason.

Figure introduced and explained

In the chat transcripts that I analyzed, the best display of typical IM lingo came from the conversations between two thirteen-year-old Texan girls, who are avid IM users. Figure 2 is a graph showing how often they used certain phonetic replacements and

Craig 5

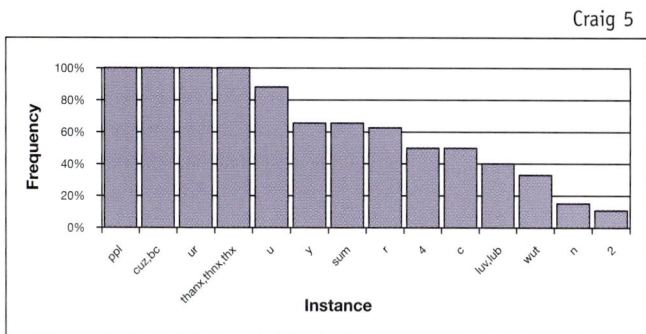

Fig. 2. Usage of phonetic replacements and abbreviations in IM.

> Figure labeled (as Fig. 2) and titled

abbreviations. On the y-axis, frequency of replacement is plotted, a calculation that compares the number of times a word or phrase is used in IM language with the total number of times that it is communicated in any form. On the x-axis, specific IM words and phrases are listed.

My research shows that the Texan girls use the first ten phonetic replacements or abbreviations at least 50 percent of the time in their normal IM writing. For example, every time one of them writes see, there is a parallel time when c is used in its place. In light of this finding, it appears that the popular IM culture contains at least some elements of its own language. It also seems that much of this language is new: no formal dictionary yet identifies the most common IM words and phrases. Only in the heyday of the telegraph or on the rolls of a stenographer would you find a similar situation, but these "languages" were never a popular medium of youth communication. Instant messaging, however, is very popular among young people and continues to generate attention and debate in academic circles.

> Discussion of findings presented in Fig. 2

My research shows that messaging is certainly widespread, and it does seem to have its own particular vocabulary, yet these two factors alone do not mean it has a damaging influence on youth

Craig 6

literacy. As noted earlier, however, some people claim that the new technology is a threat to the English language, as revealed in the following passage:

> "Abbreviations commonly used in online instant messages are creeping into formal essays that students write for credit," said Debbie Frost, who teaches language arts and social studies to sixth-graders. . . . "You would be shocked at the writing I see. It's pretty scary. I don't get cohesive thoughts, I don't get sentences, they don't capitalize, and they have a lot of misspellings and bad grammar," she said. "With all those glaring mistakes, it's hard to see the content." ("Young Messagers," par. 2)

Echoing Frost's concerns is Melanie Weaver, a professor at Alvernia College, who taught a tenth-grade English class as part of an internship. In an interview with the New York Times, she said, "[When] they would be trying to make a point in a paper, they would put a smiley face in the end [:)]. If they were presenting an argument and they needed to present an opposite view, they would put a frown [:(]" (Lee, par. 11).

The critics of instant messaging are numerous. But if we look to the field of linguistics, a central concept--metalinguistics--challenges these criticisms and leads to a more reasonable conclusion--that IM has no negative impact on a student's development of or proficiency with traditional literacy.

Scholars of metalinguistics offer support for the claim that IM is not damaging to those who use it. As noted earlier, one of the most prominent components of IM language is phonetic replacement, in which a word such as everyone becomes every1. This type of wordplay has a special importance in the development of an advanced literacy, and for good reason. According to David Crystal, an internationally recognized scholar of linguistics at the University of Wales, as young children develop and learn how words string

---

Marginal notes:

Writer returns to charges made by critics of IM

Quotation introduced with a signal verb

Block quotation presents a quotation within a quotation

Parenthetical reference uses brief title because author unknown

Transition to concept in support of thesis and in refutation of critics' claims

Linguistic authority cited in support of thesis

Craig 7

together to express ideas, they go through many phases of language play. The singsong rhymes and nonsensical chants of preschoolers are vital to their learning language, and a healthy appetite for such wordplay leads to a better command of language later in life (182).

As justification for his view of the connection between language play and advanced literacy, Crystal presents an argument for metalinguistic awareness. According to Crystal, metalinguistics refers to the ability to "step back" and use words to analyze how language works. "If we are good at stepping back," he says, "at thinking in a more abstract way about what we hear and what we say, then we are more likely to be good at acquiring those skills which depend on just such a stepping back in order to be successful--and this means, chiefly, reading and writing. . . . [T]he greater our ability to play with language, . . . the more advanced will be our command of language as a whole" (181).

Evidence presented to support the connection between wordplay and advanced literacy

Ellipses indicate omissions in quotation

If we accept the findings of linguists such as Crystal that metalinguistic awareness leads to increased literacy, then it seems reasonable to argue that the phonetic language of IM can also lead to increased metalinguistic awareness and, therefore, increases in overall literacy. As instant messengers develop proficiency with a variety of phonetic replacements and other types of IM words, they should increase their subconscious knowledge of metalinguistics.

Writer links Crystal's views to thesis about IM

Metalinguistics also involves our ability to write in a variety of distinct styles and tones. Yet in the debate over instant messaging and literacy, many critics assume that either IM or academic literacy will eventually win out in a person and that the two modes cannot exist side by side. This assumption is, however, false. Human beings ordinarily develop a large range of language abilities, from the formal to the relaxed and from the mainstream to the subcultural. Mark Twain, for example, had an understanding of local speech that he employed when writing dialogue for Huckleberry Finn. Yet few people

Another refutation of critics' assumptions

Example from well-known work of literature used as support

Craig 8

would argue that Twain's knowledge of this form of English had a negative impact on his ability to write in standard English.

However, just as Mark Twain used dialects carefully in dialogue, writers must pay careful attention to the kind of language they use in any setting. The owner of the language Web site The Discouraging Word (http://www.thediscouragingword.com), who is an anonymous English literature graduate student at the University of Chicago, backs up this idea in an e-mail to me:

> What is necessary, we feel, is that students learn how to shift between different styles of writing--that, in other words, the abbreviations and shortcuts of IM should be used online . . . but that they should not be used in an essay submitted to a teacher. . . . IM might even be considered . . . a different way of reading and writing, one that requires specific and unique skills shared by certain communities.

The analytical ability that is necessary for writers to choose an appropriate tone and style in their writing is, of course, metalinguistic in nature because it involves the comparison of two or more language systems. Thus, youths who grasp multiple languages will have a greater natural understanding of metalinguistics. More specifically, young people who possess both IM and traditional skills stand to be better off than their peers who have been trained only in traditional or conventional systems. Far from being hurt by their online pastime, instant messengers can be aided in standard writing by their experience with IM language.

The fact remains, however, that youth literacy seems to be declining. What, if not IM, is the main cause of this phenomenon? According to the College Board, which collects data on several questions from its test takers, enrollment in English composition and grammar classes has decreased in the last decade by 14 percent (Carnahan and Coletti 11). The possibility of instant messaging

---

Margin annotations:

Email correspondence cited in support of claim

Writer shows that making appropriate stylistic choices is a metalinguistic act available to users of IM

Transition to writer's final point

Evidence reveals decline in teaching of English

Craig 9

causing a decline in literacy seems inadequate when statistics on English education for US youths provide other evidence of the possible causes. Simply put, schools in the United States are not teaching English as much as they used to. Rather than blaming IM alone for the decline in literacy and test scores, we must also look toward our schools' lack of focus on the teaching of standard English skills.

I found that the use of instant messaging poses virtually no threat to the development or maintenance of formal language skills among American youths aged twelve to seventeen. Diverse language skills tend to increase a person's metalinguistic awareness and, thereby, his or her ability to use language effectively to achieve a desired purpose in a particular situation. The current decline in youth literacy is not due to the rise of instant messaging. Rather, fewer young students seem to be receiving an adequate education in the use of conventional English. Unfortunately, it may always be fashionable to blame new tools for old problems, but in the case of instant messaging, that blame is not warranted. Although IM may expose literacy problems, it does not create them.

Transition to conclusion

Concluding paragraph sums up argument and reiterates thesis

Works Cited

Carnahan, Kristin, and Chiara Coletti. <u>Ten-Year Trend in SAT Scores</u>
<u>Indicates Increased Emphasis on Math Is Yielding Results;</u>
<u>Reading and Writing Are Causes for Concern.</u> New York: College
Board, 2002.

Crystal, David. <u>Language Play</u>. Chicago: U of Chicago P, 1998.

The Discouraging Word. "Re: Instant Messaging and Literacy." E-mail
to the author. 13 Nov. 2003.

Lee, Jennifer. "I Think, Therefore IM." <u>New York Times on the Web</u> 19
Sept. 2002. 14 Nov. 2003 <http://www.nytimes.com/2002/09/19/
technology/circuits>.

Leibowitz, Wendy R. "Technology Transforms Writing and the Teaching
of Writing." <u>Chronicle of Higher Education</u> 26 Nov. 1999: A67.

Lenhart, Amanda, and Oliver Lewis. <u>Teenage Life Online: The Rise of</u>
<u>the Instant-Message Generation and the Internet's Impact on</u>
<u>Friendships and Family Relationships</u>. Washington: Pew Internet
and Amer. Life Project, 2001.

Persky, Hilary R., Mary C. Daane, and Ying Jin. <u>The Nation's Report</u>
<u>Card: Writing 2002</u>. NCES 2003-529. Washington: GPO, 2003.

"Young Messengers Ask: Why Spell It Out?" <u>Associated Press State and</u>
<u>Local Wire</u> 11 Nov. 2002. 14 Nov. 2003 <http://www.lexis-nexis.com>.

Margin labels: Heading centered; First line of each entry flush with left margin; subsequent lines indented one-half inch or five spaces; Report; Book; Email; Online newspaper article; Article in a newspaper; Report; Works Cited entries double-spaced; Government document; Article from an online database

APA, CSE, and *Chicago* Documentation

Many disciplines have their own carefully crafted documentation styles, and these styles differ according to **what information is valued most highly. Thus in the sciences and social sciences, where timeliness of publication is crucial to keeping up with the most current research, the date of publication comes up front, right after the author's name.**

—ANDREA A. LUNSFORD

APA, CSE, and *Chicago* Documentation

Chapter 56 discusses the basic formats prescribed by the American Psychological Association (APA), guidelines that are widely used in the social sciences. For further reference, consult the *Publication Manual of the American Psychological Association,* Fifth Edition. Chapter 57 deals with formats prescribed by the Council of Science Editors (formerly the Council of Biology Editors), and Chapter 58 with formats from *The Chicago Manual of Style,* Fifteenth Edition.

bedfordstmartins.com/everyday_writer To access the advice in this chapter online, click on **Documenting Sources.**

56

APA Style

DIRECTORY TO APA STYLE

APA style for in-text citations (56a)

APA style for a list of references (56c)

56a APA style for in-text citations

APA style requires parenthetical references in the text to document quotations, paraphrases, summaries, and other material from a source. These citations correspond to full bibliographic entries in a list of references at the end of the text.

1. AUTHOR NAMED IN A SIGNAL PHRASE

Generally, use the author's name in a signal phrase to introduce the cited material, and place the date, in parentheses, immediately after the author's name. For a quotation, the page number, preceded by *p.*, appears in parentheses after the quotation.

> As Fanderclai (2001) observed, older siblings play an important role in the development of language and learning skills.

> Chavez (2003) noted that "six years after slim cigarettes for women were introduced, more than twice as many teenage girls were smoking" (p. 13).

For a long, set-off quotation (one having more than forty words), place the page reference in parentheses one space after the final punctuation. For electronic texts or other works without page numbers, paragraph numbers may be used, preceded by the ¶ symbol or the abbreviation *para*.

> Weinberg (2000) has claimed that "the techniques used in group therapy can be verbal, expressive, or psychodramatic." (¶ 5)

2. AUTHOR NAMED IN A PARENTHETICAL REFERENCE

When you do not mention the author in a signal phrase in your text, give the author's name and the date, separated by a comma, in parentheses at the end of the cited material.

> One study found that 17% of adopted children in the United States are of a different race than their adoptive parents (Peterson, 2003).

3. TWO AUTHORS

Use both names in all citations. Use *and* in a signal phrase, but use an ampersand (&) in parentheses.

> Babcock and Laschever (2003) have suggested that many women do not negotiate their salaries and pay raises as vigorously as their male counterparts do.

A recent study has suggested that many women do not negotiate their salaries and pay raises as vigorously as their male counterparts do (Babcock & Laschever, 2003).

4. THREE TO FIVE AUTHORS

List all the authors' names for the first reference.

Safer, Voccola, Hurd, and Goodwin (2003) reached somewhat different conclusions by designing a study that was less dependent on subjective judgment than were previous studies.

In subsequent references, use just the first author's name plus *et al.*

Based on the results, Safer et al. (2003) determined that the apes took significant steps toward self-expression.

5. SIX OR MORE AUTHORS

Use only the first author's name and *et al.* in *every* citation.

As Soleim et al. (2002) demonstrated, advertising holds the potential for distorting and manipulating "free-willed" consumers.

6. ORGANIZATION AS AUTHOR

If the name of an organization or a corporation is long, spell it out the first time, followed by an abbreviation in brackets. In later references, use the abbreviation only.

FIRST CITATION (Centers for Disease Control and Prevention [CDC], 2003)

LATER CITATIONS (CDC, 2003)

7. UNKNOWN AUTHOR

Use the title or its first few words in a signal phrase or in parentheses. A book's title is italicized, as in the following example; an article's title is placed in quotation marks.

The employment profiles for this time period substantiated this trend (*Federal Employment*, 2001).

8. TWO OR MORE AUTHORS WITH THE SAME LAST NAME

If your list of references includes works by different authors with the same last name, include the authors' initials in each citation.

S. Bartolomeo (2000) conducted the groundbreaking study on teenage childbearing.

9. TWO OR MORE SOURCES IN ONE PARENTHETICAL REFERENCE

List sources by different authors in alphabetical order by authors' last names, separated by semicolons: (Cardone, 1998; Lai, 2002). List works by the same author in chronological order, separated by commas: (Lai, 2000, 2002).

10. SPECIFIC PARTS OF A SOURCE

Use abbreviations (*chap., p.,* and so on) in a parenthetical reference to name the part of a work you are citing.

> Mogolov (2003, chap. 9) argued that his research yielded the opposite results.

11. EMAIL AND OTHER PERSONAL COMMUNICATION

Cite any personal letters, email, electronic postings, telephone conversations, or interviews with the person's initial(s) and last name, the identification *personal communication,* and the date. Note, however, that APA recommends not including personal communications in the reference list.

> R. Tobin (personal communication, November 4, 2003) supported his claims about music therapy with new evidence.

12. WEB SITE OR WEB TEXT

To cite an entire Web site, include its address in parentheses in your text (http://www.gallup.com); you do not need to include it in your list of references. To cite part of a text found on the Web, indicate the chapter or figure, as appropriate. To cite a quotation, include the page or paragraph numbers.

> Zomkowski argued the importance of "ensuring equitable access to the Internet" (2003, p. 3).

56b APA style for content notes

APA style allows you to use content notes to expand or supplement your text. Indicate such notes in your text by superscript numerals. Type the notes themselves on a separate page after the last page of the text, under the heading *Footnotes,* centered at the top of the page. Double-space all entries. Indent the first line of each note five spaces, but begin subsequent lines at the left margin.

SUPERSCRIPT NUMERAL IN TEXT

The age of the children involved was an important factor in the selection of items for the questionnaire.[1]

FOOTNOTE

[1]Marjorie Youngston Forman and William Cole of the Child Study Team provided great assistance in identifying appropriate items for the questionnaire.

56c APA style for a list of references

The alphabetical list of the sources cited in your document is called *References.* If your instructor asks that you list everything you have read — not just the sources you cite — call the list *Bibliography.* Here are some guidelines for preparing a *References* list:

- Start your list on a separate page after the text of your document but before any appendices or notes.
- Type the heading *References,* neither italicized nor in quotation marks, centered one inch from the top of the page.
- Begin your first entry. Unless your instructor suggests otherwise, do not indent the first line of each entry, but indent subsequent lines one-half inch or five spaces. Double-space the entire list.
- List sources alphabetically by authors' last names. If the author of a source is unknown, alphabetize the source by the first major word of the title.

APA style specifies the treatment and placement of four basic elements — author, publication date, title, and other publication information.

- *Author.* List all authors' last names first, and use only initials for first and middle names. Separate the names of multiple authors with commas, and use an ampersand (&) before the last author's name.
- *Publication date.* Enclose the date in parentheses. Use only the year for books and journals; use the year, a comma, and the month or month and day for magazines; use the year, a comma, and the month and day for newspapers. Do not abbreviate.
- *Title.* Italicize titles and subtitles of books and periodicals. Do not enclose titles of articles in quotation marks. For books and articles, capitalize only the first word of the title and subtitle and any proper nouns or proper adjectives. Capitalize all major words in a periodical title.
- *Publication information.* For a book, list the city of publication (and the country or postal abbreviation for the state if the city is unfamiliar), a colon, and the publisher's name, dropping *Inc., Co.,* or *Publishers.* For a periodical, follow the periodical title with a comma, the volume number (italicized), the issue number (if appropriate) in parentheses and followed by a comma, and the inclusive page numbers of the article. For newspapers and for articles

or chapters in books, include the abbreviation *p.* ("page") or *pp.* ("pages") before the page numbers.

The following sample entries use hanging indent format, in which the first line aligns on the left and the subsequent lines indent one-half inch or five spaces. This is the customary APA format for final copy, including student papers. Note, however, that for manuscripts submitted to journals, APA requires the reverse (first lines indented, subsequent lines flush left), assuming that the citations will be converted by a typesetting system to a hanging indent format.

Books

Here is an annotated example of a basic entry for a book:

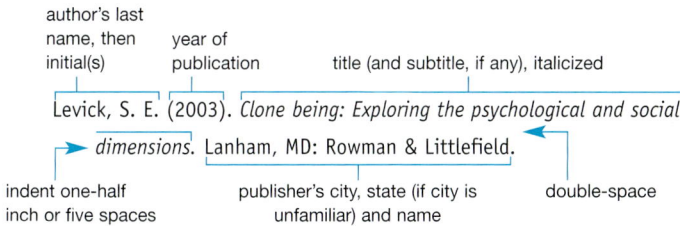

author's last name, then initial(s)
year of publication
title (and subtitle, if any), italicized

Levick, S. E. (2003). *Clone being: Exploring the psychological and social dimensions.* Lanham, MD: Rowman & Littlefield.

indent one-half inch or five spaces
publisher's city, state (if city is unfamiliar) and name
double-space

1. ONE AUTHOR

Lightman, A. P. (2002). *The diagnosis.* New York: Vintage Books.

2. TWO OR MORE AUTHORS

Walsh, M. E., & Murphy, J. A. (2003). *Children, health, and learning: A guide to the issues.* Westport, CT: Praeger.

3. ORGANIZATION AS AUTHOR

Committee on Abrupt Climate Change, National Research Council. (2002). *Abrupt climate change: Inevitable surprises.* Washington, DC: National Academies Press.

Use the word *Author* as the publisher when the organization is both the author and the publisher.

Resources for Rehabilitation. (2003). *A woman's guide to coping with disability.* London: Author.

4. UNKNOWN AUTHOR

National Geographic atlas of the Middle East. (2003). Washington, DC: National Geographic Society.

5. EDITOR

Dickens, J. (Ed.). (1995). *Family outing: A guide for parents of gays, lesbians and bisexuals.* London: Peter Owen.

6. SELECTION IN A BOOK WITH AN EDITOR

Burke, W. W., & Nourmair, D. A. (2001). The role of personality assessment in organization development. In J. Waclawski & A. H. Church (Eds.), *Organization development: A data-driven approach to organizational change* (pp. 55-77). San Francisco: Jossey-Bass.

7. TRANSLATION

Al-Farabi, A. N. (1998). *On the perfect state* (R. Walzer, Trans.). Chicago: Kazi.

8. EDITION OTHER THAN THE FIRST

Moore, G. S. (2002). *Living with the earth: Concepts in environmental health science* (2nd ed.). New York: Lewis.

9. ONE VOLUME OF A MULTIVOLUME WORK

Barnes, J. (Ed.). (1995). *Complete works of Aristotle* (Vol. 2). Princeton, NJ: Princeton University Press.

10. ARTICLE IN A REFERENCE WORK

Dean, C. (1994). Jaws and teeth. In *The Cambridge encyclopedia of human evolution* (pp. 56-59). Cambridge, England: Cambridge University Press.

If no author is listed, begin with the title.

11. REPUBLICATION

Piaget, J. (1952). *The language and thought of the child.* London: Routledge & Kegan Paul. (Original work published 1932)

12. TWO OR MORE WORKS BY THE SAME AUTHOR(S)

List two or more works by the same author in chronological order. Repeat the author's name in each entry. See also p. 424.

Goodall, J. (1999). *Reason for hope: A spiritual journey.* New York: Warner Books.

Goodall, J. (2002). *Performance and evolution in the age of Darwin: Out of the natural order.* New York: Routledge.

Periodicals

Here is an annotated example of a basic entry for an article in a journal:

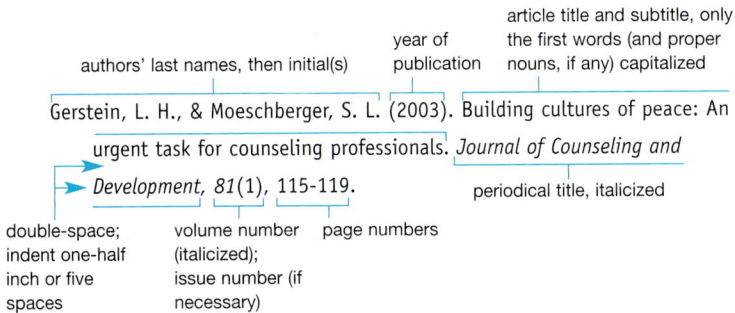

authors' last names, then initial(s)   year of publication   article title and subtitle, only the first words (and proper nouns, if any) capitalized

Gerstein, L. H., & Moeschberger, S. L. (2003). Building cultures of peace: An urgent task for counseling professionals. *Journal of Counseling and Development, 81*(1), 115-119.

periodical title, italicized

double-space; indent one-half inch or five spaces   volume number (italicized); issue number (if necessary)   page numbers

13. ARTICLE IN A JOURNAL PAGINATED BY VOLUME

O'Connell, D. C., & Kowal, S. (2003). Psycholinguistics: A half century of monologism. *The American Journal of Psychology, 116,* 191-212.

14. ARTICLE IN A JOURNAL PAGINATED BY ISSUE

Hall, R. E. (2000). Marriage as vehicle of racism among women of color. *Psychology: A Journal of Human Behavior, 37*(2), 29-40.

15. ARTICLE IN A MAGAZINE

Ricciardi, S. (2003, August 5). Enabling the mobile work force. *PC Magazine, 22,* 46.

16. ARTICLE IN A NEWSPAPER

Faler, B. (2003, August 29). Primary colors: Race and fundraising. *The Washington Post,* p. A5.

17. EDITORIAL OR LETTER TO THE EDITOR

Zelneck, B. (2003, July 18). Serving the public at public universities [Letter to the editor]. *The Chronicle Review,* p. B18.

18. UNSIGNED ARTICLE

Annual meeting announcement. (2003, March). *Cognitive Psychology, 46,* 227.

19. REVIEW

Ringel, S. (2003). [Review of the book *Multiculturalism and the therapeutic process*]. *Clinical Social Work Journal, 31,* 212-213.

20. PUBLISHED INTERVIEW

Smith, H. (2002, October). [Interview with A. Thompson]. *The Sun,* pp. 4-7.

21. TWO OR MORE WORKS BY THE SAME AUTHOR IN THE SAME YEAR

List the works alphabetically by title, and place lowercase letters (*a, b,* etc.) after the dates.

Shermer, M. (2002a). On estimating the lifetime of civilizations. *Scientific American, 287*(2), 33.

Shermer, M. (2002b). Readers who question evolution. *Scientific American, 287*(1), 37.

Electronic sources

The *Publication Manual of the American Psychological Association*, Fifth Edition, includes guidelines for citing various kinds of electronic resources, including Web sites; articles, reports, and abstracts; some types of online communications; and computer software. Updated guidelines are maintained at the APA Web site, <www.apa.org>.

The basic entry for most sources you access via the Internet should include the following elements:

- *Author.* Give the author's name, if available.
- *Publication date.* Include the date of Internet publication or of the most recent update, if available. Use *n.d.* (no date) when the publication date is unavailable.
- *Title.* List the title of the document or subject line of the message, neither italicized nor in quotation marks.
- *Publication information.* For articles from online journals, newspapers, or reference databases, give the publication title and other publishing information as you would for a print periodical.
- *Retrieval information.* For most Internet sources, type the word *Retrieved* followed by the date of access, a comma, and the word *from.* End with the URL or other retrieval information and no period. For listserv or newsgroup messages and other online postings, type *Message posted to,* followed by the name of the list or group, and the URL of the group or its archive.

22. CHAPTER OR SECTION OF A WEB SITE

To cite a whole Web site or a document from a Web site, include information as you would for a print document, followed by information about its retrieval. If no author is identified, give the title of the document followed by the date (if available), other publication information, and a retrieval statement.

> Talking about your choices. (2001). *Partnership for caring.* Retrieved January 15,
>
> 2004, from http://www.partnershipforcaring.org/HomePage/

> DotComSense: Commonsense ways to protect your privacy and assess online
>
> mental health information. (2000, January). *APA Monitor, 31,* 32. Retrieved
>
> January 25, 2001, from http://helping.apa.org/dotcomsense/

23. ARTICLE IN AN ONLINE PERIODICAL

If the article also appears in a print journal, no retrieval statement is required; instead, include the label *[Electronic version]* after the article title. However, if the online article is a revision of the print document (if the format differs or page numbers are not indicated), include the date of access and the URL.

> Steedman, M., & Jones, G. P. (2000). Information structure and the syntax-
>
> phonology interface [Electronic version]. *Linguistic Inquiry, 31,* 649-689.

> Palmer, K. S. (2000, September 12). In academia, males under a microscope.
>
> *The Washington Post.* Retrieved January 23, 2001, from http://www
>
> .washingtonpost.com

To cite an online article that did not appear in print, give the date of access and URL.

> Lou, L., & Chen, J. (2003, January). Attention and blind-spot phenomenology.
>
> *Psyche, 9*(2). Retrieved March 22, 2003, from http://psyche.cs.monash.edu
>
> .au/v9/psyche-9-02-lou.html

24. ARTICLE OR ABSTRACT FROM A DATABASE

Give the information as you would for a print document. List the date you retrieved the article and the name of the database. If you are citing an abstract, end by typing *Abstract retrieved* and the date of access and name of the database. End with the document number in parentheses, if appropriate.

Crook, S. (2003). Change, uncertainty and the future of sociology. *Journal of Sociology, 39*(1), 7-14. Retrieved January 10, 2004, from Expanded Academic ASAP database (A101260213).

Hayhoe, G. (2001). The long and winding road: Technology's future. *Technical Communication, 48*(2), 133-145. Retrieved September 22, 2001, from ProQuest database.

McCall, R. B. (1998). Science and the press: Like oil and water? *American Psychologist, 43*(2), 87-94. Abstract retrieved August 23, 2002, from PsycINFO database (1988-18263-001).

25. EMAIL MESSAGE OR REAL-TIME COMMUNICATION

Because the APA stresses that any sources cited in your list of references be retrievable by your readers, you should not include entries for email messages or real-time communications (such as IMs); instead, cite these sources in your text as forms of personal communication (see p. 419).

26. ONLINE POSTING

List an online posting in the references list only if you are able to retrieve the message from a mailing list's archive. Provide the author's name (if the author's real name is unavailable, include the screen name); the date of posting, in parentheses; and the subject line from the posting. Include any information that further identifies the message in square brackets. For a listserv message, end with the retrieval statement, including both the name of the list and the URL of the archived message.

Troike, R. C. (2001, June 21). Buttercups and primroses [Msg 8]. Message posted to the American Dialect Society's electronic mailing list, archived at http://listserv.linguistlist.org/archives/ads-l.html

For a newsgroup posting, end with the name of the newsgroup.

Wittenberg, E. (2001, July 11). Gender and the Internet [Msg 4]. Message posted to news://comp.edu.composition

27. SOFTWARE OR COMPUTER PROGRAM

PsychMate [Computer software]. (2003). Pittsburgh, PA: Psychology Software Tools.

Other sources

28. GOVERNMENT DOCUMENT

> Office of the Federal Register. (2003). *The United States government manual 2003/2004*. Washington, DC: U.S. Government Printing Office.

Cite an online government document as you would a printed government work, adding the date of access and the URL. If there is no date, use *n.d.*

> U.S. Public Health Service. (1999). *The surgeon general's call to action to prevent suicide*. Retrieved November 5, 2003, from http://www.mentalhealth.org/suicideprevention/calltoaction.asp

29. DISSERTATION ABSTRACT

If you use *Dissertation Abstracts International* (*DAI*), include the *DAI* volume, issue, and page number. If you use the UMI digital dissertation service, include the UMI number in parentheses.

> Bandelj, N. (2003). Embedded economies: Foreign direct investment in Central and Eastern Europe (Doctoral dissertation, Princeton University, 2003). *Dissertation Abstracts International, 64* (03), 1083. (UMI No. 3085036)

30. TECHNICAL OR RESEARCH REPORT

Give the report number, if available, in parentheses after the title.

> McCool, R., Fikes, R., & McGuinness, D. (2003). *Semantic web tools for enhanced authoring* (Report No. KSL-03-07). Stanford, CA: Knowledge Systems Laboratory.

31. CONFERENCE PROCEEDINGS

> Mama, A. (2001). Challenging subjects: Gender and power in African contexts. In *Proceedings of Nordic African Institute Conference: Rethinking power in Africa*. Uppsala, Sweden, 9-18.

32. PAPER PRESENTED AT A MEETING OR SYMPOSIUM, UNPUBLISHED

Cite the month of the meeting if it is available.

> Jones, J. G. (1999, February). *Mental health intervention in mass casualty disasters*. Paper presented at the Rocky Mountain Region Disaster Mental Health Conference, Laramie, WY.

33. POSTER SESSION

Barnes Young, L. L. (2003, August). *Cognition, aging, and dementia.* Poster session presented at the 2003 Division 40 APA Convention, Toronto, Ontario, Canada.

34. FILM, VIDEO, OR DVD

Moore, M. (Director). (2003). *Bowling for Columbine* [Motion picture]. United States: MGM.

35. TELEVISION PROGRAM, SINGLE EPISODE

Imperioli, M. (Writer), & Buscemi, S. (Director). (2002). Everybody hurts [Television series episode]. In D. Chase (Executive Producer), *The Sopranos.* New York: Home Box Office.

36. RECORDING

The Avalanches. (2001). Frontier psychiatrist. On *Since I left you* [CD]. Los Angeles: Elektra/Asylum Records.

56d　An abridged student research essay, APA style

An abridged version of an essay by Merlla McLaughlin appears on the following pages. It conforms to the APA guidelines described in this chapter. Note that this essay has been reproduced in a narrow format to allow for annotation.

Student Writer

Merlla McLaughlin

bedfordstmartins.com/everyday_writer　To read this essay in its entirety, click on **Student Writing.**

Leadership Roles   1 —— Shortened
title and
page number,
separated by
five spaces,
appear on
every page

Leadership Roles in a Small-Group Project ———— Title
centered
and double-
spaced

Merlla McLaughlin

Professor Bushnell

Communications 102

February 22, 2004

Heading
centered

No
indentation

Double
spacing
used

Study
described

Key points
of report
discussed

Abstract

Using the interpersonal communications research of J. K. Brilhart and G. J. Galanes as well as that of W. Wilmot and J. Hocker, along with T. Hartman's Personality Assessment, I observed and analyzed the leadership roles and group dynamics of my project collaborators in a communications course. Based on results of the Hartman Personality Assessment, I predicted that a single leader would emerge. However, complementary individual strengths and gender differences encouraged a distributed leadership style, in which the group experienced little confrontation. Conflict, because it was handled positively, was crucial to the group's progress.

Leadership Roles   3

Leadership Roles in a Small-Group Project

Although classroom lectures provide students with volumes of information, many experiences can be understood only by living them. So it is with the workings of a small, task-focused group. What observations can I make after working with a group of peers on a class project? And what have I learned as a result?

Leadership Expectations and Emergence

The six members of this group were selected by the instructor; half were male and half were female. By performing the Hartman Personality Assessment (Hartman, 1998) in class, we learned that Hartman has associated key personality traits with the colors red, blue, white, and yellow (see Table 1). The assessment identified most of us as "Blues," concerned with intimacy and caring. Because of the bold qualities associated with "Reds," I expected that Nate, our only "Red" member, might become our leader. (Kaari, the only "White," seemed poised to become the peacekeeper.) However, after Nate missed the first two meetings, it seemed that Pat, who contributed often during our first three meetings, might emerge as leader. Pat has strong communications skills, a commanding presence, and

Table 1

Hartman's Key Personality Traits

Trait category	Color			
	Red	Blue	White	Yellow
Motive	Power	Intimacy	Peace	Fun
Strengths	Loyal to tasks	Loyal to people	Tolerant	Positive
Limitations	Arrogant	Self-righteous	Timid	Uncommit-ted

Note. Table is adapted from information found at The Hartman Personality Profile, by N. Hayden. Retrieved February 24, 2004, from http://students.cs.byu.edu/~nhayden/Code/index.php

Annotations (right margin):

- Full title, centered
- Paragraphs indented
- Questions indicate the focus of the essay
- Headings help organize the report
- APA-style parenthetical reference
- Background information about team members' personality types
- Chart displays information concisely and is referred to in preceding text
- Source of table listed

displays sensitivity to others. I was surprised, then, when our group developed a *distributed style* of leadership (Brilhart & Galanes, 1998). The longer we worked together, however, the more I was convinced that this approach to leadership was best for our group.

As Brilhart and Galanes have noted, "distributed leadership explicitly acknowledges that the leadership of a group is spread among members, with each member expected to move the group toward its goal" (p. 175). These researchers divide positive communicative actions into two types: *task functions* that affect a group's productivity and *maintenance functions* that influence the interactions of group members. One of our group's most immediate task-function needs was decision-making, and as we made our first major decision--what topic to pursue--our group's distributed-leadership style began to emerge.

Decision-Making Methods

Our choice of topic--the parking services at Oregon State University (OSU)--was the result not of a majority vote but of negotiated consensus. During this decision-making meeting, several of us argued that a presentation on parking services at OSU would interest most students, and after considerable discussion, the other group members agreed. Once we had a topic, other decisions came naturally.

Roles Played

Thanks in part to the distributed leadership that our group developed, the strengths of individual group members became increasingly apparent. Although early in our project Pat was the key initiator and Nate was largely an information seeker, all group members eventually took on these functions in addition to serving as recorders, gathering information, and working on our questionnaire. Every member coordinated the group's work at some point; several made sure that everyone could speak and be heard, and one member was especially good at catching important details the rest of us were

First observations about leadership roles

Source cited to define key term for this study

Minimum of one-inch margin on all sides

Headings continue to guide reader

Discussion of the group's decision-making supports claim of distributed-leadership style

Another example of distributed-leadership style

Leadership Roles   5

apt to miss. Joe, McKenzie, Kaari, and I frequently clarified or elaborated on information, whereas Pat, Kaari, and Nate were good at contributing ideas during brainstorming sessions. Nate, Joe, and McKenzie brought tension-relieving humor to the group.

Just as each member brought individual strengths to the group, gender differences also made us effective. For example, the women took a holistic approach to the project, looking at the big picture and making intuitive leaps in ways that the men generally did not. The men preferred a more systematic process. Brilhart and Galanes have suggested that men working in groups dominated by women may display "subtle forms of resistance to a dominant presence of women" (p. 98). Although the men in our group did not attend all the meetings and the women did, I did not find that the men's nonattendance implied male resistance any more than the women's attendance implied female dominance. Rather, our differing qualities complemented each other and enabled us to work together effectively.

Social Environment

As previously noted, most of our group members were Blues on the Hartman scale, valuing altruism, intimacy, appreciation, and having a moral conscience (Hayden, "Blues"). At least three of the four Blues had White as their secondary color, signifying the importance of peace, kindness, independence, and sacrifice (Hayden, "Whites"). The presence of these traits may explain why our group experienced little confrontation and conflict. Nate (a Red) was most likely to speak bluntly. The one time that Nate seemed put off, it was not his words but his body language that expressed his discomfort. This was an awkward moment, but a rare one given our group's generally positive handling of conflict.

Conclusion

Perhaps most important is the lesson I learned about conflict. Prior to participating in this group, I always avoided conflict

Margin notes:

Transition to gender influences

Essay double-spaced throughout

Writer returns to categories defined earlier

because, as Wilmot and Hocker (1998) have suggested, most people think "harmony is normal and conflict is abnormal" (p. 9). Now I recognize that some kinds of conflict are essential for increasing understanding between group members and creating an effective collaborative result. It was essential, for instance, that our group explore different members' ideas about possible topics for our project, and this process inevitably required some conflict. The end result, however, was a positive one.

In her concluding section, writer clearly answers question posed in the introduction

Constructive conflict requires an open and engaging attitude among group members, encourages personal growth, and ends when the issue at hand is resolved. Most important for our group, such conflict encouraged cooperation (pp. 47-48) and increased the group's cohesiveness. All the members of our group felt, for instance, that their ideas about possible topics were seriously considered. Once we decided on a topic, everyone fully committed to it. Thus our group effectiveness was enhanced by constructive conflict.

As a result of this project, I have a better sense of when conflict is--and isn't--productive. My group used conflict productively when we hashed out our ideas, and we avoided the kind of conflict that creates morale problems and wastes time. Although all groups operate somewhat differently, I now feel more prepared to understand and participate in future small-group projects.

Conclusion looks toward future

Leadership Roles   7

References

Brilhart, J. K., & Galanes, G. J. (1998). *Effective group discussion* (9th ed.). Boston: McGraw-Hill.

Hartman, T. (1998). *The color code: A new way to see yourself, your relationships, and your life*. New York: Scribner.

Hayden, N. (n.d.). *The Hartman Personality Profile*. Retrieved February 15, 2004, from http://students.cs.byu.edu/~nhayden/Code/index.php

Wilmot, W., & Hocker, J. (1998). *Interpersonal conflict* (5th ed.). Boston: McGraw-Hill.

Heading centered on new page

Entries listed alphabetically by author, last name first; initials used for first and middle names

First line of each entry is flush left with margin

Subsequent lines indent

57

CSE Style

Writers in the physical sciences, the life sciences, and mathematics often use the documentation style set forth by the Council of Science Editors (CSE, formerly the Council of Biology Editors). Guidelines for citing print sources can be found in *Scientific Style and Format: The CBE Manual for Authors, Editors, and Publishers,* Sixth Edition, 1994. For citing Internet sources, the CSE endorses the *National Library of Medicine Recommended Formats for Bibliographic Citation Supplement: Internet Formats* (July 2001).

bedfordstmartins.com/everyday_writer   To access the advice in this chapter online, click on **Documenting Sources.**

DIRECTORY TO CSE STYLE

57a CSE style for in-text citations

In *The CBE Manual*, citations within an essay follow one of two formats.

- The citation-sequence format calls for a superscript number ([1]) or a number in parentheses after any mention of a source.
- The name-year format calls for the last name of the author and the year of publication in parentheses after any mention of a source. If the last name appears in a signal phrase, the name-year format allows for giving only the year of publication in parentheses.

Before deciding which system to use, check a current journal in the field, or ask an instructor about the preferred style in a particular course or discipline.

1. IN-TEXT CITATION USING CITATION-SEQUENCE SUPERSCRIPT FORMAT

In his lengthy text, VonBergen[1] provides the most complete discussion of this phenomenon.

For the citation-sequence format, you would use the same superscript ([1]) for each subsequent citation of this work by VonBergen.

2. IN-TEXT CITATION USING NAME-YEAR FORMAT

In his lengthy text, VonBergen provides the most complete discussion of this phenomenon (2003).

Hussar's two earlier studies of juvenile obesity (1995, 1999) examined only children with diabetes.

The classic examples of such investigations (Morrow 1968; Bridger and others 1971; Franklin and Wayson 1972) still shape the assumptions of current studies.

57b CSE style for a list of references

The citations in the text of an essay correspond to items on a list called *References*.

- If you use the citation-sequence superscript format, number and list the references in the order in which the references are *first* cited in the text.
- If you use the name-year format, list the references, unnumbered, in alphabetical order.

In the following examples, you will see that the citation-sequence format calls for listing the date after the publisher's name in references for books and after the periodical name in references for articles. The name-year format calls for listing the date immediately after the author's name in any kind of reference.

CSE style also specifies the treatment and placement of the following basic elements:

- *Author.* List all authors last name first, and use only initials for first and middle names. Do not place a comma after the author's last name, and do not place periods after or spaces between the initials. Do use a period after the last initial of the last author listed.
- *Title.* Do not italicize or underline titles and subtitles of books and periodicals. Do not enclose titles of articles in quotation marks. For books and articles, capitalize only the first word of the title and any proper nouns or proper adjectives. Abbreviate and capitalize all major words in a periodical title.
- *Page numbers.* For books, give the total number of pages followed by the abbreviation *p.* For articles or chapters, give inclusive page numbers.

The following sample entries use hanging indent format, in which the first line aligns on the left and subsequent lines indent one-half inch or five spaces.

Books

1. ONE AUTHOR

CITATION-SEQUENCE SUPERSCRIPT

[1] Buchanan M. Nexus: small worlds and the groundbreaking theory of networks. New York: WW Norton; 2003. 238 p.

NAME-YEAR

Buchanan M. 2003. Nexus: small worlds and the groundbreaking theory of networks. New York: WW Norton. 238 p.

2. TWO OR MORE AUTHORS

CITATION-SEQUENCE SUPERSCRIPT

[2]Wojciechowski BW, Rice NM. Experimental methods in kinetic studies. 2nd ed. St. Louis: Elsevier Science; 2003. 322 p.

NAME-YEAR

Wojciechowski BW, Rice NM. 2003. Experimental methods in kinetic studies. 2nd ed. St. Louis: Elsevier Science. 322 p.

3. ORGANIZATION AS AUTHOR

Place the organization's abbreviation at the beginning of the name-year entry and use it in the corresponding in-text citation.

CITATION-SEQUENCE SUPERSCRIPT

[3]World Health Organization. The world health report 2002: reducing risks, promoting healthy life. Geneva: World Health Organ; 2002. 250 p.

NAME-YEAR

[WHO] World Health Organization. 2002. The world health report 2002: reducing risks, promoting healthy life. Geneva: WHO. 250 p.

4. BOOK PREPARED BY EDITOR(S)

CITATION-SEQUENCE SUPERSCRIPT

[4]Torrence ME, Isaacson RE, editors. Microbial food safety in animal agriculture: current topics. Ames (IA): Iowa State Univ Pr; 2003. 416 p.

NAME-YEAR

Torrence ME, Isaacson RE, editors. 2003. Microbial safety in animal agriculture: current topics. Ames (IA): Iowa State Univ Pr. 416 p.

5. SECTION OF A BOOK WITH AN EDITOR

CITATION-SEQUENCE SUPERSCRIPT

[5]Kawamura A. Plankton. In: Perrin MF, Wursig B, Thewissen JGM, editors. Encyclopedia of marine mammals. San Diego: Academic Pr; 2002. p 939-42.

NAME-YEAR

Kawamura A. 2002. Plankton. In: Perrin MF, Wursig B, Thewissen JGM, editors. Encyclopedia of marine mammals. San Diego: Academic Pr. p 939-42.

6. CHAPTER OF A BOOK

CITATION-SEQUENCE SUPERSCRIPT

[6]Honigsbaum M. The fever trail: in search of the cure for malaria. New York:
Picador; 2003. Chapter 2, The cure; p 19-38.

NAME-YEAR

Honigsbaum M. 2003. The fever trail: in search of the cure for malaria. New
York: Picador. Chapter 2, The cure; p 19-38.

7. PUBLISHED PROCEEDINGS OF A CONFERENCE

CITATION-SEQUENCE SUPERSCRIPT

[7]Gutierrez AP, editor. Integrating biological and environmental factors in crop
system models. Integrated Biological Systems Conference; 2003 Apr 14-16;
San Antonio, TX. Beaumont (TX): Agroeconomics Research Group; 2003. 77 p.

NAME-YEAR

Gutierrez AP, editor. 2003. Integrating biological and environmental factors in
crop system models. Integrated Biological Systems Conference; 2003 Apr 14-
16; San Antonio, TX. Beaumont (TX): Agroeconomics Research Group. 77 p.

Periodicals

For rules on abbreviating journal titles, consult *The CBE Manual,* or ask
an instructor or a librarian to refer you to other examples.

8. ARTICLE IN A JOURNAL PAGINATED BY VOLUME

CITATION-SEQUENCE SUPERSCRIPT

[8]Mahmud K, Vance ML. Human growth hormone and aging. New Engl J Med
2003;348:2256-7.

NAME-YEAR

Mahmud K, Vance ML. 2003. Human growth hormone and aging. New Engl J Med
348:2256-7.

9. ARTICLE IN A JOURNAL PAGINATED BY ISSUE

CITATION-SEQUENCE SUPERSCRIPT

[9]Lau NC, Bartel DP. Censors of the genome. Sci Am 2003; 289(2):34-41.

NAME-YEAR

Lau NC, Bartel DP. 2003. Censors of the genome. Sci Am 289(2):34-41.

10. ARTICLE IN A WEEKLY JOURNAL
CITATION-SEQUENCE SUPERSCRIPT

[10]Holden C. Future brightening for depression treatments. Science 2003 Oct
31;302(5646):810-3.

NAME-YEAR

Holden C. 2003. Future brightening for depression treatments. Science
302(5646):810-3.

11. ARTICLE IN A MAGAZINE
CITATION-SEQUENCE SUPERSCRIPT

[11]Livio M. Moving right along: the accelerating universe holds secrets to dark
energy, the Big Bang, and the ultimate beauty of nature. Astronomy 2002
Jul:34-9.

NAME-YEAR

Livio M. 2002 Jul. Moving right along: the accelerating universe holds secrets
to dark energy, the Big Bang, and the ultimate beauty of nature.
Astronomy:34-9.

12. ARTICLE IN A NEWSPAPER
CITATION-SEQUENCE SUPERSCRIPT

[12]Kolata G. Bone diagnosis gives new data but no answers. New York Times 2003
Sep 28;Sect 1:1(col 1).

NAME-YEAR

Kolata G. 2003 Sep 28. Bone diagnosis gives new data but no answers. New York
Times;Sect 1:1(col 1).

Electronic sources

Although the 1994 edition of *The CBE Manual* includes a few examples
for citing electronic sources, the Council of Science Editors now recommends the guidelines set forth in the *National Library of Medicine Recommended Formats for Bibliographic Citation Supplement: Internet Formats*
<www.nlm.nih.gov/pubs/formats/internet.pdf>. The following for-
mats are based on the advice in this document. These examples use the
citation-sequence superscript system. To adapt them to the name-year
system, delete the superscripts and reorder the information in the
entries, placing the date immediately after the author's name.

The basic entry for most sources you access through the Internet should include the following elements:

- *Author.* Give the author's name, if available, last name first, followed by the initial(s) and a period.
- *Title.* For book, journal, and article titles, follow the style for print materials. For all other types of electronic material, reproduce the title as closely as possible to the wording that appears on the screen.
- *Medium.* Indicate, in brackets, that the source is not in print format by using designations such as *[Internet]* or *[database on the Internet]*.
- *Place of publication.* The city usually should be followed by the two-letter abbreviation for state. If the city is inferred, put the city and state in brackets, followed by a colon. If the city cannot be inferred, use the words *place unknown* in brackets, followed by a colon. Note that very well-known cities, such as New York or Chicago, may be listed without a state designation.
- *Publisher.* Include the individual or organization that produces or sponsors the site. It is often helpful to include a designation for country, in parentheses, after the publisher's name. If no publisher can be determined, use the words *publisher unknown* in brackets.
- *Dates.* Cite three important dates if possible: the date the publication was placed on the Internet or was copyrighted; the latest date of any update or revision; and the date the publication was accessed by you. Dates should be expressed in the format "year month day," and the date of copyright should be preceded by a *c* as in *c2000*. (In the following examples, dates are grouped together after the publisher's name. Check with your instructor to see if this style is acceptable.)
- *Page, document, volume, and issue numbers.* When citing a portion of a larger work or site, list the inclusive page numbers or document numbers of the specific item being cited. For journals or journal articles, include volume and issue numbers.
- *Length.* The length may be shown as a total page count, such as *85 p.* For much electronic material, length is approximate and is shown in square brackets, such as *[12 paragraphs]* or *[about 6 screens]*.
- *Address.* Include the URL or other electronic address; use the phrase *Available from:* to introduce the address. Only URLs that end with a slash are followed by a period.

13. ELECTRONIC JOURNAL ARTICLES

Include the authors' names; the title of the article; the title of the journal; the words *serial on the Internet* in brackets; as full a date of publication as possible; the date of access; the volume, issue, and page numbers (using designations such as *[16 paragraphs]* or *[5 screens]* if traditional page numbers are not available); and the URL.

[13]Perez P, Calonge TM. Yeast protein kinase C. J. of Biochem [serial on the Internet]. 2002 Oct [cited 2003 Nov 3];132(4):513-7. Available from: http://edpex104.bcasj.or.jp/jb-pdf/132-4/jb132-4-513.pdf

14. ELECTRONIC NEWSPAPER ARTICLE

[14]Brody JE. Reasons, and remedies, for morning sickness. The New York Times on the Web [Internet]. 2004 Apr 27 [cited 2004 Apr 30]:[about 24 paragraphs]. Available from: http://www.nytimes.com/2004/04/27/health/27BROD.html

15. ELECTRONIC BOOKS (MONOGRAPHS)

[14]Patrick TS, Allison JR, Krakow GA. Protected plants of Georgia [monograph on the Internet]. Social Circle (GA): GA Dept of Natural Resources; c1995 [cited 2003 Dec 3]. [about 216 p]. Available from: http://www.georgiawildlife.com/content/displaycontent.asp?txtDocument=89&txtPage=9

16. WEB SITE

Include as many of the following dates as possible: the date of publication (or, if this is not available, the copyright date preceded by *c*); the date of the most recent revision; and the date of access.

[15]Geology & Public Policy [Internet]. Boulder (CO): Geological Society of America; c2003 [updated 2003 Apr 8; cited 2003 Apr 13]. Available from: http://www.geosociety.org/science/govpolicy.htm

17. GOVERNMENT WEB SITE

Include a designation for the country, in parentheses, after the name of the agency or organization that publishes the site.

[17]Health Disparities: Minority Cancer Awareness [Internet]. Atlanta (GA): Centers for Disease Control and Prevention (US);[updated 2004 Apr 27; cited 2005 May 1]. Available from: http://www.cdc.gov/cancer/minorityawareness.htm

18. EMAIL MESSAGE

Include the author's name; the subject line of the message; the words *electronic mail on the Internet* in square brackets; the words *Message to:* followed by the addressee's name; information about when the message was sent and when it was cited; and the length of the message.

[16]Morrell K. Genetic testing [electronic mail on the Internet]. Message to: Corey Coggins. 2004 Mar 5, 3:16 pm [cited 2004 Mar 19]. [about 2 screens].

19. ELECTRONIC DISCUSSION LIST MESSAGE

[17]Durand M (University of Canterbury. m.durand@geol.canterbury.ac.nz). Rubidium. In: BIONET [discussion list on the Internet]. [London: Medical

Research Council]; 2003 May 30, 6:00 pm [cited 2003 Nov 21]. [about 12 lines]. Available from: http://www.bio.net/hypermail/toxicol/ toxicol.200305/0008.html

20. MATERIAL FROM AN ONLINE DATABASE

[18]Shilts E. Water wanderers. Canadian Geographic 2002 May;122(3):72-7. In: Expanded Academic ASAP [database on the Internet]. Farmington Hills (MI): InfoTrac; c2002 [cited 2004 Jan 27]. [about 17 paragraphs]. Available from: http://web4.infotrac.galegroup.com/itw/; Article: A86207443.

57c An excerpt from a student paper, CSE style

The following pages, from a research proposal by Tara Gupta, conform to the CSE guidelines described in this chapter. Just a brief excerpt of Tara's paper is shown, but all of her references are provided. Note that these pages have been reproduced in a narrow format to allow for annotation.

Student Writer

Tara Gupta

Field Measurements of
Photosynthesis and Transpiration
Rates in Dwarf Snapdragon
(*Chaenorrhinum minus* Lange):
An Investigation of Water Stress
Adaptations

Specific and
informative
title, name,
and other
relevant
information
centered on
title page

Tara Gupta

Proposal for a
Summer Research Fellowship
Colgate University
February 25, 2004

Water Stress Adaptations 2

Introduction

Dwarf snapdragon (*Chaenorrhinum minus*) is a weedy pioneer plant found growing in central New York during spring and summer. Interestingly, the distribution of this species has been limited almost exclusively to the cinder ballast of railroad tracks[1] and to sterile strips of land along highways.[2] In these harsh environments, characterized by intense sunlight and poor soil water retention, one would expect *C. minus* to exhibit anatomical features similar to those of xeromorphic plants (species adapted to arid habitats).

However, this is not the case. T. Gupta and R. Arnold (unpublished) have found that the leaves and stems of *C. minus* are not covered by a thick, waxy cuticle but rather with a thin cuticle that is less effective in inhibiting water loss through diffusion. The root system is not long and thick, capable of reaching deeper, moister soils; instead, it is thin and diffuse, permeating only the topmost (and driest) soil horizon. Moreover, in contrast to many xeromorphic plants, the stomata (pores regulating gas exchange) are not found in sunken crypts or cavities in the epidermis that retard water loss from transpiration.

Despite a lack of these morphological adaptations to water stress, *C. minus* continues to grow and reproduce when morning dew has been its only source of water for up to five weeks (R. Arnold, personal communication). Such growth involves fixation of carbon by photosynthesis and requires that the stomata be open to admit sufficient carbon dioxide. Given the dry, sunny environment, the time required for adequate carbon fixation must also mean a significant loss of water through transpiration as open stomata exchange carbon dioxide with water. How does *C. minus* balance the need for carbon with the need to conserve water?

Purposes of the Proposed Study

The above observations have led me to an exploration of the extent to which *C. minus* is able to photosynthesize under conditions

Shortened title appears next to page number

Introduction states the scientific issue, gives background information, and cites relevant studies by others; superscripts conform to CSE citation-sequence format

Headings throughout help organize the proposal

Water Stress Adaptations 6

References

[1]Wildrlechner MP. Historical and phenological observations of the spread of *Chaenorrhinum minus* across North America. Can J Bot 1983; 61:179-87.

[2]Dwarf Snapdragon [Internet]. Olympia (WA): Washington State Noxious Weed Control Board [updated 2001 July 7; cited 2004 Jan 25]. Available from: http://www.wa.gov/agr/weedboard/weed_info/dwarfsnapdragon.html

[3]Boyer JS. Plant productivity and environment. Science 1982;218:443-8.

[4]Manhas JG, Sukumaran NP. Diurnal changes in net photosynthetic rate in potato in two environments. Potato Res 1988;31:375-8.

[5]Doley DG, Unwin GL, Yates DJ. Spatial and temporal distribution of photosynthesis and transpiration by single leaves in a rainforest tree, *Argyrodendron peralatum*. Aust J Plant Physiol 1988;15:317-26.

[6]Kallarackal J, Milburn JA, Baker DA. Water relations of the banana. III. Effects of controlled water stress on water potential, transpiration, photosynthesis and leaf growth. Aust J Plant Physiol 1990;17:79-90.

[7]Idso SB, Allen SG, Kimball BA, Choudhury BJ. Problems with porometry: measuring net photosynthesis by leaf chamber techniques. Agron 1989;81:475-9.

Numbers correspond to order in which sources were first mentioned in the text, per CSE citation-sequence format

58

Chicago Style

The style guide of the University of Chicago Press has long been used in history as well as in other areas of the arts and humanities. The fifteenth edition of *The Chicago Manual of Style,* published in 2003, provides a complete guide to *Chicago* style, including two systems for citing sources. This chapter presents the notes and bibliography system. For easy reference, examples of how to format *Chicago*-style notes and bibliographic entries are shown together in 58b.

bedfordstmartins.com/everyday_writer   To access the advice in this chapter online, click on **Documenting Sources.**

DIRECTORY TO *CHICAGO* STYLE

Chicago *style for notes and bibliographic entries (58b)*

58a *Chicago* style for in-text citations, notes, and bibliography

In *Chicago* style, you use superscript numbers (^{1}) to mark citations in the text. Place the superscript number for each note near the cited material—at the end of the relevant quotation, sentence, clause, or phrase. Type the number after any punctuation mark except the dash; do not leave space between the superscript and the preceding letter or punctuation mark. Number citations sequentially throughout the text.

The notes themselves can be footnotes (each typed at the bottom of the page on which the superscript for it appears in the text) or endnotes (all typed on a separate page at the end of the text under the heading *Notes*). Be sure to check your instructor's preference. The first line of each note is indented like a paragraph (five spaces or one-half inch) and begins with a number followed by a period and one space before the first word of the entry. All remaining lines of the entry are typed flush with the left margin. Footnotes should be single-spaced with a double space between notes. All endnotes should be double-spaced.

IN THE TEXT

Sweig argues that Castro and Che Guevara were not the only key players in the Cuban Revolution of the late 1950s.[19]

IN THE FIRST NOTE

19. Julia Sweig, *Inside the Cuban Revolution* (Cambridge, MA: Harvard University Press, 2002), 9.

IN SUBSEQUENT NOTES

After giving complete information the first time you cite a work, shorten any additional references to that work: list only the author's name followed by a comma, a shortened version of the title followed by a comma, and the page number. If the reference is to the same source cited in the previous note, you can use the Latin abbreviation *Ibid.* (for "in the same place") instead of the name and title.

19. Julia Sweig, *Inside the Cuban Revolution* (Cambridge, MA: Harvard University Press, 2002), 9.

20. Ibid., 13.

21. Foner and Lewis, *Black Worker*, 138-39.

22. Ferguson, "Comfort of Being Sad," 63.

23. Sweig, *Cuban Revolution*, 21.

An alphabetical list of the sources you use in your paper is usually titled *Bibliography* in *Chicago* style. If *Sources Consulted, Works Cited,* or *Selected Bibliography* better describes your list, however, any of these titles is acceptable.

In the bibliographic entry for a source, include the same information as in the first note for that source, but omit the specific page reference. However, give the *first* author's name last name first, followed by a comma and the first name; separate the main elements of the entry with periods rather than commas; and do not enclose the publication information for books in parentheses.

IN THE BIBLIOGRAPHY

Sweig, Julia. *Inside the Cuban Revolution*. Cambridge, MA: Harvard University Press, 2002.

Start the bibliography on a separate page after the main text and any endnotes. Continue the consecutive numbering of pages. Type the title *Bibliography* (without italics or quotation marks) and center it below the top of the page. Begin each entry at the left margin. Indent the second and subsequent lines of each entry five spaces (or one-half inch). Double-space the entire list.

List sources alphabetically by authors' last names (or by the first major word in the title if the author is unknown).

58b *Chicago* style for notes and bibliographic entries

For easy reference, the following examples demonstrate how to format both notes and bibliographic entries according to *Chicago* style.

Books

1. ONE AUTHOR

1. James S. Hirsch, *Riot and Remembrance: The Tulsa Race War and Its Legacy* (Boston: Houghton Mifflin, 2002), 119.   Note

Hirsch, James S. *Riot and Remembrance: The Tulsa Race War and Its Legacy*.

Boston: Houghton Mifflin, 2002. Bibliography

2. MULTIPLE AUTHORS

2. Margaret Macmillan and Richard Holbrooke, *Paris 1919: Six Months That Changed the World* (New York: Random House, 2003), 384.

Macmillan, Margaret, and Richard Holbrooke. *Paris 1919: Six Months That Changed the World*. New York: Random House, 2003.

When there are more than three authors, it is acceptable in *Chicago* style to give the first-listed author followed by *et al.* or *and others* in the note. In the bibliography, however, list all the authors' names.

2. Stephen J. Blank and others, *Conflict, Culture, and History: Regional Dimensions* (Miami: University Press of the Pacific, 2002), 276.

Blank, Stephen J., Lawrence E. Grinter, Karl P. Magyar, Lewis B. Ware, and Bynum E. Weathers. *Conflict, Culture, and History: Regional Dimensions*. Miami: University Press of the Pacific, 2002.

3. ORGANIZATION AS AUTHOR

3. World Intellectual Property Organization, *Intellectual Property Profile of the Least Developed Countries* (Geneva: World Intellectual Property Organization, 2002), 43.

World Intellectual Property Organization. *Intellectual Property Profile of the Least Developed Countries*. Geneva: World Intellectual Property Organization, 2002.

4. UNKNOWN AUTHOR

4. *Broad Stripes and Bright Stars* (Kansas City, MO: Andrews McMeel Publishing, 2002), 10.

Broad Stripes and Bright Stars. Kansas City, MO: Andrews McMeel Publishing, 2002.

5. EDITOR

5. James H. Fetzer, ed., *The Great Zapruder Film Hoax: Deceit and Deception in the Death of JFK* (Chicago: Open Court Publishing, 2003), 56.

Fetzer, James H., ed. *The Great Zapruder Film Hoax: Deceit and Deception in the Death of JFK*. Chicago: Open Court Publishing, 2003.

6. SELECTION IN AN ANTHOLOGY OR CHAPTER IN A BOOK, WITH AN EDITOR

6. Denise Little, "Born in Blood," in *Alternate Gettysburgs*, ed. Brian Thomsen and Martin H. Greenberg (New York: Berkley Publishing Group, 2002), 245.

Little, Denise. "Born in Blood." In *Alternate Gettysburgs*, edited by Brian
   Thomsen and Martin H. Greenberg, 242-55. New York: Berkley Publishing
   Group, 2002.

7. EDITION OTHER THAN THE FIRST

7. Charles G. Beaudette, *Excess Heat: Why Cold Fusion Research Prevailed*, 2nd ed. (South Bristol, ME: Oak Grove Press, 2002), 313.

Beaudette, Charles G. *Excess Heat: Why Cold Fusion Research Prevailed*. 2nd ed.
   South Bristol, ME: Oak Grove Press, 2002.

8. MULTIVOLUME WORK

8. John Watson, *Annals of Philadelphia and Pennsylvania in the Olden Time*, vol. 2 (Washington, DC: Ross & Perry, 2003), 514.

Watson, John. *Annals of Philadelphia and Pennsylvania in the Olden Time*. Vol. 2.
   Washington, DC: Ross & Perry, 2003.

9. REFERENCE WORK

Cite well-known reference works in your notes, but do not list them in your bibliography. Use *s.v.*, the abbreviation for the Latin *sub verbo* ("under the word") to help your reader find the entry.

9. *Encarta World Dictionary*, s.v. "carpetbagger."

Periodicals

10. ARTICLE IN A JOURNAL

10. Karin Lützen, "The Female World: Viewed from Denmark," *Journal of Women's History* 12, no. 3 (2000): 36.

Lützen, Karin. "The Female World: Viewed from Denmark." *Journal of Women's
   History* 12, no. 3 (2000): 34-38.

11. ARTICLE IN A MAGAZINE

11. Douglas Brinkley and Anne Brinkley, "Lawyers and Lizard-Heads," *Atlantic Monthly*, May 2002, 56.

Brinkley, Douglas, and Anne Brinkley. "Lawyers and Lizard-Heads." *Atlantic Monthly,* May 2002, 55-61.

12. ARTICLE IN A NEWSPAPER

12. Caroline E. Mayer, "Wireless Industry to Adopt Voluntary Standards," *Washington Post,* September 9, 2003, sec. E.

Mayer, Caroline E. "Wireless Industry to Adopt Voluntary Standards." *Washington Post,* September 9, 2003, sec. E.

Electronic sources

13. NONPERIODICAL WEB SITE

13. Rutgers University, "Picture Gallery," *The Rutgers Oral History Archives of World War II*, http://fas-history.rutgers.edu/oralhistory/orlhom.htm (accessed November 7, 2003).

Rutgers University. "Picture Gallery." *The Rutgers Oral History Archives of World War II*. http://fas-history.rutgers.edu/oralhistory/orlhom.htm (accessed November 7, 2003).

14. ONLINE BOOK

14. Janja Bec, *The Shattering of the Soul* (Los Angeles: The Simon Wiesenthal Center, 1997), http://motlc.wiesenthal.com/resources/books/shatteringsoul/index.html (accessed November 6, 2003).

Bec, Janja. *The Shattering of the Soul*. Los Angeles: The Simon Wiesenthal Center, 1997. http://motlc.wiesenthal.com/resources/books/shatteringsoul/index.html (accessed November 6, 2003).

15. ARTICLE IN AN ELECTRONIC JOURNAL

15. Damian Bracken, "Rationalism and the Bible in Seventh-Century Ireland," *Chronicon* 2 (1998), http://www.ucc.ie/chronicon/bracfra.htm (accessed November 1, 2003).

Bracken, Damian. "Rationalism and the Bible in Seventh-Century Ireland." *Chronicon* 2 (1998). http://www.ucc.ie/chronicon/bracfra.htm (accessed November 1, 2003).

16. ARTICLE IN AN ONLINE MAGAZINE

16. Kim Iskyan, "Putin's Next Power Play," *Slate,* November 4, 2003, http://slate.msn.com/id/2090745 (accessed November 7, 2003).

Iskyan, Kim. "Putin's Next Power Play." *Slate,* November 4, 2003. http://slate.msn.com/id/2090745 (accessed November 7, 2003).

17. ARTICLE FROM A DATABASE

17. Peter DeMarco, "Holocaust Survivors Lend Voice to History," *Boston Globe*, November 2, 2003, http://www.lexisnexis.com (accessed November 19, 2003).

DeMarco, Peter. "Holocaust Survivors Lend Voice to History." *Boston Globe,* November 2, 2003, http://www.lexisnexis.com (accessed November 19, 2003).

18. EMAIL AND OTHER PERSONAL COMMUNICATIONS

Cite email messages and other personal communications, such as letters and telephone calls, in the text or in a note. Don't cite personal communications in your bibliography.

18. Kareem Adas, e-mail message to author, February 11, 2004.

Other sources

19. PUBLISHED OR BROADCAST INTERVIEW

19. Condoleezza Rice, interview by Charlie Rose, *The Charlie Rose Show,* PBS, October 30, 2003.

Rice, Condoleezza. Interview by Charlie Rose. *The Charlie Rose Show*. PBS, October 30, 2003.

Interviews you conduct are considered personal communications.

20. VIDEO OR DVD

20. Edward Norton and Edward Furlong, *American History X,* DVD, directed by Tony Kaye (1998; Los Angeles: New Line Studios, 2002).

Norton, Edward, and Edward Furlong. *American History X*. DVD. Directed by Tony Kaye 1998. Los Angeles: New Line Studios, 2002.

21. CD-ROM

21. *The Civil War*, CD-ROM (Fogware Publishing, 2000).

The Civil War. CD-ROM. Fogware Publishing, 2000.

22. PAMPHLET, REPORT, OR BROCHURE

Information about the author or publisher may not be readily available, but give enough information to identify your source.

22. Jamie McCarthy, *Who Is David Irving?* (San Antonio, TX: The Holocaust History Project, 1998).

McCarthy, Jamie. *Who Is David Irving?* San Antonio, TX: The Holocaust History Project, 1998.

23. GOVERNMENT DOCUMENT

23. U.S. House Committee on Ways and Means, *Report on Trade Mission to Sub-Saharan Africa,* 108th Cong., 1st sess. (Washington, DC: U.S. Government Printing Office, 2003), 28.

U.S. House Committee on Ways and Means. *Report on Trade Mission to Sub-Saharan Africa.* 108th Cong., 1st sess. Washington, DC: U.S. Government Printing Office, 2003.

58c An excerpt from a student essay, *Chicago* style

A brief excerpt from an essay by Kelly Darr follows, along with the essay's complete notes and bibliography. This essay conforms to the *Chicago* guidelines described in this chapter. Note that Kelly uses endnotes rather than footnotes; either format is acceptable in *Chicago* style. These sample pages have been reproduced in a narrow format to allow for annotation

bedfordstmartins.com/everyday_writer To read more of this essay, click on **Student Writing.**

All pages except title page numbered in upper right-hand corner

Marbury v. Madison and the

Origins of Judicial Review

Title centered and essay double-spaced throughout

    The Supreme Court of the United States is a very prestigious and powerful branch of American government today. Perhaps the most notable demonstration of the Court's power was its decision concerning the presidential election of 2000, a decision that resulted in George W. Bush becoming president.[1] The Court has not always

Source cited using superscript numeral

held this position, however. When the government system was developed in the late eighteenth century, the powers of the judicial branch were fairly undefined. In 1803, Chief Justice John Marshall, with his decision in *Marbury v. Madison,* began to define the duties of the Court by claiming for the Supreme Court the power of judicial review. Judicial review has been upheld ever since, and many people take the practice for granted. There is controversy around Marshall's decision, however, with some claiming that judicial review was not

Opening paragraph concludes with thesis in the form of two questions

the intent of the Framers. Two questions must be asked: Did Marshall overstep his bounds when he declared judicial review for the Court? If so, why has his decision been upheld for two hundred years? An examination of the actual case, *Marbury v. Madison,* and of Marshall's reasons for his decision is the first step to answering these questions.

    This case was complicated by personal and political opposition. It was brought to Court by William Marbury, whose commission as justice of the peace by John Adams was withheld by Thomas Jefferson when he became president. Jefferson's act was prompted by Adams's attempt to fill the national judiciary with Federalist judges on the eve before Jefferson took office. Due to a mistake by John Marshall himself (at the time the secretary of state under Adams), however, the commissions were not delivered. Jefferson, who did not appreciate the last-minute attempt to fill the offices with Federalists, refused to deliver the commissions after he took office. Marbury and a few other men sued James Madison, secretary of state under

Darr 6

Notes

1. *Bush v. Gore,* 531 U.S. 98 (2000), http://supct.law.cornell .edu/supct/html/00-949.ZPC.html (accessed February 8, 2004).

2. John A. Garraty, *Quarrels That Have Shaped the Constitution* (New York: Harper and Row, 1987), 7-14.

3. Ibid., 19.

4. William C. Louthan, *The United States Supreme Court: Lawmaking in the Third Branch of Government* (Englewood Cliffs, NJ: Prentice-Hall, 1991), 51.

5. Thomas J. Higgins, *Judicial Review Unmasked* (West Hanover, MA: Christopher Publishing House, 1981), 40-41.

6. *Marbury v. Madison,* 5 U.S. 137 (1803).

7. Louthan, *Supreme Court,* 51.

8. Ibid.

9. Ibid., 50-51.

10. Higgins, *Judicial Review,* 40-41.

11. Ibid., 32.

12. Ibid., 34.

Web source for court decision

First line of each note indented five spaces

Court decision

Author's last name and shortened title used for source already cited

Ibid. used to cite same source as in previous note

Darr 7

Bibliography

First line of each source flush left; subsequent lines indented five spaces

Garraty, John A. *Quarrels That Have Shaped the Constitution*. New
York: Harper and Row, 1987.

Higgins, Thomas J. *Judicial Review Unmasked*. West Hanover, MA:
Christopher Publishing House, 1981.

Bush v. Gore. 531 U.S. 1998 (2000). http://supct.law.cornell.edu
/supct/html/00-949.ZPC.html (accessed February 8, 2004).

Louthan, William C. *The United States Supreme Court: Lawmaking in
the Third Branch of Government*. Englewood Cliffs, NJ: Prentice-
Hall, 1991.

Marbury v. Madison, 5 U.S. 137 (1803).

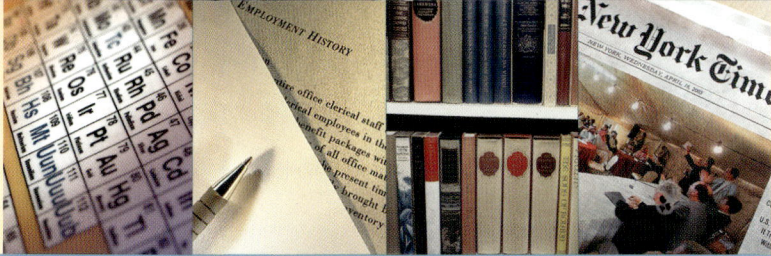

Writing in the
DISCIPLINES

Once one can write, one can
write on many topics. . . . Indeed,
[writing] may be
a chief survival skill.

–HOWARD GARDNER

Writing in the Disciplines

59

Learning to Write in Any Discipline

An instructor of multimedia and technical writing put this quotation by Steve Martin on her desk: "Writing has become what I do on a daily basis. Acting is what I do once a year." When her husband, a software developer, saw the quotation, he said: "Cool. That's a really provocative idea . . . and it's true. I write in some way every day. I don't think I even program as much as I write."

Writing is important in almost every profession, but it works in different ways in different disciplines. You may begin to get a sense of such differences as you prepare essays or other assignments for courses in the humanities, the social sciences, and the natural sciences. This chapter will help you develop the skills for writing in a variety of disciplines.

59a Analyze academic assignments and expectations.

When you receive an assignment in *any* discipline, your first job is to make sure you understand what that assignment is asking you to do. Some assignments may be as general as "Write an analysis of the group dynamics at play in your recent collaborative project for this course." (See 56d for one student's essay in response to this assignment.) Others, like this psychology assignment, will be fairly specific: "Collect, summarize, and interpret data drawn from a sample of letters to the editor published in two newspapers, one in a small rural community, and one in an urban community, over a period of three months. Organize your research report according to APA guidelines." Whatever your assignment, use the questions on the next page to analyze it.

59b Understand disciplinary vocabularies.

Entering into an academic discipline or a profession is much like entering into a conversation at a crowded party where you know no one. At

AT A GLANCE

Analyzing an Assignment in Any Discipline

1. *What is the purpose of the assignment?* Does it serve as a basis for class discussion or brainstorming about a topic? Or is the purpose to demonstrate your mastery of certain material and your competence as a writer?

2. *What is the assignment asking you to do?* Are you to summarize, explain, evaluate, interpret, illustrate, define? If you are to do more than one of these tasks, does the assignment specify an order?

3. *Do you need to ask for clarification of any terms?* Students responding to the psychology assignment on p. 461 might well ask the instructor, for instance, to discuss the meaning of *collect* or *interpret* and perhaps to give examples. Or they might want clarification of the term *urban community* or the size of a suitable sample.

4. *What do you need to know or find out to complete the assignment?* Students doing the psychology assignment need a way to analyze or categorize the letters. They also need to know how to do simple statistical analyses of the data.

5. *Do you understand the expectations regarding background reading and preparation, use of sources (both written and visual), method of organization and development, format, and length?* The psychology assignment mentions no reading, but in this field an adequate statement of a problem usually requires setting that problem in the context of other research. A student might well ask how extensive this part of the report is to be.

6. *Can you find an example of an effective response to a similar assignment?* If so, you can analyze it and perhaps use it as a model for developing your own approach to the current assignment.

7. *Does your understanding of the assignment fit with that of other students?* Talking over an assignment with classmates is one good way to test your understanding.

first you feel like an outsider, and you do not catch much of what you hear. Eventually, however, you pick up the vocabulary and begin to participate in the conversation.

Of course, this chapter cannot introduce you to the vocabulary of every field. The point is that you must make the effort to enter into the conversation. A good way to get started is to study the vocabulary of the field you are interested in. Highlight key terms in your reading or notes to help you distinguish any specialized terms. If you find only a little specialized vocabulary, try to master the new terms quickly by reading your textbook carefully, asking questions of the instructor, and looking up key words or phrases.

If you find a great deal of specialized vocabulary, any of the following procedures may prove helpful:

- Keep a log of unfamiliar or confusing words *in context*. Check the terms in your textbook's glossary or in a specialized dictionary. Students beginning the study of art, for instance, can turn to *The Oxford Dictionary of Art*. Those entering the discipline of sociology may refer to the *Dictionary of the Social Sciences*.

- Check to see if your textbook has a glossary of terms or sets off definitions in italics or boldface type.

- Try to start using or working with key concepts. Even if they are not yet entirely clear to you, working with them will help you come to understand them. For example, try to plot the narrative progression in a story even if you are still not entirely sure of the definition of *narrative progression*.

- If you belong to listservs or online discussion groups—or even if you are browsing Web sites related to a particular field—take special note of the ways technical language or disciplinary vocabulary is used there. Sometimes, you can find definitions of terms on a Web site's FAQ page.

59c   Identify the style of a discipline.

Another important way to learn about a particular discipline is to identify its stylistic features. Study pieces of writing in the field with the following questions in mind:

- How would you describe the overall *tone* of the writing? (See p. 68.)
- To what extent do writers in the field strive for an objective stance? (See 18c.)
- In general, how long are the sentences and paragraphs? (See 8d and 27a.)
- Are verbs generally active or passive—and why? (See 29g.)
- Do the writers use first person (*I*) or prefer terms such as *one* or *the investigator*? What is the effect of this choice?
- How does the writing use and integrate visual elements such as graphs, tables, charts, photographs, or maps? (See Chapters 5 and 13.)
- What role, if any, do headings and other formatting elements play in the writing? (See Chapter 13.)
- What bibliographic style (such as MLA, APA, CSE, or *Chicago*) is used? (See Chapters 52–58.)

Of course, writings within a single discipline may have different purposes and different styles. For example, a chemist may write a grant proposal, lab notebook, literature review, research report, and lab report, each with a different purpose and style.

59d Understand the use of evidence.

As you grow familiar with any area of study, you will develop a sense of just what it takes to prove a point in that field. You can speed up this process, however, by doing some investigating and questioning of your own. As you read assigned materials, ask yourself the following questions about evidence:

- How do writers in the field use precedent and authority? (See 11e.)
- What use is made of quantitative data (items that can be counted and measured) and qualitative data (items that can be systematically observed)?
- How is logical reasoning used? How are definition, cause and effect, analogy, and example used in this discipline?
- What are the primary materials—the firsthand sources of information—in this field? What are the secondary materials—the sources of information derived from others? (See 17a.)
- How are quotations used and integrated into the text? (See Chapter 19.)

59e Use conventional disciplinary patterns and formats.

You can gather all the evidence in the world and still fail to produce effective writing in your discipline if you do not know the field's generally accepted formats for organizing and presenting evidence. Again, these formats vary widely from discipline to discipline and sometimes from instructor to instructor, but patterns do emerge. The typical laboratory report, for instance, follows a fairly standard organizational framework whether it is in botany, chemistry, or parasitology. A case study in sociology or education or anthropology likewise follows a typical organizational plan.

Chapters 60–62 go into detail about several kinds of writing common in various disciplines.

bedfordstmartins.com/everyday_writer For information on multidisciplinary invention techniques, go to **Links** and click on **The Art and Craft of Writing.** For other multidisciplinary resources, click on **Writer's Almanac.**

60

Writing for Literature and the Other Humanities

Literature and other subject areas in the humanities deal with what it means to be *human*. Literary critics analyze and interpret texts portraying the human condition. Historians reconstruct the past. Philosophers raise questions about truth, knowledge, beauty, and justice. Scholars of languages learn not just to speak but to inhabit other languages and cultures. In these and other ways, those in the humanities strive to explore the human experience.

AT A GLANCE

Reading and Writing about Literature and the Other Humanities

- *Be clear about the purpose of a piece you are reading or writing.* The two common purposes of written works in the humanities are to inform and to argue. For example, a historian studying census records from the period of the Black Plague may intend to provide helpful information on the development of the disease. Or the historian may argue that one or more practices played a particularly important role in the spread of the plague.

- *Become an active, engaged reader.* Strong readers of texts in the humanities consistently pose questions and construct hypotheses as they read, going beyond the surface information and "talking back" to texts. They might ask themselves, for instance, why a writer is making some points or choosing particular examples but omitting others.

- *Become familiar with the kinds of texts common to the humanities.* Humanities instructors may expect you to read and write many types of essays and arguments, such as analytic essays (also called critical analyses), case studies, dialogues, personal journals, position papers, research papers, response pieces, and summaries.

- *Understand the essential difference between primary and secondary sources.* Primary sources typically are firsthand accounts, records of events, and artifacts. Diaries, letters, data from experiments, and historical documents are common primary sources. Secondary sources are texts written *about* a primary source or are in some other way one step removed from the main source. Encyclopedias, books by historians, and biographies are typical secondary sources. (17a)

Texts in the humanities reflect writers' concerns with the related skills of self-expression, analysis, and argument. Common assignments that make use of these skills include summaries, response pieces, position papers, critical analyses, and research-based projects. Some of the assignments, such as summaries and analytic essays, encourage looking very closely at a particular text, while others, such as research projects and case studies, call for going well beyond a primary text.

For papers in literature, modern languages, and philosophy, writers often use the documentation style of the Modern Language Association; see Chapters 52–55 for advice on using MLA style. For papers in history and other areas of the humanities, writers often use the documentation style of the University of Chicago Press; see Chapter 58 for advice on using *Chicago* style.

bedfordstmartins.com/everyday_writer For more on writing in the humanities, go to **Links** and click on **Writing in the Disciplines.** For other multidisciplinary resources, click on **Writer's Almanac.**

60a Read literature actively.

Although you are most likely to read and write about literature in English classes, you may encounter stories, poems, and essays in a number of other disciplines in the humanities. To successfully analyze and interpret such texts, you must ask questions and actively participate in the process of making meaning.

60b Consider the special terms for literary analysis.

The following elements of literature often appear in literary analyses. Becoming familiar with these terms will help you understand and write about literature.

Terms about sounds in a literary work

alliteration the repetition of an initial sound to create special emphasis or rhythm, as in this sentence from Eudora Welty: *Monsieur Boule inserted a delicate dagger in Mademoiselle's left side and departed with a posed immediacy.*

meter the rhythm of verse, as determined by the kind and number of feet (groups of syllables) in a line. Iambic pentameter indicates five feet of two syllables, with the stress falling on the second of the two, as in

U / U / U / U / U /
An aged man is but a paltry thing.

onomatopoeia the use of words whose sounds seem to resemble, or echo, their meaning: *hiss* or *sizzle,* for example.

Reading Literature to Write about Literature

Read the work for an overall impression.

- Read slowly and carefully, with a pen in hand.
- Make sure you can describe the basic plot, action, or sequence of events.
- Underline any unfamiliar words, and look them up in a dictionary.
- Freewrite for fifteen minutes or so about your initial response to the work. (See 6b.)

Reread and annotate the work.

- "Talk back" to the work by writing comments and questions in the margins.
- Make a note of anything that seems remarkable, memorable, out of place, puzzling, or ineffective.
- Underline repeated sounds, words, or images that seem important.

Review your thoughts and notes.

- Make a list of your most interesting marginal comments.
- List two or three questions about the work that you would like to answer in a paper.
- Freewrite a brief response to each of these questions.

---

rhyme scheme   the pattern of end rhymes in a poem, usually designated by the letters *a, b, c.* A Shakespearean sonnet typically follows a rhyme scheme of *abab cdcd efef gg.*

rhythm   in metrical poetry, the beat or pattern of stresses; in prose, the effect created by repetition, parallelism, and variation of sentence length and structure.

stanza   a division of a poem: a four-line stanza is called a quatrain; a two-line stanza, a couplet.

QUESTIONS TO ASK ABOUT SOUND

How does a poet's use of rhyme, meter, and other sound effects contribute to what you see as the poem's meaning? How do sentence rhythms and sounds underscore significant details in a story?

Terms about imagery in a literary work

Imagery is the general label applied to vivid descriptions that evoke a picture or appeal to other senses.

allusion an explicit or indirect reference in one work to another work or passage (for instance, a biblical passage) or to a person, place, or historical event.

figurative language a departure from the ordinary or standard use of words that enriches description and creates a special effect. Figures of speech include analogy, hyperbole, metaphor, simile, and personification. (See 39d.)

symbolism the use of one thing to represent other things or ideas, as the American flag symbolizes patriotism.

QUESTIONS TO ASK ABOUT IMAGERY

What images does the author use and what is their effect on you? How do any recurring images reinforce what you see as the work's meaning? How do metaphors and similes contribute to the work? What symbols does the author use, and how do they relate to the work's themes?

Terms about narrative elements in a literary work

characters the people in a story, who may act, react, and change during the course of the story.

implied author the sense of a pervasive authorial presence that is created by the text, as distinct from the narrator or from the real author. In *The Adventures of Huckleberry Finn,* for example, the real author is the flesh-and-blood Samuel Clemens (or Mark Twain); the implied author is the distinctive authorial presence that emerges for us as we read the novel.

irony the suggestion of the opposite, or nearly the opposite, of what the words usually mean, as in saying that being caught in a freezing downpour is "delightful."

narrator the person telling a story, who may be a character within the story or an omniscient voice with a point of view outside the story itself. In *The Adventures of Huckleberry Finn,* the narrator is Huck himself. In poetry, the narrator is known as the speaker.

plot the structure of actions or events in a text, which reveals the conflicts among or within the characters. Authors frequently use chronological order but often include flashbacks to past events. Traditionally, the plot begins with exposition, which presents background information; rises to a climax, the point of greatest tension; and ends with a resolution and dénouement (a French-derived term originally meaning "unraveling" or "unknotting"), which contain the outcome.

point of view the perspective from which a work is presented—in fiction, by a narrator outside the story or a character speaking in first or third person; in poetry, by the speaker of the poem.

setting the scene of a literary work, including the historical time, physical location, and social situation.

theme   a major and often recurring subject or topic; the larger meaning of a work, including any thoughts or insights about life or people in general.

tone   the narrator's or speaker's attitude (for instance, serious or ironic), conveyed through specific word choices and structures.

QUESTIONS TO ASK ABOUT NARRATIVE ELEMENTS

How convincing is the narrator's interpretation of events, and how does this affect your understanding of the work's themes? How does the protagonist, or main character, change during the course of the narrative? How do any conflicts between characters drive the plot forward and reinforce the work's themes? How does the setting of the work contribute to the development of its themes?

In writing about literature, you may need to use other terms that haven't been mentioned here. If necessary, consult a glossary of literary terms in print or online, such as *The Bedford Glossary of Critical and Literary Terms* or LitGloss <bedfordstmartins.com/litgloss>.

60c   Develop an interpretation and thesis in response to literature.

A good understanding of literary terminology will help you begin to analyze and interpret a particular work and formulate a thesis—the main point or claim you wish to make in your essay. Think of your thesis as answering a question about some aspect of the work. The guiding question you bring to a literary work will help you decide on a critical stance or approach toward the work. You can adopt a text-based stance, which builds an argument by focusing on specific features of a text; a context-based stance, which focuses on the context(s) surrounding a work; a reader-based stance, which focuses on the response of a particular reader to a text; or a combination of these approaches. (See the chart on the next page.)

A student literary analysis

An abridged version of an essay by Melissa Schraeder appears on the following pages. Taking both a text-based and a context-based stance, Melissa analyzes gender relations in Toni Morrison's *Beloved.* Because her audience—her classmates—had read the work, she chose not to review the plot in detail. She states her thesis and then substantiates it by citing passages from the primary source, the novel, as well as from secondary sources. Note that Melissa uses the present tense to dis-

Student Writer

Melissa Schraeder

DEVELOPING A CRITICAL STANCE

Type of Stance	Questions to Ask
Text-based	• What is the genre of the work—detective fiction? tragic drama? lyric poetry? Why is the form of the work significant? • What is the point of view, and who is (are) the narrator(s)? How reliable and convincing does the narrator seem? • What do you see as the major themes of the work? How do such elements as plot, setting, character, imagery, and sound support these themes? What can a close reading reveal about the theme(s)?
Context-based	• How does a consideration of the work's historical context contribute to an understanding of its themes? • How does information about the author's life affect your understanding of the work? • How are differences of gender, race, and class represented in the work? Does the text reinforce or challenge cultural stereotypes?
Reader-based	• Who are the readers the writer seems to address? Do they include you? • How do you, as a reader, respond to the different elements of the text? • How are readers from different cultural backgrounds (race, gender, class) likely to respond to the work?

cuss literary events. The essay follows the MLA guidelines described in Chapters 52–55. Note that it has been reproduced in a narrow format to allow for annotation. (For another MLA-style student essay, see Chapter 55.)

bedfordstmartins.com/everyday_writer   To read this essay in its entirety, click on **Student Writing.**

Schraeder 1

Melissa Schraeder

Professor Cheryl Glenn

English 205 Essay 3

April 24, 2004

"He Wants to Put His Story Next to Hers":

Gender in Toni Morrison's <u>Beloved</u>

Toni Morrison's <u>Beloved</u> is a novel about the transformation of individual identities and of the communal identity of African American Ohioans, a transformation most closely connected to a new understanding of gender relations. Morrison explores the power relations between male and female masters and male and female slaves, paralleling the individual stories of two former slaves--Sethe and Paul D--in order to highlight the common pain in their experiences. Linking these stories together through the threads of sexual exploitation and exclusion from the typical gender roles of whites, Morrison criticizes the traditional values associated with white male dominance. Out of this critique, she offers a new model of gender for African Americans, a model based on the shared suffering of an enslaved past and the shared struggle for a future of freedom and equality.

The history that Morrison offers in <u>Beloved</u> crosses geography and generations as she brings two new characters into an African American community in Ohio. Sethe is attempting to start a new life there, and Paul D returns to Ohio after being imprisoned at a forced labor camp for runaway slaves. Soon Beloved, the matured ghost of Sethe's infant daughter (the baby girl that Sethe murdered rather than see re-enslaved) appears. Sethe and Paul D begin to recall their memories of slavery, as Sethe attempts to explain her murder of Beloved to Paul D and, more important, to Beloved herself.

Much of the history of racial suffering that Morrison retells includes episodes of sexual violence, as Pamela Barnett's work on <u>Beloved</u> has emphasized (73-75). This history is consistent with the

Name, instructor's name, title of course and assignment, and date are all at left margin, double-spaced

Title centered

Double space between title and first paragraph

Indent first sentence of paragraph

Opening paragraph concludes with thesis statement

Second paragraph offers a brief overview of novel's plot

Reference to a critical study, with page numbers immediately following

Schraeder 2

larger body of literature written about and by enslaved African American women. For example, Harriet Jacobs's <u>Incidents in the Life of a Slave Girl</u> (which, according to "Judgment Day" on PBS Online's <u>Africans in America</u> Web site, was "one of the first open discussions about the sexual harassment and abuse endured by slave women") offers a firsthand account of the sufferings caused by sexual exploitation. The anonymous, colonial-era painting called <u>Virginian Luxuries</u> depicts sexual harassment and physical violence as common liberties taken by slave owners (see Fig. 1). Thus, the descriptions of sexual violence in <u>Beloved</u> have very real historical precedents (Morrison 74).

In the lives of African American women, violence made motherhood a double burden: they not only had to watch their

Fig. 1. <u>Virginian Luxuries</u>, Abby Aldrich Rockefeller Folk Art Center, Williamsburg. This painting illustrates the combined gender and race power that white males had over African American women and men like Sethe and Paul D.

(Margin annotations:)

Student's last name and page number in upper right corner of every page

Paragraph provides historical context

Parenthetical reference directs readers to figure

Parenthetical reference for in-text citation

Figure helps support the point being made. Note that it is labeled "Fig. 1" and that title, painter, and source are cited using MLA style.

Schraeder 3

children suffer under slavery or see them sold off at young ages, but
they also knew that many of their children were conceived through
hate instead of love. While Beloved is not conceived through rape,
Sethe does offer the fear of white rape and the desire to protect her
children as an explanation for her decision to kill. "Whites might
dirty <u>her</u> all right, but not her best thing, her beautiful magical best
thing--the part of her that was clean" (Morrison 296). Morrison
suggests, moreover, that motherhood is only one of many conventional gender roles that were denied to African American women.

In her depiction of Paul D, Morrison points out that African
American males suffered abuse similar to that of African American
females. Paul D's memory of the homosexual favors he and the other
African American men were forced to perform upon white labor
prison guards suggests that the dominant male role often depended
on racial difference instead of mere sexual difference. In other words,
Paul D's encounters with sexual violence illustrate that in a white-
male-to-black-male scenario, the black male is often gendered
feminine while the white male takes on the dual position of male
dominance and white supremacy.

Unlike Sethe's struggle with womanhood under slavery, which
focuses on exclusion from specific feminine roles, Paul D's struggle is
marked by a confusion over what it means to be a man. Paul D
increasingly questions the worth of the ideals of manhood--such as
independent action, self-sufficiency, physical strength, and
eloquence--since these are denied to him by slavery.

In recalling the maxim of the slave owner named Schoolteacher
that "definitions belonged to the definers--not the defined," Paul D
decides to define his own conditions for manhood instead of allowing
a white man to name them for him (Morrison 225). First, he decides
to turn inward, shutting out the white-dominated world that
threatens and diminishes his existence. Soon, however, Paul D's love
for Sethe begins to soften these protective measures as he imagines

Discussion of female gender role begins

Present tense used for literary events

Direct quotation

Discussion of male gender role begins

Elements of plot recounted as evidence of Paul D's transformation

Schraeder 4

that they might be able to live a conventional married life together. Yet the confusion caused by Beloved and the anger and pain caused by Sethe's story of murdering Beloved force Paul D to reconsider both white ideals of manhood and his own self-protective attempts to maintain a separate sense of African American manhood.

Struggling under the power that Beloved has over him, Paul D attempts to convince Sethe to bear a child with him, as "a solution: a way to hold on to her, document his manhood and break out of the girl's spell--all in one" (Morrison 151). For Sethe, however, the idea of pregnancy is a sign of Paul D's jealousy and a desire to expand his control over her, her daughter Denver, and Beloved.

Textual evidence supports explanation of Paul D's behavior

When Paul D finally can accept Sethe's actions and Beloved begins to disappear back into the spirit world, Sethe and Paul D undergo a final transformation that resolves their conflicts over gender power. In the end, when Paul D returns to Sethe and offers to both care for and listen to her, Morrison writes that "his coming is the reverse route of his going," suggesting both a careful retracing of steps or revisiting of mistakes and a healing erasure of pain (Morrison 318).

Beloved's final depiction of Sethe and Paul D is remarkable for the two ways it reenvisions gender. First, Morrison establishes a plane of gender equality and mutual respect, as suggested by the narrator's voicing of Paul D's thoughts: "He wants to put his story next to hers" (Morrison 322). Second, Morrison folds the values of self-knowledge, self-worth, self-love, and self-respect into the gender roles of Sethe and Paul D. After the pain of his past, Paul D realizes that "only this woman Sethe could have left him his manhood," and Sethe finally stops fighting her past as she hears the words that only Paul D would speak: "You your best thing, Sethe. You are" (Morrison 322). Through these deeper understandings of one another's gendered histories, Sethe and Paul D transform the agony of the past into the knowledge necessary to order the present and the power to shape the future.

Quotation from text support claim about reenvisioning gender

Summary of argument and restatement of thesis

Schraeder 5

Works Cited

Barnett, Pamela. "Figurations of Rape and the Supernatural in — Work in an anthology
Beloved." Toni Morrison: Beloved. Ed. Carl Plasa. New York:
Columbia UP, 1998. 73-85.

"Judgment Day." Africans in America. 1998. PBS Online. 16 Apr. 2004 — Document from the World Wide Web
<http://www.pbs.org/wgbh/aia/part4/4p2923.html>.

Morrison, Toni. Beloved. 1987. New York: Knopf, 1998. — Republished book

Virginian Luxuries. n.d. Abby Aldrich Rockefeller Folk Art Center, — Anonymous painting found on Internet
Williamsburg. Common Place. 18 Apr. 2004 <http://
www.common-place.org/vol-01/no-04/slavery/bontemps.shtml>.

60d   Learn the scope of the other humanities

In humanities disciplines other than literature, the interpretation and creation of texts are also central. The nature of these texts may vary: an art historian may "read" a painting by Leonardo Da Vinci; a philosopher may analyze a treatise by John Locke or Emmanuel Kant. But whether the text being studied is ancient or modern, literary or historical, verbal or visual, textual analysis plays a critical role in all of the reading and writing that people in the humanities undertake.

For sample pages from a student essay that uses *Chicago* style, see 58c.

> **bedfordstmartins.com/everyday_writer**   For more examples of writing in the humanities, click on **Student Writing.** For additional information, go to **Links** and click on **Writing in the Disciplines.** For other multidisciplinary resources, click on **Writer's Almanac.**

61

Writing for the Social Sciences and the Natural Sciences

The social sciences and the natural sciences call for systematic, observable studies—in offices, labs, and the field. Such studies might involve why people vote, how children learn, where birds migrate, or thousands of other phenomena. Regardless of what they are analyzing, however, both social scientists and natural scientists know that what they write, from a first grant proposal to a final scientific paper, is central to their efforts.

> **bedfordstmartins.com/everyday_writer**   For more on writing in the social sciences and natural sciences, go to **Links** and click on **Writing in the Disciplines.** For other multidisciplinary resources, click on **Writer's Almanac.**

61a   Learn the scope of the social sciences.

The social sciences—which may include psychology, anthropology, political science, speech communication, sociology, economics, and education—attempt to identify and explain patterns of human behav-

---

AT A GLANCE

Reading and Writing about the Social Sciences

- *Learn to deal with both quantitative and qualitative studies.* Quantitative studies emphasize statistical information—from surveys, polls, experiments, and tests—which is often presented in graphs and charts. As you read, question the information. You might ask, for example, *Do these statistics apply to people in general or to only a particular group?* Qualitative studies are more subjective because they rely on interviews and observations. When reading a qualitative report, you might ask, *Is the writer's argument consistent with the interviews, or is the writer jumping to conclusions?*

- *Become familiar with the kinds of writing social scientists do.* Like students and scholars in other areas, social scientists often analyze the works of others—for example, in position papers, book reviews, and literature reviews (that is, reviews of other studies related to a research topic). Social scientists also write about their own research—for example, in research reports, case studies, or ethnographies (studies of particular cultures).

- *Become familiar with the structural elements common to research reports in the social sciences.* Your instructor may ask you to include some or all of the following sections in a paper you write: abstract (an overview of the findings), introduction, review of literature, methods *or* procedure (an explanation of research techniques), results, discussion, conclusion, references.

- *Write clear, unbiased prose with everyday but precise language.* Use the active voice as often as possible. When describing research results, use the past or present perfect tense (the study *showed,* the study *has shown*). When explaining the implications of research, use the present tense (for future research, these findings *suggest*).

- *Learn the terminology of the social sciences.* Recognize, however, that some terms you use in everyday speech, such as *group* or *identity,* can have specialized meanings in the social sciences.

- *Learn the style of social science writing.* Use *I* and *we* only to mean yourself and colleagues—not people in general. For the most part, literary techniques such as irony are inappropriate in social science writing. While metaphors can be helpful in explaining a complicated concept, use them carefully.

ior. The social sciences share with the humanities an interest in what it means to be human and with the natural sciences the goal of relying on systematic studies and quantifiable evidence.

For papers in the social sciences, writers often use the documentation style of the American Psychological Association; see Chapter 56 for advice on using APA style. For a student research essay that uses APA style, see 56d.

bedfordstmartins.com/everyday_writer   For more examples of writing in the social sciences, click on **Student Writing.** For additional information, go to **Links** and click on **Writing in the Disciplines.** For other multidisciplinary resources, click on **Writer's Almanac.**

AT A GLANCE

Reading and Writing about the Natural Sciences

- *Remember that striving for objectivity is very important in the natural sciences.* Scientists study phenomena through carefully controlled experiments and often use specialized instruments so that they can generate reliable data.

- *Become familiar with disciplinary terms, and use them accurately.* Refer to dictionaries of scientific terms if you need help with unusual words or with commonly confused words or word parts, such as *absorption/adsorption* and *quasi/semi.*

- *Recognize the value of charts, graphs, models, and other visuals to scientific writing.* When you use figures or tables to present data, be sure to add titles and numbers to your visuals and to include appropriate column headings, labels, and captions. Be sure as well to *comment on* such data in the text of your report.

- *Become familiar with the kinds of writing natural scientists do.* For example, natural scientists write research or grant proposals (to secure funds for research), lab notebooks (to record ongoing experiments), literature reviews (to analyze research on a specific topic), and research reports and lab reports (to detail one's own research).

- *Become familiar with the structural elements common to scientific papers.* Depending on the type of writing you are doing, instructors may ask you to include some of the following elements or sections: an abstract (overview), introduction or statement of purpose, literature review, list of materials, budget, time-line, explanation of methods, results, discussion, conclusion, and list of references.

- *Learn the style of scientific writing.* Use clear, straightforward prose, and avoid seldom-used abbreviations that can make scientific writing difficult to read. In general, use the present tense for research reports. Use the past tense, however, when you are describing specific experimental methods and observations or citing research published in the past.

- *Use the passive voice if appropriate.* Much scientific writing focuses on what is being studied rather than on the person doing the studying. In some circumstances, then, you may want to use the passive voice: *the grey wolf was driven from its native habitat; seedlings were dispersed over hundreds of acres.*

61b Learn the scope of the natural sciences.

The term *natural sciences* encompasses both the life sciences—such as biology and botany—and the physical sciences—such as chemistry and geology. Scientists in these disciplines want to understand how the physical and natural worlds work. More than many other scholars, natural scientists are likely to leave the privacy of their office or lab to engage in fieldwork and experimentation. Writing—whether done in the lab or the field—is central to their work.

For papers in the natural sciences, writers often use the documentation style of the Council of Science Editors; see Chapter 57 for advice on using CSE style. For sample pages from a student essay that uses CSE style, see 57c.

bedfordstmartins.com/everyday_writer For more examples of writing in the natural sciences, click on **Student Writing.** For additional information, go to **Links** and click on **Writing in the Disciplines.** For other multidisciplinary resources, click on **Writer's Almanac.**

62

Writing for Business

Writing assignments in business classes serve two related functions. While their most immediate goal is to help you master the theory and practice of business, these assignments also try to prepare you for the kinds of writing you will face when you enter the world of work after college. For this reason, students in *every* discipline need to know how to write effective business memos, emails, letters, résumés, and reports.

62a Learn the scope of business writing.

Thanks to technology, a team of businesspeople researching a topic now has almost unlimited access to information. Writers in business need to negotiate a huge stream of print, electronic, and online information and to evaluate that information for its usefulness. They are aware that time constraints and deadline pressures affect decisions about *what* to read

Effective Business Communication

- *Be clear.* Use simple words and straightforward sentences with active verbs. Use topic sentences to help readers follow your points.
- *Be concise.* Use the words you need to make your point but no more. Don't give readers information they don't need. Try to keep paragraphs fairly short—in general, six lines or fewer.
- *Be complete.* Include all the information readers need. You don't want them to have to call or write you for important, but missing, details.
- *Be courteous.* Write in a friendly, conversational tone, but don't be overly casual. Imagine how you would respond if you were the reader.
- *Be correct.* Use a spell checker, and then proofread carefully.

and write as well as about *how* to do so. Good business writers also realize that they are working increasingly in a global arena. As a result, they need to be sensitive to the cultural contexts of what they read and write, since what is considered polite in one culture may be considered rude in another. (For more on reading and writing in a global context, see Chapter 36.)

No matter what medium they are working within, writers in business—like writers everywhere—need to consider their purpose, audience, style, tone, medium (print, electronic, online), document design, and use of visuals. Business writers who do this can respond more effectively to the challenges of communication in the twenty-first century.

62b Use a conventional format for memos and emails.

Memos, a common form of print or electronic correspondence sent within and between organizations, tend to be brief, often dealing with only one subject.

The following memo, written by Michelle Abbott and Carina Abernathy, presents an analysis and recommendation to help their employer (Jenco) make a decision.

Student Writer

Student Writer

Michelle Abbott

Carina Abernathy

MEMO

Date: January 30, 2004

To: Rosa Donahue, Sales Manager

From: Michelle Abbott & Carina Abernathy, *MA CA* — Initials of senders added in ink
Sales Associates

Subject: Taylor Nursery Bid

As you know, Taylor Nursery has requested bids on a 25,000-pound order — Paragraphs not indented
of our private-label fertilizer. Here is our analysis of Jenco's costs to fill
this special order and a recommendation for the bidding price. — Opening paragraph clearly states memo's purpose

The total cost for manufacturing 25,000 pounds of the private-label — Most important information clearly emphasized
brand for Taylor Nursery is $44,075. This cost includes direct material,
direct labor, and variable manufacturing overhead. Although our current
equipment and facilities provide adequate capacity for processing this special order, the job will involve an excess in labor hours. The overtime
labor rate has been factored into our costs.

The absolute minimum price that Jenco could bid for this product without
losing money is $44,075 (our cost). Applying our standard markup of 40% — Initial recommendation presented to employer
results in a price of $61,705. Thus, you could reasonably establish a price
anywhere within that range.

In making the final assessment, we advise you to consider factors relevant
to this decision. Taylor Nursery has stated that this is a one-time order.
Therefore, the effort to free this special order will not bring long-term — Double spacing between paragraphs
benefits.

Taylor Nursery has requested bids from several competitors. One rival,
Eclipse Fertilizers, is submitting a bid of $60,000 on this order. Therefore,
our recommendation is to slightly underbid Eclipse with a price of — Final recommendation
$58,000, representing a markup of approximately 32%.

Please let us know if we can be of further assistance in your decision on — Closing builds good-will by offering further help
the Taylor Nursery bid.

AT A GLANCE

Effective Memos

- Write the date, the name of the recipient, your name, and the subject on separate lines at the top.
- Begin with the most important information: get right to the point.
- Try to involve readers in your opening paragraph by focusing on how the information you convey affects them.
- Focus each paragraph on one idea pertaining to the subject.
- Emphasize specific action—exactly what you want readers to do, and when.
- Make sure your style and tone fit the audience and purpose of your memo.
- Use attachments for detailed supporting information.
- Attempt to build goodwill in your conclusion.
- For print memos, write your initials next to your name.

Email is a form of brief communication used continually in business, industry, and the professions. Traveling instantaneously to individuals and groups anywhere in the world, at any hour, an email message follows a format much like that of a memo. (For guidelines for and an example of effective email, see Chapter 12.)

62c Use a conventional format for letters and résumés.

When you send a business or professional letter, you are writing either as an individual or as a representative of an organization. In either case, and regardless of your purpose, a business letter should follow certain conventions.

One particular type of letter, the letter of application or cover letter, often accompanies a résumé. The purpose of a letter of application is to demonstrate how the experiences and skills you outline in your résumé have prepared you for a particular job. The following letter of application for a summer internship was written by Nastassia Lopez.

Student Writer

Nastassia Lopez

LETTER OF APPLICATION

↓ 1"

Nastassia Rose Lopez ——————————— Nastassia
523 Brown Avenue   creates a
Stanford, CA 94305   letterhead
650-326-6790 / nrl87@hotmail.com   for her letter
                                                                              and provides
                                                                              contact
                                                                              information
February 1, 2004

Mr. Price Hicks
Director of Educational Programs and Services ——————— Inside
Academy of Arts and Sciences   address with
5220 Lankersheim Blvd.   full name,
North Hollywood, CA 91601   title, and
                                                                              address

Dear Mr. Hicks: ——————————————————— Salutation
                                                                              addresses
                                                                              a specific
                                                                              person
I am an enthusiastic Stanford student who believes that a Development
Internship at the Academy of Arts and Sciences would greatly benefit both the — Opening pro-
Academy and me. A Los Angeles native in my first year at Stanford, I'm a seri-   vides infor-
ous student who is a hard worker. My current goal is to comprehend the full   mation about
scope of the entertainment industry and to learn the ropes of the craft.   Nastassia
                                                                              and lists her
                                                                              major goals
As an experienced writer, I am attracted to the Development Department because
I am curious to learn the process of television production from paper to screen. Provides
In high school, I was enrolled in Advanced Placement Writing, and I voluntarily background
took a creative writing class. At Stanford, I received High Honors for maintain- information to
ing an excellent grade-point average across all my classes, including several   illustrate her
writing-intensive courses.   skills and the
                                                                              strength of
                                                                              her interest
My passion for writing, producing, directing, and *learning* is real. If my application is accepted, I will bring my strong work ethic, proficiency, and creativity to
the Academy.

Thank you very much for your time and consideration. My résumé is enclosed,
and I look forward to hearing from you.

Sincerely yours,

Nastassia Rose Lopez ——————————————————— Four line
                                                                              spaces for
Nastassia Rose Lopez   signature

AT A GLANCE

Effective Letters

- Use a conventional format. Many letters use the block format, in which all text aligns at the left margin. Some writers prefer a modified block format, aligning the return address, date, close, and signature flush left with the center of the page. You have the further option of centering each line of the return address, as the student writer does on p. 483.

- Whenever possible, write to a specific person rather than to a general *Dear Sir or Madam.*

- Open cordially, and be polite—even if you have a complaint.

- State the reason for your letter clearly. Include whatever details will help your reader see your point and respond.

- If appropriate, make clear what you hope your reader will do.

- Express appreciation for your reader's attention.

- Make response simple by including your telephone or fax number or email address and, if appropriate, a self-addressed, stamped envelope.

While a letter of application emphasizes specific parts of a résumé, the résumé itself summarizes your experience and qualifications and provides support for your letter. An effective résumé is brief, usually one or two pages.

Research shows that employers usually spend less than a minute reading over a résumé. Remember that they are interested not in what they can do for you but what you can do for them. They expect a résumé to be printed neatly on high-quality paper or formatted neatly on a Web page or in an electronic file. In all cases, your aim is to use clear headings, adequate spacing, and conventional formats that will make your résumé easy to read. Such conventions may be hard to accept because you want your résumé to stand out, but a *well-written* résumé with a *standard format* is the best way to distinguish yourself.

Your résumé may be arranged chronologically (in reverse chronological order) or functionally (around skills or expertise). Either way, you will probably include the following information:

1. *Name, address, phone and fax numbers, and email address,* often centered at the top.
2. *Career objective(s).* List immediate or short-term goals and specific jobs for which you realistically qualify.
3. *Educational background.* Include degrees, diplomas, majors, and special programs or courses that pertain to your field of interest. List honors and scholarships and your grade-point average if it is high.

4. *Work experience.* Identify each job—whether a paying job, an internship, or military experience—with dates and names of organizations. Describe your duties by carefully selecting strong action verbs for a hard-copy résumé and nouns for a scannable résumé. Highlight any of your activities that improved business in any way.

5. *Skills, personal interests, activities, and honors.* Identify your technology skills. List hobbies, offices held, volunteer work, and awards.

6. *References.* List two or three people who know your work well, first asking their permission. Give their titles, addresses, and phone or fax numbers. Or simply say that your references are available on request.

7. *Keywords.* Labels and terms that an employer might use to search for a job candidate are important to include if your résumé is submitted electronically and might become part of a database.

The following résumés were written by Dennis Tyler Jr. The second one is formatted for scanning; since many employers now enter résumés into databases to be searched and sorted, take careful note of how Dennis prepared a scannable résumé.

Student Writer

Dennis Tyler Jr.

bedfordstmartins.com/everyday_writer   For more examples of business and professional writing, click on **Student Writing.** For additional information, go to **Links** and click on **Writing in the Disciplines.** For other multidisciplinary resources, click on **Writer's Almanac.**

RÉSUMÉ

Name in boldface and larger type size

DENNIS TYLER JR.

CURRENT ADDRESS	PERMANENT ADDRESS
P.O. Box 12345	506 Chanelle Court
Stanford, CA 94309	Baton Rouge, LA 70128
Phone: (650) 498-4731	Phone: (504) 246-9847
Email: dtyler@yahoo.com	

Position being sought

CAREER OBJECTIVE   Position on editorial staff of a major newspaper

EDUCATION

Educational background

9/00–6/04   **Stanford University,** Stanford, CA
BA, ENGLISH AND AMERICAN STUDIES, June 2004

9/02–12/02   **Morehouse College,** Atlanta, GA
STANFORD STUDY EXCHANGE PROGRAM

Work experience relevant to position being sought

EXPERIENCE

6/03–9/03   **Business Scholar Intern,** Finance, AOL Time Warner, New York, NY
Responsible for analyzing data for strategic marketing plans. Researched the mergers and acquisitions of companies to which Time Inc. sells advertising space.

1/02–6/03   **Editor-in-Chief,** *Enigma* (a literary journal), Stanford University, CA
Oversaw the entire process of *Enigma.* Edited numerous creative works: short stories, poems, essays, and interviews. Selected appropriate material for the journal. Responsible for designing cover and for publicity to the greater community.

8/02–12/02   **Community Development Intern,** University Center Development Corporation (UCDC), Atlanta, GA
Facilitated workshops and meetings on the importance of home buying and neighborhood preservation. Created UCDC brochure and assisted in the publication of the center's newsletter.

6/02–8/02   **News Editor,** *Stanford Daily,* Stanford University, CA
Responsible for editing stories and creating story ideas for the newspaper. Assisted with the layout for the newspaper and designs for the cover.

Talents and honors not listed above

SKILLS AND HONORS

- Computer Skills: MS Word, Excel, PageMaker, Microsoft Publisher; Internet research
- Language: Proficient in Spanish
- Trained in making presentations, conducting research, acting, and singing
- Mellon Fellow, Gates Millennium Scholar, Public Service Scholar, National Collegiate Scholar
- Black Community Service Arts Award, 2003–2004

REFERENCES   Available upon request

SCANNABLE RÉSUMÉ

Dennis Tyler Jr.

Current Address
P.O. Box 12345
Stanford, CA 94309
Phone: (650) 498-4731
Email: dtyler@yahoo.com

Permanent Address
506 Chanelle Court
Baton Rouge, LA 70128
Phone: (504) 246-9847

Keywords: journalist; journal editor; literary publishing; finance; community development; design; leadership; newspaper writer; PageMaker; Spanish; editor-in-chief

Education
BA in English and American Studies, June 2004, Stanford University, Stanford, CA
Morehouse College Study Exchange, fall 2002, Atlanta, GA

Experience
Business Scholar Intern, fall 2003
Finance, AOL TimeWarner, New York, NY
Data analyst for strategic marketing plans. Researcher for the mergers and acquisitions of companies to which Time Inc. sells advertising.

Editor-in-Chief, 2002–2003, Enigma (a literary journal), Stanford University, CA
Oversaw the entire process of Enigma. Editor for numerous works: short stories, poems, essays, and interviews. Content selection for the journal. Cover design and publicity to the greater community.

Community Development Intern, fall 2002
University Center Development Corporation (UCDC), Atlanta, GA
Workshops on the importance of home buying and neighborhood preservation. Publication responsibility for UCDC brochure and the center's newsletter.

News Editor, summer 2002, Stanford Daily, Stanford University, CA
Story editor for the newspaper. Layout and cover design for the newspaper.

Skills and Honors
Computer skills: MS Word, Excel, PageMaker, Microsoft Publisher; Internet research
Language: Proficient in Spanish
Trained presenter, researcher, actor, singer
Mellon Fellow, Gates Millennium Scholar, Public Service Scholar, National Collegiate Scholar
Black Community Service Arts Award, 2003–2004

References
Available upon request

Annotations:

Each phone number or email address on a separate line

Standard typeface (Times Roman) and type size used

Keywords listed to aid in computer searches by employers

No underlining, italics, boxes, borders, or columns

White space used to mark off sections

Verbs converted to nouns wherever possible

Keywords used in body of résumé wherever possible

For MULTILINGUAL Writers

The story of the American people, the story of the peoples native to this continent and of those who immigrated here **from every corner of the world,** is told in the rich accents of Cherokee, Spanish, German, Dutch, Yiddish, French, Menomenie, Japanese, Norwegian, Arabic, Aleut, Polish, Navajo, Thai, Portuguese, Caribbean creoles, and scores of other tongues.

–HARVEY DANIELS

For Multilingual Writers

For Multilingual Writers

63

U.S. Academic Conventions

Xiao Ming Li, now a college teacher, reports that before she first came to the United States, she had been a "good" writer in China—both in English and Chinese. When she became a college student in the United States, however, she struggled to figure out what her teachers expected of her writing in English. Although she used appropriate words and sentence grammar, her instructors seemed to expect her to write in a whole new way, which she could not, at first, grasp.

Xiao and other multilingual students facing new writing expectations often need to call on writing-center tutors or instructors to help them write more effectively in their classes. In short, resourceful students actively tackle the question of how to write "U.S.A. style."

Of course, there is no one style of writing in any culture and surely not in the United States. Even the variety of English often referred to as "standard" covers a wide range of styles (see Chapter 38). In addition, writing styles vary considerably from field to field. In spite of this wide variation, you can learn the basic style called for most often in U.S. college writing. To begin to become an effective writer in American English, consider some of the expectations prevalent in the United States about readers, writers, and texts.

63a Understand expectations about readers.

U.S. college instructors expect you to be an actively engaged reader—to respond to class readings and to offer informed opinions on what the readings say. Such highly active reading may seem unusual or even impolite to you, but it will not seem so to your instructors and many of your classmates. Keep in mind that instructors are not asking you to be negative or combative. Rather, they want to know that you are engaged with the text and the class.

AT A GLANCE

U.S. Academic Style

- Use conventional grammar, spelling, punctuation, and mechanics. (Chapters 28–51)
- Make explicit links between ideas. (Chapter 8)
- Use an easy-to-read type size and typeface, conventional margins, and double-spacing. (Chapter 13)
- State your claim explicitly, and support it with examples, statistics, anecdotes, and authorities of various kinds. (Chapter 11)
- Carefully document all your sources. (Chapters 52–58)
- Consistently use the appropriate level of formality. (36f and 39a)
- Use conventional idioms. (Chapter 66)
- Use conventional academic formats, such as research projects, literary analyses, and position papers. (Chapters 59–62)

Here are other expectations many college instructors have about what good reading involves:

- Good reading calls for understanding the overall content of a piece and being able to summarize it.
- Good reading calls for understanding each sentence, making direct connections between sentences and paragraphs, keeping track of repeated themes or images, and figuring out how they contribute to the entire piece.
- Good reading requires you to note the author's attitude toward and assumptions about the subject. Then you can speculate on how the attitude and assumptions may have affected the author's thinking.
- Good reading means distinguishing between the author's stance and how the author reports on the stances of others. Keep an eye open for the key phrases an author uses to signal an opposing argument: *while some have argued that, in the past,* and so on.
- Good reading goes beyond content to notice organizational patterns, use of sources, and choice of words.

63b Understand expectations about writers.

Establishing authority

In some cultures, what students write is supposed to reflect—not differ from—what they are learning. These cultures consider teachers a very important source of knowledge and, hence, authority. One Japanese student, for example, considered it rude to challenge a teacher: "Are you ever so smart that you should challenge the wisdom of the ages?"

In contrast, instructors in the United States typically view students as in the process of establishing themselves as authorities, as writers who create new knowledge based on their own thinking and on what others have said, and as constructive critics. What does "establishing authority" mean in practice?

- Assume that your opinions count (as long as they are informed rather than tossed out with little thought) and that your audience expects you to present them.

- Draw conclusions based on what you have read, and offer those conclusions.

- Build your authority by citing the works of others. (See 36e and 59d for more information on the use of evidence.)

Being direct

U.S. college instructors will most often expect you to get to your main point quickly and to be direct throughout a paper. Good writing prepares them for what is coming next, provides definitions, and includes topic sentences. (See Chapter 36 for a description of the organization that American instructors generally prefer in student papers.) One recent cross-cultural study concluded that German instructors, on the other hand, more readily accept digressions and even some obscurity as a sign of the writer's scholarship.

To achieve directness in your writing, try the following strategies:

- Avoid overqualifying your statements. Instead of saying *I think the facts reveal,* come right out and say *The facts reveal.*

- Avoid digressions. If you use an anecdote, be sure that it relates directly to your main point.

- Make your transitions from point to point obvious and clear. The first sentence of a new paragraph should reach back to the paragraph before and then look forward to what is to come.

- Sometimes you will also want to use summary statements between sections, especially if your paper is longer than two or three pages.

63c Understand expectations about your texts.

Your instructors hold different expectations for the different kinds of written work you produce in U.S. colleges—from brief in-class writing to longer papers written outside of class.

In-class writing

When you respond to short-answer questions and write very brief essays for in-class exams, you need to display the knowledge you have learned in the course. On such exams, then, demonstrating that you know the material is more important than developing new or original ideas about it.

You can overcome the problem of running out of time on an exam by preparing carefully in advance.

- Review all the material carefully.
- Anticipate the questions, and write practice answers to them.
- Explain—either orally or in writing—the material you will be tested on to someone unfamiliar with it.
- Do some timed writing right before class to get your writing muscles warmed up.
- Finally, once the test begins, prepare a very brief outline to guide you. Such an outline can help you organize your thoughts and keep you on track.

Long essay questions and formal papers

For long essay questions and, especially, for formal papers, be sure to provide plenty of evidence—specific details in support of your points. These details can include examples, precedents, statistics, definitions, or occasionally even anecdotes, but to be effective these details need to be as specific as possible and related to the point you are making.

On some long-essay exams, you will be expected to show your familiarity with assigned readings by mentioning evidence put forth by the authors of those readings. When you write research papers, you need to go even further by formally citing all your sources and documenting them carefully. You may be used to relying on sources without mentioning them; while that is an old and time-honored tradition in some cultures, in U.S. academic writing, it almost always results in a charge of misuse of sources or even of plagiarism. Your instructors will expect you to acknowledge every source you use, even if you are only paraphrasing or summarizing it rather than quoting it directly. (See also Chapters 19 and 20.)

bedfordstmartins.com/everyday_writer   For sample "U.S.A. style" essays, click on **Student Writing.**

64

Nouns and Noun Phrases

Everyday life is filled with nouns and noun phrases: orange juice, the morning news, a bus to work, meetings, pizza, email, Diet Coke, errands, dinner with friends, a chapter in a good book. No matter what your first language is, it includes nouns. This chapter will focus on some of the ways English nouns differ from those in some other languages.

64a Know how to use count and noncount nouns.

The nouns *tree* and *grass* differ both in meaning and in the way they are used in sentences.

> The hill was covered with trees.
> The hill was covered with grass.

Tree is a count noun, and *grass* a noncount noun. These terms do not mean that grass cannot be counted but only that English grammar requires that if we count grass, we express it indirectly: *one blade of grass, two blades of grass,* not *one grass, two grasses.*

Count nouns usually have singular and plural forms: *tree, trees.* Noncount nouns usually have only a singular form: *grass.*

Count nouns refer to distinct individuals or entities: *a doctor, a book, a tree; doctors, books, trees.* Noncount nouns refer to indeterminate masses or collections: *milk, ice, clay, blood, grass.*

COUNT	NONCOUNT
people (plural of *person*)	humanity
tables, chairs, beds	furniture
letters	mail
pebbles	gravel
grains	rice
facts	information
suggestions	advice

Some words can be either count or noncount, depending on meaning.

COUNT	Before there were video games, children played with *marbles.*
NONCOUNT	The floor of the palace was made of *marble.*

When you learn a noun in English, you need to learn whether it is count, noncount, or both. The following print and online resources can help:

Cambridge Advanced Learner's Dictionary
Oxford Advanced Learner's Dictionary
Collins Cobuild English Dictionary
Dave's ESL Café <www.eslcafe.com>
ESL go.com <www.eslgo.com>
ESLflow <www.eslflow.com>
English-Zone.com <www.english-zone.com>

64b State singular and plural forms explicitly.

Look at this sentence from a traffic report:

All four bridges into the city are crowded with cars right now.

This sentence has three count nouns; one is singular (*city*), and two are plural (*bridges, cars*). If you speak a language with nouns that generally have no distinct plural forms (for example, Chinese, Japanese, or Korean), you might feel that no information would be lost if the English sentence were *All four bridge into the city are crowded with car right now.* After all, *four* indicates that *bridge* is plural, and obviously there would have to be more than one car if the bridges are crowded. But English requires that every time you use a count noun, you ask yourself whether you are talking about one item or more than one and that you choose a singular or a plural form accordingly.

Since noncount nouns have no plural forms, they can be quantified only with a preceding phrase: *one quart of milk, three pounds of rice, several bits of information.* In these cases, the noun remains singular.

64c Use determiners appropriately.

A noun together with all its modifiers constitutes a noun phrase. For example, in *My adventurous sister is leaving for New Zealand tomorrow,* the noun phrase *my adventurous sister* consists of two modifiers (*my* and *adventurous*) and the noun *sister.*

Words like *my, our,* and *this* are determiners, which are common and important words in the English language. Determiners come before nouns to identify or quantify them.

COMMON DETERMINERS

- the articles *a/an, the*
- *this, these, that, those*

- *my, our, your, his, her, its, their*
- possessive nouns and noun phrases (*Sheila's, my friend's*)
- *whose, which, what*
- *all, both, each, every, some, any, either, no, neither, many, much, (a) few, (a) little, several,* and *enough*
- the numerals *one, two,* etc.

Using determiners with singular count nouns

Every noun phrase containing a singular count noun must begin with a determiner.

▶ *my*
  adventurous sister
  ^

▶ *the*
  big, bad wolf
  ^

▶ *that*
  old neighborhood
  ^

If there is no reason to use a more specific determiner, use *a* or *an: a big, bad wolf; an old neighborhood.*

    Notice that every noun phrase need not begin with a determiner, only those that involve a singular count noun. Noncount and plural count nouns sometimes have determiners, sometimes not: *This grass is green* and *Grass is green* are both acceptable, though the former refers to a specific grassy area and the latter to grass in general.

Remembering which determiners go with which types of noun

- *This* or *that* goes with singular count or noncount nouns: *this book, that milk.*
- *These, (a) few, many, both,* or *several* goes with plural count nouns: *these books, those plans, a few ideas, many students, both hands, several trees.*
- *(A) little* or *much* goes with noncount nouns: *a little milk, much affection.*
- *Some* or *enough* goes with noncount or plural count nouns: *some milk, some books; enough trouble, enough problems.*
- *A, an, every,* or *each* goes with singular count nouns: *a book, every child, each word.*

64d Use *a, an,* or *the* to convey your intended meaning.

The articles *a, an,* and *the* can be challenging to multilingual speakers. Many languages have nothing directly comparable to them, and languages that do have articles differ from English in the details of their use.

Using the

Use the definite article *the* with nouns whose identity is known or is about to be made known to readers. The necessary information for identification can come from the noun phrase itself, from elsewhere in the text, from context, from general knowledge, or from a superlative.

             the
▶ **Let's meet at fountain in front of Dwinelle Hall.**

The phrase *in front of Dwinelle Hall* identifies the specific fountain.

▶ **Last Saturday, a fire that started in a restaurant spread to a neighboring**
                                The store
dry-goods store. ~~Store~~ was saved, although it suffered water damage.

The word *store* is preceded by *the,* which directs our attention to the information in the previous sentence, where the store is identified.

                             the
▶ **Professor to student in her office: "Please shut door when you leave."**

The professor expects the student to understand that she is referring to the door in her office.

             the pope
▶ **The Vatican says ~~Pope~~ is expected to visit Africa in October.**

Since there is never more than one living pope, his identity is clear.

          the
▶ **Will is now best singer in the choir.**

The superlative *best* identifies the noun *singer.*

Using a *or* an

Use *a* before a consonant sound: *a car.* Use *an* before a vowel sound: *an uncle.* Pay attention to sounds rather than to spelling: *a house, an hour.*

    A or *an* tells readers they do not have enough information to identify what the noun specifically refers to. The writer may or may not have a particular thing in mind but in either case will use *a* or *an* if the reader lacks the information necessary for identification. Compare the following sentences:

▶ **I need *a* new *parka* for the winter.**
▶ **I saw *a parka* that I liked at Dayton's, but it wasn't heavy enough.**

The parka in the first sentence is hypothetical rather than actual. Since it is indefinite to the writer, it clearly is indefinite to the reader and is used with *a,* not *the.* The second sentence refers to a very specific actual parka, but since the writer cannot expect the reader to know which one it is, it is used with *a* rather than *the.*

If you want to speak of an indefinite quantity, rather than just one indefinite thing, use *some* with a noncount noun or a plural count noun.

▶ **This stew needs** *some* **more** *salt.*

▶ **I saw** *some plates* **that I liked at Macy's.**

Zero article

If a noun appears without *the, a* or *an,* or any other determiner (even if it is preceded by other adjectives), it is said to have a zero article. The zero article is used with noncount and plural count nouns: *cheese, hot tea, crackers, ripe apples* (but not *cracker* or *ripe apple*). Use the zero article to make generalizations.

▶ **In this world nothing is certain but death and taxes.**

–BENJAMIN FRANKLIN

> The zero article indicates that Franklin refers not to a particular death or specific taxes but to death and taxes in general.

Here English differs from many other languages—Greek or Spanish or German, for example—that do use the definite article to make generalizations. In English, a sentence like *The snakes are dangerous* can refer only to particular, identifiable snakes, not to snakes in general.

It is sometimes possible to make general statements with *the* or *a/an* and singular count nouns.

> *First-year college students are* confronted with many new experiences.
>
> *A first-year student* is confronted with many new experiences.
>
> *The first-year student* is confronted with many new experiences.

These sentences all make the same general statement, but the emphasis of each sentence is different. The first sentence refers to first-year college students as a group, the second focuses on a hypothetical student taken at random, and the third sentence, which is characteristic of formal written style, projects the image of a typical student as representative of the whole class.

64e Arrange modifiers carefully.

Some modifiers precede the noun, and others follow, and you need to learn both the required and the preferred positions for modifiers in order to know what can go where.

- Phrases or clauses follow the noun: *the tiles on the wall, the tiles that we bought in Brazil.*
- Determiners go at the very beginning of the noun phrase: *these old-fashioned tiles. All* or *both* precedes any other determiners: *all these tiles.* Numbers follow any other determiners: *these six tiles.*
- Noun modifiers go directly before the noun: *these kitchen tiles.*
- All other adjectives go between determiners and noun modifiers: *these old-fashioned kitchen tiles.* If there are two or more of these adjectives, their order is variable, but there are strong preferences, described below.
- Subjective adjectives (those that show the writer's attitude) go before objective adjectives (those that merely describe): *these beautiful old-fashioned kitchen tiles.*
- Adjectives of size generally come early: *these beautiful large old-fashioned kitchen tiles.*
- Adjectives of color generally come late: *these beautiful large old-fashioned blue kitchen tiles.*
- Adjectives derived from proper nouns or from nouns that refer to materials generally come after color terms and right before noun modifiers: *these beautiful large old-fashioned blue Portuguese ceramic kitchen tiles.*
- All other objective adjectives go in the middle, and adjectives for which a preferred order does not exist are separated by commas: *these beautiful large decorative, heat-resistant, old-fashioned blue Portuguese ceramic kitchen tiles.*

As you probably realize, the endless noun phrase in the last bulleted item is a monstrosity that would be out of place in almost any conceivable kind of writing. You should always budget your use of adjectives.

bedfordstmartins.com/everyday_writer   For exercises, go to **Exercise Central** and click on **Nouns and Noun Phrases.**

65

Verbs and Verb Phrases

When we must act, verbs tell us what to do—from the street signs that say *stop* or *yield* to email commands such as *send* or *delete*. Verbs can be called the heartbeat of prose, especially in English; with rare exceptions, you cannot deprive an English sentence of its verb without killing it. If you speak Russian or Arabic, you might not find anything wrong with the sentence *Where Main Street?* But unlike those and many other languages, English sentences must have a verb: *Where is Main Street?* This chapter will focus on some of the ways English verbs differ from verbs in other languages.

65a A review of verb phrases

Verb phrases can be built up out of a main verb (mv) and one or more auxiliaries (29b).

> My cat *drinks* milk.
>
> My cat *is drinking* milk.
>
> My cat *has been drinking* milk.
>
> My cat *may have been drinking* milk.

Verb phrases have strict rules of order. If you try to rearrange the words in any of these sentences, you will find that most alternatives are impossible. You cannot say *My cat drinking is milk* or *My cat have may been drinking* milk. The only permissible rearrangement is to move the first auxiliary to the beginning of the sentence in order to form a question: *Has my cat been drinking milk?*

Auxiliary and main verbs

In *My cat may have been drinking milk,* the main verb *drinking* is preceded by three auxiliaries: *may, have,* and *been.*

- *May* is a modal, which must be followed by a base form (*have*). (65d)
- *Have* indicates that the tense is perfect, and it must be followed by a past participle (*been*).
- *Been* (or any other form of *be*), when it is followed by a present participle (such as *drinking*), indicates that the tense is progressive.
- When a form of *be* is followed by a past participle, as in *My cat may have been bitten by a dog,* it indicates passive voice.

Auxiliaries must be in the following order: modal + perfect *have* + progressive *be* + passive *be.*

> **PERF**
> ┌ **PASS** ┐   **MV**
> ▶ Sonya *has been invited* to stay with a family in Prague.

> **PERF**
> ┌ **PROG** ┐   **MV**
> ▶ She *has been taking* an intensive course in Czech.

> **MOD**
> ┌ **PROG** ┐   **MV**
> ▶ She *must be looking* forward to her trip eagerly.

Only one modal is permitted in a verb phrase.

> MOD   MV
▶ Sonya *can speak* a little Czech already.

> MOD
> ⌐PROG¬   MV
▶ She *will be studying* for three more months.

> *will be able to speak*
▶ She ~~will can speak~~ Czech much better soon.
>   ^

Every time you use an auxiliary, you should be careful to put the next word in the appropriate form.

Modal + base form

Use the base form of the verb after *can, could, will, would, shall, should, may, might,* and *must.* (See Chapter 29.)

▶ Alice *can read* Latin.

▶ Paul *should have* studied.

▶ They *must be* going to a fine school.

In many other languages, modals like *can* or *must* are followed by the infinitive (*to* + base form). Do not substitute an infinitive for the base form in English.

▶ Alice can ~~to~~ read Latin.

Perfect have + past participle

To form the perfect tenses, use *have, has,* or *had* with a past participle. (See Chapter 29.)

▶ Everyone *has gone* home.

▶ They *have been* working all day.

Progressive be + present participle

A progressive form of the verb is signaled by two elements, a form of the auxiliary *be* (*am, is, are, was, were, be,* or *been*) and the *-ing* form of the next word: *The children are studying.* Be sure to include both elements.

> *are*
▶ The children studying in school.
>   ^

> *studying*
▶ The children are ~~study~~ in school.
>   ^

Some verbs are rarely used in progressive forms. These are verbs that express unchanging conditions or mental states rather than deliberate actions: *believe, belong, hate, know, like, love, need, own, resemble, understand.* (See Chapter 29.)

Passive *be* + *past participle*

Use *am, is, are, was, were, being, be,* or *been* with a past participle to form the passive voice.

▶ **Tagalog *is spoken* in the Philippines.**

Notice that with the progressive *be* the following word (the present participle) ends in *-ing,* but with the passive *be* the following word (the past participle) never ends in *-ing.*

▶ **Meredith *is* studying music.**
▶ **Natasha *was* taught by a famous violinist.**

If the first auxiliary in a verb phrase is *be* or *have,* it must show either present or past tense, and it must agree with the subject: *Meredith has played in an orchestra.*

Notice that a modal auxiliary never changes form to agree with the subject.

can
▶ **Michiko ~~cans~~ play two instruments.**
   ^

65b Use present and past tenses carefully.

Every English sentence must have at least one verb or verb phrase that is not an infinitive (*to break*), a present participle (*breaking*), or a past participle (*broken*) without any auxiliaries.

In some languages, such as Chinese and Vietnamese, the verb form never changes regardless of when the action of the verb takes place, and the time of the action is simply indicated by other expressions such as *yesterday, last year,* and *next week.* In English, the time of the action must be clearly indicated by the tense form of each and every verb, even if the time is obvious or indicated elsewhere in the sentence.

could not
▶ **During the Cultural Revolution, millions of young people ~~cannot~~ go to**
were   ^
school and ~~are~~ sent to the countryside.
   ^

In some languages (Spanish, for example), words end in either a vowel sound or a single consonant sound, not in one consonant sound followed by another. Remember to add the -*s* of the present-tense third-person singular and the -*ed* of the past tense.

>   *called*   *lives*
> ▶ **Last night I ~~call~~ my aunt who ~~live~~ in Santo Domingo.**
>   ^   ^

Using direct and indirect discourse

Changing direct quotations to indirect quotations can sometimes lead to inappropriate tense shifts. If the verb introducing the indirect discourse is in the present tense, the verb in the indirect discourse should also be in the present tense.

> DIRECT   She said, "My work *is* now complete."
>
> INDIRECT   She *tells* me that her work is now complete.

If the verb introducing the indirect discourse is in the past tense, stick with tenses that refer to past time in the indirect discourse.

>   *had received*
> ▶ **She told me that her exams were over and that she ~~receives~~ the highest**
>   ^
> **score in her class.**

If, however, the introductory verb is in the past tense but the information that follows holds true in the present, then shifting to a present-tense verb is acceptable.

> ▶ **She *told* me that her work *is* as exciting as ever.**

65c   Understand perfect and progressive verb phrases.

The perfect and progressive auxiliaries combine with the present or past tense, or with modals, to form complex verb phrases with special meanings. In particular, you should learn to recognize sentences in which you must use the perfect or progressive rather than a simple tense (29e).

Distinguishing the simple present and the present perfect

> ▶ **My sister *drives* a bus.**

The simple present (*drives*) merely tells us about the sister's current occupation. But if you were to add the phrase *for three years,* it would be incorrect to say *My sister <u>drives</u> a bus for three years.* You need to set up a time frame that includes both the past and the present, so you should use the present perfect or the present perfect progressive.

> ▶ **My sister *has driven* a bus for three years.**
> ▶ **My sister *has been driving* a bus for three years.**

Distinguishing the simple past and the present perfect

▶ Since she started working, she *has bought* a new car and a DVD player.

The clause introduced by *since* sets up a time frame that runs from past to present and requires the present perfect (*has bought*) in the subsequent clause. Furthermore, the sentence does not say exactly when she bought the car or the DVD player, and that indefiniteness also calls for the perfect. It would be less correct to say *Since she started working, she bought a new car and a DVD player.* But what if you should go on to say when she bought the car?

▶ She *bought* the car two years ago.

It would be incorrect to say *She has bought the car two years ago* because the perfect cannot be used with definite expressions of time. In this case, use the simple past (*bought*).

Distinguishing the simple present and the present progressive

When an action is in progress at the present moment, use the present progressive. Use the simple present for actions that frequently occur during a period of time that might include the present moment (though the simple present does not necessarily indicate that the action is taking place now).

▶ My sister *drives* a bus, but she *is taking* a vacation now.
▶ My sister *drives* a bus, but she *takes* a vacation every year.

Many languages, such as French and German, use the simple present (*drives, takes*) for both types of sentence. In English, however, the first sentence above would be incorrect if it said *but she takes a vacation now.*

Distinguishing the simple past and the past progressive

spent
▶ Sally ~~was spending~~ the summer in Italy.
   ^

You might be tempted to use the past progressive (*was spending*) here instead of the simple past, since spending the summer involves a continuous stretch of time of some duration, and duration and continuousness are typically associated with the progressive. But English speakers use the past progressive infrequently and would be unlikely to use it in this case except to convey actions that are simultaneous with other past actions.

▶ Sally *was spending* the summer in Italy when she *met* her future husband.

Use the past progressive to call attention to past action that went on at the same time as something else.

65d Use modals appropriately.

The nine basic modal auxiliaries are *can, could, will, would, shall, should, may, might,* and *must.* There are a few others as well, in particular *ought to,* which is close in meaning to *should.* Occasionally *need* can be a modal rather than a main verb.

The nine basic modals are the pairs *can/could, will/would, shall/should, may/might,* and the loner *must.* In earlier English, the second member of each pair was the past tense of the first. To a limited degree, the second form still functions as a past tense, especially in the case of *could.*

▶ Ingrid *can* ski.

▶ Ingrid *could* ski when she was five.

But for the most part, in present-day English, all nine modals typically refer to present or future time. When you want to use a modal to refer to the past, you follow the modal with a perfect auxiliary.

▶ If you have a fever, you *should* see a doctor.

▶ If you had a fever, you *should have seen* a doctor.

In the case of *must,* refer to the past by using *had to.*

▶ You *must* renew your visa by the end of this week.

▶ You *had to* renew your visa by the end of last week.

Using modals to make requests or to give instructions

Modals are often used in requests and instructions. Imagine making the following request of a flight attendant:

▶ *Will* you bring me a pillow?

That sentence expresses your request in a demanding manner, and the flight attendant might resent it. A more polite request acknowledges that fulfilling the request may not be possible.

▶ *Can* you bring me a pillow?

Another way of softening the request is to use the past form of *will,* and the most discreet choice is the past form of *can.*

▶ *Would* you bring me a pillow?

▶ *Could* you bring me a pillow?

Using the past of modals is considered more polite than using their present forms because it makes any statement or question less assertive.

Now consider each of the following instructions:

1. You *can* submit your report electronically.
2. You *may* submit your report electronically.
3. You *should* submit your report electronically.
4. You *must* submit your report electronically.
5. You *will* submit your report electronically.

Instructions 1 and 2 give permission to submit the report electronically but do not require it; of these, 2 is more formal. Instruction 3 adds a strong recommendation; 4 allows no alternative; and 5 implies, "Don't even think of doing otherwise."

Using modals to indicate doubt and certainty

Modals can also indicate how confident the writer is about the likelihood that what is being asserted is true. Look at the following set of examples, which starts with a tentative suggestion and ends with an indication of complete confidence:

Please sit down; you *might be* tired.

Please sit down; you *may be* tired.

Please sit down; you *must be* tired.

65e Use participial adjectives appropriately.

Many verbs refer to feelings—for example, *bore, confuse, excite, fascinate, frighten, interest.* The present and past participles of such verbs can be used as ordinary adjectives (28m). Use the past participle to describe a person having the feeling.

▶ The *frightened* boy started to cry.

Use the present participle to describe the thing (or person) causing the feeling.

▶ The *frightening* dinosaur display gave him nightmares.

Be careful not to confuse the two types of adjectives.

      interested
▶ I am ~~interesting~~ in African literature.
    ^

                    interesting.
▶ African literature seems ~~interested.~~
                    ^

bedfordstmartins.com/everyday_writer   For exercises, go to **Exercise Central** and click on **Verbs and Verb Phrases.**

66

Prepositions and Prepositional Phrases

If you were traveling by rail and asked for directions, it would not be helpful to be told to "take the Chicago train." You would need to know whether to take the train *to* Chicago or the one *from* Chicago. Words such as *to* and *from,* which show the relations between other words, are prepositions. Not all languages use prepositions to show such relations, and English differs from other languages in the way prepositions are used. This chapter provides guidelines for using prepositions in English.

66a Use prepositions idiomatically.

Even if you usually know where to use prepositions, you may have difficulty from time to time knowing which preposition to use. Each of the most common prepositions, whether in English or in other languages, has a wide range of different applications, and this range never coincides exactly from one language to another. See, for example, how English speakers use *in* and *on*.

> The peaches are *in* the refrigerator.
>
> The peaches are *on* the table.
>
> Is that a diamond ring *on* your finger?

If you speak Spanish

The Spanish translations of these sentences all use the same preposition (*en*), a fact that might lead you astray in English.

> *on*
> ▶ Is that a ruby ring ~~in~~ your finger?
>   ^

There is no easy solution to the challenge of using English prepositions idiomatically, but the strategies on the next page can make it less troublesome.

66b Use two-word verbs idiomatically.

Some words that look like prepositions do not always function as prepositions. Consider the following two sentences:

> ▶ The balloon rose *off* the ground.
> ▶ The plane took *off* without difficulty.

AT A GLANCE

Using Prepositions Idiomatically

1. Keep in mind typical examples of each preposition.

IN **The peaches are *in* the refrigerator.**

There are still some pickles *in* the jar.

Here the object of the preposition *in* is a container that encloses something.

ON **The peaches are *on* the table.**

The book you are looking for is *on* the top shelf.

Here the object of the preposition *on* is a horizontal surface that supports something with which it is in direct contact.

2. Learn other examples that show some similarities and some differences in meaning.

IN **You shouldn't drive *in* a snowstorm.**

Here there is no container, but like a container, the falling snow surrounds and seems to enclose the driver.

ON **Is that a diamond ring *on* your finger?**

A finger is not a horizontal surface, but like such a surface it can support a ring with which it is in contact.

3. Use your imagination to create mental images that can help you remember figurative uses of prepositions.

IN **Michael is *in* love.**

Imagine a warm bath in which Michael is immersed (or a raging torrent, if you prefer to visualize love that way).

ON **I've just read a book *on* computer science.**

Imagine a shelf labeled "Computer Science" on which the book you have read is located.

4. Try to learn prepositions not in isolation but as part of a system. For example, in identifying the location of a place or an event, the three prepositions *in, on,* and *at* can be used.

    At specifies the exact point in space or time.

AT **There will be a meeting tomorrow *at* 9:30 AM *at* 160 Main Street.**

Expanses of space or time within which a place is located or an event takes place might be seen as containers and so require *in*.

IN **I arrived *in* the United States *in* January.**

5. *On* must be used in two cases: with the names of streets (but not the exact address) and with days of the week or month.

ON **The airline's office is *on* Fifth Avenue.**

I'll be moving to my new apartment *on* September 30.

In the first sentence, *off* is a preposition that introduces the prepositional phrase *off the ground.* In the second sentence, *off* neither functions as a preposition nor introduces a prepositional phrase. Instead, it combines with *took* to form a two-word verb with its own meaning. Such a verb is called a phrasal verb, and the word *off,* when used in this way, is called an adverbial particle. Many prepositions can function as particles to form phrasal verbs.

The verb + particle combination that makes up a phrasal verb is a tightly knit entity that usually cannot be torn apart.

> ▶ The plane took without difficulty . ~~off.~~
>   *off*

The exceptions are the many phrasal verbs that are transitive, meaning that they take a direct object (28l). Some transitive phrasal verbs have particles that may be separated from the verb by the object.

> ▶ I *picked up my baggage* at the terminal.
> ▶ I *picked my baggage up* at the terminal.

If a personal pronoun is used as the direct object, it must separate the verb from its particle.

> ▶ I *picked it up* at the terminal.

Some idiomatic two-word verbs, however, do not operate like phrasal verbs.

> ▶ We *ran into* our neighbor on the train.

In such verbs, the second word is a preposition, which cannot be separated from the verb: *We ran our neighbor into on the train* would be unacceptable. *Ran into* seems to consist of the verb *ran* followed by the preposition *into,* which introduces the prepositional phrase *into our neighbor.* Yet *to run into our neighbor* is different from a normal verb + prepositional phrase, such as *to run into the room.* If you know the typical meanings of *run* and *into,* you can interpret *to run into the room.* Not so with *to run into our neighbor;* the combination *run + into* has a special meaning ("find by chance") that could not be determined from the typical meanings of *run* and *into.* Therefore, *run into* must be considered a two-word verb but one that has much more in common with verbs followed by prepositions than with phrasal verbs. Such verbs as *run into* are called prepositional verbs.

Prepositional verbs include such idiomatic two-word verbs as *take after,* meaning "resemble" (usually a parent or other older relative); *get over,* meaning "recover from"; and *count on,* meaning "trust." They also include verb + preposition combinations in which the meaning is predictable but the specific preposition that is required is less predictable;

these prepositions must be learned together with the verb (for example, *depend on, look at, listen to, approve of*). There are also phrasal-prepositional verbs, which are verb + adverbial particle + preposition sequences (for example, *put up with, look forward to, give up on, get away with*).

bedfordstmartins.com/everyday_writer For exercises, go to **Exercise Central** and click on **Prepositions and Prepositional Phrases.**

67

Clauses and Sentences

Sound bites surround us, from Nike's "Just do it" to Apple Computer's "Think Different." These short simple sentences may be memorable, but they don't tell us very much. Ordinarily, we need more complex sentences to convey meaning. The sentences of everyday discourse are not formed in the same way in every language. This chapter will focus on clauses and sentences in English.

67a Express subjects explicitly.

English sentences consist of a subject and a predicate. This simple statement defines a gulf separating English from the many languages that leave out the subject when it can easily be inferred. Not English. With few exceptions (for example, commands with implied but not stated subjects), English demands that an explicit subject accompany an explicit predicate in every sentence. Though you might write *Went from Yokohama to Nagoya* on a postcard to a friend, in most varieties of spoken and written English, the extra effort of explicitly stating who went is not simply an option but an obligation.

In fact, every dependent clause must have an explicit subject.

▶ They took the Acela Express to Boston because *it* was fast.

English even requires a kind of "dummy" subject to fill the subject position in certain kinds of sentences. Consider the following sentences:

▶ *It* is raining.

▶ *There* is a strong wind.

If you speak Spanish

Speakers of Spanish might be inclined to leave out "dummy" subjects. In English, however, *it* and *there* are indispensable.

It is
▶ ~~Is~~ raining.
    ^

   There is
▶ ~~Has~~ a strong wind.
    ^

67b Express objects explicitly.

Transitive verbs typically require that objects—and sometimes other information—also be explicitly stated (28l). For example, it is not enough to tell someone *Buy!* even if it is clear what is to be bought for whom. You must say *Buy it for me* or *Buy me the watch* or some other such sentence. Similarly, saying *Put!* or *Put it!* is insufficient when you mean *Put it on the table.*

67c Be careful of English word order.

In general, you should not move subjects, verbs, or objects out of their normal positions in a sentence. In the following sentence, each element is in an appropriate place:

SUBJECT VERB OBJECT   ADVERB
▶ **Mario left Venice reluctantly.**

This sentence would also be acceptable if written as *Mario reluctantly left Venice* or as *Reluctantly, Mario left Venice,* but note that only the adverb can be moved. The three key elements of subject, verb, and object should be moved out of their normal order only to create special effects.

If you speak Turkish, Korean, or Japanese

In these languages, the verb must come last. Even if you have no difficulty adjusting to a different position for the verb in English, your recognition of the fact that word order can vary from one language to another should alert you to other possible problems.

If you speak Russian

Because Russian permits a great deal of freedom in word order, you must remember never to interchange the position of subject and object (*Venice left Mario reluctantly* is not acceptable English). In general, also avoid separating the verb from its object (*Mario left reluctantly Venice*). (For more on subjects and objects, see 28k and l.)

67d Use noun clauses appropriately.

Examine the following sentence:

> In my last year in high school, my adviser urged that I apply to several colleges.

This is built up out of two sentences, one of them (B) embedded in the other (A):

A. In my last year in high school, my adviser urged B.

B. I (should) apply to several colleges.

When these are combined as in the original sentence, sentence B becomes a noun clause introduced by *that* and takes on the role of object of the verb *urged* in sentence A. Now look at the following sentence:

> It made a big difference that she wrote a strong letter of recommendation.

Here the two component sentences are C and D:

C. D made a big difference.

D. She wrote a strong letter of recommendation.

In this case, the noun clause formed from sentence D functions as the subject of sentence C so that the combination reads as follows:

> That she wrote a strong letter of recommendation made a big difference.

This is an acceptable sentence but somewhat top-heavy. Usually when a lengthy noun clause is the subject of the sentence, it is moved to the end. The result is *Made a big difference that she wrote a strong letter of recommendation*. If you speak Italian or Spanish or Portuguese, you might see nothing wrong with such a sentence. In English, however, the subject must be stated. The "dummy" element *it* comes to the rescue.

> *It made*
> ▶ ~~Made~~ a big difference that she wrote a strong letter of recommendation.
> ^

67e Know how to choose between infinitives and gerunds.

Knowing whether to use an infinitive (*to read*) or a gerund (*reading*) in a particular sentence may be a challenge to multilingual writers (28m). The hints that follow will make this task easier.

INFINITIVE
▶ My adviser urged me *to apply* to several colleges.

GERUND
▶ Her *writing* a strong letter of recommendation made a big difference.

Why was an infinitive chosen for the first sentence and a gerund for the second? In general, *infinitives* tend to represent intentions, desires, or expectations, while *gerunds* tend to represent facts. The gerund in the second sentence calls attention to the fact that a letter was actually written; the infinitive in the first sentence conveys the message that the act of applying was something desired, not an accomplished fact.

Using gerunds to state facts

▶ Jerzy *enjoys going* to the theater.
▶ We *resumed working* after our coffee break.
▶ Kim *appreciated getting* candy from Sean.

In all of these cases, the second verb form is a gerund, and the gerund indicates that the action or event that it expresses has actually happened. Verbs like *enjoy, resume,* and *appreciate* can be followed only by gerunds, not by infinitives. In fact, even when these verbs do not convey clear facts, the verb form that follows must still be a gerund.

▶ Kim *would appreciate getting* candy from Sean, but he hardly knows her.

Using infinitives to state intentions

▶ Kumar *expected to get* a good job after graduation.
▶ Last year, Fatima *decided to become* a math major.
▶ The strikers have *agreed to go* back to work.

Here it is irrelevant whether the actions or events referred to by the infinitives did or did not materialize; at the moment indicated by the verbs *expect, decide,* and *agree,* those actions or events were merely intentions. These three verbs, as well as many others that specify intentions (or negative intentions, like *refuse*), must always be followed by an infinitive, never by a gerund.

Understanding other rules and guidelines

A few verbs can be followed by either an infinitive or a gerund. With some, such as *begin* and *continue,* the choice makes little difference in meaning. With others, however, the difference in meaning is striking.

▶ **Carlos was working as a medical technician, but he** *stopped to study* **English.**

The infinitive indicates that Carlos intended to study English when he left his job. We are not told whether he actually did study English.

▶ **Carlos** *stopped studying* **English when he left the United States.**

The gerund indicates that Carlos actually did study English but later stopped.

The distinction between fact and intention is not a rule but only a tendency, and it can be superseded by other rules. Use a gerund—never an infinitive—directly following a preposition.

▶ **This fruit is safe for** ~~to eat.~~ *eating.*

▶ **This fruit is safe** ~~for~~ **to eat.**

▶ **This fruit is safe for** *us* **to eat.**

Checking when to use an infinitive or a gerund

A full list of verbs that can be followed by an infinitive and verbs that can be followed by a gerund can be found in the *Collins Cobuild English Dictionary.* See also the other resources listed on p. 496.

67f Use adjective clauses carefully.

Adjective clauses can be a challenge to multilingual writers. Look at the following sentence:

▶ **The company** *Yossi's uncle invested in* **went bankrupt.**

The subject is a noun phrase in which the noun *company* is modified by the article *the* and the adjective clause *Yossi's uncle invested in.* The sentence as a whole says that a certain company went bankrupt, and the adjective clause identifies the company more specifically by saying that Yossi's uncle had invested in it.

One way of seeing how the adjective clause fits into the sentence is to rewrite it like this: *The company (Yossi's uncle had invested in it) went bankrupt.* This is not a normal English sentence, but it helps to demonstrate a process that leads to the sentence we started with. Note the following steps:

1. Change the personal pronoun *it* to the relative pronoun *which: The company (Yossi's uncle had invested in which) went bankrupt.* That still is not acceptable English.
2. Move either the whole prepositional phrase *in which* to the beginning of the adjective clause, or just move the relative pronoun: *The company in which Yossi's uncle had invested went bankrupt* or *The company which Yossi's uncle had invested in went bankrupt.* Both of these are good English sentences, the former somewhat more formal than the latter.
3. If no preposition precedes the relative pronoun, substitute *that* for *which* or leave out the relative pronoun entirely. *The company that Yossi's uncle had invested in went bankrupt* or *The company Yossi's uncle had invested in went bankrupt.* Both of these are good English sentences, not highly formal but still acceptable in much formal writing.

Speakers of some languages find adjective clauses difficult in different ways. Following are some guidelines that might help:

If you speak Korean, Japanese, or Chinese

If you speak Korean, Japanese, or Chinese, the fact that the adjective clause does not precede the noun that it modifies may be troublesome, both because such clauses precede nouns in the East Asian languages and because other modifiers, such as determiners and adjectives, *do* precede nouns in English.

If you speak Farsi, Arabic, or Hebrew

If you speak Farsi, Arabic, or Hebrew, you may expect the adjective clause to follow the noun as it does in English, but you might need to remind yourself to change the personal pronoun (*it*) to a relative pronoun (*which* or *that*) and then to move the relative pronoun to the beginning of the clause. You may put a relative pronoun at the beginning but mistakenly keep the personal pronoun, thus producing incorrect sentences such as *The company that Yossi's uncle invested in it went bankrupt.*

If you speak a European or Latin American language

If you are a speaker of some European or Latin American languages, you are probably acquainted with adjective clauses very much like those of English, but you may have difficulty accepting the possibility that a relative pronoun that is the object of a preposition can be moved to the beginning of a clause while leaving the preposition stranded. You might, therefore, move the preposition as well even when the relative pronoun is *that,* or you might drop the preposition altogether, generating such incorrect sentences as *The company in that Yossi's uncle invested went bankrupt* or *The company that Yossi's uncle invested went bankrupt.*

Finally, the fact that the relative pronoun can sometimes be omitted may lead to the mistaken notion that it can be omitted in all cases. You cannot omit a relative pronoun that is the subject of a verb.

▶ Everyone *who* invested in that company lost a great deal.

67g Understand conditional sentences.

English pays special attention to whether or not something is a fact or to the degree of confidence we have in the truth or likelihood of an assertion. Therefore, English distinguishes among many different types of conditional sentences—that is, sentences that focus on questions of truth and that are introduced by *if* or its equivalent. The following examples illustrate a range of different conditional sentences. Each of these sentences makes different assumptions about the likelihood that what is stated in the *if* clause is true; each then draws the corresponding conclusion in the main clause.

> If you *practice* (or *have practiced*) writing frequently, you *learn* (or *have learned*) what your chief problems are.

This sentence assumes that what is stated in the *if* clause may very well be true; the alternatives in parentheses indicate that any tense that is appropriate in a simple sentence may be used in both the *if* clause and the main clause.

> If you *practice* writing for the rest of this term, you *will* (or *may*) understand the process better.

This sentence makes a prediction about the future and again assumes that what is stated may very well turn out to be true. Only the main clause uses the future tense (*will understand*) or some other modal that can indicate future time (*may understand*). The *if* clause must use the present tense, even though it too refers to the future.

> If you *practiced* (or *were to practice*) writing every single day, it *would* eventually *seem* much easier to you.

This sentence casts some doubt on the likelihood that what is stated will be put into effect. In the *if* clause, the verb is either past—actually, past subjunctive (29h)—or *were to* + the base form, though it refers to future time. The main clause contains *would* + the base form of the main verb.

> If you *practiced* writing on Mars, you *would find* no one to read your work.

This sentence contemplates an impossibility at present or in the foreseeable future. As with the preceding sentence, the past subjunctive is used in the *if* clause, although past time is not being referred to, and *would* + the base form is used in the main clause.

> If you *had practiced* writing in ancient Egypt, you *would have used* hieroglyphics.

This sentence shifts the impossibility back to the past; obviously you are not going to find yourself in ancient Egypt. But since past forms have already been used in the preceding two sentences, this one demands a form that is "more past": the past perfect in the *if* clause and *would* + the present perfect form of the main verb in the main clause.

bedfordstmartins.com/everyday_writer   For exercises, go to **Exercise Central** and click on **Clauses and Sentences.**

Acknowledgments

Cover credits: Station wagon with bumper stickers: © Mark Gibson / Index Stock Imagery; Receiving email message on mobile phone: © Nick Koudis / Getty Images; Menu: © Thinkstock LLC; Man circling help wanted Ads: © Royalty-Free/CORBIS; For sale by owner sign: © David Buffington / Getty Images; Neon open sign over boutique: © Photodisc Collection.

Part-opening credits (left to right): **Pages 1 and 3:** John Foxx/fotosearch; Amelia Kunhardt/The Image Works; Brand X Pictures/fotosearch; Greer & Associates, Inc./SuperStock. **Pages 23 and 26:** Arne-Kristian Mertens/transit; Steve Hamblin/ Alamy; Corbis/fotosearch; EyeWire (Photodisc)/fotosearch. **Pages 99 and 101:** Photodisc/fotosearch; Royalty Free/CORBIS; Brand X Pictures/fotosearch; Photodisc/ fotosearch. **Pages 137 and 139:** Thinkstock/fotosearch; Photodisc/fotosearch; Goodshoot/fotosearch; David Young-Wolff/PhotoEdit. **Pages 181 and 183:** Rachel Epstein/PhotoEdit; Eric Fowke/PhotoEdit; Corbis/fotosearch; Bill Aron/PhotoEdit. **Pages 207 and 210:** Richard Cummins/SuperStock; Thinkstock/fotosearch; Corbis/fotosearch; Photodisc/fotosearch. **Pages 275 and 277:** Thinkstock/fotosearch; Photodisc/fotosearch; Jeff Greenberg/PhotoEdit; Photodisc/fotosearch. **Pages 315 and 318:** Robert Brenner/PhotoEdit; Peter Hvizdak/The Image Works; Tony Free-man/PhotoEdit; Lew Lause/SuperStock. **Pages 365 and 367:** Photodisc/fotosearch; Corel/fotosearch; Brand X Pictures/fotosearch; Spencer Grant/PhotoEdit. **Pages 413 and 415:** Photodisc/fotosearch; Photodisc/fotosearch; FogStock/Alamy; Brand X Pictures/fotosearch. **Pages 459 and 461:** Photodisc/fotosearch; Eric Kamp/ IndexStock; David Forbert/SuperStock; Rudi Von Briel/PhotoEdit. **Pages 489 and 491:** Michael Newman/PhotoEdit; David Maenza/SuperStock; Murat Ayranci/ SuperStock; Jeff Greenberg/PhotoEdit.

Other credits: **Page 3:** Comstock/fotosearch; **page 6:** © Royalty-free/CORBIS; **page 9:** © Royalty-free/CORBIS; **page 33:** Courtesy www.adbusters.org; **page 34** (top left): © Bettmann/CORBIS; **page 34** (top center): © John S. Pritchett; **page 34** (top right): © Bettmann/CORBIS; **page 44** (top): © Royalty-free/CORBIS; **page 44** (bottom): © Royalty-free/CORBIS; **page 45:** (top): © Lippincott Williams & Wilkins, 2004; **page 45** (bottom): © Bettmann/CORBIS; **page 52:** © Royalty-free/CORBIS; **page 54:** © Royalty-free/CORBIS; **page 55:** © Bettmann/CORBIS; **page 78:** *Atlanta Journal Constitution,* September 18, 2001. By permission of Mike Luckovich and Creators Syndicate, Inc.; **page 108:** Reproduced by permission; **page 110** (top): © 1996–2004 National Geographic Society. All rights reserved. Reproduced by permission; **page 110** (middle): © 2003 Mars, Incorporated. www.colorworks.com. All rights reserved; **page 110** (bottom): © 2004 Bartleby.com. www.bartleby.com. Reproduced by permission; **page 116,** "Democracy" cartoon: Ares. www.caglecartoons.com/espanol; **page 116,** photo: Brand X Pictures/fotosearch; **page 117,** jumping whale: © Copyright 2002 Underwater Video Services. All rights reserved. www.underwatervideo.co.za. Reproduced by permission; **page 120:** Copyright © 2004 Acterra, a 501 © (3) nonprofit. www.actura.org. Reproduced by permission; **page 121:** Copyright © 1995–2004 by the West Coast Environmental Law Research Foundation, 1-800-330-WCWL, 1001–207 West Hastings Street, Vancouver, BC V6B 1H7, Canada. www.wcel.org. Reprinted by permission; **page 148:** © 2003 Google. www.google.com. Reprinted by permission; **page 161:** excerpt from pp. 909–34 in *Human Rights Quarterly* 25 (2003). © 2003 by The Johns Hopkins University Press. Reprinted by permission; **page 163:** Copyright © 2004 by the National Audubon Society, Inc. www.audubon.org; **page 275:** Emily

Index

·

Student Writing Directory

IN THE BOOK

Student writing samples throughout this book provide models for analysis and class discussion. The numbers below refer to a chapter number or section of a chapter.

ON THE WEB SITE

You'll also find the following collection of additional student writing on this book's companion Web site. Go to **bedfordstmartins.com/everyday_writer** and click on **Student Writing.**

ARGUMENT WRITING

RESEARCHED WRITING

Advice for Considering Disabilities

On the pages noted below you will find advice for making texts accessible to readers with disabilities and resources for writers with disabilities.

For Multilingual Writers

Revision Symbols

Some instructors use these symbols as a kind of shorthand to guide you in revision. The numbers refer to a chapter number or a section of a chapter.

abb	abbreviation *49a–g*		//	faulty parallelism *8e, 23*
ad	adjective/adverb *31*		para	paraphrase *18d, 19*
agr	agreement *30, 33f*		pass	inappropriate passive *24c, 29g*
awk	awkward			
cap	capitalization *48*		ref	unclear pronoun reference *33g*
case	case *33a*			
cliché	cliché *9b, 39d*		run-on	run-on (fused) sentence *34*
co	coordination *22a*			
coh	coherence *8e*		sexist	sexist language *33f, 37b*
com	incomplete comparison *21c*		shift	shift *24*
			slang	slang *39a*
concl	weak conclusion *8f, 20b*		sp	spelling *40*
cs	comma splice *34*		sub	subordination *22b*
d	diction *39*		sum	summarize *18d, 19*
def	define *8c*		t	tone *9b, 18c, 39a, 39d*
dm	dangling modifier *32d*		trans	transition *8e, 27b*
doc	documentation *52–58*		u	unity *8a*
emph	emphasis unclear *25*		vague	vague statement
x	example needed *8b–c*		verb	verb form *29a–d*
rag	sentence fragment *35*		vt	verb tense *29e–h*
s	fused sentence *34*		wv	weak verb *29*
yph	hyphen *51*		wrdy	wordy *26*
ic	incomplete construction *21b–e*		ww	wrong word *9b, 39a–b*
			,	comma *42*
ntro	weak introduction *8f, 20b*		;	semicolon *43*
it	italics (or underlining) *50*		. ? !	period, question mark, exclamation point *44*
			'	apostrophe *45*
jarg	jargon *39a*		" "	quotation marks *46*
lc	lowercase letter *48*		( ) [ ] —	parentheses, brackets, dash *47a–c*
lv	language variety *38*			
mix	mixed construction *21a*		: / ...	colon, slash, ellipsis *47d–f*
mm	misplaced modifier *32*			
ms	manuscript form *13*		∧	insert
no ,	no comma *42j*		∩	transpose
num	number *49h–j*		⌣	close up
¶	paragraph *8*		X	obvious error

CONTENTS